JENNY McLEOD

JENNY McLEOD
A LIFE IN MUSIC

Norman Meehan

TE HERENGA WAKA
UNIVERSITY PRESS

Te Herenga Waka University Press
PO Box 600, Wellington
New Zealand
teherengawakapress.co.nz

A catalogue record is available from the
National Library of New Zealand.

ISBN 9781776921171

Printed in Singapore by Markono Print Media Pte Ltd

For Robert Hoskins

Contents

Preface

Jenny McLeod's life and work are well documented in articles and profiles published in newspapers and periodicals, and there are chapters about her in a couple of books too. In this biography, these accounts have been supplemented by a number of mostly unpublished interviews that writers and broadcasters conducted with Jenny between 1968 and 2021, all of which shed light on Jenny's thinking and outlook at particular times in her life.

As well as talking about her life and music, Jenny also wrote about them. Her prose includes programme notes and performance guidelines for her compositions, music theory, personal recollections of her early life and of musicians she'd met, family history and genealogy, public addresses of various kinds, and a number of searching essays. She wrote a great deal of poetry (of which only a small portion has been published) and many, many letters to friends and loved ones. These were also important sources in the preparation of this biography.

To fill out the picture, I spoke to and corresponded with many of Jenny's friends and colleagues. Their recollections and insights were valuable and often telling. These sources, and all of those listed above, are referenced in the endnotes and bibliography.

By far the most important source for this book, however, was Jenny herself. A great deal of this biography emerged from our conversations (which began in 2019 and continued, on and off, for two or three years) and our correspondence. All together that amounted to several hundred pages of single-spaced text. Jenny also saw various drafts of the manuscript during the writing, and offered many comments and corrections – a further seventy pages on just the first draft. Her responses ranged from delight ('Well, I never! This is all news to me' and 'I'd completely forgotten about that!') to dismissive ('Bullshit!' and 'You've made this up! It isn't what I said at all').

The result is an account richly furnished with Jenny's own words and recollections, analyses and interpretation. Many of these words are from published sources and Jenny's extensive deposits in the Alexander Turnbull Library, Wellington, but the majority come from our interviews and correspondence, and all unattributed quotes are from those exchanges.

So, a great deal of the narrative is in Jenny's voice. However, that voice speaks from different moments in her life. I have drawn on letters and essays, as well as interviews and poems, from across her career, and over the years her thinking about many things evolved as her priorities shifted. For this reason, I have included a number of endnotes that qualify particular remarks with the views she adopted in later years.

Complementing Jenny's account are the voices of people who have known and, in many cases, worked with her. These voices sometimes sound a different note or emphasise an alternative viewpoint. My aim has been to honour Jenny's recollections and interpretation, but also welcome other perspectives by admitting different voices with their own take on events.

In an essay called 'Aspects of Myth and Reality: Some Personal Notes' Jenny wrote that we all have our own private store of beliefs, beliefs that can be 'shared and discussed in an atmosphere where there is no "right" or "wrong" view'. These different beliefs, she suggested, can be added to a communal store in which, even where there is divergence, 'each voice can be recognised nonetheless as having its own truth and authenticity'. She likened this rich pageant of voices to a braided river, because approaching a conversation in that way 'recognises a legitimate place for every voice'.[1]

What I hope emerges from this confluence of voices is a narrative that gestures towards the ways in which Jenny's life and work are intertwined. An artist's life can be made comprehensible when examined in the context of their work. Conversely, an artist's creative output, when viewed through the lens of their experiences, often becomes more vivid and colourful. That art and life might be mutually constitutive was an idea Jenny was comfortable with: 'Who you are matters as much as what you create,' she said to me, 'the one directly informs the other, and vice versa.'

Introduction

In 1993 Jenny was invited to compose music for the Sing Aotearoa festival hosted on Maungārongo Marae in Ohakune. There she met and quickly became close to a number of Ngāti Rangi, including Joan Akapita, a much-respected kuia. As their friendship blossomed, Joan suggested Jenny might like to join them for their annual canoe trip down the Whanganui River. The Tira Hoe Waka – coming together to paddle – is generally only for members of Whanganui River iwi, and Jenny was honoured to be invited. She jumped at the chance.

The purpose of the journey is spiritual learning, and 'particularly to teach the young people their tribal lore and heritage, so they can learn who they are'. Matiu Māreikura, Joan's brother and a kaumātua among Ngāti Rangi, had explained to Jenny that knowing who you are is very important, and that only then do you 'cast a long shadow'.[1] In a 1996 essay, Jenny described her experiences at the beginning of the journey:

> This 'casting a long shadow' puzzled me. But when I'm formally welcomed, along with all my ancestors, at the Taumarunui marae (our setting-off point), indeed I do feel something like my own 'shadow' grow quite perceptibly. It's very new, to find myself somehow 'enlarged' and fortified by those of mine who went before me, through their invisible presence in my life being so directly acknowledged as a reality (and as a matter of course) by the tangata

whenua here, whom I've not met before. Suddenly I'm proud of my
people, of who I am – I actually feel taller.[2]

While Jenny identified strongly with Māori, particularly from the
mid-1990s onwards, she did not lose sight of her own forebears: the
McLeod clan on her father's side, and the Perrin line from which her
mother descended. Both families had mottos: 'Hold Fast' is emblazoned
on the McLeod crest; 'Be Watchful' was, Jenny understood, the Perrin
family motto, one she interpreted as 'Stay Awake'. These were values
she cherished to the end of her life, that 'from the beginning I took on
and look on as my own. They stayed with me and can qualify, I think,
as major subliminal supports in the many times of personal and musical
difficulty that confronted me.'

1

Beginnings

There wasn't a great deal of music in the McLeod household when Jenny was very young, but close to eighty years later she could recall listening to the wind-up gramophone, particularly to recordings made by her maternal grandfather, John Halford Perrin. His versions of 'The Floral Dance' and 'The Laughing Policeman' were 78s she heard over and over. 'I still feel the warmth the memory brings of being surrounded or embraced by the flimsy old crackle-hissy maternal grandpa voice.'

John Halford Perrin was a capable bass–baritone – capable enough to be 'one of the first in New Zealand to make a wind-up gramophone recording'.[1] He sang with his older brother Ernest and their father, John Edmund Perrin, in the first Palmerston North All Saints (Anglican) Choir. Ernest was also Drum Major for the Palmerston North Garrison Band, and two of Ernest and John's sisters, Rachel and Gertrude, were fine sopranos who sang in the local Orchestral Society's programmes.

John Halford sang in the Methodist church choir, too, doing so in order to be near Eliza Jamieson. In due course, the two were married. Writing up her family history, Jenny noted, 'If [Eliza] hadn't married my grandfather, I sometimes reflect, but had married instead Joe Nielsen from Hawera, whom she *almost* married, then neither I nor the New

Zealand pianist Margaret Nielsen (who taught me and was later my good friend and colleague in the Victoria University Music Department) would ever have been born. Whether she knew it or not, Eliza's decision was for music.'[2]

Grandpa John was a builder and joiner and a master carver. In his teens he began working for his father, a partner in the firm Meyrick, Perrin & Oakley, which did much of the early building in the new Manawatū settlement of Palmerston North. Although there are photos of Grandpa John holding baby Jen in his arms, she remembered meeting him only once, as he lay near death on a hospital bed. But she came to know him through his work – the hard-chiselled lines and curves of the wood he had shaped; 'his lions, and heads, and horses always looked like real lions, heads and horses . . . they were beautifully done, perfectly proportioned and finished' – and his workshop, which she explored as a child. Shortly before he was claimed by tuberculosis, he had designed and carved wooden horses for the Foxton Beach merry-go-round. He 'also painted and named each horse. The two I remember were St Geneviève – *my* horse that I always wanted to ride – and St Cloud.'

John Halford built a home for Eliza and himself on Palmerston North's Foxton Line. It was right next door to Eliza's family home – where Great-grandpa Gideon Jamieson, who had emigrated from Shetland, lived – and on land that Eliza's father had made over to the young couple as a wedding gift. Grandpa John named it Lerwick House to mark his wife's Shetland origins. And he modelled it after Shetland dwellings: the upstairs more like an attic than a full upper storey, and the staircase small and narrow. 'I didn't recognise this until I visited Shetland years later,' Jenny recalled, 'feeling immediately at home when I found the cousins' houses there were just like Nanna's.'

Jenny loved to stay at Lerwick House during the summer holidays, and, with her brothers, explored its nooks and crannies, the narrow wooden staircase cupboard, the attic-like bedroom with its gables and beams where they slept. 'There was a feeling of care about the house itself. You could feel – in the dark, comfortable lustre of a rich varnish, or in the turn of wood on an architrave, or window ledge, or mantle, or the finish on a panel – that this house was crafted and shaped by someone who took a real pleasure in doing his work well.'[3]

Years after her grandfather died, Jenny recalled standing in his workshop at the back of the house, where the smell of sawdust and wood and leather offered her 'the sense of hard but rewarding toil, of purposeful activity, a feeling that here something real had gone on'. There she felt a powerful connection to him – as if he had just stepped out – and later came to believe 'the artistic tradition was handed on to me most immediately from him'.[4]

> My very earliest memory, long before I had learned to talk, is of lying in a warm, gentle light in my cot, and being handed down from the dark, something bright and shining, with a beautiful, intricate pattern on it that utterly captivated me, and which I somehow knew was of great significance for *me*. This turned out later to be a small silver christening mug, with my name engraved on it in italics by my grandfather – his gift to his first grandchild. And so, the very first thing I remember is a feeling of wonder at something new and strange, something *beautiful*.[5]

Jenny's mother, Lorna Bell Perrin, inherited some of her father's artistic leanings. Born in Palmerston North in 1915, Lorna attended the local West End School and, consistent with her middle-class upbringing, studied classical piano with local teacher and Austrian émigré Howel Edward Gunter. She had a fondness for the music of the day too, and would eventually fill her piano stool with albums of popular songs from the 1920s and '30s: 'Red Sails in the Sunset', 'If You Knew Susie' and the like. Later in life she took up guitar and was a reliable singer. In the late 1950s she was a founding member of Neil Colquhoun's Levin group, the Song Spinners, recording three LPs of New Zealand folk songs with them: *Songs of the Whalers* and *Songs of the Gold Diggers* in 1959, and *Songs of the Gum Diggers* in 1960. 'Our mum sings a little solo ("Tuapeka Gold") on one of these albums, though (like me) she was really not a soloist. Her voice there is a wee bit shaky – the song sounds intimate, like a lullaby rather than a "performance" as such.'

While Lorna was fond of music and a competent performer, she was most powerfully drawn to crafts and the plastic arts. 'My mother clearly inherited Grandpa's love of making things,' Jenny said. 'She had a good eye for balance and proportion, was talented at drawing and painting and was exceptionally good with her hands.'[6]

After her father died, Lorna made certain she inherited his tools and put them to use making things that astonished her children: a ten-inch replica of a Ford Prefect, painted bright yellow, with doors and a bonnet that opened and closed, and an electric motor that powered it across the floor; accurate models of King Henry VIII and Queen Elizabeth I in elaborate historical dress; a two-foot-high Garter King-of-Arms in his red heraldic costume, accurate to the finest detail (including gold embroidery and trimmings, and the royal mace on a cushion), with which she won a British Commonwealth doll competition.

She won many competitions – and some very tidy prizes, including a brand-new Toyota Corolla, for making an apron, of all things – and did her best to help her children follow in her footsteps. Jenny recalled: 'Mum would always ask me first whether I wanted to enter this or that competition – her own idea, not mine – and only after I'd decided I did, would she declare that now I had to finish the job to the best of my ability, and there would be no giving up or sloppiness.' In this way she instilled in her children a value Jenny thought Lorna had probably learned from her father: namely, 'the inherently high standard of work we came naturally to expect of ourselves, simply as a matter of self-respect. I learned from her that in order to excel you must do more than is expected. When Mum had finished her competition work, she would always go on to present her entry in some immaculate, exceptional way that would take a lot more time and would naturally impress and draw attention to the outstanding quality of the whole thing.' Doing as well as she could, and going the extra mile, became the habits of a lifetime:

> As the first and oldest child, I probably came in for the main brunt
> of this education, and I do not for a moment regret it, even though
> it involved hours of painstaking work, of endless mistakes and
> corrections, of slaving into the night until one was dropping from
> exhaustion and one's eyes could barely focus, and fits of crying, not

wanting to go on, but going on anyway, since you had already put so much work into the bloody thing (whatever it happened to be) that you were not going to waste it all by giving up now. In this way I won one or two painting competitions myself, and my mother taught me a high level of concentration, perseverance and dissatisfaction with all but one's best efforts – valuable lessons indeed, and the more so for one's having learned them so young.[7]

Another lesson Lorna passed on to her daughter was one picked up from her piano teacher, whom she liked and looked up to: 'Mr Gunter may not have taught her much about music, but he did teach her, as she said more than once, never to expect gratitude from anyone – a sentiment with which I fully concurred, even at quite a tender age.'[8]

A confident, vivacious young woman, Lorna moved to Wellington after leaving school, working as a secretary and shorthand typist at the Treasury. In those days she rode a motorcycle, wore a leather jacket, drank shandies and smoked cigarettes: 'She never disclosed how she met my father but I suspect I might have been on the way when they decided to get married.'[9] Although Jenny knew her mother as an ostensibly devout Methodist with puritanical tendencies, 'she could sometimes shock us by coming out with a filthy joke'.

Jenny's father, Ronald D'Arcy McLeod, was from a branch of the McLeod clan who settled in New Zealand somewhat later than the Perrins (who arrived in 1842). Landing in Dunedin from Glasgow, Ronald's grandfather, John Sherer McLeod, along with his chemist brother William, established the Sunlight Soap factory there in 1884. Ronald's father, Alan Sherer McLeod, one of thirteen children, was welcomed into the family business. Alan fathered nine children – of whom Ronald was the eighth – before being dispatched by the firm to Fiji in search of indigo dye for their soap. Once there, he took to the bottle and absconded to an outer island with a local woman; he remained there for the rest of his life. A short time later, Alan's wife, Elizabeth Janet (Jeanetta) McLeod (née Dorreen), likewise took flight, abandoning her children in Auckland. Ronald was subsequently raised by his oldest sister, Maisie.

Ron, as he was known to his friends (although Maisie and Netta, his youngest sister, called him Mick), left school at fourteen to go to work. Jenny thought he had never recovered from the emotional turmoil of his childhood, and once described her father as the quietest man she had ever known: 'Dad was not a good talker. Most of his life he had three kids and a wife, none of whom ever shut up, so he had no room to speak. He never had an extended conversation with any of us.'

A keen sportsman – flat feet may have circumvented wartime conscription but posed no problems on the golf course – and a skilful driver, Ron loved cars and owned more than twenty in his lifetime.[10] Jenny said, 'He taught me to drive, how to swim, how to ride a bike, how to play tennis and golf. He taught me that, even as the littlest boy in a family of nine, you could actually get along in this life. And he did.' Although there were musicians in his extended family – his nephews Ronald McLeod and Paul Person were professional singers – and Ron showed an interest in music, he seems to have had little aptitude for it.[11]

A Timaru childhood

Jennifer Helen McLeod, the first of Ron and Lorna's three children, was born in Wellington in November 1941. When she was six weeks old the family moved to Timaru, settling in Otipua Road, close to the city's southern boundary. It was a fortuitous choice for Lorna – Kay Harding, an old friend and also a young mother, lived close by. Jenny said, 'Until we moved to the north side of town, the Hardings' was always a place of huge merriment, mischief and fun, and like a second home for me and my two little brothers. Kay's oldest daughter Philippa, whom we all knew as Pip, remained a lifelong friend.' Pip was a few years older than Jenny and extremely musical – a fine pianist and cellist who later became a Suzuki expert and played for decades with the Sydney Symphony Orchestra.

The home environment Lorna and Ron created for Jenny and her brothers, Perrin (b. 1943) and Craig (b. 1945), was comfortable and outwardly happy. 'Dad regularly organised outstanding weekend family picnics,' Jenny said, 'with a great spread always provided by Mum: ham, egg, tomato sandwiches; bacon and egg pie; and my favourite, sausage and stuffing pie made with sweet short pastry.' Driving to the river or the beach for the day was a frequent activity during Timaru's warm summer weekends and when the family holidayed in the North Island.

Prior to commencing school, Jenny had only a little experience – and next to no first-hand knowledge – of music. There was no piano or guitar in the house, and the only music she recalled beyond Grandpa John's recorded performances was her mother singing nursery rhymes. 'Dad never sang,' she said, 'not even in the bathroom.' Although she learned songs from Lorna – the most memorable was 'Golden Slumbers', which she in turn sang to her toys – Jenny's pathway to active music making didn't properly begin until her arrival, aged five, at Timaru South School, a fifteen-minute walk from the family home. Pinned to the wall above the blackboard and around another wall of the Primer One classroom were long stretches of brown paper, about a metre high, on which was painted a large music staff with black musical notation. 'This was almost a transcendental moment for me – an epiphany. I had never seen these strange marks before and had no idea what they meant, but I knew instantly and for sure they were there *for me* . . . I showed no outward sign and said nothing to anyone – this was my private secret – but inside I was almost bursting with excitement.' Jenny observed that these marks were the same as the much smaller ones in the book on the classroom piano, and quickly worked out that the sounds that emerged from the piano were somehow linked to them. Her teacher was a friend of Lorna's, so Jenny felt confident to go to her after school and say, 'Allie, can you teach me what those are?'[12]

In less than an hour, Jenny learned to read music – 'it just came very naturally to me; it was like a language that I already knew, an inborn proclivity' – and began staying after school to play the piano. News of this development was passed on to Lorna, and as soon as Ron could afford to buy one, a piano arrived in the McLeod home. A kind of compulsion took hold of Jenny, and she spent a great deal of her spare time playing the instrument.

After the family moved to a house built for them in Newman Street on the north side of town, Jenny had a few piano lessons from a Mrs Dugdale but mostly worked on her own. She played through a beginners' classical repertoire – her mother had retained a few books from her own studies with Mr Gunter – as well as hymns and albums of the popular songs her mother still liked, although Jenny didn't recall ever hearing Lorna play them. As a student of music, she was off to a terrific start.

Her career as a performer began a little less gloriously. 'My first [musical] memory is not of doing well. It's of <u>not</u> doing well at something. I can remember my first public performance. I think I must have been six or seven and I was supposed to play "The Elves Dance". I was paralysed with fright. So, I stopped playing and I just got up and announced to the audience, "I've got stage fright," and I went off the stage again.'[13] This setback hardly diminished her appetite for music. She remembered:

> After school, aged twelve or thirteen, I used to look up in books and write down biographies of all these composers and stick them to the back of their music that I had copies of – details of what happened in their lives. That's a strange thing to do unless you're going to be rather involved with music. I used to play their pieces too, and I recall being very cross whenever my mother, who was preparing dinner (or 'tea'), would call out to me when I was in the middle of a piece, 'It's ready; come and eat.' And I would think, 'No way, I'm going to finish my piece first.' So, I might be halfway through quite a long sonata movement and the rest of the family would have to endure me banging my way through the rest of it until I was ready to come and eat.

Early inspiration came from a young Dutch woman called Anna who lived with the McLeod family for about six months, assisting around the house after Lorna broke her shoulder on a family skiing holiday. 'Anna used to regularly play Chopin – meaning, she could only play the A major *Polonaise* (the "Military"), but she played it all the time – and I liked it.' And when their neighbours the Einhams had a visit from the Southgate family, Jenny encountered a young man only a little older with a similar passion for music. William Southgate (b. 1941) would go on to become an internationally regarded conductor and composer, but his first musical steps were made at the piano: 'Bill Southgate played "The Little White Donkey" really well on our piano and I liked that. So, I got the music and learned that. Bill Southgate and Pip Harding were the first real musicians that I had any real contact with.'[14]

Jenny's musical interests weren't limited to the classical repertoire for piano. 'The [Highland] pipes resonated within me,' she said later in life, 'and still do in a very singular way, like something of my own "out there" that is calling to me, and that I cannot ignore or deny.' She was able to make sense of this early fixation when she discovered, years later, that the Clan MacLeod was responsible (by way of the MacCrimmons) for the existence of what she thought of as one of the world's noblest musical traditions: Highland pipe music. Aged about nine her greatest musical ambition was to be a drummer with a pipe band. She was too small to carry a pipe-band snare drum, so her parents purchased a child-sized equivalent for her. 'I taught myself by ear a military drum pattern, practicing my rolls until they sounded good enough, and was duly appointed Marchwiel Primary School Drummer. Twice a day I stood outside playing my little drum while all the kids marched into their classrooms: my first "musical job".'[15]

Jenny took to school easily. As a result of her mother's instruction, she and her brothers were able to read and write long before they arrived there. She found the environment, with its emphasis on learning, welcoming, and the headmaster and his wife were friends of her parents. Seeing them in the school playground made her feel at home from the outset. 'All of my schooldays were exceedingly happy ones,' she recalled. 'Most of my schooling took place under good teachers whom I regarded as my friends, and so learning itself was natural.'[16]

Jenny's brothers Perrin and Craig were also musical; both were choir boys in the Anglican church in Timaru. The three of them made their own childhood fun by putting on performances. 'Whispering Hope' was a favourite, played for visiting relatives with Jenny at the piano accompanying her boy soprano brothers. 'Even as young as ten or so, there was nothing strange to me in grabbing my little brothers, always my willing slaves – "Let's have a concert" – then going round knocking on doors and inviting all the neighbours, who duly came and paid their shilling to sit in little rows on our terrace (to the surprise of our parents, whom I didn't bother to ask) and watch some weird and hilarious concoction of ours.'[17]

Later, as teenagers, the three of them would sing together while doing the dishes, improvising harmonies to the 1950s pop songs they had learned from the radio. Craig's musical training had begun on the violin; later, he turned his attention to trumpet and voice, performing with both the national and Wellington youth orchestras, and as a baritone soloist with the London Bach Society.

Perrin had exceptional aural skills and a superb memory, and played piano very well by ear most of his life. At one time he even took work as a cocktail pianist. Jenny recalled:

> When I came home – I was already at Vic, in my first year, and had got to know a much bigger range of music than I knew before I went there – I used to like to sit and play the piano. I knew that my family was also listening and I liked to play for them. And then a day or two later I would come back and discover my brother playing, by ear, Schubert, chunks of the later B-flat Sonata. He would play Scarlatti, the 'Cat Fugue' – learned the whole thing painfully from the music and memorised it. He played whatever he liked that he'd heard me play. Very gifted.

Jenny was fond of her brothers and felt a kinship with them. The three of them often wondered how it was they could have been born to parents so different from themselves. Jenny recalled witnessing a quarrel between Ron and Lorna over the kitchen table one evening when she was five or six: 'I was shocked and amazed to find my mother was crying – something I had not seen before. Mum had been the centre, the apotheosis of my whole little world, and here she was crying – and crying about money. Dad said we were running short. But how could you cry about money? Even as a child I knew at once and for certain that money was not to be cried about.' She concluded that her parents 'didn't really know what life was about. For the rest of their lives, I took everything they said with a grain of salt.'

Her doubts about her parents' preparedness for life were possibly fuelled by her perception of the coolness of their relationship; they didn't even seem to like one another. As far back as Jenny could remember her parents had separate beds, and later separate bedrooms, and Ron once disclosed to her, 'I've never seen your mother naked.' Lorna's excessive modesty, even prudishness, was later matched by her prim disapproval of Ron's drinking: she may have enjoyed a shandy or two as a young woman in Wellington, but as a Methodist mother of three Lorna was a teetotaller. Ron was not an alcoholic, but Lorna joined Al-Anon, a support group for Alcoholics Anonymous, and prowled the house looking for concealed booze. Ron took to hiding flagons of sherry in the garage, which Lorna would duly uncover, marking the level to monitor how much he was drinking. Jenny described the situation: 'The poor bugger. It plagued his life, I'm sure. In that context no one can drink sensibly.'[18]

Ron, for his part, maintained strict control over the family's finances, and refused Lorna's requests for household appliances that would have made home life easier. Silently outraged, Lorna took a job and opened her own bank account. She never forgave Ron his tightfistedness and in her will left him absolutely nothing, not even the Toyota Corolla she had won in a sewing competition, and that he drove as he nursed her during her final illness. At one point – after the children had left home – she separated from Ron and moved to Britain to get away from him. In London she undertook secretarial work and attended courses at the Royal College of Needlework. In due course she returned to New Zealand, and to the home she shared with Ron. Jenny used to say that Lorna hated her husband so much, she couldn't live without him.

'They couldn't help it if they didn't much like each other,' Jenny reflected. 'It didn't mean that they were incapable of loving their children. They did indeed love us, and really, I would never have wanted a different upbringing.' Jenny was an inquisitive child, and headstrong, and the security of her home environment undoubtedly fostered her growing self-reliance. She said, 'My father told me (when I asked him much later) that I was already "very independent" even as a young child.'

That independence impelled her to embark on what she called a 'mission of mischief'. Under the stairs she and her brothers had a Smoking Club, complete with a minute book in which they recorded what they smoked. It was the beginning of Jenny's inveterate fondness for smoking. In the ceiling beneath the roof, she and her brothers established a Nudist Club; on hot days they would climb among the rafters and take their clothes off. Jenny also pinched money from her father's cloth cash bag and used the eight stolen florins to buy comics for her and her brothers. Seventy years later she still remembered the 'gentle, hurt, surprised look on Dad's face when he told me I should have just asked and he would have given me the money. But he wouldn't have,' she added.

Ron's generosity might not have extended to the florins in his purse, but he was lavish with the vacations he provided for his family. Jenny remembered 'terrific holidays every year, all over the country – skiing, swimming, canoeing, fishing at lakes, rivers, mountains, beaches. As children we would never have known our country as well without Dad doing all this.' Most summers the family travelled north by car from Timaru, taking the Lyttelton ferry to Wellington and driving on to Foxton Beach where Jenny's grandfather had built a modest beach house he'd called 'Wharepuni'. Spartan, comfortable, of unlined corrugated iron, and smelling of sand and salt and tussock and dry pine needles, it was where Jenny spent many Christmas holidays. There was a harmonium in the house, so the summer wasn't entirely without music, but those holidays were primarily about the river and the beach.

One summer when she was eight or nine, Jenny was almost swept out to sea while canoeing alone near the mouth of the Manawatū River. Her father and a friend were able to get out to her in another boat and haul her back to shore, but the incident – coupled with a near-drowning she had experienced as a youngster picnicking with her family in Canterbury – left her with a lifelong respect for the sea. She told me that in forty years living at Pukerua Bay she had swum just once, although insisted the coldness of the water was the main reason she stayed on the beach. 'To this day,' she wrote in 1992, 'though I love the sea and am not easily prised from my home alongside it, I would never dream of going out on it alone. I much prefer to sit and gaze at it for hours through the window, where I know I am safe. So much for all my brave sea-faring ancestors.'[19]

Those summers on the Horowhenua coast must have reminded Ron how much more agreeable the weather was in the North Island. During Jenny's first year at Timaru Girls' High School, he decided he had had enough of being cold, and arranged for the family to leave Canterbury and move north to Levin.

2

Levin | Horowhenua College

When Ron arrived in Timaru in 1941, he opened and ran the local Singer Sewing Machine Company store, where he was responsible for sales, servicing and repairs. After the war he owned and operated a bookshop on the town's main street, modelled on his older brother Ken's bookshop in Rotorua. Lorna was the reader in the household (at least until her children arrived) and was especially fond of Dickens. As far as Jenny was aware, her father knew very little about books. When he married Lorna, he had a complete set of Alexandre Dumas but had probably not read more than two or three of them. Jenny could not recall ever seeing her dad curled up with a book. That said, reading books and selling books are not the same thing, and Ron's Timaru bookshop was successful.

With the decision to move north, Ron sold his Timaru business to Whitcombe & Tombs and, on arriving in Levin in 1954, bought out Stannard's, a bookshop on Oxford Street. This he operated successfully as McLeod's Bookshop until he retired in the mid-1960s. The shop was to be a boon for Jenny and her brothers, as books that didn't sell in the annual sale usually ended up at home. Jenny said, 'I read them all, and my mum's old books: *What Katy Did* and *Anne of Green Gables*. I read everything in the house, but it was a very motley collection.'[1]

Jenny's interest in music would become a consuming passion in Levin. Her early music education had been primarily self-directed. Fleetingly, there were lessons with Mrs Dugdale in Timaru, and in Levin with Mrs Maher, 'but she never taught me anything, and neither did the old girl in Timaru. I used to pick whatever I wanted to learn, then I would learn it and take it along and play it to them, and they would say "Oh, that's lovely dear." They didn't teach me anything about how to play the piano.' The usual disciplines of the instrument were anathema to Jenny. She despised scales and technical exercises – 'that was all terribly dull' – preferring her piano technique, such as it was, to develop through the pieces she played. She later conceded, 'That's not the way to become a good pianist, although I always got by. There's a good deal of bluff in my piano playing.'[2]

Bluff may well have been an indispensable attribute given the wide variety of music she played over the next six or seven years. Equally valuable was her ability to easily sight-read almost anything. Levin, home to fewer than six thousand in the early 1950s, might seem an inauspicious place to begin a musical career, but the range of Jenny's musical activities during her years there was remarkable. She played piano and (eventually) organ for church services, weddings, receptions and funerals, and for a regional performance of Handel's *Messiah* in Palmerston North's All Saints Church (where her grandfather had been a member of the congregation). She sang in three choirs, and accompanied solo instrumentalists and singers, local revues and shows, choruses, operettas and high school assemblies. She was a pianist at talent quests and parties and played, mainly by ear, for country-hall socials. Jenny also played piano accordion, recorder, drums and, later, clarinet. She could even manage a version of 'St. Louis Blues' on her brother Craig's trumpet, learned by ear from a Louis Armstrong record. At about fifteen she picked up guitar and played rock and roll songs with her brothers in the front room at home, and recalled yodelling 'Wake Up Little Susie' for a literally captive audience at the Kohitere Boys Training Centre, a juvenile detention facility just south of Levin.

The range of her musical activities called for a broad repertoire, and she became adept at playing classical music as well as folk songs, hymns, anthems, opera, show tunes and old-time dance music. When the Levin Little Theatre put on *Amahl and the Night Visitors*, she accompanied her brothers in a production that her mother and Perrin helped to costume and stage. She was so heavily involved in the local scene, she later speculated that 'there would've been quite a bit less musical life in Levin without me'.

Finding sheet music for all these activities was made easier thanks to her excellent relationship with the local music store, Jenness's, a few doors up from her father's bookshop. 'Anything that I fancied, that I came across maybe on the radio or whatever, I would go down to Jenness's. He was amazing. He had these little books: I'd say "Can you get me this?" and he'd get his little book out and say "Yeah" and he would get it.'

Music of every kind and from all over the world arrived for her at Jenness's. The ease with which she could sight-read such a broad range of music meant she felt entirely at home in an extremely wide variety of styles. She also felt no desire to make distinctions between them: 'There was really no dichotomy for me. Most of the time I didn't have a teacher, so I just played whatever I liked. I didn't distinguish if it was classical or if it was pop music.' That failure, or perhaps refusal, to distinguish between the various kinds of music she was involved with almost certainly formed the basis of her lifelong eclecticism. Jenny also attributed her catholic tastes to her lack of formal musical training in small-town New Zealand:

> I'd lived in a fairly provincial sort of circle. I lived in Timaru for 12 years, then I lived in Levin. So, I never had any sort of enlightenment as to the musical world at all. My tastes hadn't developed at all. I hadn't even thought about the distinction between what one might call 'good' and 'bad' music. I brought myself up musically, on various Romantic works. I was very fond of Chopin, Beethoven, a little Bach [but] I had no consciousness of style or period – it meant nothing to me. I could listen to a piece composed in the 20th century and not even notice that it was any different from a piece written by Chopin.[3]

This early recognition that music was not better or worse for being categorised or shoehorned into a particular genre – the real point for her, she later said, was whether she liked it – became a hallmark of Jenny's career as a composer. When she was invited to deliver the annual Douglas Lilburn Lecture in 2016, she asked, early on in her address, 'What? No tradition?' – a response, perhaps, to Lilburn's lament that mid-century (Pākehā) New Zealand lacked a living musical tradition of its own. She went on: 'In the 'fifties, small-town kiwi-land seemed to have just about every tradition', which she then listed, concluding with: 'To me it was all one *huge* tradition, a riotous profusion! And all of it mine!'[4]

Jenny may have felt as if all of that music was hers to possess, but it would be fair to say music also possessed her. If she wasn't playing hockey after school, she was holed up in the front room at home, playing piano, playing and cataloguing her records, reading about the lives of the composers whose work she loved. She described this as a 'largely private dream world' where 'I shut the door and nobody else ever came into the front room.'[5]

The level of her commitment to music, and the determination with which she pursued it, are evidence of her steadfastness, of her dog-with-a-bone tenacity, her obsessiveness. Asked about his sister's most striking characteristic, Craig McLeod singled out her 'devotion to an idea – let's work on it, let's work it out, let's do it – and motivation like I've never seen. She's had that ability to get rid of everything else in life and just focus exactly on what she wanted to do, and do it. I think that was her greatest gift, actually.'[6]

For all her commitment to music, Jenny was unable to study it formally in her senior years at Horowhenua College. 'I wanted to do School Cert music – I was the only one who did want to – but they made me choose between French and Music and I thought, "Well, I've done music on my own up until now; I can manage to do that on my own, but I can't do French on my own." So, I did French.' There were, however, plenty of opportunities outside regular classes to make music – in the lunch hour; before or after school – and it was Jenny's good fortune that Christopher Small was the school's music master.

Small had grown up in nearby Palmerston North, and after university study in Dunedin and Wellington returned to teach at Horowhenua

College from 1953 to 1958; his service there coincided almost exactly with Jenny's time at the school. After winning a government bursary, Small travelled to the United Kingdom in 1961 to study composition. He remained there to lecture at a number of universities, and wrote several books, the most influential of which was *Musicking*, named for the word he coined to denote any activity involving or related to musical performance. 'To music,' Small reckoned, 'is to take part, in any capacity, in a musical performance, whether by performing, by listening, by rehearsing or practicing, by providing material for performance (what is called composing), or by dancing.'[7] He extended this definition to include the work of roadies who set up venues and move pianos, the writers of programme notes, ticket-takers and even those who clean the theatre after the audience has gone home. This definition is inclusive in the extreme, and certainly at odds with more traditional economies of musical value that privilege composition and performance and would characterise the role of audiences (let alone ticket sellers) as being of little account.

It's unlikely these ideas informed Small's teaching during the 1950s – they were the product of many years' engagement with the musical establishment – but it is likely the egalitarian values that underpin his later thinking were a part of his character even during his first years teaching. Jenny's own compositional practice evolved to reflect these values, and her output is notable for the considerable quantity of music she wrote for amateur performers. In a country as small as New Zealand that is perhaps understandable, but it is easy to link the kind of inclusiveness Jenny's catalogue exhibits to Small's advocacy for music-making that invites universal participation.

An open invitation to participate was certainly central to Small's work at Horowhenua College. In addition to teaching core music, he helped stage shows at the school and ran an extracurricular choir. Jenny described herself as his 'right-hand-man', playing the piano parts he wrote for her in arrangements he prepared expressly for the school choir. Jenny recalled that she and Small enjoyed a mutually supportive, collegial relationship: 'He was a better pianist than me but he had to turn to me when he needed to conduct something, so he always made sure that we kept on good terms. He used to write me really nice accompaniments; he always made them interesting and fun to play.' By all accounts it was an excellent choir. 'We were terribly proud of our choir; nobody would have missed our lunchtime practices. We adored Chris, loved all this work, and loved to do well. Nothing made us happier than the sight of his face, all shy and red, each time we had won the inter-school competition, when we knew we had done well, and knew he was terribly pleased with us, though he rarely said very much.'[8]

Exposure to Small's teaching and example were formative for Jenny, although she was hardly an uncritical acolyte. Before she'd heard a note of Arnold Schoenberg's music, Small expressed his dislike for the German composer's work: he couldn't stand serial music or the avant-garde and condemned it in core music classes. 'He thought the whole business would collapse if funding was withdrawn,' Jenny said. 'I'd never heard it so I couldn't judge, but already I was aware of a sort of evil presence, in Chris's terms anyway. It didn't affect me because Chris and I were more like colleagues.'[9] What did affect Jenny was Small's determination to make music where he was, for the people around him. 'I surely absorbed from [him] an awareness that it was good to tailor things to suit the specific conditions, and that people liked having music written for them (I liked it myself) – to say nothing of experiencing the joy of a group enterprise carried through to fruition and success.'[10]

An introduction to te ao Māori

In Timaru Jenny had little contact with Māori. Levin, in the heart of Horowhenua with its rich and complex history of Māori occupation, was an altogether different experience. At school Jenny was surrounded by Māori students, many of whom had to travel from Ōtaki and other nearby towns, and she became particularly friendly with those in her hockey team, among them Amy Taylor. 'Amy and I were close and very good friends. We were strong players and loved the game. We would travel with the hockey teams, both for school and later a whole bunch of us were Horowhenua hockey reps as well, so there were not only inter-

school matches, but also provincial matches to which we travelled, to
Wellington, Palmerston North.'

Through Amy – whose grandfather was a Ngāti Raukawa rangatira –
and other Māori students, Jenny heard haka and action songs, and was
immediately drawn to them. She joined the school's Māori Club, which,
in the absence of any Māori teachers on the staff, was run by students.

> With the Māori Club, it was my friend Amy Taylor – who became
> Amy Brown, the inventor of worm farms – she was the one who
> knew everything. She seemed to be teaching and organising
> everything, everyone just did what she said. This means that our
> tikanga was from Ngāti Raukawa. There was no president or
> secretary or treasurer or anything – you wouldn't usually find such
> 'officers' in a kapa haka group, which is essentially what our Māori
> Club was. Amy was wonderful and she played the piano for the
> club. When she wanted to do something on stage, she would get me
> to play the piano; when she played the piano I was on the stage, so I
> knew all the tunes and the harmony and the words.

It never occurred to her to wonder why she was the only Pākehā in the
club. 'But they never made me feel any different. I really enjoyed their
company. They never felt like "them" – it was just all "us". Always good-
natured, lots of laughs, and much fun and joy at our practices.'

At Amy's invitation, Jenny attended a Ngāti Raukawa gathering at the
beautifully carved Rangiātea Church in Ōtaki, the oldest Māori Anglican
church in Aotearoa. It was one of her first immersive experiences in te ao
Māori. Jenny remembered 'sitting on the floor in the church aisle during
the welcome ceremony, and then I went home with Amy to her place
and three of us spent the night laughing, and telling jokes and stories in
Amy's big old double bed. That was great. I only went there once, but
that once was enough to know there was a Māori world. Any Māori in
those days who had a life on the marae didn't talk about it. The only way
you would find out about life on the marae would be to go to a marae.'

Jenny's experience of Māori life and culture deepened as she progressed
through high school. As a senior student she eventually captained the

hockey team, which traditionally performed Te Rauparaha's haka 'Ka Mate' before each game. Jenny learned that Ngāti Raukawa women enjoyed privileges not shared by women in other iwi, such as speaking on the marae and performing the haka. 'It's not always the case that the captain leads the haka, but as the captain who knew the haka (Amy had taught me the whole thing), I led the haka. To lead the haka is one of the world's great experiences. It's just fantastic.'

Aged sixteen, and at her mother's suggestion, Jenny applied for an American Field Service scholarship, and was awarded the opportunity to travel to the United States for a final year of high school. It seemed to Jenny that a part of her role as an AFS scholar (and as such, a representative of Aotearoa) should be to introduce American Midwesterners to Māori culture. She spoke about this with Amy, who in turn consulted her whānau, who supported the idea; they even crafted a piupiu (flax skirt), pari (woven bodice) and headband for Jenny. Amy taught her the double long poi, and Jenny learned the words to the action songs and haka she would perform during her year away.

This early engagement with and growing love for te ao Māori was to become the basis of a lifelong relationship from which many friendships and musical projects would emerge. Later in life she reflected:

> As a kid I wasn't particularly religious or spiritual, which may puzzle some people who saw what I did later, but I had a sense of the Māori as a blessed people. I didn't mention this to anyone, but I used to look at Māori faces, and I liked what I saw there. Because I thought of them as a blessed people didn't mean I had to go and become a Māori, it didn't mean anything – it was just what I observed, I just thought of them like that. That makes a big space in your heart for Māori people, just to think of them as a blessed people.

A year abroad

In 1958 Jenny travelled to the US, having been assigned to live with a 'comparable' family in Decatur, Illinois, and attend high school there.

On arriving she experienced something akin to culture shock: she found the locals incurious, and their ignorance of the world beyond the US, or even just the world beyond Decatur, startling. While amused that they were impressed with her 'command of the English language' and by a common belief that New Zealand was close to Greenland, she was disconcerted to be among people who had never seen the sea. 'What can you possibly make of the world if you've never seen the sea?' she wondered. And she found the political conservatism of the Midwest bewildering. It was four years since Joseph McCarthy had been censured by the US Senate, but the anti-communist sentiment he had inspired was still widespread. 'This was the late '50s, anti-communist, McCarthyism and all that stuff. They were looking for communists under the bed. I couldn't understand it. Socialism is (or was then) like a dirty word in America which still strikes me as very strange; here it just means doing the right thing by everybody else. People who can't afford things, well, you help them.'[11]

As an AFS scholar Jenny was often invited to speak at social clubs as a kind of ambassador from New Zealand. At those gatherings, dressed in her piupiu and pare, she would tell stories, play guitar while singing action songs, and demonstrate Te Rauparaha's haka and the double long poi. 'I thought I had a duty,' she later said, 'to show these Americans a bit of real Aotearoa, which I didn't doubt I knew.'[12]

Although she may have found Illinois' social and political worlds somewhat alien, the musical contexts in which she landed were more familiar. The Jewell family with whom she lived had a daughter close to Jenny's age, Carole Ann, an 'American sister' for the year. They shared a room and a love of music. Carole Ann was a capable pianist who could sight-read easily, and she and Jenny often played duets and other piano music for four hands – which could be challenging given there was only one piano in the house and the music sometimes required a second.

With around fifteen hundred students, Stephen Decatur High School, which Jenny and Carole Ann both attended, boasted two senior choirs, a women's choir, various a cappella groups and, this being the US, a big band. In this rich context, Jenny was involved in a great deal of music making. She played piano for a production of Oscar Straus' operetta

The Chocolate Soldier (in which Carole Ann played the female lead), as well as singing with, and accompanying, choral groups performing light and popular music. The music those groups performed was challenging – usually commercial arrangements of technically demanding material – but the students could all sight-read and the standard of performance was high. In fact, Jenny felt the students were able to perform the music as proficiently as – and in exact imitation of – adult choirs, and the tightness of their ensemble work eclipsed what she had experienced in New Zealand by a considerable degree. As impressive as the achievements of these groups were, they also revealed a kind of homogeneity that was in stark contrast to her choral experiences with Chris Small:

> I enjoyed all this and was impressed by it at the time, [but] I realise now that our Horowhenua College choir was actually much more fun. High school choirs and adult choruses all over America were singing exactly the same arrangements as our Decatur High choirs; but at Horowhenua we had our *own* arrangements, 'specially for *us*, that *nobody* else knew how to do, and which wowed the whole province. There were no adult choirs who sang, or who *could* sing, the way our choir did.[13]

In the United States Jenny learned a lot about singing, particularly in a cappella settings, and part-writing for standard jazz ensembles. From her art teacher, Justine Bleeks, she also gained an important insight into the ethics of creativity.

> After visiting New York with my American family, I presented to Miss Bleeks some pages of pen-and ink sketches I had taken from commercial New York postcard photographs. Her sharp eyes immediately spotted this. She told me I must never do this again; that basically I was stealing somebody else's composition and, if necessary, I should use my own photos. She tore up all my sketches and made me do some more – a fairly dramatic gesture. I was a bit shaken, as such a thought had never entered my head, but I never sailed so close to the wind again.[14]

And there were lessons in matters of the heart, too. Decatur High might have had some good-looking boys, but it was Dolores with whom she was really in love. 'Being occasionally just as capable of falling in love with a woman as with a man,' Jenny said, 'I fell passionately in love with my sports teacher. Noticing she was the object of my tender affections, Dolores invited me to her small apartment, where I could not fail to observe the large double bed decorated with imitation flowers that, clearly, she shared with her female sports-teaching partner. Oh dear, the sinking heart.' Letting her down gently, Dolores was to become a supportive friend, and gave Jenny an inscribed copy of Kahlil Gibran's *The Prophet*, 'which I quite took to for a while and treasured'.

Jenny was sorry to leave Decatur and the friends she had made there, but she was glad to return to Aotearoa when her year was up: 'I had been extremely homesick, especially for the sniff of the sea and the whole country here: I desperately missed it.'

Land girl

On her arrival back in New Zealand in 1959, Jenny's parents expected her to go on to university. She had been dux in her fourth year at Horowhenua College and recipient of an AFS scholarship; it seemed certain she would 'do a Bachelor of Arts degree and become a teacher' – the educational catchcry of the day. Jenny had other ideas. Her time away had made her realise that while she missed friends and family, it was New Zealand's physical environment – big skies, proximity to the sea, the smells and colours of the country – she had missed the most. That longing for the land triggered in her a somewhat romantic desire to get closer to it. She set aside immediate plans for university and took a job at a horticultural research station just south of Levin.

Funded by the New Zealand government, the Levin Horticultural Research Centre was established in the 1940s to conduct research on commercial plants.[15] When Jenny started in 1959, there was a staff of about twenty-five. She began in the glasshouses but was soon out among the vegetables. 'Half the time I'd be measuring stuff with callipers and writing down which variety of vegetable had the best growing record; they were all getting different kinds of fertiliser and this and that. Or else I was sneaking a sleep under the trees because I was out in the fields and nobody knew what I was doing or was keeping up with it.' There were the usual pranks played on new staff – Jenny was asked to scale a wind turbine with a huge spanner in order to 'wind it up' – and strawberry fights in the packing shed; the work was hardly onerous and the company agreeable. When Marjorie, the only other woman on the staff, left her post as librarian to marry Jenny's boss, John Goldie, Jenny was moved indoors to run the library and keep records.

Music wasn't entirely absent from this environment. She shared the office with others, including Jeff Hyde, who liked music and was also a good whistler. 'He knew a lot of the same music I did so we used to have competitions whistling our way through *Eine Kleine Nachtmusik* and stuff like that; who could get from beginning to end?'

Away from work, Jenny maintained an active musical life. She regularly accompanied performances around the Horowhenua region and had a few private piano lessons with Ian Harvey, who had taken over as the music teacher at Horowhenua College on Christopher Small's departure: 'Ian Harvey taught me mainly the meaning of rubato.'

Knowing that she would eventually go to university, Jenny decided to take a couple of extramural papers through Palmerston North University College: English Literature; and Greek History, Art and Literature. While the Greek paper was 'interesting enough, but not interesting enough to be studying for a pass', English Literature was much closer to her heart. She enjoyed engaging with the set texts and found the course stimulating. Among the delightful discoveries of the paper were several twentieth-century poets: 'One of our set poets was e.e. cummings. Well, I just loved cummings, still love him, and I did Auden, Eliot. It was a nice little handful.'

After eighteen months, work at the Levin research centre lost its allure and Jenny was ready for change: 'I got all of the land urge out of me,' she said. 'I've hated gardening ever since.'[16] In the summer of 1960/61, as she began to think about heading off to university, her old friend from Timaru, Philippa Harding, got in touch. Pip, a fine cellist, suggested

Jenny join her at the Summer School of Music, held at St Peter's School outside the small Waikato township of Cambridge, for a couple of weeks of music.

The Cambridge Summer School of Music first ran in 1946 under the direction of Owen Jensen as part of Auckland University College's Adult Education Centre. A success from the outset, it was to be held annually until the late 1980s. New Zealand composer Douglas Lilburn presented his watershed paper 'A Search for Tradition' the first summer it ran, and from 1947 onwards instruction in composition as well as performance was offered at the school. It was a hothouse environment. Performers and composers from around New Zealand came to live in, or to pitch tents in the school grounds; they renewed old friendships and forged new ones, and made and experienced music together. In her first year at Cambridge, Jenny – who had not yet decided to study music at university and had no conscious aspirations to become a composer – joined the piano class run by Wellington pianist Doris Sheppard. She described the whole experience as 'a revelation: ten days where everybody was as mad about music as I was, and we did nothing but music all day and half the night long; it was like heaven on earth.'[17]

It was at the summer school that Jenny first encountered serial music, an opportunity for her to make up her own mind about Chris Small's bête noire.

> I remember Robin Maconie coming out to one of the evening concerts to play the Webern *Variations for piano* in a long night shirt with a funny little cap on and sunglasses and he sat down and he played this Webern, without any music, and I listened to this with my ears just popping out of my head and I thought, 'He's making it up.' The first time I thought it was a joke but then he played it again and I could tell it was the same piece and so I thought, 'No, he's memorised it, it was written down, somebody wrote it.' So, there was a big question mark hanging there.[18]

The community, the performing, hearing music and sounds she had not encountered before was life-changing. 'Everyone kept saying I had to be a teacher, and this still goes on in the provinces; if you have any brains at all you have to get a BA and be a teacher. You couldn't go off doing silly things like music.'[19] Cambridge changed everything: 'After I went to my first Cambridge Summer School, before I went to varsity, I thought "Oh blow it, I'm not going to be a school teacher, I'm going to do music", because Cambridge was great.'[20]

3

Victoria University College

Victoria University College in Wellington, a college of the University of New Zealand, served a little over three thousand students in 1961 when Jenny first enrolled there.[1] The Music Department was small but lively, and was considered the hub of composition in New Zealand. Douglas Lilburn was a senior lecturer and shared teaching duties with composer David Farquhar. Pianist Margaret Nielsen had joined them the previous year to teach keyboard and aural skills. Although she did not offer piano lessons to performers, she was a constant fixture in the department's free lunch-hour concerts.

The school was led by Frederick Page, who had been appointed Professor of Music a few years earlier. He had begun teaching at Victoria in 1946, and described the buildings on first impression as like 'an institution for bad girls'.[2] The physical environment had not improved a great deal in the intervening years and when Jenny arrived the Music Department was housed in the old Chemistry wing: 'pretty dilapidated – bits of plaster used to fall off the ceiling as you walked up the stairs – but it was a wonderful atmosphere'. If the accommodation was down-at-heel, it was compensated for by the first-rate art on the walls: Page was on the pictures committee of the university and, having an excellent eye (he was also married to painter Evelyn Page), had been able to acquire some choice canvases for the Music Department. 'On the back wall of the Vic music room,' Jenny remembered, 'hung a very substantial McCahon painting of Otago Peninsula, which over the years infused our whole lives as students – and for some of us later, as staff. There were New Zealand paintings all over the place, something we took completely for granted.'

Through her Methodist connections in Wellington, Lorna McLeod found her daughter a flat in Majoribanks Street on the slopes of Mount Victoria. Jenny immediately sought to inject herself into the city's musical life and joined the choir of the Wesley Methodist Church in Taranaki Street, a short walk from her new home. Her membership of the church choir was short-lived, and the Methodists did nothing to sanitise her appearance: she arrived at Victoria on a motorbike, and – like her mother twenty-five years earlier – sporting wild hair and a leather jacket, and smoking relentlessly. The motorbike didn't last long – Wellington was too cold and windy, and the trip back to Levin just too far on a small and unreliable bike – and she got about on foot or by bus, taking the train when she felt the need to visit home. To her mother's chagrin Jenny made a habit of not letting her family know when she was returning, preferring to arrive unannounced: 'I liked to just turn up and see that everybody was happy to see me.'

To support herself Jenny took a part-time job in the mornings, sewing buttonholes and belts in a factory on Manners Street, halfway between home and the university. The business was owned and run by Ernst Neuer, an Austrian Jew who had emigrated during the rise of Nazism; a qualified medical doctor, he was unable to practise in New Zealand because his training was not recognised. His wife Sarah (and sometimes their daughter Ruth, also a music student at Victoria and a good friend to Jenny) worked alongside him in the factory. Their relationship was nothing like that of Ron and Lorna McLeod, whose emotions were bottled up and voices seldom raised. Arguments of cyclonic intensity between Neuer and his wife would erupt completely unexpectedly – shouting and screaming, tears and recriminations – and subside just as quickly. 'Those rows shocked the hell out of me,' Jenny said, 'because my parents never had a row in front of anybody; though they were profoundly uncomfortable with each other a lot of the time, which you could feel. Because my parents never had rows, I was never in the habit of hearing rows, so I had to get used to this . . . After a while I didn't turn a hair.'[3]

Jenny's decision to pursue music rather than English at Victoria was not prompted by a desire to study with New Zealand's foremost composer; she enrolled with aspirations for a career in performance: 'I thought I was going to be a concert pianist. Grand dreams.'[4] In fact, she'd had no intention of studying composition at all, and had not composed a note of music. 'I thought all composers were dead. Not long before coming to Vic I bought a record that had some Lilburn and I was shocked to find that composers were not all dead; there he was when I went down there.'[5] Her belief that composition belonged to the past may have been partly attributable to an experience she'd had a few years before she moved to Wellington.

> When I was still at home, I thought I was writing my first piece, because I dreamed this piece. When I woke up, I thought 'Oh, write it down – don't lose it.' I was quite excited – I thought, 'So this is what it is to be a composer!' After I had written it down, it turned out that Handel had written it already. My mother had a few classical pieces which she used to learn from her piano teacher in Palmerston North, Mr Gunter, and I found these albums later on as I was just kind of teaching myself. I discovered the piece that I thought I had written was actually in there and I had played it – cos I was quite good at sight-reading – once or twice, maybe. It was completely accurate. I can still remember it and I could still write it down. I was ever so disappointed when I discovered that I hadn't written it first.

During the early 1960s, Victoria offered a Bachelor's degree in Music without named specialisations – one did not graduate as a composer, musicologist or performer, but simply with a BMus. Students primarily studied history and literature, harmony and counterpoint, although there were a few courses in related executant activities including composition, musicianship and orchestration. Performance activities such as playing an instrument or performing in an orchestra or choir did not then attract academic credit. Students wishing to continue to learn an instrument did so outside of the department. During her first year in Wellington Jenny studied piano with Doris Sheppard, building on the foundation they had laid at the Cambridge Summer School. Jenny thought her a good teacher but found her a challenging personality, 'neurotic and possessive about her students'.

With almost no formal training, Jenny's preparation for a music degree was patchy. She had worked through a few music rudiments books and gone over the Grade 5 music theory syllabus, although hadn't bothered to sit the exam. She did, however, have an excellent ear and was able to recognise almost everything she was shown in class, even if the names were unfamiliar. 'When I got to varsity it was just a matter of, "Oh, that's what that's called", you know, and I found it really very easy . . . I didn't think of it as training, I was thirsty for music, to get into it more. It was curiosity to get to know more . . . I began to realise how much music I just didn't know, [that] I didn't even know was there. So, it was just indulging my appetite, basically.'[6]

The small size of the Music Department meant students got to know one another well, forming an easy and energetic esprit de corps. The cohort included people Jenny had met at the Cambridge Summer School of Music the previous summer, such as violist Evelyn Killoh and pianist/composer Robin Maconie – a second-year student when Jenny arrived – who went on to become a world authority on the music of Karlheinz Stockhausen. Among those joining her in the first-year class in 1961 was Te Puoho Kātene (then known as Paul), who had started a Fine Arts degree at Canterbury before his love of choral singing led him to abandon his paintbrushes and move to Victoria to study music. Also in her cohort were trombonist Roy Murphy and pianist John Charles, musicians who had played jazz with drummer (and later screen actor) Bruno Lawrence in their teens; young composers including Ray Twomey, and Ian MacDonald and Gary Mutton, who wrote piano pieces that Jenny would go on to perform. 'Both Ian and Gary wrote their little sets of piano pieces for me,' she remembered. 'I was touched, and they were dear, gentle little pieces.'

The Victoria University Music Society, run by students and supported by the music faculty, was very active. In Jenny's first year the society presented Anton Webern's *Variations for piano, Op. 27* (performed by the society's secretary-treasurer, Robin Maconie), as well as recordings of electronic music by Karlheinz Stockhausen and Herbert Eimert.[7] While music from abroad was programmed, the society was equally committed to performing student compositions; during the three years Jenny studied at Victoria, works by Ray Twomey, Kit Powell, Robin Maconie and Gary Mutton, as well as some of her own pieces, were performed.

Jenny quickly became involved in the society, and she assisted Robin and society president Evelyn Killoh and others in staging events. Many of the students were able performers, but it was sometimes necessary to get players in from outside to supplement their number. 'We got players from the orchestra and paid them by selling the recordings to Radio New Zealand [then the New Zealand Broadcasting Corporation, NZBC]. That worked out well, and they played our pieces.' Jenny's involvement continued across her time at Victoria and in 1963 she served as the society's president.

As well as the student-run Music Society concerts, there were departmental lunch-hour recitals featuring performances by both students and faculty. Between them, these series offered students plenty of opportunity to perform. Jenny made her solo debut during her first year, performing Chopin's *Barcarolle*. She also performed with ensembles, including a June 1961 performance of a Handel organ concerto (on the music room Steinway – the Handel had no pedal part) with an orchestra conducted by David Farquhar.[8] It was 'in a simple key . . . attractive, and also not too difficult' – perfect for a first-year student soloist.

Jenny formed a trio with good friend and cellist Sue Smith and student violinist Peter Verhoeven (later replaced by violinist Murray Grönwall, who lectured in the French Department). The group played many Haydn piano trios at Victoria and participated in one of the annual

University Games Easter tournaments, performing Beethoven's 'Ghost' trio. At the same event she also performed Schubert's piano duet *Fantasy in F minor* with Murray Brown. 'A wonderful piece,' she said. 'We gave such a great performance that day. Nothing Murray and I did before or after was ever quite as good.'

Jenny also sang in the university choir conducted by Robert Oliver. Their performance of Bach's *Magnificat* at St Peter's Church just down the hill from the campus was another memorable occasion. There were concerts to attend as well: orchestral music presented by the National Orchestra in the Town Hall; and more adventurous fare from the Wellington branch of the International Society for Contemporary Music (ISCM).

Established in 1950 by Fred Page, pianist Dorothy Davies and violinist Francis Rosner, and with support from the Department of Internal Affairs, the local branch of the ISCM had nominated Igor Stravinsky as its patron, a nomination to which he responded favourably in 1957.[9] The society promoted twentieth-century music and bravely sought to engage the New Zealand public with Stravinsky and Bartók, Boulez and Stockhausen, and various points between. They also presented music by New Zealand composers: Dorothea Franchi, Larry Pruden, Ronald Tremain, Edwin Carr, Robin Maconie, David Farquhar, Douglas Lilburn and others.

As a first-year student, Jenny became the official page turner for the Wellington Chamber Music Society. As such, she was invited to post-concert parties in the homes of Wellington's émigré community. 'I got to know Arthur and Lisl Hilton, Fred and Lotte Turnovsky and others really quite well in this way. Dr J.C. Beaglehole and his wife Elsie were also staunch chamber supporters, who had post-concert parties at their house, too.' Over the next few years, she was to meet all the visiting chamber artists and turned pages whenever they needed it. 'It was a whole other world I had never experienced before, and I completely thrived on it. I loved it.'

The richness of the cultural milieu in which she found herself was exactly what she had hoped for. The 'heaven on Earth' she had discovered at the Cambridge Summer School of Music was to be her daily experience during her first years of study at Victoria.

'Try writing a little piece'

Jenny had easily met the academic challenges of high school. She'd had no trouble with her studies in the United States either: 'As top senior student at Stephen Decatur High I happily relinquished the role of valedictorian to local top student Ed Bryant in return for a piano solo at our graduation ceremony – Chopin's "Revolutionary" Etude – which then earned me the offer of a piano scholarship I had to decline (under AFS rules) from the local Professor of Music at Millikin University.' Her nimble intelligence, coupled with an excellent ear, meant that even in the absence of theoretical preparation for university music study, she was undeterred by the demands of the curriculum. She was also confident and resilient: at high school her nickname had been 'Bounce' because 'Whatever happened to me, I could bounce back.' Confidence and intelligence are useful attributes for managing life's setbacks, but in Jenny's case they also fuelled her suspicion of rules. 'Auras of authority never went down very well with me,' she said.

Jenny's scepticism and contrary nature may well have been a reaction to the generally uncritical conformity she had encountered in both small-town New Zealand and Decatur, Illinois. In those socially conservative settings, people seemed eager to tell her what was acceptable and what was not, what was good and what was bad. 'It just seemed to me that they didn't know what they were talking about. Somehow my instincts told me that they didn't really know that something was bad; it was just what they'd inherited.' As a result, she was reluctant to accept anything at face value: 'I was quietly – quietly enough that I never got caught – extremely rebellious against any kind of authority, whether at school or [with] anything that I just thought was a load of bullshit.'

There were downsides to this scepticism: 'Anything that I was told not to do because it was bad for me,' Jenny said, 'I would just shut my mouth tight and I would think, "Yes, and we'll see about that." I would not believe them until I'd tried it for myself. So, I got into all sorts of trouble that I didn't need to, because I just didn't believe them.'

Jenny's contrarian tendencies were never far from the surface in her interactions with her teachers. Candidates for the BMus degree studied harmony and counterpoint, with Douglas Lilburn and David Farquhar teaching Palestrina and species counterpoint in the first year, and Bach in the second year. Due to some irregularity in teaching rotations, Jenny studied with Lilburn both years.

When I was being ladled all this stuff – the great authorities and all these ancient scores and what have you – I just thought 'Oh, yes?' And if I ever found an opportunity to play a trick on one of my teachers, I did. We used to have all these old Dutch scores of Palestrina in burnt sienna, brown print. We had heaps of them at Vic, and I used to study them a bit. One day I discovered parallel fifths in Palestrina and I thought, 'This is fantastic.' So, I memorised the passage. In my next first-year counterpoint assignment I put an exact replica of this situation into my tutorial – these were one-to-one tutorials – which Douglas was supervising. I was just sitting there beside him waiting for him to discover this. He always used to spend hours looking at your work and he wouldn't say anything. He would just sit there – he didn't sit at the piano and try to play it so he could understand what it said – he was just reading it in his head. After a long, long time he said, 'You can't do that.' And I said, 'What?' So, he showed me my – and Palestrina's – parallel fifths. And I said, 'Palestrina did it.' He said, 'He did not.' I said, 'Yes, he did,' and I showed him the original score, which completely flabbergasted him and shut him up. And he took that score away and he went and talked to David about it and a couple of weeks later he said to me, 'I talked to David about that and we decided it was a misprint.' You can't imagine what fun it was for me to do that. And I agree, of course it was a misprint, but I wasn't going to let on; what are the chances of finding something like that in print and getting them to fall for it?

Lilburn wasn't the only faculty member Jenny was determined to have a bit of fun with. When Fred Page assigned a fugue-writing exercise, Jenny's piece concealed a passage from *Auld Lang Syne*. 'When he'd finished looking at my fugue – he said, "Very good, very good" and waved me away airily – I took my pencil and I pointed to the tune in there. That was great fun. He laughed. And he took the score and showed it to the others.'

Harmony and counterpoint, keyboard and aural skills, and the examination of selected works – Bach, Beethoven, Schubert – formed the central planks of Jenny's early years of study. Composition was not formally offered until the third and fourth years of an Honours degree. Even so, Douglas Lilburn encouraged students to write music during their first two years. In addition to Counterpoint I, for which weekly technical exercises were assigned, Lilburn also taught harmony classes. In that context, he would suggest to his students that they 'try writing a little piece' during the term holidays. 'That was as far as it got,' Jenny said. 'He would then look at what you did.' With Lilburn's encouragement, Jenny composed a small piece for piano. 'It, sort of, came out quite well and I quite liked it, so I thought, "I'll do some more".'[10]

Completed during her first term at Victoria, *Piano Suite* was the first of many pieces she would compose while a student. A work of five short movements, it was also one of the very few pieces of her own she would perform publicly – at an evening concert in the Music Department arranged by the Music Society. At Lilburn's prompting she began to compose music regularly and made her first foray into setting poetry as song.

Jenny had derived a great deal of pleasure from the English paper she had taken extramurally the previous year and developed a fondness for modern poets, in particular e.e. cummings. As far back as her fourth-form year at Horowhenua College she had been receptive to poetry, thanks in part to English teacher Allan Cargo. 'I always liked teachers who could have a bit of fun. One day [Allan Cargo] stood up in class and read a poem about Mr McCloud by Ogden Nash, whose lines never matched each other in length but always rhymed at the end. There was this whole poem about Mr McCloud and the last line was "I'm just a McCloud with a silver lining." I adored that. If I didn't like poetry before that, I liked it afterwards.'

From Ogden Nash to e.e. cummings is a leap, and Jenny confessed to finding cummings' poems impenetrable at first: 'I'd had awful trouble with them; it took me ages. I didn't understand what symbolism was and consequently I read these e.e. cummings poems thinking "What's it about?" I had to go to my Methodist minister – because I knew he had an English degree – and I took this poem to him and asked him to explain to me what it meant.' Armed with an understanding of symbolism, Jenny discovered meaning, as well as a rich musicality, in cummings' poetry; it's unsurprising she chose his words to set to music. The three poems she sculpted into songs that year were: 'somewhere i have never travelled, gladly beyond any experience'; 'i carry your heart with me (i carry it in my/heart)'; and 'anyone lived in a pretty how town'.

Pleased with the resulting songs, Jenny decided to have them performed at a Music Society concert. In Levin she'd shared organ-playing duties for the St John's Methodist Church with Maureen Spencer, a woman closer to her mother's age who was also a good singer.

> I asked her if she would learn my e.e. cummings songs and come down to Wellington to Vic and sing them. So, she did. I didn't realise at that time that this was not quite what they were expecting from students in the Vic Music Department. If you'd written some songs, it would be usual to ask another student to sing them. Fred and Douglas were particularly impressed, because this woman from nowhere – from Levin – came and sang my new songs. I played the accompaniment. I think it was the enterprise that impressed them.

Page and Lilburn were also impressed that a student in her first year of study would set verse by a writer considered to be at the cutting edge of contemporary poetry. The day after the performance, Page handed Jenny a volume of cummings' work.[11] He, and Lilburn too, had a keen interest in the arts beyond music, and enjoyed friendships with some of the country's finest poets, writers and painters. Discovering that Jenny shared their appetite for poetry quite likely enriched their growing friendship with her.

In fact, the relationships among staff and students were generally very open and convivial. Jenny recalled:

My teachers at university – Margaret Nielsen, David Farquhar, Douglas Lilburn, Freddy Page – there were only four of them and they all knew each other outside being on the staff. There were not many students back in those days so we got to know each other. They used to invite us to their parties – we didn't invite them to ours and they had the good sense not to come – but I went to all their parties and this way I got to know all the other artists around Wellington. I remember [painter] John Drawbridge and [sculptor] Tanya Ashken, for instance, people that I would otherwise never have met, but I met them in that purely human context and not an academic context; and in the context of wonderful, good food. A very literate group; well-educated and self-educated a lot of the time, well-read people. Margaret was a good jazz pianist. [In California] she'd looked after [Dave] Brubeck's kids and studied with Darius Milhaud. Get Margaret in her cups and she would sit there, improvising jazz. Her specialty number was the 'Black Watch Night Beetle' which she sang as she played. David was hilarious and would play Gershwin's arrangements of his own songs; fiendishly difficult, but he loved those.

While Jenny felt a strong connection to Margaret and David, it was her relationships with Fred and Eve Page, and with Douglas Lilburn, that defined her early years in Wellington and would mark her life most deeply.

Fred Page's initial impressions of Jenny may have been mixed – it wasn't every day a young woman arrived at the Music Department riding a motorbike, clad in leather and smoking like she'd invented it – but when he discovered how musical she was he quickly warmed to her. He began by loaning her books from his extensive collection, initially poetry by e.e. cummings and, in time, all kinds of things. 'Fred always took an interest in what I was reading and sometimes he would turn up with a book under his arm and just say "Have a look at this." Had it not been for him, I would not have read the things I did read. He just used to feed me whatever it was he was reading himself.'

Jenny's expanding literary taste also had a positive benefit for Levin, where her father still ran his bookshop. 'Penguin books were big in those days. Dad didn't used to stock much of them, but I came back from Vic one day and said, "Dad, where're the Penguins?" Well, next time I came he'd got a great big stand of Penguins: he had the best Penguin stock on the coast. That was because of Fred, basically.'

Fred Page also took charge of Jenny's musical education. When her piano teacher Doris Sheppard refused her time off lessons during the exam period, Jenny walked out on her. 'Hearing of this, Freddy directed me, in that lordly manner of his, to prepare a prelude and fugue every week and come to his study for a lesson. For the rest of my student career these lessons continued. Payment was out of the question. In this way I learned most of Bach's *Well-Tempered Clavier* and much of Mozart.'[12]

Soon enough Jenny was spending time with the Pages at their weekend retreat in Waikanae, a house in the modernist style designed for them by Austrian architect Ernst Plischke. She would drive Fred (and sometimes Eve, when Eve wasn't making her own way there) the hour or so north on a Friday night and spend the weekend with them. Jenny described them as fantastic cooks who would prepare exquisite meals while she mowed the lawns or cared for the roses. Weather permitting, they would eat this 'simple peasant food', as Fred liked to call it, under the large mulberry tree in the centre of the freshly cut lawn. Along the outer sides of the corner property were lime trees, and their reflected light 'invested the whole place with a sort of heavenly radiance,' Jenny said. 'Eve did a lot of her paintings out there, and wherever we now see wonderful outdoor sunlit leafy greens and yellows in her work, we can usually recognise the Waikanae lime trees.'

As a regular guest for meals at Fred and Eve's Wellington home in Hobson Street, Jenny met artists such as Janet Paul, and writers including Charles Brasch and Rewi Alley. 'Fred and Eve would introduce me to all these other people who were making lovely things, or writing things or just being provocative.' One of them was the poet Denis Glover, whom Fred took Jenny to meet a few years later when Glover was living on the Kāpiti Coast.

> We stopped outside Denis's little cottage at Paekākāriki and banged
> on the front door. Nothing. We went round the back and banged

again. Still nothing. As we started to leave, a figure with a purple
face and a monumental black eye came scurrying out, with cries
of relief, explaining confusedly that he had thought we were the
trumpeter returned, who had already beaten him up for pinching
his trumpet – which, he hastened to add, he had not done. This
was Glover. He led us into the living-room, a few feet from the
sea-front. All the windows were shut, the sun poured in, and it was
sweltering. All afternoon [Glover's wife] Kura and Denis cursed
each other roundly (and all their respective absent relatives), over-
filled us and themselves with lukewarm draught beer, and played
endless 78s of Caruso. Hurling insults and witticisms, Denis
performed magnificently. It was like walking into a Dostoyevsky
novel.[13]

Reflecting on what her relationship with the Pages meant to her, she
later wrote:

They taught me a whole lot more about quality – quality in art,
in books, in film, in music, in food, in conversation, in laughter
– in short, quality in living. From Fred and Eve, I learned how to
really look, to really listen, and to really taste. They had an unerring
instinct for beauty, for what is fine and real, and loved nothing
better than to live with it all around them, in the most unassuming
and natural ways, and to introduce it to the young.[14]

As well as nurturing Jenny's love and respect for the arts and for living,
Fred Page was an important role model in the way he so profoundly
respected people. 'But it was this about Freddy that I loved,' she wrote,
'and for which I held him in the highest moral regard: his sheer love
of the human spirit, his life-long concern that it should broaden,
deepen, become stronger, more compassionate, more dynamic – just
more . . . For him, the person was paramount.'[15]

Jenny was very fond of her parents, and recognised that they had
offered her a solid foundation from which to start out in life, but it was
clear to her that they couldn't teach her what she most needed to learn.

'Eventually I said as much to Mum, who then even agreed with me.' She had long since stopped asking for her parents' advice and, when it was offered, didn't consider taking it. At one point she said she did not even think of Ron and Lorna as her real parents. She told them that the Pages were her substitute parents, people who could give her what she needed, and 'they took it very well – they weren't offended – and they loved my substitute parents'.[16] Lorna and Ron were indeed charmed when they met the Pages. Ron had taken up painting – Jenny suggested this as a form of therapy to combat the depression he suffered during those years – and Eve found merit in his work, complimenting him and encouraging him to continue. Craig McLeod too had struck up a friendship with Fred 'when one weekday afternoon they discovered each other as the only two in the audience at a new continental film in town, having both skipped the same music tutorial to go to it'.[17]

By Jenny's account, her love for these 'substitute parents' appears to have been reciprocated. 'Freddy and Eve', she wrote, 'looked on me as a daughter (they loved my brothers, too) and we remained the dearest of friends right up until their respective deaths.'[18] Sebastian, Fred and Eve's son, was a little older than Jenny, and years later he admitted to her that he and his sister Anna 'were a bit envious at [Jenny] supplanting their place as a child'.

Douglas Lilburn was also a friend, a role model and a teacher to Jenny. However, her relationship with Lilburn was of a different order. When Jenny had argued with Doris Sheppard about time off lessons during exams, Doris 'became extremely annoyed and accused me of being "in love with Freddy Page". She wasn't so wrong, in fact – I was actually in love with Douglas. But nobody knew that, or so I thought, apart from Douglas himself, who knew this from quite early on – it was no secret to him.'

Jenny admitted she had 'fallen in love' more than once purely because of an aspect of a person's character: one man's love for his children; the purity of another man's love for his wife. 'I just loved to see these things in people, especially men, in whom pure unadulterated love seems not to be such a common thing.' With the benefit of many years' hindsight, she came to see that:

I really loved Douglas because of his commitment and dedication as an artist; and as an undergraduate student, never before had I seen this at such a high level – even though I wasn't always so mad about all the work he produced. But he *was* a composer, a real one. And the question of one's being a real composer or not was of great importance to me. So here was Douglas, very seriously a real composer. Of course, in Levin I knew Chris Small too, and he was a composer – and well, I'd been in love him too, natürlich – but Lilburn was a much more serious matter. My whole being was intrinsically wound up with that awareness.

Jenny suspected her attachment to Lilburn during her early years at Victoria was probably something akin to 'worship', a feeling likely reinforced by Lilburn's considerable regard for her. 'Lilburn saw something in me, that was clear – although this was true of Fred too – and Douglas supported me, he took me seriously as a composer. He had got me into it all in the first place, and then it was him who asked me back to teach at Vic – he organised all that.'

The affection she felt for Lilburn was a secret she understandably kept close – Lilburn was her teacher, a member of the music faculty. Even so, her feelings for him did find expression in music. 'One of those early [e.e. cummings] songs, "somewhere i have never travelled", was written for the Douglas Lilburn I had fallen in love with.'

Returning to Cambridge

Jenny enjoyed the environment and the community she had discovered as a music student in Wellington, and thrived on exposure to new music and ideas. One of the highlights of her first year was hearing Ralph Vaughan Williams' *Fantasia on a Theme by Thomas Tallis*, a recording of which Lilburn had played in class.[19] It's a ravishing work, and Jenny was both smitten by it – 'What a piece. I had never heard a piece that went on and on and on and was just so glorious' – and determined to imitate it: 'As soon as I heard that I thought, "I could write one of those".'

The university did not then have a regular orchestra, so the best opportunity students had to hear their orchestral music performed was at the Cambridge Summer School of Music, where the performance of student works was a priority. After the delights of her previous visit, Jenny had been set on returning anyway, but the chance to have an orchestral work performed reinforced her intention and saw her put time aside to attempt to 'write one of those'.

For her second summer in Cambridge, Jenny decided to forgo piano classes and instead joined the composers, taught in 1962 by Ron Tremain. Other class members included Robin Maconie, Kit Powell and National Orchestra clarinettist Ken Wilson from Wellington, and John Rimmer from Auckland. Tremain had been associated with the school almost since its inception, studying with Douglas Lilburn in the early years and returning as a tutor after completing a doctorate at London's Royal College of Music. As a young composer at the Cambridge Summer School, he had understood the need to prepare music during the preceding year if there was to be a hope of its being performed at Cambridge. Composer Larry Pruden (who had also attended Cambridge in the 1950s, and succeeded Tremain as the school's composition teacher in 1963) also understood this: 'Each year I made a special effort to write a new piece for Cambridge knowing that it would be put into somewhat inadequate rehearsal but at least here was a chance to immediately assess one's work.'[20]

The students in Tremain's charge in 1962 had followed this example. John Rimmer described what happened in the composition classes:

> It very much depended on what the student composers had done during the year and what they took to Cambridge . . . The tutor would look through the whole piece – or most of a piece – if you'd written something especially for the school, but it only really worked if you'd done a substantial part of a piece and took it down to Cambridge for them to look at. And then [you'd have] to try and get a performance there.[21]

The number of concerts held over the summer season meant there were plenty of opportunities to have pieces performed. Kit Powell recalled the intensity of activity. The days began, he said, with lessons for the various groups – choir, orchestra, early music, instrumental lessons, composers' group – which continued after lunch, occupying normal school hours.

> Then, before the evening meal there was a concert, often from the pupils, and after the meal another, often from pupils and tutors. Immediately after the evening concert the hall was cleared for a dance, with live music of course, and after the dance there was either a party (usually outside) or, more often, a copying session. One must remember that this – early '60s – was before the invention of the photocopier, and so all orchestral works which the composers had brought with them and which had been approved for performance had to have instrumental parts. A big group of students (not just from the composers' group) would sit round a large table with the score in the middle and copy parts, some directly from the score, others would make further copies of string parts. This would continue into the small hours of the morning.[22]

Jenny remembered that the composers not only stayed up until all hours to help one another write out parts for the orchestra but also assisted with performances. Depending on what was needed, it could be all hands to the pump: Robin Maconie recalled being dragooned into the orchestra to play double bass, receiving last-minute instruction on the instrument from Arthur Broadhurst, the headmaster of St Peter's School.[23] The demands made of composers were usually a little more modest, however. Jenny said Larry Pruden 'would arrive with a trailerload of percussion instruments and the composers would play those with the orchestra. I remember playing the bass drum in Borodin's *Second Symphony*. It was awesome.'

The orchestral piece Jenny had prepared for the summer of 1962 was called *Pastorale*. 'It was more than somewhat influenced by that gorgeous Vaughan Williams' *Fantasia on a Theme by Thomas Tallis*. I loved the big build-up in there, so my *Pastorale* piece was via Vaughan Williams . . . as much as I could manage it.' In the composers' class she had the opportunity to finesse the piece and wrangle a performance. And the performance was pretty good. 'That was fantastic,' she recalled. 'What was so great was that it sounded the way I had imagined it.' William Walden-Mills, the national advisor in school music, was also impressed with the work; he asked Jenny for the music and had the National Secondary Schools' Orchestra perform the piece.

Experiences like these were catalytic in Jenny's drift towards a life composing music. She was discovering the pleasure of writing music and the satisfaction of hearing that music performed. She was also learning that composing – having 'to go through this whole process against a deadline and not be sure until after you had heard it whether a piece would actually work' – was a nerve-wracking business. It was excellent training, and the presence of an orchestra in Cambridge 'was the great incentive for me to write a piece, even though I never thought of myself as a composer . . . The *Cambridge Suite* I would never have written if it hadn't been for Cambridge. And I would never have written the *Little Symphony*.'[24]

Although the orchestra at Cambridge included tutors – who were often members of the National Orchestra or other professional players – it was mainly made up of students, with a few ring-ins. Their performances could be a little uneven, and John Rimmer remembered, 'They tended to vary quite a lot, but thinking back one was always thrilled to get a live performance. So, I think the rough spots tended to be smoothed over by the experience.'[25] Jenny, however, was positive about the quality of the performances, saying 'They were excellent. They were very good performances.' Her favourable recollections, likely of performances of her own works, were possibly a function of her awareness of the musicians at her disposal and her determination to prepare music specifically for them, a trait that would become a hallmark of her mature compositional practice: 'None of the pieces I wrote for them were too hard; I knew who I was writing for. I mean, [the parts] kept them busy, but they played them very well. Most of the time the music wasn't very hard to listen to . . . the *Cambridge Suite* and the *Little Symphony* are both very easy pieces.'[26]

The *Cambridge Suite*, composed during Jenny's second year at Victoria and performed at the beginning of 1963, is a longer and more varied work than *Pastorale*. There's evidence in this piece of her university studies, as well as the music she had been listening to before she went to Victoria. The 'Introduction' bounces along – clarinet, flute and legato violin melodies gliding over the skipping pizzicato strings. Jenny likened it to LeRoy Anderson's *Plink, Plank, Plunk!* – 'a fun pizzicato piece I liked as a youngster. I once requested this during a radio request session, only silly me thought it was called "Flink, Flank, Flunk", for which I was roundly reproached by the announcer.' The second movement, 'Interlude', Jenny thought of as a kind of homage to the first of Benjamin Britten's 'Four Sea Interludes' from *Peter Grimes*. There might be a whiff of Debussy in there, too. Britten also makes his presence felt in the third, 'Musette', and fourth, 'Passacaglia', movements, as does J.S. Bach. 'I was blown away as a student by the Bach *Passacaglia in C minor*,' Jenny said, 'and also by Dido's magnificent aria "When I am laid in earth" from Purcell's *Dido and Aeneas*. My own passacaglia here is much less classical however.'

The final and fittingly named 'Galop' movement makes a friendly wave to Bartók, and there might be hints of a pre-serial Stravinsky (or even his teacher Rimsky Korsakov) in this music. The movement includes 'an episode based on my first ever (authentic) composition, a little piano piece written after my first term at Vic . . . I don't know where that score ended up, but the piece included here I remembered by heart.'

It is certainly attractive music, and melodies pop up all over the show, including in the trumpet parts, much to the delight of Jenny's brother Craig, who attended the school in 1963. 'I'd complained to her,' he recalled, 'that us trumpeters never got any good tunes to play, particularly with Mozart and Haydn, the mid-classical period – dominants and octaves was all you got to play – so she wrote me a wonderful trumpet part in her *Cambridge Suite*.'[27]

With its warm surfaces, appealing melodies and thirteen-minute duration, it was an easy piece to programme and was duly selected by the NZBC Concert Orchestra for performance.[28] That was quite a coup for a student in 1963; it was heard on the radio alongside music by her teachers Larry Pruden and Douglas Lilburn the following year.[29] Musicologist Richard Hardie detected in the *Cambridge Suite* elements he attributed to Lilburn's influence, perhaps in the pastoral quality of some of the string writing. Jenny didn't think so. 'No Lilburn influence at all,' she said. 'There was never a great deal of that in my music, and it came only many years later.' Perhaps what Hardie heard was evidence of Lilburn and Jenny's common influences – Ralph Vaughan Williams in particular, but probably Benjamin Britten too – evidence of the continuities that are part and parcel of the creative process.

Little Symphony, the orchestral piece that Jenny composed during her third and final year at Victoria for performance the following summer in Cambridge, also drew on the music she was learning about in her classes. When she heard Stravinsky's *Symphony in C* she liked it immediately:

> I realised that you could write a whole series of symphonies if you wanted to – that would all be little *Symphonies in C* and [yet] completely different pieces – and so I said to myself 'I can write one of those too.' I was still a student, a third-year student, when I wrote my *Little Symphony*. It was done completely intuitively, just from my feeling for Stravinsky's. So that's the main reason why it sounds however it sounds; there's a lot in there that is identifiably Stravinskian.

Jenny derived considerable satisfaction from realising she could use Stravinsky's *Symphony in C* as a starting point for her own music and felt that doing so brought her closer to him and his work: 'I could count on the fingers of one hand the composers who were very close to me, and Stravinsky was one of them.'

She had been able to get pretty close to Stravinsky himself when he visited Wellington in 1961, and was at Wellington airport when he landed there.

> Our friend and fellow-student Robin Maconie had invented and prepared all the little signs on sticks that we held: 'I dig Ig' was his idea. A group of us from the Victoria University Music Society went to greet the truly great one . . . He was very cheerful and gracious. Later Fred Page approached him at his hotel, and explained that

a group of (National Orchestra) players up at the university was 'having difficulty with his *Octet*' and 'could Stravinsky perhaps help?' Oh, the cheek of that Freddy. But behold, Igor immediately dropped everything and accompanied Fred up the hill to the rehearsal, where indeed he did help to the extent at least that the scheduled performance took place without any mishap.[30]

Like the *Cambridge Suite* from the previous year, the *Little Symphony* also enjoyed remarkable success for a student work; it too was recorded for broadcast by the NZBC Concert Orchestra. The *New Zealand Listener* described it as 'unashamedly tonal' and noted Stravinsky's influence. Jenny explained that the first and final movements make use of sonata form, a nod to the neo-classical qualities of Stravinsky's pre-serial music, and confessed, 'I can cheerfully state that this piece is of no significance whatever in the contemporary scene.'[31]

It wasn't only her orchestral music she heard performed in Cambridge. In 1964, her final year there as a student, she was able to secure a performance of her *String Trio*.[32] In three movements, the trio is an altogether cooler work than the *Little Symphony*, making use of serial technique and more contrapuntal writing than is evident in the works she was then composing for larger forces. The austerity of the piece, along with its dissonance, make it rather less approachable than her jauntier orchestral music. Jenny recalled:

> My string trio, which is a little darker, was played there. I remember hearing a couple of old ladies behind me, who didn't know that I was the one who had written it, talking about my *String Trio* and one of them said to the other, 'How she must have suffered.' They were talking about the music, and the sound of the music made them feel that I must have suffered. Actually, at the time it made me laugh; it doesn't make me laugh so much now . . .[33]

For composers, the opportunity to hear performances of their own pieces was undoubtedly one of the main attractions of the Cambridge Summer School, but there were plenty of other benefits to being in attendance. Jenny also learned a great deal about writing for particular instruments by seeking the advice of the excellent performers present: 'John Kennedy – Nigel's father, a wonderful cellist – used to come and coach cello. Marie Vandewart, Michael Wieck, they were really good people and they gave very good advice if you wanted it.'

Jenny may have listened to such advice, but she didn't always take it. Full-time immersion in music and study at Victoria had given her increasing confidence in the compositional choices she was making, and she was happy for those choices to be at odds with prevailing trends or with the opinions of her teachers. In 1962 Ron Tremain, then a senior lecturer in music at Auckland University, ran the composition classes at Cambridge and expressed some hesitation about one of the pieces Jenny had brought to the school that summer. As well as *Pastorale*, she had prepared a setting of T.S. Eliot's poem 'Virginia' from his *Landscapes* cycle.[34] 'I had used what Ron contended was a cliché but to me – and by the time I got to second year at Vic – I still liked it, and I still wanted to do it. The way I cadenced the whole song was using a very common kind of progression, but it didn't offend me the way I think it offended Ron. I think he wanted me to change it, but I refused to change it.'

The number of musicians and composers arriving at St Peter's for the school grew each year, and by January 1964 the *Auckland Star* reported that more than two hundred were in attendance.[35] The bucolic setting – waking each morning in tents to the sounds of birds and cattle – combined with youthful company, mild weather and a shared passion for music coalesced into an intense social experience. Jenny remembered, 'We might stay up all night, often in quite large groups, just laughing and talking.' Composer Jack Body recalled the 'summertime holiday atmosphere' of the place and 'all kinds of crazy things that one does in summertime' being part of the experience.[36] Some lasting friendships were formed: Jenny forged a lifelong bond with composer Dorothy Freed, and cemented her friendship with cellist Pip Harding, whom Jenny described as 'an earlier example for me of the sort of musical life that was possible'. She worked alongside and so got to know Robin Maconie, Barry Johnstone, Kit Powell, John Rimmer and Larry Pruden. There were briefer dalliances, too. Jenny told Tim Dodd,

'There was many a moon-light flit. It was a bit like ship-board life and deep and passionate friendships would form in a very short time, and be consummated, also.'[37]

Her brother Craig recalled that at Cambridge, 'It was such fun, and everyone was getting laid.'[38] This kind of lightness characterised Jenny's attitude to the liaisons she enjoyed at the Summer School: they were not serious matters, simply a pleasurable complement to the carefree holiday atmosphere, summer weather and music:

> Certain players who had played with me, or played or heard my music and been moved, or had played other music that we listened to together – certain keenly erotic music, such as Schubert's Cello Quintet – would occasionally end up in my bed, where we would play again recordings of this music as proceedings advanced. 'Free love' was pretty much in the air when I was a student at Vic, and certainly at St Peter's Cambridge Summer Music School. It all seemed very natural. True, a tutor there once told me I wouldn't be in his bed if his wife had been there, but that was all okay with me. These affairs were not long-lived.

'Free love' may have been in the air in the early 1960s, but for Jenny the link between sex and music was longstanding:

> I had been sexually (and to me delightfully) interfered with by the fingers of a strange young man after my parents misguidedly left me alone as a bathing-suited four-year-old at the Manawatū River estuary at low tide. When I told them of this very beautiful and wonderful thing that had just happened to me down at the beach, my father leapt up yelling 'What?!' and raced off to the beach to find the obliging young man and possibly kill him. Clearly Dad didn't think it was so lovely – but he wasn't there. I was, and remained, a very surprised four-year-old, knowing and remembering exactly what I'd felt – obviously my father had to be wrong. I never suffered any subsequent guilt-ridden delusion as to the apparently 'forbidden' nature of such feelings.

The sexual awakening Jenny experienced that day was shortly followed by her arrival at school, where she had her first deep encounter with music. Both were intensely private experiences and she quickly associated them with one another. 'The "secret" nature of sexual arousal and my love of music meant the two were already well connected in my own mind as my biggest secrets. Possibly my recurring attraction to childhood in my music (something commented on by others, and something I never quite understood myself) also came from these early inner epiphanies, whose double effects on my soul drove me almost unconsciously for so long.'

As enchanting as the friendships and liaisons Jenny enjoyed at Cambridge may have been, and as important as it was for her to compose and hear performances of the four works premiered there, perhaps the most significant event of her four summer seasons at the school was hearing French composer Olivier Messiaen's *Quartet for the End of Time*:

> I remember vividly the calm, sunny late afternoon at the Cambridge Music School, when the visiting English cellist John Kennedy met in the gym at St. Peter's with an interested few, only about four or five of us, to play a tape of the *Quatuor pour la fin du temps*. This was the first time Messiaen's music had ever been heard in this country, even on tape. It was to be a decisive moment, not only for me, but also for Robin Maconie who was there as well. My feelings upon hearing this music were indescribable. I was completely stunned, in a way that I had never been before by any music I'd ever heard. I knew immediately that I had to get myself to Paris, and get to this man.[39]

Robin Maconie, also in St Peter's gymnasium that afternoon, recalled, 'It was certainly a revelation to me.'[40] Graduating from Victoria the following year, he won an Internal Affairs studentship and travelled to France, where he attended Messiaen's classes at the Paris Conservatoire.

Jenny still had a degree to finish and so returned to her studies in Wellington, but with her eyes set firmly on Messiaen and his music. She ordered the score of his piano piece *Cantéyodjayâ* and practised it incessantly. 'Douglas heard me on the music room Steinway and appeared at the door very interested and curious to find out what it was – the first Messiaen he had ever heard as well. After that he wrote his *Nine Short Pieces for Piano* in which the Messiaen influence is notable.' *Cantéyodjayâ* was a challenging work and, Jenny confessed, beyond her abilities as a pianist. Nevertheless, she performed it that year in a Wellington ISCM concert: 'Fred insisted,' she later said. It was, Jenny thought, the first public performance of Messiaen's music in New Zealand, even if a somewhat wayward account of the work. 'But enthusiasm can sometimes work wonders,' she said, 'and I got through it without any major disasters.'[41]

Jenny also ordered a copy of Messiaen's 1944 treatise *Technique de mon langage musical* and began to make her way through it, seeking to grasp how he conceived his music. On hearing Messiaen's *Quartet*, she'd had the impression that music such as Lilburn's was, by comparison, somehow 'black and white' – austere, even 'dried up'. Messiaen had revealed a new world of musical colour to her. 'I loved the colours. I hadn't the faintest idea how he made them but I knew I would like to know how to do that.'[42] She found parts of his treatise excessive, eccentric, even outrageous, but that did not alter her plans to head for Paris. 'It simply made it all the more necessary that I should go there and find out for myself just who it was that was capable of all this.'[43]

Graduation

Messiaen's music may have been an increasingly consuming presence in her life that year, but she also had an Honours portfolio to assemble. Given the warm reception her orchestral music had enjoyed at Cambridge the previous summers (both *Pastorale* and the *Cambridge Suite* were selected for subsequent performance), it is somewhat surprising that she chose to populate her portfolio with pieces that mobilised smaller forces and, in particular, songs. *Epithalamia*, for baritone and piano, is a setting of a poem by New Zealand writer and academic William Broughton, the older brother of David, a childhood friend in Timaru. 'David and I used to play together after school: climbing macrocarpa trees, Cowboys and Indians, and a great stack of dead branches within which we had our hideout.' *Epithalamia*'s text, less whimsical than Jenny's memory of David, discloses Broughton's disillusionment with organised religion, and Jenny's music, dark and spare and somehow forbidding, mirrors the disappointed tone of the words. In retrospect, she came to see that her choice of *Epithalamia* was more significant than she realised at the time:

> I was drawn to Bill's text not only because I knew him a little from my childhood. The title 'Epithalamia' signifies songs or poems celebrating a marriage. As I recall it now, this short cycle essentially describes a kind of retreat, or turning away from, or discarding of (so-called) religion in favour of the artist's 'marriage' to his or her craft. I related to this pretty easily at the age of twenty or so, and I was attracted to the idea of devotion to one's craft; it was something good, it felt right, and I liked it. But I was still too young to grasp anything like its full meaning. At the time I was not yet even sure that I was or would be a composer. How could I really dedicate myself or be 'wedded to' something of which I was still in my heart so uncertain?

The dialectic Broughton's text establishes – religion or spirituality set in opposition to the work of the artist – was one that Jenny would navigate for many years. Finding a point of balance between the two was something she would only really achieve in late middle age.

Also included in the portfolio was *Song for the Nativitie*, a Christmas carol. 'It was written,' Jenny said, 'for the Wellington Harmonic Society at the request of their then conductor Peter Zwartz, who was also a friend of mine. I didn't write the words, but have no idea now who did write them.' Looking back, Jenny was somewhat dismissive of the work. 'I thought I would look it up in my APRA list of registered works, but it isn't there. I never even registered it. That shows you how much importance I attached to it.'[44] She described it as 'pretty studenty'.

The last of the songs is a setting of e.e. cummings' 'what a proud dreamhorse', from his 1935 collection *No Thanks*. It's one of those cummings poems in which words tumble one over another in a kind of joyful fertility dance. There's a copy of the score – along with the rest of the music included in Jenny's Honours portfolio – lodged in the Victoria University library, but Jenny said, 'Well, I've never seen it since, never been performed. I'd be quite interested to hear it.'

Completing the portfolio was the instrumental *String Trio*, which was performed the following year at the Cambridge Summer School by Michael Wieck, Winifred Styles and Marie Vandewart. Loosely serial and cool, the work nevertheless includes some lovely textures and pleasing melodies (particularly in the second movement), and the music possesses an attractive forward motion, even during the slower passages. The final movement, a fugue with a mournful first subject that returns again and again, gives *String Trio* a satisfying if somewhat wintry denouement.

Her Bachelor of Music (with First Class Honours) complete, Jenny set her sights on Paris.[45] To save for the trip, she took work with the New Zealand Post Office, inheriting the Box Hill, Khandallah, round from her university friend Jack Richards, who later rose to international prominence as an expert in foreign and second-language teaching, and whose publishing successes enabled him to become a generous supporter of the arts. The poet James K. Baxter had an adjacent walk in Ngaio, and Jenny sat beside him in the sorting room every morning.[46] 'I rubbed elbows literally with Jim every day, and soon I was also driving us both out to our mutual walks after sorting the mail, dropping Jim off at Ngaio on my way north to Khandallah.' She described her morning encounters with Baxter in 2016: 'Far from silent, Jim kept on loudly, cheerfully addressing the world, without lifting his head. And the same all the way in the car till I dropped him off at Ngaio. None of us could understand a word of what he said (though his English was fine) – so nobody ever replied. We just got used to him.'[47]

Baxter wasn't always so entertaining. There were regular gatherings of artists, writers, musicians (and often a few students) at the Western Park pub on Tinakori Road before the bar closed at 6 p.m. One evening, Jenny recalled,

We had all moved on to a party in a flat on Tinakori Hill, belonging (I think) to [writer] Louis Johnson, and were mostly fairly merry. Somehow Jim and I ended up in a fond embrace. Later Jim reported to Louis that I had 'nearly sucked his tongue out of his head', cheeky bugger – making me out to be some sex-starved nutter. I did it because he wouldn't stop. When he failed to respond to my many 'that's-enough' and 'I'm-finding-it-hard-to-breathe' moves, and with the whole thing happening in the middle of the room in full view of everyone, I got mad. I thought, 'Damn you, Baxter, you're not going to forget this in a hurry!'

She did not maintain contact with Baxter beyond her time as a postie, but did set one of his poems, 'My love came through the city', as a 'godsong' during the 1990s: 'A simple, rather folk-like poem that I liked a lot,' Jenny said. 'One of those rare, almost epic ballads that can touch the nerve, or the bone of a people – and fruit of the later Jerusalem Jim, less full of himself (or of booze) as "The Poet".'[48]

Getting to Paris was an expensive business in 1964. Fred Page had proposed Jenny for a university postgraduate scholarship, a considerable grant, which she was awarded. He also suggested she apply to the Queen Elizabeth II (QEII) Arts Council for financial assistance. To her delight, her application was successful. However, she was not permitted to take up both grants, so opted for the larger sum offered by the latter. 'The money was great,' she said, 'enough for travel, plus all living expenses (good food, rent) and extra travel. And this was for two years.' In her application she had not specified what she would be studying, only that she had chosen Messiaen as her teacher. The Arts Council had simply assumed she would study composition when they granted her the bursary. 'I thought, "Well, that's that. I'd better go."'[49]

Confident she would indeed be able to travel as planned, Jenny made an effort to understand what was needed to gain admission to Messiaen's class. It was helpful that Robin Maconie had preceded her to Paris, and Jenny was in contact with his sister, Heather Kerr, who had also studied music (and English) at Victoria. Prior to Robin's arrival in Paris in 1963, visitors had been permitted to attend Messiaen's classes as 'observateurs', but in a letter to Heather, Robin advised that the rules had changed; students were now required to pass a test in order to be admitted to the class. Part of the test in 1963 involved fugue writing: 'Fugue writing was a specialty of French scholarship,' Robin said, 'and I was not very good at it, but my sense of absolute pitch was exceptional and I successfully named every note of a 12-tone chord Messiaen arpeggiated across the breadth of the keyboard.'[50]

Armed with this knowledge, Jenny decided she had better bone up on fugue writing. She had already taken Fred Page's class and had some understanding of entries, stretto, episodes, the stuff of fugues. Even so, she thought it prudent to prepare as thoroughly as possible, and so had a look in the Victoria University library. There she found *Traité de la fugue* by the French composer and teacher André Gedalge. It was written in French and four centimetres thick, and Jenny reckoned she had better things to do with her remaining time in Wellington than grind through an arcane tome on contrapuntal technique, even if it was the standard text (in France) on writing fugues. She decided to put off reading the book until she was on the boat to Europe: what else was there to do for six weeks aboard ship?

> My friend Derek Sanders – we used to spend a lot of time together; we played duets – Derek said, 'I'll steal it for you from the library.' I'd had a look at it: it was in French, and no one had ever taken it out anyway; I couldn't imagine that anyone was ever going to read it at Vic. So, I said 'OK'. He threw it out the window and I just caught it on the other side. So we could say I took it: yes, I did. But I saved someone else from a horrible fate. I mean, at Vic, they never would have used it.

Gedalge's *Traité de la fugue* was one of three books Jenny packed when she departed. Also in her bag was Walter Piston's *Orchestration*, the textbook Lilburn had recommended to his students. Her third inclusion was to prove important to her personally and, later, professionally: Allen Curnow's 1960 anthology *The Penguin Book of New Zealand Verse*. The volume opened with Reverand Richard Taylor's nineteenth-century translations of Māori creation poetry from the Whanganui region: 'I loved it so much that I took it with me.'

There was one final composition to complete before leaving for Europe, although it's one she preferred to forget. Jenny subsequently described it as 'the worst piece I ever wrote' and withdrew it from circulation a few years later. *Diversions For Orchestra* was a two-movement work commissioned by Peter Zwartz for the Wellington Youth Orchestra, which he conducted.

> Peter paid me £25 to write it, only he left everything until the last moment before I was due to leave for Europe, so it was the hastiest piece I ever wrote. One night during these last few days, while walking down to the Zwartzs' house, I was accosted by a nutcase energetically exposing himself under a street-light, so became involved with police interviews and reports. Thus, I was also somewhat distracted from the task at hand. Douglas heard the WYO play the piece soon afterwards and told me eventually it was a 'terrible piece', whereas Peter thought it was 'quite a good piece'. I never heard it played myself but was well aware that the first of its two movements particularly left a good deal to be desired. (The second, a set of variations, was not so bad in fact, but it still got thrown out with the first).[51]

In the New Zealand winter of 1964, Jenny McLeod may have been about to head halfway around the world to study with Olivier Messiaen, a musician receiving commissions to write music for performance, and have recently graduated with a First Class Honours degree in composition, but she did not feel like a composer; did not think of herself as a composer. Her engagement with composition had been for fun, for the joy of it, and while she adored music generally, and found the work of writing and hearing her music performed stimulating, she did not yet see composition as a vocation.

This did not dilute the seriousness with which she applied herself to her music, however, and the works she completed before leaving New Zealand are impressive achievements. Study at Victoria had certainly aided her development, although perhaps less for the instruction she received than for the music she was exposed to. Naturally, some of the music she experienced at Victoria was composed by her teachers, and commentators including Mark Jones and Richard Hardie have detected the influence of David Farquhar and Douglas Lilburn in her early music. Jones suggests that Jenny's song cycle *Epithalamia* discloses David Farquhar as an influence, along with Benjamin Britten, and Hardie suggests the *Cambridge Suite* and the *Little Symphony* offer evidence of Lilburn's influence on her writing.[52]

Those comparisons are probably fair – parts of the *Little Symphony* do bear surface resemblances to passages in Lilburn's *Overture: Aotearoa*, and *Epithalamia* seems to know something about Farquhar's song for baritone, 'Death Shall Have No Dominion', a setting of John Donne's text. But those local associations were likely eclipsed by what she was learning from the music of Igor Stravinsky and Béla Bartók, early music by Arnold Schoenberg and Anton Webern, and Englishmen Ralph Vaughan Williams and Benjamin Britten. Certainly, her teachers influenced the music she was listening to, and this was to have a significant effect on what she wrote, but it is not clear that their own music provided her all that many clues. Jenny said, 'Anybody who's ever had contact with Douglas finds it a profound contact. It was something about his seriousness, his commitment to what he was doing, and I'll never forget the atmosphere at the first performance of his *Third Symphony* and going around to his party afterwards. It gave a reality to contemporary music that I was just taken up by.'[53] But this speaks of Lilburn in terms of his personality and his habits – of his influence on Jenny as a person – rather than of the lessons Jenny may have drawn from his compositional practice. Still, 'he was the person whose study you'd walk into to have your tutorial', and it's understandable that his fingerprints are evident here and there in Jenny's first compositions.

This early music – the *Cambridge Suite, String Trio, Epithalamia*, the *Little Symphony* – does sound like the sum of its influences rather than the work of a composer with an identifiable personal voice. Perhaps what distinguishes Jenny's early work from that of so many other young composers is how well she was able to assemble those disparate influences into a coherent whole. The skill with which she did so was likely down to her excellent ear and her ability to metabolise what she heard through the filter of a keen musical intelligence. Nonetheless, the question of imitation versus innovation remains, and a few years later she speculated: 'Was I just a reasonably talented student who could pastiche other people's music or did I have original talent?'[54] Travelling to Europe where she could test herself against some of the best young composers in the world was a good way to find out.

4

Europe | Paris

At Victoria Jenny had become friendly with Cecilia Wilson. She vividly recalled their first meeting: 'Cecilia had angelic long blonde hair, and she played the harp: "She was a picture," said Fred. Robin Maconie gallantly wrote a part for her in one of his pieces and Cecilia came over to the music room to play it, so this was where I first met her.' Cecilia was a student of French, and recalled that 'everybody knew everybody' at the university in those days.[1] She too was planning to travel to Paris in the winter of 1964 and work there for a year. Jenny and she booked passage together on the Sitmar line vessel, *Castel Felice*.

In June the entire McLeod family travelled to Auckland to farewell Jenny at the docks. Her brother Craig recalled that Douglas Lilburn was also there, surprising the McLeods when, 'in front of all of us, the whole family, there's Lilburn enfolding Jenny in his arms and giving her this loving, romantic kiss'. Craig had suspected that Jenny had strong feelings for Lilburn, feelings which as far as he knew had gone unrequited, and he interpreted Lilburn's display as evidence of romantic interest. Jenny was less surprised by her teacher's embrace and said, 'It wasn't the first time we had kissed. One thing I did take unmistakably from Douglas's various responses . . . was that he wanted me to come back to him.' It would not be the last time that Jenny experienced strong feelings for a gay or bisexual man.

Sailing by way of Southeast Asia and the Suez Canal, Jenny and Cecilia shared a cabin with two others. Cecilia was horribly seasick at first but Jenny was fine – one of the few passengers to have breakfast on the first day out. There were stops along the way, with the opportunity to disembark in Suez and travel overland to Port Said, taking in various antiquities en route, including the Pyramids of Giza and the National Museum in Cairo where Tutankhamen lay encased in glass. And there was plenty of time on the trip to study Gedalge's *Traité de la fugue*, although the experience was far from satisfactory.

> I began to read this bloody book and my heart just sank further and further – it was unbearably academic. The teacher's examples were . . . this is where the lost composer ends up: writing textsbooks with his own examples as the music. It was just so awful I couldn't bear it, so I hurled it over the side. [It's] now resting where it deserves at the bottom of the Indian Ocean.[2]

After six weeks at sea, Jenny and Cecilia left the ship in Naples. From there they travelled overland through Italy, with stops in Rome and Florence, then took the train to France.

Jenny had forged some lasting relationships aboard ship. Writer James McNeish was among the passengers, and he and Jenny were to develop a warm friendship. They kept in touch, and while in Europe travelled together from London to Salzburg for a ski trip. Back in New Zealand Jenny occasionally stayed with McNeish at Te Maika on the Kāwhia Harbour, and saw him in Wellington from time to time until his death in 2016.

Jenny also became close to Barbara Einhorn, an Otago graduate on her way to begin doctoral study in Berlin. Barbara was a good violinist, and she and Jenny got together in the mornings aboard ship to play duos – Bach, Mozart, Corelli: 'The sort of music played by university students of classical music,' Jenny recalled. They subsequently spent time together in Paris and had a memorable holiday in Scotland the following summer. Another Otago graduate, Anna Justice, also became a lifelong friend. Anna settled in Switzerland, becoming a chronobiologist at the University of Basel and a pioneer in light therapy for winter depression.

Olivier Messiaen

Arriving in the City of Light – La Ville Lumière – was an experience of love at first sight. It was September, and 'Paris was fabulous,' Jenny said. 'Paris is my city: Sainte Geneviève was the patron saint of Paris, and that was my name. When I got there, it was like magic because Paris looked just like I thought it would. I loved the French language and I felt completely at home there.'

One of their first ports of call was Cecilia's friend Bernard Lajarrige, a French actor and comedian with whom she had stayed on a previous visit. Bernard and his wife Pauline Simon, daughter of the well-known French painter Lucien Simon, lived with their children in what had formerly been the Simon family home. When Cecilia enquired if they knew of anywhere she and Jenny could rent, they offered them the big room downstairs.

The big room downstairs was somewhat spartan by New Zealand standards. Cecilia remembered, 'We had a cold tap, so we would go and have a bath once a week in their apartment, which was further up.'[3] However, their location at 3-bis rue Cassini in the 14th arrondissement, with the Observatoire de Paris almost next door, was exceptional. The Sorbonne, where Cecilia was studying part time, was a short walk away, and the theatres and concert halls where they spent weekend evenings, both together and separately, were seldom more than a few Métro stops from home.

The old Paris Conservatoire, where Jenny was to commence study in October, was a little further, perhaps half an hour by Métro with a change at Châtelet. The buildings – formerly a Jesuit college – were unprepossessing: dingy grey-green walls, completely bare and grimly academic. The music rooms at Victoria at least had wonderful art on the walls. At the Paris Conservatoire: almost nothing, just 'some vast ancient crepuscular nonsense on the main wall of the orchestra hall,' Jenny said. No wonder Debussy was unhappy there. Still, this dispiriting setting did nothing to dampen Jenny's hopes to study with the composer of *Le Quatuor pour la fin du temps*.

Messiaen's reputation as a teacher was of the highest order, and European mid-century modernism owes much of its shape to his pupils, Karlheinz Stockhausen, Pierre Henry, Luc Ferrari, György Kurtág and Iannis Xenakis among them. Something of the energy and excitement of his classes was recalled by one of his most famous students, Pierre Boulez:

> It is hard to date exactly this unique experience and harder still to place it in a precise context . . . Dates seem irrelevant to what was rather an atmosphere – an epic birth, heroic days, an intellectual idyll! It was a time of exploration and liberation, an oasis of simplicity in the surrounding desert of contrivance and fabrication. Names that were all but forbidden, and works of which we knew nothing, were held up for our admiration and were to arouse our intellectual curiosity – names that have since made quite a stir in the world. It was not only Europe that was honoured in our spirit of inquiry: Africa and Asia showed us that the prerogatives of 'tradition' were not confined to any one part of the world and, in our enthusiasm, we came to regard music as a way of life rather than an art: we were marked for life.[4]

Boulez had studied with Messiaen in the 1940s, initially privately and later in the harmony classes Messiaen taught at the Conservatoire. By the time Jenny studied with him, some of the urgency of the post-war years would certainly have dissipated, but Messiaen remained an engaged and lively teacher, and his reputation meant that a great many students applied for his classes. Only twenty – fifteen French students and five foreigners – were accepted into the class each year, and selection was on the basis of how candidates performed during the first two weeks of instruction, open to all-comers. Competition was intense. Jenny had been expecting a fugue-writing test of the kind Robin Maconie had encountered the previous year, but instead Messiaen subjected applicants to ear tests and oral (and aural) spot analyses as he selected those who would remain to study with him.

Messiaen was a small man, slightly stooped – Jenny described him as well-upholstered. He wore glasses and (usually) a brightly coloured shirt under braces and an otherwise sensible old-style double-breasted suit jacket. Jenny liked him immediately. In an essay she wrote to mark his passing in 1992, she recalled their first meeting:

> He took my hand warmly when I introduced myself, and asked if I knew 'Monsieur Maconie' . . . But a grave problem soon presented itself, all the same, namely, that for the rest of the first few weeks I hardly understood a word my teacher said. I had some high school French, but the spoken language is quite another kettle of fish. Not only did I not understand the questions, when he was testing us, but I also had no idea what the French equivalents were for all the conventional musical terms that I knew perfectly well in English. (His own book had hardly been conventional.) Of necessity, I picked these up pretty fast, by guesswork and by listening to the French students' answers, and then resorted to the low tactic, whenever I understood a question, of answering it, whether or not it was me that he had asked. This no doubt did not endear me to my fellow-students, but he must have sensed my despair, for when he finally read out the list, after weeks of this torture, my name was on it.[5]

Messiaen was in the habit of changing the content of his course from year to year, focusing on material that suited the needs or proclivities of the students he had selected. At the beginning of the course he would throw out a few suggestions of what they might look at, talk with students a little and choose the year's content accordingly. In 1964, piano music was the topic of study.[6] That selection, Jenny would learn later, was made 'largely on the basis of "the looks on the pupils' faces". I didn't realise at the time how carefully he studied the faces of his new pupils and decided that this one needed such-and-such a "stimulus" and that one needed such-and-such a remedy, and so on.'[7]

Classes in 'Analysis, rhythm and aesthetics', as they were known, were three hours long and took place four days a week. Messiaen's instruction consisted largely of his performance and analysis of many of the piano works considered important to the classical canon: all twenty-three Mozart piano concertos; all thirty-two Beethoven piano sonatas; most of Chopin's piano music; Debussy's compositions for piano; Webern's Op. 27; and Boulez's *Deuxieme sonate*. On occasion Messiaen's wife, the concert pianist Yvonne Loriod, would join him and they would perform various Mozart piano concertos on two pianos.

The approach Messiaen adopted in class was not at all prescriptive, and his effectiveness as a teacher was the result of a passionate engagement with (and expert knowledge of) his materials, contagious enthusiasm, and lucid explanations of what he heard in the music, the latter often called out above the piano as he played through the pieces being studied. 'He did not even try to "teach" us, really. He simply let us know the way he saw (heard) things – which was revelation enough, as far as I was concerned – and from there we could make up our own minds.'[8]

To provide context for the music he taught, he referred to works beyond the piano repertoire: he spoke often of Stravinsky's *The Rite of Spring* – which he held to be one of the great masterpieces – along with Mussorgsky's *Boris Godunov* and Debussy's *Pelléas et Mélisande*. The breadth, expertise and passionate seriousness of Messiaen's teaching was life-altering for Jenny:

> He completely changed my conception of music – resonance, colour, texture, rhythmic cells, accentuation, Gregorian chant, Greek rhythms, all interspersed with constant references to poetry and literature. It was a whole new world and I lapped it up . . . He often relayed to us the inner colours he saw when he heard particular harmonies, and we came to take this as a matter of course, duly writing down 'blue-violet', 'red-orange with green', and so on, all over our scores, though we poor blind ones saw not a thing.[9]

Although Messiaen had written a great deal of music for piano, that year he made little reference to his own compositions in class.

It's possible this was because the composers he most loved – whom he frequently said were Debussy, Mozart and Chopin – offered more than enough material to populate a survey of piano music. The previous year, when the subject of study had been religious music, he had included some of his own works, analysing *Trois petites liturgies*, *Livre d'orgue* and *Catalogue d'oiseaux*.[10] Perhaps he felt his contributions to the piano literature were less significant than his religious works. Or perhaps there simply wasn't enough time to get to them. In any case, while he was quite convinced by the approaches and materials he had developed for his own compositional practice, 'he was not in the least bit insistent that his own ideas were the best'.[11]

Messiaen may not have proposed his own music as the object of study the year Jenny was in his class, but he did provide an opportunity for the students to hear his music in performance. Messiaen's friend, the novelist André Malraux, was then Minister of Culture, and in that capacity commissioned from him a work on the theme of death. Messiaen, a devout Catholic, composed *Et expecto resurrectionem mortuorum*. The premiere was to be held in La Sainte-Chapelle, once the private chapel of the kings of France, on the Île de la Cité in central Paris, and was by invitation only. Messiaen, however, ensured the invitation was extended to his pupils and accompanied them on a chartered bus to the performance.

La Sainte-Chapelle with its fifteen vast stained-glass windows in the upper chapel is one of Paris's architectural treasures. This was to be Jenny's only visit there: '[T]he luminosity and colour and radiance were breath-taking. And so was the sound, when it began – and not only for its harmonies and rhythms and timbres. For its sheer volume (entirely wind, brass and percussion) in that stupendously reverberant space quickly rose to such truly devastating levels that I soon began to fear this priceless glass was in very real danger of shattering.' Jenny, and the windows, survived the onslaught, and she remembered the performance as 'an occasion (not the only one) on which Messiaen innocently succeeded in scaring me half to death. I was terribly relieved when it was all over and the place was still intact.'[12]

Ordinarily it would have been an easy matter to hear Messiaen's music in Paris – he was organist at the church of the Sainte-Trinité and played there every Sunday. Unfortunately, in 1964 the organ was being restored, and Jenny was not to hear him improvise on the instrument until a return visit in the 1980s.[13] But she did travel to the Donaueschingen Festival to hear the premiere of *Couleurs de la Cité Céleste*, a memorable work that included the songs of the tūī and the bellbird, likely transcribed from a box-set recording of New Zealand birdsong Robin Maconie had given to Messiaen the previous year.

As important as Messiaen's music was to her, it was Messiaen the man, and the values he exemplified in the way he lived, that were to have the greatest influence on Jenny:

> Those who judged him to be simply naïve completely misread him, and also underestimated the nature and extent of his generosity and kindness to others (particularly to other composers). For it was not, as some imagined, that he did not see their faults. Indeed, he saw them perfectly clearly – he simply ignored the shortcomings and focussed on the best in people. This quality – I can only describe it as his goodness – his utter transparency, the complete (and completely natural) absence in him of any malice or guile, were what I loved in him perhaps above all. Together with the originality of his mind and his prodigious musical gifts, this made him not only one of the world's greatest teachers but also one of the world's great spirits – a teacher in the truest sense of the word.[14]

Later, she reflected:

> To spend so much time in the immediate presence of an essentially great and good human being is a rare and profoundly affecting thing. What rubs off on you can hardly be put into words. At the deepest level it is something from which you never recover. 'Marked for life' is how Boulez put it, and that is true. What you apprehend is as much about love as it is about anything else. Who you are matters as much as what you create. Good luck to those who think it is only what you create that matters. The one directly informs the other, and vice versa.

Piano Piece 1965

Although her study at the Conservatoire was consuming, it occupied only twelve hours weekly. This left Jenny with plenty of time for other things, including work on her own music. In Paris, much of that effort was focused – fittingly, considering the topic of study in Messiaen's class – on a piece for solo piano. Jenny had become acquainted with Arnold Schoenberg's ideas about dodecaphonic (or 'serial') music at Victoria, and she described the work she composed in Paris, *Piano Piece 1965*, as 'kind of Schoenbergian'. She added, 'I had used a series in something I wrote for my folio at Vic, but [*Piano Piece 1965*] was the biggest piece I wrote using the 12-note series.'[15]

Schoenberg, as a mid-career composer, had sought to write music that was not anchored to a particular key or tonality – music subsequently described as 'atonal'. He was to systematise an approach to writing atonal music with what has been called 'twelve-tone technique' because all twelve tones (or notes) of the chromatic scale are sounded as often as one another in the system, none assuming greater importance than any other. Schoenberg's general principle – an idea very much of its time – was to thwart the hierarchies of the old tonal system: a sort of 'musico-political communism'. The system was adopted and championed by his students, notably Anton Webern and Alban Berg, and later by composers including Pierre Boulez, who adapted it and took it to a deeper level, and the American, Milton Babbitt.

Schoenberg's system involved composing with pitch material drawn from a tone row or series, an ordered set of the twelve pitches of the chromatic scale, which could then be manipulated by various means. It was fundamental to Schoenberg's approach, and consistent with his aspiration that no note assume greater importance than any other, that notes could not be repeated until all the other notes in the chromatic scale had been sounded. Jenny, not especially keen on rules or the 'aura of authority', adopted what she found useful from Schoenberg's ideas, but mixed this with other approaches that interested her – and did so with scant regard for some of Schoenberg's fundamentals. The piece she composed is in fact derived from a single tone row, but she also embraced ideas she had picked up from others, including Pierre Boulez.

Boulez had been a student of Messiaen both privately and at the Paris Conservatoire, and his compositions, conducting, and outspoken positions on modern music made him one of the dominant figures of classical music in Europe after World War II. Jenny would have first encountered his music courtesy of Fred Page. During a visit to Europe in 1958, Page had heard Boulez's chamber work *Le Marteau sans maître* and befriended the composer, bringing scores of his music back to New Zealand.[16] By the time Jenny moved to Europe, Boulez was inescapable: 'At the time, in the eyes of the younger generation, Boulez was "king" in Paris. He could do no wrong – we all adored him, and we went along ecstatically to all the Domaine Musical concerts, which were real ear openers.'[17]

For *Piano Piece 1965*, Jenny adopted Schoenberg's dodecaphonic system, composing a twelve-tone row and subjecting it to the kinds of manipulations he had pioneered, including using a twelve-tone matrix.[18] From Italian composer Luciano Berio she appropriated some of the formal properties of *Cinque variazioni* ('Five variations'); it too was a serial piece, and was a model to her in respect of the five sections she used to organise her material. (When Jenny showed Berio her score for *Piano Piece 1965* the following year, he was critical, claiming it was too varied. Jenny was amused but unperturbed by his response.)

Boulez's *Le Marteau sans maître* also offered important clues as Jenny composed her piece. She 'saw that he had broken up his series into different little cells . . . that add up to the twelve-notes' and was enchanted by the idea (and sound) of 'lots of little cells in a series; it brought the series to life'. In particular, this approach gave her licence to repeat notes, in violation of one of Schoenberg's foundational principles: 'I just didn't like Schoenberg's way of, "You have to repeat all the notes each time before you get around to the same one again." That's just not musical. Harmony is created by little floats of notes, and they need to be repeated in order to create the impression of a harmony.'

Jenny had thought that in treating each cell 'as a harmonic cell, where the notes could come in different orders', she was applying Boulez's technique of frequency multiplication. In fact, she had misunderstood his system, and it would be some years before she fully grasped the substance of his ideas on this matter. Even so, Jenny's misapprehension was fruitful: 'You can be mistaken in the way you understand something and it can still provide fuel for your own pieces.' In January 1965 she wrote to Fred Page: 'Am in the throes of a new piano piece – more serial than anything I've written to date, but still not at all a consistent use of [serial technique]. My head is buzzing with theories about duration and rate of harmonic change. Yes – surprise! I still think in terms of harmony.'[19]

In his analysis of *Piano Piece 1965*, Richard Hardie identified Jenny's use of repeated notes and her penchant for breaking the series into a number of smaller cells. He also noted her skilful use of rhythmic motifs to provide a measure of consistency – and perhaps some sort of coherence – across the work.[20] Rather than five sections (as Jenny thought of it), Hardie identified nine, the concluding four sections being loose reflections of the opening four, and all turning on the fulcrum of the central fifth section. To his eye and ear this gave the work an arch-shaped trajectory. Hardie's findings seem entirely reasonable and he certainly provided ample evidence for his claims. To the casual listener, however, many of the properties he identified will be, at best, only faintly audible. What is readily apparent is the pleasing ebb and flow of the music: perhaps aural evidence of the symmetry Hardie identified on the page. That symmetry is especially clear in the ways warm sounds contrast with more dissonant splashes of colour; turbulent episodes are counter-balanced by tranquil passages. It's all woven together with a beguiling musicality, too. Hardie categorised the piece as a serial work that made use of non-serialised components, and concluded that Jenny 'does not let herself get caught in the restricting shackles of strict twelve-tone technique. As a result, she is able to include unique and personal features in *Piano Piece 1965* that reveal her skill as a composer.'[21] One of the unique and personal features Hardie discovered was a pair of errant notes, pitches that he couldn't make sense of in terms of serial procedure. 'Every note in the piece can be attributed to permutations of the original row, except for two notes,'

Richard said. 'When I asked Jenny about these, she looked at me with that mischievous twinkle in her eyes and said, "I just liked the sound of those notes there."'[22]

Paris wasn't all work and study. Jenny and Cecilia went to shows, theatre and concerts together, including a memorable ballet performance of Stravinsky's *The Rite of Spring* conducted by Pierre Boulez. (Jenny was so arrested by the production she returned each night for four nights and went again during the return season.)[23] They also regularly socialised with Philip Knight and John Langdon. Philip had studied French at Victoria while Jenny and Cecilia were there, and in Paris 'was doing this doctorate on "L'art pour l'art", art for art's sake,' Cecilia said. 'He and John used to have parties; they made a concoction they called Mother's Milk which was vile and *so* strong. And they used to take us off to these gay nightclubs.'[24] To get there, Jenny recalled, 'We rode across Paris in the Metro wearing our Indian saris (that we had bought in Ceylon). One night at a transvestite place down at Les Halles, Cecilia and I were nearly attacked by the local prostitutes, who thought we were the competition. Philip and John saved us.' Jenny also got to know Douglas MacDiarmid, the New Zealand painter who had lived in France since around 1950 and whom she had first met through Douglas Lilburn. She was to remain in contact with MacDiarmid for the rest of his life, exchanging many letters with him. 'He was the sort of person with whom, whenever contact resumed, even after many years, it seemed that no time had passed at all and we simply picked up right where we had left off.'

Thanks to Ron McLeod's generosity, Jenny and Cecilia's activities weren't limited to the city: 'He bought me a Citroën 2-chevaux, one of those funny-looking little beetle cars with two motorbike engines, in which Cecilia and I travelled around France, and I later took to Germany, England and Scotland.' In a letter to Lilburn written during their Easter holiday in the south of France, Jenny said of camping: 'I enjoy it, and so far, anyway, haven't encountered any of the hazards I was worried about, though we sleep with a hatchet between us, just in case! One night some mad animal came and ate all our cheese, otherwise nothing irregular. I think it was a sheep – do sheep eat cheese?'[25]

During the Christmas break of 1964 Jenny travelled to Dunvegan Castle on the Isle of Skye. There she stayed with Dame Flora MacLeod, then chief of the Clan MacLeod, who had extended an invitation to visit when she was hosted by Jenny's family in Levin while on a world tour in the mid-1950s. Dame Flora, her daughter Joan Wolrige-Gordon and grandson John, who was later to become the 29th chief of the Clan MacLeod, welcomed Jenny royally. She recalled:

> There were only four of us there at Dunvegan (apart from the staff), and John was only a few years older than me . . . his mother and grandmother were the 'oldies', so we were naturally thrown together. He showed me round, took me for long walks and long conversations on the moors . . . At the Paris Conservatoire we had embarked on a tour de force analysis of all Mozart's piano concertos, and Messiaen's wife Yvonne Loriod had been coming to our classes to play all of them, with Messiaen accompanying her as the 'orchestra' on a second piano. It was a revelation, and I had taken a few of these scores with me to Dunvegan, where I found an excellent small grand piano in the large drawing room. John loved music, and though he wasn't in the room I could sense him listening in the background as I played my own versions of some of this heavenly music. John was great company, had trained as an actor and singer at LAMDA [London Academy of Music and Dramatic Arts]. I felt he was like an older brother, we found the same things funny. I liked him immensely . . . we were kindred spirits, I felt, we shared something touching and profound and unspoken.

A second visit was soon pencilled into her diary.

Returning to France in January, Jenny resumed classes at the Conservatoire. The year concluded with a final examination, the *concours*, in late June, at which students presented their own analysis of a work previously analysed in class by Messiaen to a jury of examiners. Jenny elected to address every note of Beethoven's *Piano Sonata No. 27, Op. 90*. Given the complexity of her analysis and her, at times uncertain, grasp of the technical French she needed to deliver it, she found it necessary to memorise her presentation. This she rehearsed with Messiaen at his apartment – something he requested of all his students.

> I romped through it happily, and as I'd hoped, Messiaen was highly delighted and surprised – he thought it was 'formidable!' And off I skipped. But a few days later as I romped through it a good deal less happily before The Jury in the hall, the very imposing chairman (who I believe was the director himself) suddenly asked me a question. Horrors! It didn't even sound like French, it sounded like complete gobbledygook. This was not in my plan. I was dumbstruck. What could I do?! Obviously, I wasn't supposed to ask *him* any questions . . . Instead I did the Forbidden. Turning helplessly to Messiaen, who was sitting apart, and to whom I was on no account to speak – he'd warned us all so explicitly – I lowered my voice and confided to him my unexpected predicament. Immediately, to my joy, he did the forbidden too. 'She didn't understand the question!' he waved and called out though he wasn't supposed to speak either. It was repeated much more slowly and clearly, and turned out to be French after all – also dead easy; and soon I was out of there, thank God. I was very glad later that I did work hard for this. We were evidently forgiven for breaking the rules: to my considerable surprise I won a second prize (together with Paul Méfano).[26]

Most students attended Messiaen's class for two years, and the generous funding Jenny had received from the Arts Council meant she could have done so. However, as wonderful as the experience of studying with Messiaen was, Jenny found that her allegiance had shifted away from him, and towards the music and thought of his most celebrated former students: Pierre Boulez and Karlheinz Stockhausen. 'It was fashionable among my classmates,' she later wrote, 'to laugh, and complain, and speak of Messiaen as "too old-fashioned",' and she too hungered for the excitement and boldness of the new music being pioneered in Europe at the time. In 1992 Jenny confessed, 'There was so much about Messiaen that I did not get into anything like a proper perspective until many years later, after I had got my priorities a bit straighter', but in the summer of

1965 her first wish was to place herself in the midst of the avant-garde.[27]
On completing her year at the Paris Conservatoire, Jenny travelled with
several of her classmates – Michel Decoust, Maurice Benhamou and
Solange Ancona – to Basel, where they had enrolled as observers in a
summer course on conducting that Boulez was leading there.

5

Europe | Basel, Darmstadt, Cologne

Although Pierre Boulez was at first acclaimed for the music he wrote, over time his renown as a conductor may have rivalled or perhaps even eclipsed his reputation as a composer. He had first conducted a professional orchestra in the mid-1950s; by 1965 he had led some of Europe's finest ensembles and begun to establish ties to orchestras in the United States. The course Jenny and her friends attended in Basel was jointly organised by Boulez and his long-time friend and patron, Paul Sacher. Lasting three weeks and with sessions running all day and well into the night, teaching was focused on conducting and analysis. Jenny recalled:

> There were sessions where Boulez spoke and instructed a small handful of younger conductors, including Heinz Holliger and Boris de Vinogradov – though these were off-the-cuff talks, not lectures as such – and other sessions where they rehearsed with Boulez and the orchestra. The whole group of students was maybe thirty strong, with the rest of us (who paid less) as observers. About half a dozen of us came from Messiaen's preceding Paris Conservatoire class. There I also first met American flautist David Johnson who later travelled with me to attend Stockhausen's course in Cologne.

For his part, Sacher funded the presence of the Basel Symphony Orchestra at workshops and concerts, where works studied and performed included Stravinsky's *The Rite of Spring*, Schoenberg's *Five Pieces* and Boulez's own *Le Marteau sans maître*.

Overall, the course in Basel was an odd experience for Jenny, who was struck by the indifferent quality of quite a few of the professional conductors in attendance. In an article for *Composer* magazine, she reported their unexpected lack of musical experience: 'Some arrived without knowing the score they proposed to conduct, some could beat the bars but had no conception of the music . . . In some cases they were not even aware of the music! Wrong notes, parts missing. Nothing disturbed them.'[1]

When she'd arrived in Europe, Jenny had been acutely conscious of her inadequacies as a musician. She had been pleasantly surprised to find she could foot it with her fellow students at the Paris Conservatoire, but had not expected to find the kinds of musical shortcomings evident in Basel amongst European professionals. Given the opportunity to test herself against international standards of excellence, she was encouraged to find she wasn't too far off the pace: 'I didn't take myself very seriously before then because I really wasn't sure what sort of talent I had . . . When I got to Europe, I discovered I wasn't as stupid as perhaps I thought I was. I was just as clever as most of my contemporaries there, except of course for the very experienced ones, and I decided I needn't be worried about them. I didn't need to be inhibited by thinking I wasn't as good as them. And that boosted me and gave me lots of self-confidence.'[2]

It was perhaps that burgeoning self-confidence which galvanised Jenny to confirm her enrolment in a course commencing later in the year in Cologne, directed by Karlheinz Stockhausen. She wrote to Fred Page from Basel advising him of her decision, adding, 'Am beginning to wonder how much good all the analysis of scores I've been doing lately is doing me – I just forget it all anyway and have to think it out again every time I come back to the score. Still, I get a kick out of doing it.'[3]

From Basel, Jenny drove to Darmstadt in Germany in her little Citroën. 'It was,' she remembered, 'cheering to depart from various countries (intending never to return) leaving unpaid traffic tickets behind one – especially the outrageous Switzerland, where a citizen once even grabbed and lectured me when I ventured to step out against the traffic lights.' She was also thrilled to be attending one of the premier events for contemporary music, the Darmstädter Ferienkurse – the Darmstadt Summer Course.

Held over the last ten days of July, the course that year included performances of music by Charles Ives, Anton Webern, György Ligeti, Mauricio Kagel, Peter Schat and many others. There were also addresses by musicologists Theodor Adorno and Carl Dahlhaus, and composers including Earle Brown, Ligeti and Boulez.[4]

Fred Page and Douglas Lilburn had preceded Jenny to Darmstadt, and both had strong reactions to the experience. Page had first attended the Summer Course in 1958 and was overwhelmed. He claimed that afterwards nothing was the same, and confessed that, while there, 'I began to wonder whether I could ever listen to orthodox music again.'[5] Lilburn's reactions were a little more conflicted. He didn't like the certainty of the addresses, 'reacting sharply against an authoritarian tone in composition lectures when the authority is simply that of the composer–lecturer, the subject his own recent work, the terminology individual, and the logic based on questionable premises'. And he actively disliked some of the music, which he said 'upsets my ears and all my notions of music'. But he was encouraged by the alertness and concentration of the audiences, the excellence and 'purposeful virtuosity of the players' and, finally, by the energy of Darmstadt compared with the 'boredom of an epigonic Society for the Promotion of New Music concert I heard at Cheltenham. Whatever one thinks of this Darmstadt world there is no denying its vitality, assurance and conviction nor the exhilaration of its search into new sounds.'[6]

While Jenny's attendance at Darmstadt was motivated by her own search for new sounds, it was probably mostly driven by her desire to hear more from Boulez. She had first heard his music – in the form of *Le Marteau sans maître* – in a Domaine Musical concert in Paris, and again in Basel where Boulez talked about the work and conducted it: 'It's an amazing piece; wonderful. For it's the kind of piece I didn't think about technically – I did at a certain point, but after that I forgot about the

techniques of it – just the sound of it. I could just put myself into that
sound and never want to come out. It's like supreme meditation; a work
of the gods.' Even so, it was Boulez's thought which most fascinated her.
Her first-hand encounters with his ideas at his lectures and workshops
were complemented by reading his essays and articles, something she
would do for the rest of her life. She said:

> When Boulez says something, I really listen, because he said the
> things I wanted to hear; he said things that just resonated with me;
> he'd say things in a way that nobody else said them. And that would
> be like a big confirmation for me. Part of why I have such high
> esteem for him is that he often seemed to read my own mind; he'll
> say something about a situation, a composer or something – might
> be dead, might be alive – and I'll think, 'I've always had that sort
> of feeling myself, but nobody else has said it.' And when you hear
> someone saying something that comes from right inside of you,
> that's an extraordinary feeling. The feeling is 'Listen to that!' because
> what else is he going to say that is going to come from right inside
> of you? I've never had that experience with any other living person.
> I would keep coming across them as I read his books: 'Yes! I agree
> with you.'

It wasn't just that Boulez's observations mirrored Jenny's; his reasons
for so thinking were also congruent with her own. Boulez, for example,
had been critical of French composer Hector Berlioz's harmonic
sense, which he found clumsy. Jenny had studied Berlioz's *Symphonie
Fantastique* during her third year at Victoria and been discomfited by
his harmony, suspecting 'that there was something wrong with it. Then I
discovered he was a guitarist and that explained it. And then I discovered
that Boulez had felt the same thing. These kinds of things connect you
to someone else; when you find you've had private ideas along the same
lines as someone else.'[7]

This kind of validation must have been important for a young
composer making her first steps, but there was also much to learn from
Boulez. Exposure to his ideas expanded Jenny's compositional palette

(for example, the ideas she applied to *Piano Piece 1965*) and led her to re-examine music she had formerly been impatient with. 'He used to encourage us to confront all the things that we didn't like about music, and take them into ourselves and understand them better and get some inspiration in that direction, too. That's right up my alley – try to open yourself.' Ultimately, perhaps it was Boulez's intellectual rigour and the brilliance of his mind that were most compelling: 'To me, everything he ever did, there's such quality in it, there's real thought behind the things that he's done: in [his] music and the kinds of techniques he developed for himself; the things that he wrote.'

At Darmstadt, Boulez himself conducted music by Charles Ives, Anton Webern and his pupil, the Dutch composer Peter Schat. He also presented a lecture on form in 'New Music' and was on hand for a performance of his 1958 composition for orchestra, *Doubles*. In spite of that, Jenny left the Summer Course with a somewhat agnostic view of the New Music community: 'I wasn't that impressed with Darmstadt. I'd been buying copies of *Die Reihe* – the avant-garde journal – and I made mental notes of anything I didn't understand. I went around at Darmstadt asking people what it meant, and nobody had any idea what it meant.'[8] Consequently, she became 'increasingly disillusioned with the whole thing because it seemed to me that there were quite a lot of people who were there for suspect reasons and did not know what was going on at all'.[9]

Jenny's summer of Boulez wasn't yet over. Immediately following the Darmstadt school, Boulez travelled to the Edinburgh International Festival, where he featured as both a composer and a conductor for the first full-scale retrospective of his music. Needless to say, Jenny went to see and hear him in action. There, to her surprise, she bumped into Messiaen. He was delighted to see her and, introducing her to composer Michael Tippett, claimed her as his pupil.

> Finally, when we were saying goodbye, I had to tell him that no, alas, he wouldn't be seeing me back in Paris, I was going on to Germany the next year. His face fell momentarily (the moment I'd been dreading), but straight away he was wishing me well, and I was very relieved. When I was in Cologne with Stockhausen the

following year, I went back to Paris and heard him doing again the famous analysis of *The Rite of Spring* which had so influenced Boulez (whose own analysis I'd already heard in Basel). After you had been in Messiaen's class, you were always welcome as a friend to drop in on any future classes, and once again I was greeted with joy.[10]

Jenny's visit to the Edinburgh Festival was followed by a return trip to Skye, this time in the company of Barbara Einhorn:

> We camped on a very isolated Skye farm where the farmer and his wife only spoke Gaelic. Still, they generously insisted on giving us milk and eggs, meanwhile thinking us completely mad. We were there for weeks. However, we had made the mistake of putting up our tents in a dry creek-bed, and awoke one morning to heavy rain on the canvas above, and a fresh creek pouring through the tent below our stretchers. Very quick and wet pack-up, drove to Edinburgh, where we camped again and went to the Festival, only to return one night after a concert, to find there had been a big storm and our tent had blown down, everything (bedding and all) was soaked. So, we sat up all night in the car and started knitting the fantastic Scottish wool we had bought the day before by the light of our camping-gas lantern.

It was a perfect summer holiday for Jenny, a tranquil interlude to break up the musical intensity of the academic year in Paris and the summer festival season, and the New Music course she was about to commence in Cologne.

Karlheinz Stockhausen

In 1963, at the invitation of the Rheinische Musikschule, Karlheinz Stockhausen had founded the Cologne Course for New Music. He designed the course and was its principal instructor, but each year he invited other specialists to join him on the faculty. The year

Jenny participated in the course, composers Luciano Berio and Henri Pousseur, and composer and conductor Michael Gielen, were teaching too. Stockhausen had also enlisted some of the very best interpreters of New Music to contribute to the programme: pianist Aloys Kontarsky, vibraphonist/percussionist Christoph Caskel and cellist Siegfried Palm delivered masterclasses and were on hand to perform. These three were members of the Stockhausen Ensemble, the composer's dedicated performance group.

Jenny arrived in Cologne in the early autumn of 1965 and settled into lodgings recently vacated by Robin Maconie – a sparsely furnished room just outside the south portal of the city wall, Am Chlodwigplatz, and above a coffee shop named after the proprietor, Jupp Geyr.[11] She found Cologne unfriendly – cold and grey and intolerable. Her neighbour in the building was constantly unpleasant and rude to her and her guests; walking one day on the street a stranger pulled her ponytail for no reason. 'The October Festival was absolutely obscene,' she told musicologist Suzanne Court. 'The Germans are so repressed, and then suddenly for one day a year they go mad and drink wildly and tell filthy stories. The way they enjoy themselves is hardly enjoyable . . . Of course, at that time it was only about 20 years after the war and they were still digging up mass graves. I hated Germany so much, and in particular Cologne.'[12]

Study at the Course for New Music wasn't exactly a cakewalk either. After the gentle and self-effacing Messiaen, Stockhausen was quite a shock. Jenny described him as 'incredibly egotistical, incredibly obsessed with his own work. Messiaen was the opposite; in the year that I studied with him he hardly mentioned his own work at all. Stockhausen was incapable of talking about any music other than his own.' She found what he had to say about his music terrifically interesting, but his preoccupation with his own oeuvre meant 'he wasn't interested in the music of anyone else, including his students'.[13]

That year there were close to forty students enrolled in the course, some of whom had been Jenny's classmates in Paris: 'There were about four or five of us who went from Paris to Basel for Boulez's course, then we went to Darmstadt, and then we went to Cologne.' Jenny said that 'whether working with him or not, everyone in those days was listening to Stockhausen', so it is little wonder young composers were eager to study with him. In 1965 those young composers included trumpeter Jon Hassell, who later collaborated with La Monte Young and Brian Eno; and Irmin Schmidt and Holger Shüring (known professionally as Holger Czukay), who went on to co-found the experimental rock group Can. When the new cohort of students arrived that year, Stockhausen was in the middle of rehearsals for his new work *Momente*: 'We spent our first few weeks with him in the rehearsals and he'd show us how he composed it, the thinking behind it.'

At a personal level, study with Stockhausen was a mixed bag for Jenny. She found him 'kind of moody. A bit unpredictable; you never quite knew what he was going to be like when he turned up for a class.' On one occasion, at a party Stockhausen threw for his students, one or two of them suggested to him that he was 'just like Wagner. And Stockhausen, looking very innocent, [said] "No, I'm not." Yes, he was – very like Wagner.'[14] That kind of egoism can be hard to take but Jenny thought it understandable, and perhaps even forgivable, in such a visionary musician: 'He was constantly and literally so full of inspiration that he couldn't have been otherwise. Ideas simply poured out of him; I never knew such a thing.'

The most cogent lessons Jenny took from her time studying with Stockhausen were to do with the ideas he developed for his pieces, and the processes he activated to bring them into being. That each piece he made sounded so different from the others testified to his capacity to consistently arrive at viable new concepts and procedures. She remembered his explanation of *Momente*: 'What was most interesting to me was how he was kind of making autobiographical music, and the range of what he was treating as music. He would take bits of this and that, or mimic things that had happened in his own life, and turn them into little bits of music and then put all these little bits together. The structure was really interesting.'

In other pieces – *Mikrophonie 1*, for example – an instrument might be specified but the performer's instructions indicated procedures rather than specific notes or durations. In this way the performers' decisions and interpretive proclivities, usually in the background, were moved to the foreground; any meaning the work possessed could be said to reside as much in the process of the music-making as in the sounding object that resulted. Such approaches to composition were a very long way from the *Cambridge Suite*, but for Jenny fascinating, nonetheless.

Stockhausen's preoccupation with ideas and processes, with concepts being at least as important as how the pieces sounded, with interesting structures and new ways of putting things together, was also some distance from the kinds of ideas Jenny had encountered during her studies with Messiaen. It was more than a few steps along from what she had learned from Boulez, too. Boulez, for all his avant-garde credentials, was, in Jenny's view, 'more traditional than Stockhausen. Anyone who could say Bach was the greatest composer, which [Boulez] did say, well, you're not a progressive.' Stockhausen was progressive: 'If you're going around with your head full of spaces awaiting interesting structures, or new ways of doing things, of putting things together, then Stockhausen – he's the one. That was what he was trying to do; he wasn't trying to write beautiful pieces. I don't think he was; that's not the way he talked. He correctly understood the most important aspects of his own work.' And it was from Stockhausen's well of ideas that Jenny received the impetus that led her to write one of her best-known works.

For Seven

The animating spark for the chamber work *For Seven* (originally called *Fourches* but soon renamed[15]), came one day during class when Stockhausen mentioned he 'was thinking about a piece made entirely of *accelerandi* and *ritardandi* [getting faster; getting slower]'.[16] Jenny recalled that he 'said to our small class, of about ten of us maybe, "There you are: I've given you an idea." And I thought it was a bloody good idea.' It may have been a good idea, but it was also a very bare-bones idea, and the first challenge was to work out how to translate that notion into music.

To do so Jenny needed to draw on much of her musical training as well as her recent European experiences, developing for herself the

concepts she would ultimately deploy in composing the work. She began
by working out durations, making use of a number of simple ratios:

> My own use of numerical ratios in *For Seven* came first from the
> whole idea of the piece being based on *accelerandi* and *ritardandi*,
> which in strictest terms can themselves only be notated in terms of
> numerical ratios (that is, rather than having them simply unwritten
> but improvised by the performer, for example). Then as soon as the
> thought of numerical ratios came into my mind, I also thought, 'Ah!
> Natural pitch intervals are also expressed as numerical ratios (from
> the harmonic series)' – namely, interval ratios – which I knew well
> enough from studying acoustics back at Vic. Only then did it occur
> to me that I could also use these same ratios to predetermine the
> relative lengths of the musical sections.[17]

Using these ratios to determine the overarching shape of the piece,
Jenny arrived at a formal arrangement comprising three large movements,
the first and last of which were structurally palindromic, pivoting on a
longer middle movement. Each of those three movements was divided
into smaller sections, some of which – including the middle section of
the middle movement, the axis on which the entire piece turned – were
themselves palindromic. This approach to formal organisation – 'serial
proportions within proportions on multiple scales' was how Robin
Maconie described it – can be found in Stockhausen works such as
Zyklus (1959), and earlier compositions too, such as Webern's *Variations
for piano, Op. 27* (1936).[18]

Each section, and there are thirteen of them, was host to different
combinations of the eight instruments (for seven players) Jenny had
chosen for the work. Those instrument choices were governed by the
available musicians, including members of Stockhausen's ensemble on
site at the Cologne course. This left Jenny with 'a bunch of empty bars,
so to speak, that were going to get filled with music, but I knew where
the changes were going to be'.

The melodic lines she composed, consisting of pitches generated by
means of the same simple ratios she had used to produce the durations

and formal demarcations, were then transformed using an idea she had picked up from Boulez. He had suggested that a monophonic (that is, one-note-at-a-time) line could be combined with or superimposed upon another (similar or dissimilar) monophonic line: 'Boulez told us he had got this idea originally from Bach, who in his solo instrumental lines would typically combine several different voices so as to imply a three- or four-part harmony within a single line.' Such combinations obscured the original line and could, depending on the lines being aggregated, result in music of considerable abstraction. *For Seven* possesses passages in which the apparently chaotic music generated through these superimpositions resembles the serial music Jenny had studied in Paris and Basel, but it is not by any stretch of the imagination a serial work.

A final idea that shaped *For Seven*, and that was somewhat innovative for the time, corresponded to an approach Stockhausen had used writing *Momente*. In that work, 'he kind of graduated textural things so it went from what he called amorphous background music, background sound, and things would gradually come into the foreground.' The foreground music Jenny composed (using numerical ratios) was highly structured and served clear-cut melodic and rhythmic purposes. It contrasts with the more textural background, which is comprised of passages less differentiated in terms of melody and rhythm. These background passages were composed using chromatic material that foreshadowed the harmonic substance of her music theatre pieces *Earth and Sky* and *Under the Sun*, as well as the Tone Clock music Jenny would begin to write in the late 1980s. They also bore a resemblance – in that they were more textural than melodic/rhythmic – to the music of the Polish school, composers such as Witold Lutosławski and Krzysztof Penderecki. The backgrounds act as accompaniment to a number of virtuosic, concerto-like sections across the work; they also occasionally offer up material that migrates into the foreground, mainly as decoration.

In the thick of working on the piece, Jenny wrote to Fred Page, telling him:

> Am working very hard on my first (and last, probably!) 'European piece' for a small chamber ensemble, which, if it's ready in time, and

with a bit of luck, will be played by Kontarsky, Palm, Caskel et al in a concert next March. It's doing me the world of good, I find, to have to plan out a complete work <u>before</u> I start writing it, and also, with much of the interest concentrated on variety of colour, I'm learning a tremendous amount about instruments.[19]

Jenny described *For Seven* as an extremely technical piece, the composition of which she found sorely testing: 'I was just so glad to get it finished. It took three months and that was hard, hard slog for me because I'd never written anything so complicated.' It was also challenging to play, something Jenny was conscious of as she composed the work.

There has often enough been a kind of 'teaching' element to some of my composing, especially where advanced professional performers were concerned. As well as trying to make the most of their uncommon technical skills, I would try to 'stretch' them a little bit, so they might learn something a bit new. For example, in *For Seven (Fourches)*, where I was writing for a handful of the then greatest contemporary exponents in the world (Christoph Caskel, Siegfried Palm, Aloys Kontarsky) I used largely graphic durations (space = time), which Siegfried coped with by adding his own musical durations to each bar. And I had Caskel play vibraphone with two sticks in each hand, which he told me was a first – and in fact for the first performance (Cologne 1966), Caskel in his own 'special' vibes section missed out one of the layered legato voices, apologising that he hadn't had time to practise it properly. It was there in all his later performances, however.

The use of graphic notation was still in its infancy when Jenny composed *For Seven*. She was aware of the techniques, and had seen Berio's *Sequenza III* score, but had not made use of the approach to conform to any trend or to declare her allegiance to the avant-garde; her reasons were entirely practical: 'Graphic notation was just the simplest, most flexible way I could think of to notate the resulting durations – and also, I thought, the easiest way for the performers to read them and play them – therefore the best solution for that particular piece.'

Given the complexity of the compositional processes Jenny used to arrive at *For Seven*, it might have been music exclusively for the slide-rule and lab-coat brigade. In fact, for all its abrupt shifts, dark textures and abstract sounds, it is music that is easy to listen to, not at all po-faced. With hindsight, Jenny thought 'It's a bit like a tūī. It has plenty of chortles in it, and is a good-natured, lively sort of piece.'

While still in Cologne, Jenny sent a copy of the score to Witold Lutosławski, hoping he might be prepared to teach her.

> He got in touch with me when he was in Cologne and we had a meeting at his hotel. He told me he couldn't teach me anything. I'm pretty sure it was because with the Poles all their work to start with was in the background; it was all quasi-amorphous. It was not nearly so much distinctive foreground music . . . And I'm pretty sure that's why – because of the range of technical details that I had put in [*For Seven*] – he felt he couldn't teach me anything.

For Seven was first performed by the Stockhausen Ensemble at a concert to mark the conclusion of the Course for New Music in Cologne in March 1966. Jenny was on hand to hear it and thought it went pretty well. The piece was well reviewed in the *Frankfurter Allgemeine Zeitung* by prominent German critic H.H. Stuckenschmidt, much to Fred Page's delight when he read about it in a Wellington newspaper. 'Stuckenschmidt had featured at Darmstadt,' Jenny said, 'and had written a small but widely known and translated book, *Twentieth Century Music*, which I had read myself as a student after Fred recommended it. So, the support of such a voice was gratifying and encouraging, to say the least.'

That year *For Seven* was performed twice more, both times under conductor Bruno Maderna: at Darmstadt and at the Berlin Festival.[20] Fred Page was in Berlin on sabbatical at the time and was astonished to hear Maderna conducting the Stockhausen Ensemble performing 'a furiously contemporary piece in the heart of the European avant-garde, Fred's *ne plus ultra* of New Music', a piece by one of his own students. A short while later in Warsaw he met a number of Polish composers. They had seen the score of *For Seven* – Lutosławski had shown it to them – and had also attended the Berlin Festival partly so they could hear the work. Jenny recalled that when they learned he was from New Zealand, 'they asked Fred if he knew me, and he replied sonorously, "I was her teacher." They were "suitably impressed" according to Fred, and couldn't do enough for him.'

Jenny had not really expected the work to receive a New Zealand performance, such were the technical demands the music made on performers. But that didn't stop Douglas Lilburn selecting it as one of the first scores to be published by Victoria University's Wai-te-ata Press in 1967. 'This despite the fact,' Jenny said, 'that he thought it was a piece "without any rhythm". I explained it was just a different kind of rhythm.' The work was eventually performed in New Zealand, in 1992, and has since been performed both there and in America and Europe numerous times.

Jenny described *For Seven* as 'my high European effort'. Making it had been tremendously challenging, however: 'It just about killed me, it was really hard work writing it.'[21] And as pleased as she was with the results, she felt ambivalent about the idiom in which she found herself working. She had written to Fred Page: 'And in the middle of all this busy humming avant-garde world I wonder really where I fit in, in spite of the fact that, for the moment at least, I've thrown myself into it boots and all. Ultimately, I think I shall look for something more free, more basic and (most important) less complex – I've just tried to explain this to Lutosławski, who I think has found one solution.'[22]

She also expressed dissatisfaction with her European work to Douglas Lilburn, telling him, 'That's not the music I want to write, but I just had to show them that I could do it too.'[23] At some level, Jenny seemed to need to prove to *herself* that she could do it as well. 'It was the only avant-garde piece that I ever wrote . . . But [doing] that meant that I had come to terms with what was required to be a genuine composer in a way. At least of serious music.'[24]

While the desire to prove herself may have been a key driver of her engagement with European avant-garde approaches, there were other important factors motivating her decision to do so in Cologne.

For one, she had an ensemble that included some of the world's finest musicians available to play her music, an opportunity anyone serious about composition would want to seize. She was also genuinely curious about the new music and how it was put together, a result perhaps of her fondness for (at least some of) Webern's music, and her appetite for the intellectually rigorous approaches advocated by composers such as Stockhausen and Boulez. She was also motivated by Boulez's encouragement to confront the things she disliked. It was good to do so, Jenny came to understand, 'because there may be something in there for you'. She might have been ambivalent about the compositional techniques she had learned and the music that arose from them at the time, but in the years to come some of the ideas and practices she had developed through that careful, challenging and rigorous work were to manifest in fruitful ways in her music.

Jenny's mixed feelings about the music she was making in Europe may also have been shaded by the restlessness she had felt living in Cologne. That was partly the result of cultural dislocation – she found the people very different from New Zealanders, very different even from those she had met in Paris, and often unfriendly (the musicians were friendly, thankfully) – but it was also to do with missing home. Early on in Cologne, 'a kind of grey place', she could spend entire weekends holed up in her room above Jupp Geyr's coffee shop with a bottle of white wine, whistling or yodelling her way through Bach's G major cello Prelude or losing herself completely in English translations of the Tolstoy and Dostoyevsky novels she bought at the local railway station. 'I liked it. I was never lonely but I was profoundly homesick for my country; not for anybody in particular, but for my country. Just the smell of the place, the sea, the sky, the mountains.' She found enormous solace in Allen Curnow's *Penguin Book of New Zealand Verse*, which she had taken with her to Europe, and was particularly captivated by Richard Taylor's translations of Māori creation poetry included in the volume:

There's nothing like being stuck in some black hole in Cologne with a Māori book that is so close to your heart. It was closer than Genesis, I felt. I don't remember actively comparing them but it was.

Somehow, it's very personal, because it's very abstract. Those very beginnings – the nothing: Te Pō and Te Kore – what comes out in Taylor's version is incredibly abstract, only in being so abstract it is exactly human, because [those texts] talk about the consciousness – our consciousness. I felt so close to it that I couldn't not take it with me. I only took two books with me: one was Piston's *Orchestration*, the other one was *The Penguin Book of New Zealand Verse*.

She may have missed the land and sea and sky of Aotearoa but, 'Ah, somehow that was all there in that creation poetry, so I loved it. It just sang to me really in an environment like post-war Cologne.'

Back to the family

Finishing the Course for New Music in March, Jenny travelled, by way of Paris, to London, where her younger brother Craig had settled the previous year. Living and working in the UK for a spell has been, and arguably remains, a rite of passage for young people from New Zealand. More surprising – although perhaps not to her children – was Lorna's decision to travel to Britain with him: 'She wanted to get away from my father because he was driving her mad.'[25]

In the spring of 1966, Perrin joined Jenny, Craig and Lorna there. Perrin had exhibited an early interest in clothing and fabrics that Lorna had been pleased to support. 'When Perrin was ten years old,' Jenny said, 'Mum bought him a tiny little sewing machine that actually worked, thus helping to establish his life's path. He eventually became a fashion designer in Auckland, after a cutter–designer apprenticeship under the better-known Dutch immigrant designer Robert Leek at the Levin menswear factory of Austrian Kurt Hager. In London Perrin worked for Mary Quant for a few years. He was a very good dress designer.'

When Jenny arrived in the summer of that year it was close to a complete family reunion, and she was delighted by her brothers. In a letter to Douglas Lilburn, she wrote: 'Happy and mildly surprised to find they've turned into rather nice people, with something in their heads, and something to say, and the same absurd sense of humour, and altogether we have a good deal in common. All the more surprising, we conclude, considering our parents!'[26] Work commitments tied Craig to London, but a desire to acquaint themselves with their family origins saw Jenny, Lorna and Perrin travel north.

> Mum had already arranged to visit family in Shetland. Perrin had a penfriend, Mrs Perrin (of Lea and Perrins Worcestershire sauce), who lived in the Hebrides on the Isle of Lewis. She invited him to come and stay with her. To his great delight, and embarrassment, a Highland piper greeted him at the wharf and piped him all the way to her house. Meanwhile I went with Mum to the Shetland Islands where we stayed in the countryside with our aged cousin Agnes, near the small town of Walls. Agnes lived in an ancient crib or cottage, where she still burned peat slabs, cut and dried by herself, in a wide fireplace where a dried side of smoked mutton was hanging. She had only had the power on for three weeks.

Jenny and her mother found, still standing, the partly ruined cottage of Gideon Jamieson, Lorna's great-grandfather who had been brought out to New Zealand in the 1870s by his sons. 'In Walls, to my surprise and joy, my own great-great-Grandpa was still remembered and talked of as the Bible-Basher, and there was still his old cottage, with its odds and ends lying around just as he had left it – nobody had touched it in nearly a hundred years. No graffiti, no vandalism.' They also met relatives from Gideon's line of the family:

> Peter Tait Jamieson was a fisherman, with grizzled face and unforgettable blue North Sea eyes. His wife, like many Shetland wives, wore their knitting belt all day long, so they could fill in every available waiting moment during the housework or cooking with their traditional Shetlands knitting (similar to so-called Fair Isle knitting, except that only natural wool colours are used, of all shades from deep to light). They taught Mum how to do this as well, and she knitted various traditional items on her return.

Jenny's interest in her family roots, already pronounced, grew more concentrated through getting to know her extended family in Shetland. Some years later she compiled an extensive family history.[27]

Jenny's bursary was due to finish in August that year, but an invitation to teach at Victoria University foreshortened her stay in Europe. Farewelling her brothers and mother in London, she flew back to New Zealand in June.

6

Junior Lecturer | Journeyman Composer

Jenny's return to New Zealand in the middle of 1966 was timed to coincide with the second semester at Victoria. Fred Page was taking a sabbatical over the second half of the year and teaching cover was needed in his absence. Douglas Lilburn had advocated for Jenny's appointment and a short while later a lectureship in music was advertised. The excellence of Jenny's pedigree and the high regard in which she was held by other staff members saw her application find favour. She began work as a permanent faculty member at the beginning of 1967.

As an inexperienced lecturer Jenny was given responsibility for some of the lower-level courses delivered to large classes, first-year harmony and music history in particular:

> My very first lecture to a good-sized history class turned out to be a nerve-racking affair: my plan was to devote the last twenty minutes to playing a recording – but the big old Music Room record player gave up the ghost the moment I began. What to do? Stuck in front of a class to whom I had absolutely nothing left to say, 'Talk among yourselves!' I yelped, rushing out the door in a cold sweat, hoping that Douglas might save me. He came back and told them 'Miss

McLeod' had 'recently been in Europe and surely there was plenty they'd like to ask her?' – and all was well.

The teaching she most enjoyed was to small groups of postgraduate students. In these seminars she taught analysis, although by assigning work that the students presented to their peers she ensured they contributed at least as much to proceedings as she did. The music covered was all from the twentieth century, and she generally began the course by looking at Stravinsky's *Le Sacre du printemps*. Lyell Cresswell, who was in Jenny's class in 1968 and went on to a very successful composing career based in the UK, recalled, 'Each of us prepared a small section to discuss at the next class, but we didn't get much beyond the start of the second part because there was so much to talk about. It was taking up too much time and we had to get on with the other pieces.'[1]

Stravinsky aside, the classes focused mainly on twelve-tone music – Schoenberg, Webern, Boulez – systematic compositions responsive to the kinds of analysis Jenny had encountered in Europe. Cresswell recalled that Webern's *Konzert Op. 24*, which they studied, was 'very clear in the use of the twelve-note row and we concentrated mainly on listing all the various statements of it, and talking about its make-up. With [Boulez's] *Structures* again it was a question of working out the system.'[2] Although Jenny was personally interested in the compositional approaches that had to some extent supplanted serial techniques, and had begun to adopt some of those ideas in her own work – the use of amorphous textures evident in *For Seven* and related to the work of Lutosławski and Penderecki, for example – she did not include those approaches in her teaching. She did suggest the students listen to such music, however. 'Recordings of new works by Lutosławski, Penderecki and other Poles were brought to our attention at that stage too,' Cresswell said, 'but we didn't look at them. I suppose they didn't fit with Jenny's point of view at the time. I have a picture in my mind of her going dewy-eyed whenever the names of Boulez and Messiaen were mentioned.'[3]

Jenny had many excellent students in her first years at Victoria, although she was particularly fond of the small group of Honours students she taught in 1968. As well as Lyell Cresswell, the class included Elizabeth Kerr, Ian Harris (who played cor anglais with the NZBC Symphony Orchestra), Denis Smalley and Gordon Burt (both of whom had come up from Christchurch). All of them were to go on to do significant musical work in New Zealand and abroad.

> They were a brilliant class in music analysis, which they became very good at [and] which kept me on my toes. I used to work just as hard as they did, a bit harder because I had come from Boulez and Messiaen and Stockhausen and Berio, Henri Pousseur, all these people. I'd come back and brought all these tidings of great joy. These students were just so happy. They loved to find out these sorts of things; they just found them out by themselves with a bit of encouragement. And they used to do their own analyses; I would be all ears to see what they thought or had discovered. Lyell's work on Webern's *Konzert Op. 24* was amazingly thorough.

The energy and commitment Jenny brought to the classroom meant students were soon caught up in the music they were studying. Organist and composer Roy Tankersley, a member of her 1969 analysis class, recalled: 'It was exciting. Her enthusiasm and passion to unwrap contemporary music scores was infectious. We delved into Webern, Schoenberg and in particular *The Rite of Spring*.' Roy remembered an anecdote Jenny told of Stravinsky taping the score of *Le Sacre* to the walls of his apartment and snipping out one or two sections to get the overall balance right. 'I don't know if there is any truth in this, but . . . [that] prompted me to take graph paper and coloured pencils for themes, and outline Part One.'⁴

At times Jenny and her students would grow sick of the university classrooms. Elizabeth Kerr remembered 'analysis classes on the rocks at Oriental Bay or in the pub', Jenny 'driving her class members there in the back of her old VW Beetle.'⁵ Some days, Jenny recalled, 'we used to end up at the George having a beer or two while we were still having our class.' But 'we were not wasting our time at the George or sitting down on the rocks; it was all really tremendously well-spent time, for all of us.'

Jenny's involvement in departmental life extended beyond her teaching. As a pianist she participated in lunchtime concerts. Lyell Cresswell remembered: 'At one lunchtime concert in the old music room at Victoria Jenny and Fred gave a lively performance of Stravinsky's arrangement for four hands of *Le Sacre du printemps*. They bounced up and down on the piano stool capturing the spirit of the piece, if not the accuracy.'[6] Jenny's recollection was that the performance was reasonably accurate. 'The main trouble here,' she said, 'was that Freddy kept jamming his foot down on the sustain pedal, so that I had to keep kicking it off. As a pianist he always did this whenever he started to get carried away.'

In terms of writing music, Jenny had in effect completed her apprenticeship in Europe and, as a journeyman composer, was ready to make her own way. Before leaving New Zealand, her music had worn its influences quite baldly. It is easy enough to listen to the *Cambridge Suite* and hear traces of Benjamin Britten, or to detect Stravinsky's shadow over the *Little Symphony*. The training and experience she acquired in Europe saw the music that had informed her early works bed down, become somehow metabolised, so that it was less clear where her influences petered out and her own voice as a composer began to assert itself. Like all artists, composers are (to begin with, anyway) the sum of their influences; no one creates art ex nihilo. However, there does come a point when artists with something to say subsume all that they have learned and weave those lessons into garments of their own design.

Back in New Zealand this is what Jenny began to do. The music that was to exercise the greatest influence on her had stabilised to a handful of key composers and significant works. 'I never felt any need for any more than that,' she said. Those composers were, for the most part, unsurprising: Stravinsky's music had become a part of her musical DNA; so too had Bartók's, 'just certain pieces, like *Music for Strings, Percussion and Celeste*, the string quartets, or just a kind of general Bartókian language'. She also recognised that Webern and Schoenberg had got under her musical skin: 'It's early Webern and Schoenberg that I preferred. With Webern his full serial stuff is fascinating, but Schoenberg, I liked his earlier music better than when it went twelve-note.' George Gershwin's music – which Jenny, like her colleague David Farquhar, loved to play – was a less obvious influence, although perhaps it became more apparent in the works she composed during the 1980s.[7] Benjamin Britten was clearly part of the mix too, and Jenny said she 'very much liked *Serenade for Tenor, Horn and Strings. A Ceremony of Carols* is a brilliant collection of carols. They're wonderful. There's the *Sinfonia da Requiem, Peter Grimes, Turn of the Screw*, and bits of the *War Requiem* I like.'

Douglas Lilburn, Olivier Messiaen and Pierre Boulez also made their mark on Jenny as a composer, but their traces are not so easily discernible in the surface detail of her work from those years. While some commentators have detected Lilburn's influence on Jenny's music, she was not convinced his example was particularly significant in respect of how her music actually sounded. Messiaen and Boulez, on the other hand, were to have profound effects on her music, but the seeds they had planted were still taking root in the late 1960s and it would be years before the fruit of their influence became apparent.

The first music Jenny composed after returning to New Zealand was to accompany theatrical productions. Prior to leaving for France, she had composed music for the Victoria Drama Club, preparing incidental music for their 1963 production of Shakespeare's *Troilus and Cressida* directed by Roger Savage. Now she was to write incidental music for the Drama Club's William Austin production of *Twelfth Night*. Jack Richards, who had made way for Jenny in the New Zealand Post Office in 1964, said, 'I remember auditioning for *Twelfth Night* and part of the reason I got the part I did was because I was the only one who could sing Jenny's music.'[8] He'd played the clown, and Jenny said that even after more than fifty years, 'Jack can still sing his opening song.'

Jenny also prepared incidental music for a Downstage Theatre production of *Hamlet*. Richard Campion, the director, requested that the music be scored for saxophone quartet, 'for its sleazy sound; not what I would have chosen myself', Jenny recalled. There was also a radio commission: incidental music for James K. Baxter's play *Mister Brandywine Chooses a Gravestone*.

This kind of writing on demand was to become characteristic of her work for the next few years; it may have been that, for the moment, she lacked an inner compulsion to compose. (It may simply have been that she lacked time, being fully occupied with her teaching responsibilities during her first year or two back in Wellington.) The music she had written prior to 1967 was driven by the imperatives common to fledgling composers: the desire to learn, to acquire technique and develop craft, to try ideas, to simply have the experience of writing some music and then hearing it played. Her time in Europe had been a kind of finishing school where she further advanced her knowledge and technique but also, and perhaps just as importantly, tested herself against international standards of composition. Having satisfied herself that she could hold her own amongst her contemporaries on the international scene, the pressing question became not 'Can I compose?' but rather, 'What shall I compose?' For Jenny, as for most self-aware composers, that was to become a fundamental – and perhaps existential – question. And as she slowly made progress towards an answer that satisfied her, she was content to write the music people asked her to write. The theatre and radio music she prepared in 1967 was modest in scope and impact, but the next piece she was asked to compose unexpectedly promoted her to the status of a 'household name' in New Zealand.

Earth and Sky

During the 1960s, schools in the Wairarapa established an annual music festival that was coordinated by the local branch of the New Zealand Educational Institute. In 1964 the festival mounted a production of Benjamin Britten's one-act opera *Noye's Fludde*, composed for amateur performers and particularly children.[9] In 1967 it occurred to conductor Peter Zwartz that Jenny would be an ideal person to compose a work for their 1968 event. 'Without asking me,' Jenny recalled, 'he talked them into asking me to write something for this festival.'

In the years immediately preceding this commission, Jenny had been primarily focused on composing music for highly skilled professional performers and progressive, knowledgeable audiences. Writing a work for Wairarapa school-children to perform to an audience largely comprised of their parents called for an altogether different kind of music. And to succeed, it called for a subject the children could relate to.

When commissions arrived on her desk, Jenny's habit was to consider what she had already been thinking about to see if it might serve the new project. With the Māori creation poetry that had nourished her so profoundly in Germany fresh in her mind – it had by then become something sacred to her, she said – she knew she had her starting point. 'I used something that was close to my heart, and it was perfect timing because [*Earth and Sky*] was the first real thing that happened after I came back from Europe. It was the first opportunity that cropped up and I thought, "Ah, children; Ah, nature; the Creation poetry".'[10]

The abstraction of the poetry – the whakapapa of creation: Te Kore; Te Pō; Te Ao-Marama – was part of what Jenny found so appealing in the genealogy these texts detailed. It had not previously occurred to her that children might be well placed to convey this, but as soon as she thought of it, 'children seemed the perfect ones to tell it; the best way to tell it – all the abstract stuff'. That abstraction was harnessed to a natural setting – an unspoiled Creation – which she also thought would make sense to her young performers: 'We gave them something that they could immediately connect with, like trees and birds and plants.'

For Jenny, the nature of the commission immediately implied the need for a strong theatrical element. In Stockhausen's classes there had been a lot of talk about theatre, and she had become aware of the exciting and innovative approaches to performance being pioneered on the Continent: 'I had come from where there were happenings – the New York and European Happenings were happening at the time that I was over in Europe – all kinds of strange experimental things were going on that ended up under the umbrella of theatre. So, when I got back here it was easy and I never thought twice about not doing it. I thought it was just perfect – the way to use whole bunches of kids and put a narrator in when you wanted one.'

Jenny's willingness to embrace a theatrical approach was tempered by her concern that the show genuinely worked as children's theatre; that it not be a watered-down version of adult theatre. She told Suzanne Court, 'I wasn't trying to create anything new – I was trying to make something work for the children without them having to say lines, because I knew that wouldn't work.'[11]

What Jenny was convinced would work was an invitation to the children to use their imaginations, and to engage them across a wide range of performance activities. She told music commentator Owen Jensen that the show was 'a combination of various theatrical and musical elements. I haven't found a name for it – there isn't one, I don't think. It combines speech, mime, creative movement, orchestral sounds, vocal sounds. It's probably not as "way out" as it might sound because it has to be simple for children to learn.'[12] She explained her approach:

> I kept thinking of the sort of things that I would like to do were I in the situation of a child on stage and, considering the aptitudes of various children, tried to separate the various things. So, if they're good at dancing, there's something for them to do; if they're good at painting, there's something for them to do; speaking, singing and so on, and we can separate things out like that rather than expect one child to be able to do everything.[13]

Jenny also wanted all the children – the actors, speakers, dancers, choristers, musicians – on stage, 'being the sea, being the trees, being this and that. They did that really well; the ones who actually played snails and various critters, and the teenage boys – 1st XV types – playing gods with masks that my mother made.' These masks, designed by Perrin and fabricated from papier-mâché by Lorna (who by now had returned to the home she shared with Ron), were large and colourful and exactly fit for purpose. 'The masks were perfect, marvellous. Freddy and Eve couldn't get over them. And wonderfully sturdy – they survived at least two productions and seasons.'

To prepare her libretto, Jenny first drew on Richard Taylor's translations of Māori creation poetry, 'the very beginning part of the creation; that's the bit that got me best. From the nothing, Te Pō, and the sea coming up. About the first half-hour of *Earth and Sky* is the very beginning, and then we move on to Tāne and the battle of the gods and so on.' As rich as Taylor's text was, Jenny felt she needed more material. There were some books available – Antony Alpers' *Maori Myths and Tribal Legends Retold* had been published a few years earlier – but she also investigated the holdings in the Alexander Turnbull Library. Repeated visits to the library led her to the accounts of many different tribal traditions. Particularly useful were the stories gathered in the histories complied by ethnographer Elsdon Best. Jenny also read Polynesian accounts of the Creation, learning about the deeds of Māui, a significant figure in the origin stories of Polynesia.

Although Jenny's reo Māori was not at that stage strong, she was dissatisfied with some of the translations she saw. Where the Turnbull Library records included the original Māori texts, she re-translated those passages, using the parts that spoke to her most powerfully as she crafted her libretto. She hoped, given the neglect Māori culture appeared to be suffering in New Zealand at the time, that her work might bring back into the world of the living these ancient Māori and Polynesian genealogies.

The completed libretto offered Jenny a compelling narrative arc on which to hang her music. Before composing a note, however, it was necessary to determine the forces, the instruments, for which she would write. Tuned percussion of various sorts had considerable appeal to her, not only because they corresponded to the ancient provenance of the stories but also because they were instruments children could easily learn to play. She settled on a large group of tom-toms and xylophones – instruments that were hardly to be found lying around primary school music rooms. Consistent with her mother's can-do attitude, and a New Zealander's inclination to use whatever was to hand to fashion whatever was needed, Jenny set the Wairarapa schools community the task of building them:

> They didn't have xylophones but I thought, 'Well, their dads can make xylophones.' So, I sent them a few instructions – how to tune this and that, how to line them all up – and blimey, the dads got right into it and they made twelve [xylophones]. I found out from books on African music how to turn [barrels] into drums, so I just let the dads know and they got into it and, lo and behold, half of our orchestra was xylophones and tom-toms made by the dads.

Aware of the problems posed by amateur string players, Jenny elected to omit violins, violas, cellos and basses from her instrumental palette. Instead, she deployed local brass players ('Our brass bands,' Jenny said, 'were some of the best in the world, so I thought we could get the brass band to come and play') and woodwinds, supplementing local flautists, clarinettists, oboe and bassoon players with a few students who came up from Wellington to fill out the section. There were a couple of pianos and an organ too, and Jenny reckoned, correctly, that there would be one or two good local pianists up to the task.

The music Jenny composed for the production was tailored to respond to the Māori origins of her texts: 'In *Earth and Sky* I used quasi-Māori chants that I made up myself, and that various Māori people thought were Māori. They said "Oh, I haven't heard that one." I would keep my mouth shut.'[14] Beyond this, the music primarily reflected the kinds of systematic approaches she championed in her teaching. Her experiences with Stockhausen had affirmed the value of processes in musical composition, and such processes had become a significant preoccupation for her. 'Before I write a piece,' she told Owen Jensen, 'I have an idea – now, this is an intellectual idea, I admit it – to get across, a certain musical process that I want to explore. And it happened in this opera that I was exploring all kinds of symmetrical relationships, vertically and horizontally.'[15] Some years later Jenny told Elizabeth Kerr, 'I was obsessed with symmetries – Webern had enhanced this for me – and in *Earth and Sky* symmetry plays a part on all sorts of levels. Symmetrical chords, the whole first piece is symmetrical in terms of the bar structure, in one place the melody mirrors itself underneath and so on.'[16]

Those symmetrical relationships were not of concern to the audience – they were not even the concern of the performers – they were mobilised to serve the purposes of the composer. Writing music on the basis of an idea like this, Jenny said, 'gives me a language. From that I build up the material that I'm going to use. This has nothing to do with communication yet, but you have to start somewhere and accumulate your material somehow. You can't just draw a bit of this and a bit of that; there has to be some system, some unity.'[17]

Another technique she used as she worked on *Earth and Sky* was related to an idea she had deployed when composing *For Seven*. That work was influenced by Stockhausen's *Momente* to the extent that she had composed both foreground and background music, and allowed for some traffic between them. 'But it wasn't only Stockhausen,' Jenny recalled. 'You see, Boulez had talked in similar terms about [Debussy's] *Jeux*; that you could find this kind of distinction between foreground and background. So, foreground and background were part of the thinking of the time.' The background music in *For Seven* was developed using chromatic triads.[18] Like the music of Witold Lutosławski and some of his Polish contemporaries, this background music was 'quasi-amorphous' in sound, and the role it fulfilled was primarily textural, rather than melodic or rhythmic. 'And the background in *For Seven*,' Jenny said, 'became the foreground in *Earth and Sky* . . . If I hadn't done those pieces in Europe, I couldn't have written *Earth and Sky* because I wouldn't have had the experience of dealing with what I was thinking of as more "background" sounds.'

Despite the complexity of some of this music, and its chromatic nature, it was accessible, in part because it was so rhythmically direct: 'It was different from *For Seven* because in *Earth and Sky* there's nothing but beat, beat, beat.'[19]

Earth and Sky begins with drums and claves, young actors assembling to chant in honour of Tāne, the god of forests and birds. A 'Song of Joy' declares the beauty of Aotearoa, and the singers invoke the great god Io to lift the tapu of silence so that the creation story may be told. In the second scene of Act One, Te Kore, the nothing, is replaced by Te Pō, the darkness, from which emerge the land and the gods of Earth and sky.[20] The gods dance but cannot separate the Earth mother, Papatūānuku, from the sky father, Ranginui. That task falls to Tāne. In Act Two, Tāne clothes the sky with celestial bodies and populates the land with plants and animals. The gods squabble and damage his handiwork, but he is able to effect repairs and in time is provided with a wife, Hine, by Tiki, the maker of humankind. In the final act and after many generations, Māui's feats are described – taming the sun god and bringing fire to the world – but he is unable to subdue death. At his passing, the people lament him. The songs and chants are in te reo Māori and in English, and the action is tied together by a pre-recorded narration in English.

More than a story set to music, *Earth and Sky* was conceived and performed as a kind of total theatre – 'Gesamtkunstwerk of the South Pacific' was how composer Denis Smalley described it – and the music was accompanied by plenty of colourful action on stage: theatrical lighting and dancing, costumes and masked gods.[21] 'Words, music and spectacle are all equally important,' Jenny wrote in a 1993 essay, adding that director 'Peter Tulloch's contribution was as great as mine.'[22] Tulloch and Jenny enjoyed a close working relationship, and he later recalled that although he had been associated with many new works, 'Never have I experienced the generosity that Jenny offered me nor the clarity of vision.' Over the course of rehearsing the show his direction became intimately attuned to Jenny's wishes: 'Much of the work came from the actor/dancers in the choirs, but I always knew when it was "right". Initially I'd get a "thumbs up", which diminished to a head nod, a wrinkle of the nose, and finally I didn't even need to look for her approval – one simply knew!' Tulloch's work on the show was so effective in bringing Jenny's vision to life, he was called upon to direct a second season in Tauranga the following year, and three years later to direct her subsequent children's music theatre piece, *Under the Sun*.[23]

Earth and Sky was performed in Masterton for the Wairarapa Primary Schools Music Festival in September 1968, with Dobbs Franks as musical director. About 250 school-children performed to a rapt audience and the work was immediately heralded as a watershed moment in New Zealand music. Prime Minister Keith Holyoake was on hand for the opening performance and thought the show 'terrific, superb'. He told reporters, 'It is a long time since I was so excited and so stirred and I think this experience was shared by everyone here tonight.'[24]

Reviewing the performance for the *New Zealand Listener*, Cameron Hill reported: 'Not since Stravinsky conducted the final section of his *Firebird* in Wellington, have I experienced the same raw thrill as I did during the "Invocation to Io" scene.' Hill commented favourably on Jenny's composition, believing it to be music 'that even the youngest schoolchildren can understand, feel and learn from'. There were aspects of the performance he thought less than perfect – some stumbles by individual instrumentalists, and passages 'where the action does not sufficiently sustain the story'. But he concluded his review by saying, '*Earth and Sky* is a major work – perhaps Jenny McLeod will no longer be called the "young New Zealand composer" – and it speaks with a universal tongue.'[25] The enthusiasm of some music reviewers bordered on breathless: 'Such was the impact of this work that the event could better be described as a blast-off'; and, from London, '*Earth and Sky* must surely be one of the most ambitious works ever written for children . . . a new force has come into New Zealand music.'[26]

Playwright Bruce Mason believed *Earth and Sky* to be one of those rare productions that 'create instant astonishment', and that Jenny's libretto 'beautifully blended awe and robust humour' while 'avoid[ing] the heavy biblical tramp of most English transliterations of the Maori creation story'. Mason also suggested that *Earth and Sky* had importance beyond being entertaining or well done. As he saw it, Māori culture had been 'defused of all its sacred and numinous qualities' and consigned to the junk-heap by European occupation. 'What Miss McLeod has done is to reclaim image, concept and myth from the junk-heap and infuse it with a new sense of reverence and awe, in which we can all participate. It is a noble achievement.'[27]

It wasn't only music critics and cultural commentators who were won over by *Earth and Sky*. Michael Morrissey, who played Tāne and Māui in the Masterton production, recalled, 'being stunned by how affected the audience was, and feeling the perfect performer's satisfaction that not only were rehearsals fantastic but the audience loved the show.'[28] One of Jenny's fondest memories of the Masterton season was of how her father – whom she would never have described as musical   responded:

> When he came down to the first performance I watched him, because I was sitting a bit further back in the upstairs, and he was in the first row upstairs. And my father, who was always a bit of a child, I don't think he knew what hit him that night. I watched him as the kids started coming in from the different doors and singing and playing their little drums and stuff, and he just edged his way

to the front of his seat, just about falling over the balcony. He didn't move; he just stayed like that the whole time.

That first performance 'finished with an audience response of 30 seconds of absolute silence and a standing ovation'.[29]

Although Jenny was delighted by the intensity of the positive response to *Earth and Sky*, it did take her somewhat by surprise: 'It was just so much more than I thought it was going to be.' Asked why she thought it had worked so well, she said, 'Partly it was the kids. There was just sort of no barrier between them and the audience. They got right into the heart of it without any inhibitions whatever, and there was no doubt that it was *our* thing that we were doing in New Zealand.'[30]

The kids might have played an important role, but Jenny recognised that the power of the Māori poetry, the original inspiration for the show, was also vitally important. 'It's because of where it comes from: it is the whole ethos and output of an entire people, of an entire tradition with thousands of years behind it.' Her main contribution, she felt, was that of a facilitator, accommodating the meeting of two powerful forces: 'Given all this – the combined impact of many children, united and at their best; and of our uniquely blessed Māori voice, at its deepest in this supremely living creation poetry – it would be wrong to attribute too much of the show's success to me personally. A focal point for two such powerful energies, it could hardly fail, provided I didn't do anything too wrong.'[31]

The creation of *Earth and Sky*, then, was down to the collaborative efforts of those involved, rather than the inspired jottings of the composer. As Jenny cheerfully acknowledged, 'There isn't in fact all that much music in it', and she didn't believe the show could be placed in a tradition that implied substantial and skilful composition married to exemplary performance skills. Given how far it lay from conventional notions of opera or musical theatre, Jenny asked, 'Is it even art, then? Certainly,' she affirmed, 'but *our* art, more than *my* art – something nobody in the world but us could do, or even come close to doing. It was this that people sensed, and this is why they rightly rejoiced and took pride in it.'[32]

Interest in *Earth and Sky* – and in Jenny, too – was considerable, and both were covered extensively in the media. With so much public attention, it was almost inevitable that there would be further seasons over the next few years: in Tauranga in 1969, again directed by Peter Tulloch and with Dobbs Franks conducting; in Auckland in 1970, produced by Ian Mune and with musical direction by Ian Harvey (whom Jenny first met when he replaced Christopher Small as the music teacher at Horowhenua College in the late 1950s) and Kathleen McRoberts; and in Christchurch in 1971, produced by Neta Neale and with musical direction by Robert Field-Dodgson.[33] The Auckland season at the Mercury Theatre was Jenny's least favourite staging – too sophisticated, too much symbolism, the school kids sitting passively in rows behind (instead of being actively on) the stage, dancing of 'the tutu ilk' – but also attracted the most intense media scrutiny. Queen Elizabeth II and members of the royal family attended a gala performance during the season and demand for tickets was through the roof. Eventually a computer was enlisted to select which of the two thousand applicants might be offered a seat from among the seven hundred available.[34]

Although Jenny felt enormous respect for the Māori traditions celebrated in the show, she'd had little direct contact with Māori. 'When I wrote *Earth and Sky*,' she said in 2002, 'I didn't know there *was* a Māori culture. I'd been at school with Māori, and had some good Māori friends, but I didn't realise the extent of the Māori world.'[35] As a result, she had not consulted Māori about the content of the show. Such an omission seems unthinkable in the new century, and Jenny later said, 'I would never dare touch a subject like that now.' Even so, and after many years of reflection, she felt that she had not been wrong to undertake the project; that her motivation for writing *Earth and Sky* in the 1960s had been good:

> I didn't do that for any wrong reason either; I did it because I loved that poetry; I loved it so much I took it with me when I went to study in Germany. I respond to it as the deepest root in my life. I feel very close to certain individuals but this feeling is different. I

just fed on it and it kept me sane in the middle of that crazy time. I still feel like that and actually, that is what has saved me from ill fortune. I believe that, had my motives been less pure than they were – and are – all sorts of things could have gone wrong. And all sorts of things tried to go wrong but they never did.[36]

The second season of *Earth and Sky*, in Tauranga, was embraced by local Māori, who, Jenny recalled, 'were right into it . . . They were all happy and they were putting on the opening night and they invited the Māori Queen and they sat me next to [her].' At the end of the first act, Te Arikinui Dame Te Atairangikaahu turned to Jenny and said, 'The name of Io is not to be spoken indoors.' Jenny recalled, 'She said this to me without any other explanation at all, very directly, seriously and gravely, and completely out of the blue – these were the only words she spoke to me, there was no other conversation.' The Māori Queen's unexpected response, and the gravity and seriousness with which she expressed it, were a cause for concern: the last thing Jenny wanted was for the work to give offence or violate sacred traditions. 'Later on, after the first night, there was a move among the Tauranga Māori elders and what they did was formally say a karakia to protect the whole production.' The Tauranga season, and subsequent seasons in Auckland and Christchurch, proceeded without incident or misfortune.

Although *Earth and Sky* was not staged after the Christchurch production in 1971, it remained an important work for Jenny, and was still vivid in her memory more than twenty years later when she became close to Ngāti Rangi of the Maungārongo Marae in Ohakune. At the invitation of her friend Joan Akapita, Jenny joined the Tira Hoe Waka, the river iwis' annual canoe journey down the Whanganui River from Taumarunui to the coast. The participants – around one hundred and ten the first year Jenny made the trip – stayed on various marae all the way down the river. Each night after the evening meal there would be a karakia, led by whichever group was the host that particular day and on that particular marae. One evening early in the trip the hosts chanted the ancient words she had used for *Earth and Sky*. Jenny couldn't believe her ears. 'I never dreamed I was ever going to hear that because I thought it was dead. Then I was in a fit of shame and guilt that I had taken and used something that was living still.' Jenny knew she would have to confess to her friends that she had used these ancient words in her music theatre piece, but didn't know how to broach the matter.

A year or two later, Jenny was approached by Waipukurau journalist and writer Hilary Pedersen, representing a group who wanted to stage *Earth and Sky*. Jenny recalled: 'I thought, I can't let it happen without going to talk with the Whanganui people, and I didn't know how to do it – I was very nervous. I told the people from Waipukurau that they couldn't do it unless the Whanganui people said it was OK. Then I waited until the signs were right.'[37] A short time later, while staying in Hawke's Bay, Jenny woke during the night and thought, 'I have to go to Ohakune in the morning. So I went, without even ringing them to see who was there – they were often away at tangi and things. But all the people I needed to talk to, the three main ones, were all there at the marae.'[38]

Many years later, Jenny remembered the experience clearly:

> So, I sat down and talked with them for about an hour. The minute I started to speak tears began rolling down my cheeks, completely silent tears. I just kept weeping all the time I was saying all this; it didn't affect my speech or anything. I just sat there and told them what I did and explained that when I did it, I thought I was bringing it back to life; that I wanted it to come back. Anyway, I'd done this and I was very sorry. Then I said [that] these people in Hawke's Bay wanted to do it all again and I realised I couldn't let that happen without talking to Whanganui and seeing how they might feel about it. They didn't say anything; they sat there and listened. There was no hostility, just deep attention – [it felt] to me as if the ancestors were there with us, listening. By the time I finished Matiu Māreikura, their leader – he's like my brother – said what a good thing it was that I had come and asked them and put this before them because that meant that I was family. Then he said I was right to think that I was bringing it back because he said there was only one place this creation poetry had stayed alive, and that

was on the upper Whanganui. Down the lower end, the city end, it had completely died. Then he said, when the Waipukurau idea came up, 'You'd better let me see what words you've used in case you've used words that are too sacred to be used.' So, I came home and I let him have the booklet from the recording, it had all the words in it, and I didn't hear back from him for months. The Hawke's Bay thing fell through but I was [in Ohakune] again at Christmas, three, or four, or five months later. I asked Matiu how did he get on with the words and he said to me, 'Did you have a problem with it?' I said, 'No. You wanted to make sure I didn't use any words that were too sacred.' He said, 'Oh, no. That's all right; you explained everything.' That was it. That was the blessing that I got. Although it hasn't been done again since then, I wouldn't worry because I got their blessing completely.

Although the opportunity to have the work performed again failed to materialise, Jenny's re-engagement with it at a time when she had drawn close to Māori led her to the conclusion that structural change was needed. 'I realised that I'd ended it in the wrong place. I'd ended *Earth and Sky* in the spirit world, because it ends with the death of Māui [and] spirit voices. I realised I should have ended it in this world, I should have brought it back from the spirit world.'[39] She composed a new ending to achieve that objective, adding a new concluding chorus and final haka. And like many composers who revisit their work, she found 'quite a few untidy details, so I tidied it all up'.[40]

Earth and Sky may have only had a brief life in the New Zealand performance repertory, but it has endured in the memories of those who participated in the productions. In her later years Jenny continued to receive messages from people she had forgotten – or in some cases not personally met – reminding her of something about the work, or to explain that participation in the show inspired them to pursue a life in the arts. *Earth and Sky* lived on in the LP recording of Auckland's Mercury Theatre production, released by Philips in 1970. And it has lived on as a thread in Aotearoa New Zealand's cultural matrix, particularly for the way it celebrated Māori traditions. Jenny remembered her surprise and joy when, at a humanities conference in the early 1990s, Māori advocate and educator Keri Kaa 'got up, and she welcomed *Earth and Sky* first; she welcomed the work of art before the people, and I thought that was really something.'

7

Professor of Music

During her early years as a staff member in the Music Department, Jenny had focused her attention on the content and delivery of the courses she taught. She was committed to finding ways to make her teaching relevant to students, and was especially eager that instruction accommodate some of the ideas she had encountered during her time in Europe, as well as the trends she saw as most important in contemporary culture, notably interest in popular and non-Western music. Fred Page shared some of the same ambitions, particularly with respect to contemporary Western classical music, and in 1969 asked Jenny to undertake an academic reorganisation of the music curriculum. Jenny agreed, having no idea that Douglas Lilburn had redrafted the curriculum just a few years earlier, in 1964: 'I'd been away for two years and on my return had noticed no great sign of anything different from what I was familiar with.'

Jenny's failure to recognise the changes Lilburn's new curriculum had on the overall programme was partly a function of the singular focus she placed on her own teaching: other than the Honours analysis class, the courses for which she was responsible appeared to be the same as those she had taken as an undergraduate. She was also largely unconcerned with the degree as a holistically conceived programme of study: 'Until Fred asked me, I was not even interested in the degree structure, had never really given it a second thought, and was by no means concerned with any sort of push to open things up or "make things new" or whatever. I only started giving it all some real consideration after Fred had requested me to.'

When Page charged Jenny with revising the curriculum, he did not advise her of Lilburn's relatively recent work on the programme and did not supply her with any of the relevant documentation. Perhaps he assumed she already knew, or that Lilburn (who was overseas at the time) had told her. Whatever the reason, when combined with Jenny's academic administrative inexperience – a more experienced person would have checked the current University Calendar and spotted Lilburn's revisions – it was to be a damaging oversight.

Jenny used as a starting point the pre-1964 degree documents with which she was familiar, and which she had on her shelves. What she proposed was significantly different from the degree she herself had completed in 1963 but not so very different from the degree structure Lilburn had drawn up. Where her proposal differed from Lilburn's curriculum was largely around how content was disposed.

Jenny concentrated study of the materials of music – harmony, counterpoint, fugue, technical analysis – into three 'Composition' papers. These might include composition exercises, but their purpose was primarily to ensure students intending to formally study composition at Honours level were thoroughly prepared to do so. 'Both Messiaen and Boulez,' Jenny said, 'considered that you couldn't really teach composition as such (I mean, that composers can't be taught how to compose) – but that analysis of, and listening to, other musical scores was the most effective way for a composer to learn (in addition to trying to practise writing music oneself, of course).' Jenny also made these Composition papers (and thus, this content) elective in the degree. Her proposal required only that Music I, II and III – papers concerned with the history and literature of music – remain mandatory. This achieved two things: first, students were able to exercise more choice in what they studied (Lilburn's degree mandated five specific papers; Jenny's only three); second, the groundwork was laid for the later development of a degree that allowed students to major in music history and literature (otherwise known as musicology), or composition, or performance.[1]

When she mentioned the curriculum changes she was proposing to her colleague David Farquhar, he explained 'how everything had to go through the Law Draftsman as well as the Arts Faculty, and how all of this was so difficult to cope with that "me, on my own" (he implied) would never manage it.'

> I thought, 'We'll see about that.' So, I worked out beforehand what I needed to do so that the faculty would pass everything and I just re-wrote the BMus regulations, re-wrote the courses, introduced various new courses and prepared the regulations in the legal language. As a matter of fact, they passed it all . . . Fred took me along to the faculty meetings and I just explained it and not a question was raised and it all went through just like that.[2]

News of the degree changes reached Douglas Lilburn in London. He was sickened to hear of it, at least in part because his overseas leave that year was only for fifteen weeks, yet 'there was no hint of this impending change before I left'.[3] Lilburn's once friendly and mutually supportive relationship with Page had soured during the 1960s. Page's decision to task Jenny with the curricular redesign while Lilburn was abroad further damaged that relationship, but also implicated Jenny in the downward spiral of their decaying friendship. Where there had formerly been respect and love, Lilburn appears to have become suspicious of Jenny and her motivations.[4]

It's possible Page's decision to ask Jenny to redraft the curriculum was the result of some changing circumstance within the university, or was triggered by a chance remark in a Professorial Board meeting. Perhaps he had looked over Lilburn's curriculum and thought it could be further improved with some new ideas and fresh thinking. In Jenny's view, 'Fred would honestly have had only the future of the Music Department and of music itself at heart' in asking her to do this work. In light of Page and Lilburn's history – 'Douglas and Fred had a long and true friendship from Christchurch days, and Douglas was earlier the first person Freddy had hired to teach alongside him after he was appointed to get the Vic Music Department started,' Jenny said – and how wounded Page was at Lilburn's subsequent withdrawal, it is extremely unlikely Page asked Jenny to undertake the review as a rebuke to Lilburn or his work.

Nevertheless, Lilburn did take umbrage. Lilburn's biographer Philip Norman provides examples of Page's behaviour during the 1960s that Lilburn found increasingly hard to take.[5] Jenny, too, conceded 'the somewhat "Olympian" attitude Freddy could affect' might have damaged Lilburn and Page's relationship, but she said that while Page might have been thoughtless, she never found him to be spiteful. Sadly, and particularly as events might have concluded much more amicably had Jenny, Lilburn and Page simply talked things through, Jenny's own friendship with Lilburn eventually broke down.

> My close relationship with Douglas came to an end one evening when Fred was there. I ventured to suggest something perfectly sensible and suddenly Douglas lost his cool completely. He indicated angrily that I was talking rubbish and he 'had a quarter of a century on me'. (I think the real trouble was more that I had ceased to be a 'worshipper'.) Anyway, at this I too grew angry; I didn't respect anyone simply because of their age – for me respect had to be earned, and if it was to be mutual, Douglas was not showing much at the time. I returned his disrespect by telling him short and sweet to 'Get stuffed!', upon which he flew into an utter rage. I'd never seen such a thing – even down at the Neuers' belt-and-buckle factory – and nor have I ever seen anything like it since. Douglas jumped to his feet and shouted dramatically at me to 'leave this house and never come back!' It was like theatre or Dostoyevsky come to life. I was shocked and devastated, muttering 'Don't worry, I won't,' as I stalked out – and later weeping bitter tears on Freddy's shoulder in the car, in the dark.

In 1970 Fred Page announced his retirement from the university. Jenny, along with her colleagues, felt that Lilburn would be the ideal person to take on the role of Professor of Music. When she raised it with him, Lilburn said he did not intend to apply. The previous year, angry at Page's behaviour over the curriculum redesign, he had tendered his resignation. The university, it would seem, was reluctant to lose so prestigious a staff member and eventually offered him a personal chair in music, oversight of the Electronic Music Studio and a salary consistent with his needs. This position he accepted gratefully, and he was happy to largely withdraw from the life and running of the department.[6] Learning that Lilburn did not intend to apply for the position Page was vacating, Jenny thought, 'I don't know if David's going to apply but just for the hell of it, I'm going to apply. I never dreamed I would get it.'

Jenny's application detailed her musical successes and the academic administrative skill she had acquired in reorganising the curriculum, and was supported by a very favourable reference from Olivier Messiaen.[7] It was an impressive application for such a junior staff member and saw her appointed, at the age of twenty-eight, as New Zealand's youngest ever university professor. It would have helped that Page supported her application, too – 'Fred said he told the [appointing committee] that my second prize in Messiaen's class was the equivalent of a "Silver Medal at the Olympics".' David Farquhar, although perhaps disappointed not to be offered the role, agreed with Page that Jenny was the department's most exceptional graduate.[8] The appointment had some surprising consequences: 'Douglas had a personal chair,' Jenny said, 'but as head of the department I was his senior and I was David's boss.'[9]

Jenny's appointment excited quite a bit of interest in the press, and there were plenty of interviews and articles marking her rise to the professoriate; the progressive ideas she was bringing to the department – some of which had been shared by Fred Page – made good copy. In 1971 she explained her plans for the department to Jill McCracken of the *New Zealand Listener*: 'What I would like to do is not so much change what's there at the moment, though that of course needs modifying, but to start courses which are a bit more relevant. We need courses in musical communication and musical sociology, to find out why and how music fits into various cultures.'[10] She advocated for greater links between the drama and music departments at the university, and believed broadly based study preferable to what she saw as the excessively narrow focus of the conservatory model of music education.

> Conservatories are out of date. I object to the whole conservatoire mentality. They are behind the times, thinking in the past. There is still the idea of training people to be concert artists, to be soloists. I don't see any sense in this. I think the concert artist and the concert as it exists today are slowly and surely dying out. Look at the orchestras around the world. They're so unhappy most of them, including ours, and it's just part of the terrible circumstances of being a professional musician. These people lose their enthusiasm and their spontaneity because it's inevitable – rehearsals all the time, dud conductors, not having any say and playing the same old stuff over and over again. I wouldn't want to advise anybody to go into that sort of life.[11]

As the incoming professor, her vision for Victoria's Music Department involved de-emphasising the kinds of professional focus favoured by conservatories, and prioritising the communitarian aspects of music-making. She thought it vitally important that musicians created 'music with a meaning for the whole community'.[12] She told Rosemary McLeod of the *Sunday Times* that music degrees, as they were then constituted, were outdated because they were not calibrated to meet the needs of the general population: 'The community and the institutions are tuned to different stations.'[13] Jenny's dissatisfaction with art music had been bubbling under the surface since her time in Europe. Perhaps her experiences with *Earth and Sky* – an example of what was possible when communities cooperated in the creation of music by and for the people who lived in them – had reinforced her conviction that community-based music was a credible and possibly necessary alternative to (and maybe even replacement for) art music by and for professionals.

Another area she saw as ripe for development was the study of non-Western music. With Fred Page's support she had introduced such study into the curriculum (with her 1969 revisions), but she was eager to expand those offerings. This was in part because engaging with music from other cultures cast useful light on the music of the West: 'I've come to realise the great lack in our own music is its lack of relationship with non-musical concepts. Non-Western music is closely related to actual concepts of life. Indian music is the pure expression of Hindu philosophical concepts.'[14] She had been taking classical Indian drum lessons from Dr C.G. (Balu) Balachandran and was well placed to appreciate this; she was eager for students in the programme to enjoy similar opportunities. To that end, she planned to augment the non-Western music courses then on offer – in Indian and North African music – and host non-Western musicians as visiting specialists with the help of university grants.[15]

Jenny was also eager to expand the department's curriculum by offering popular music studies. She wanted to encourage students to 'write, sing and think pop', and believed, 'Pop music is the community music of today. Some of it is very good. And the fact that most of it has words helps to give it meaning.'[16] Such enthusiasm for popular music may have surprised her colleagues, but hers was not a starry-eyed, uncritical appreciation of the genre. In a letter to poet Kevin Ireland some years later, she decried the 'glossy pop (or pap) of "A Whiter Shade of Pale", which is certainly crap of the most appealing kind to a certain undiscriminating taste'. She remained positive, however, about the 'real heart' she identified in 'the best sixties rock, that came from the blues, from black Africa, and that was not a wrong direction in my view'.[17] As a newly appointed Professor of Music she thought, 'Local pop productions are so good it seems absurd that we don't discuss them at university.' And so, before terribly long, that was where they were being discussed.

Not all of the changes Jenny instituted were as potentially contentious, and she said, 'We shall certainly go on giving the basic traditional training; there is no one else to do it.'[18] This included an ongoing expansion of instrumental performance study for academic credit, which Page and Lilburn had introduced in 1965: 'By the time I was back there teaching, [violinist] Ruth Pearl and [pianist] Diny Schramm were full-time instrumental tutors. Others were added gradually – for example, Gavin Saunders on viola – but mostly they were part-time, and often also NZSO principals. Diny retired at the same time as Fred, and I appointed Judith Clark as permanent full-time piano tutor, a position she held until her own retirement.'

The development of the curriculum coalesced in the degree structure Jenny finally locked into place in 1972 – a BMus with three concentrations of study: history and literature, performance, and composition. This was the model other universities in New Zealand also adopted.[19] Composer Ross Harris, who joined the music faculty while Jenny was at the helm, recalled that though the curricular development of the early 1970s was driven by Jenny, it also felt natural.

That's not to say everything Jenny instituted as Professor of Music was a good idea. She wondered, for example, if the fiercely analytical bias she embraced in her own courses was entirely healthy, and observed that introducing credit for activities like choir – formerly voluntary and extra-curricular – might have taken some of the fun out of university life. But other aspects of her legacy as head of department, such as the creation of the three majors and the growing emphasis placed on ethnomusicology, were to remain positive features of the department into the new century.

The time needed to develop and implement these curricular changes was considerable and was to keep her fairly busy over the next few years, but before she could get her teeth properly into this, she had a new commission to think about.

Under the Sun

The year Jenny assumed a professorial role at Victoria University, 1971, was also the centenary year for her mother's home town, Palmerston North. Civic and community groups began planning several years in advance of the celebrations, which ultimately included public parades, interdenominational church services and community garden parties. A Centenary Collection of New Zealand paintings was acquired by the Palmerston North Art Gallery and a special postage stamp was issued. There was even a visit from the Queen.[20] Morva Croxson, a leader in establishing music therapy in New Zealand, was appointed to head the Palmerston North Centennial Music Committee. The mayor, Brian Elwood, suggested she 'think big'. Hearing that *Earth and Sky* was to be performed in Masterton, she and Helen Caskie, a friend and local composer, decided to go along. They 'were very impressed, particularly noting the involvement of children. The whole thing was fresh and lively and honestly New Zealand.'[21]

Captivated by what she had seen and heard, Morva floated the idea of commissioning a work from Jenny for the centennial celebrations. The commission, which Jenny accepted, was not particularly prescriptive. 'A broad-brush approach was taken, though we did discuss what had impressed us at Masterton,' Morva recalled. 'We wanted to involve a full cross-section of the people offering good music programmes in schools and the Palmerston North Teachers College, plus local choral and instrumental groups. There was a lot of talent in the city.'[22] Making use of all that local talent called for a huge cast of musicians and performers – during 1970 Jenny was predicting there would be about five hundred people in the cast – and a large performance space. The organisers settled on the city's Pascal Street stadium.[23]

Given the forces being marshalled, Jenny formulated a suitably epic proposal for the work. Provisionally titled *Starsong*, it had as its subject 'the beginning and end of the world – and everything in between'.[24] She developed the piece along similar lines to *Earth and Sky*, thinking of it as music theatre, and writing a libretto, which included a great deal of narration, before composing any music. She felt that once the dramatic context of the show had been finalised, composing the music would be straightforward. And besides, given the scale of the production, she envisaged that 'In many places the music will be subsidiary and attention will be focussed on shifting levels, with music-dancing, projected pictures and mass movement.'[25] With the script completed, Jenny felt the remaining challenges were largely logistical and technical. Morva Croxson agreed:

> There were lots of challenges, but surprisingly few real problems. The community bought into the concept of a grand scale musical happening in the sports stadium, of all places. People came out of the woodwork with offers of help or links to the right person to do something. The army clad the roof to stop the rain and wind noises

plus organised latrines; rag and bone merchants lent sacks to line the slatted pens and improve warmth, heaters were lent and wired up, builders added a small vestibule to the main entrance to have space for incoming patrons and the ticket office. A stage was created for the pop group and an upper walkway added to allow the projection of children's art work.[26]

Of course, there was still music to write, and quite a bit of it too, given the show would be two hours long and called for four orchestras, four massed children's choirs and two small mixed adult choirs. Jenny's approach to the task involved a great deal of thought prior to writing the score, developing a concept of the sound she was after: 'Once you've got that,' she said, 'the thinking work is done, more or less, and it's a question of getting it on paper – which doesn't depend on mood as far as I'm concerned. One sits down and does it, that's all.'[27]

Simply sitting down and doing it was not trivial. The final score filled five thick volumes and weighed close to eight kilograms. Pianist and répétiteur Bruce Greenfield, who was sharing a house with Jenny towards the end of 1970 when she was writing the music, was still astonished at Jenny's capacity for work more than fifty years later:

> I have never witnessed anything like that. She wrote that piece in four weeks. She plotted it all out before the four weeks – orchestration and that sort of stuff – and then she did not leave the house, she barely slept, for four weeks. I used to take meals in and tidy up, take her drinks and food and stuff, but she just kept at it; she kept at it until it was all done. It was all inside her – she didn't have to work anything out – it all just came out. It was a gigantic piece, it had four orchestras and four choirs and the score, as you can imagine, was vast. We had to carry it around in suitcases.[28]

To work with that kind of intensity required considerable focus and single-mindedness – qualities Jenny seemed to possess in abundance: 'When she was composing *Under the Sun*,' Bruce recalled, 'she had a little electric alarm clock beside her bed. It had obviously gone off while she was having a light snooze, and she got up and got a pair of scissors and cut the cord of the electric clock. I walked into the room and found her somewhat dazed – she'd had a 240-volt shock and the scissors were melted – but she just got up and started composing again.' Bruce, who was to marry Jenny in 1973, said of that period, 'That's when I fell in love with her, really. I admired creative genius at that level, it just dazzled me.'[29]

While the music composed for *Earth and Sky* primarily owed a debt to her studies in Europe, the music Jenny prepared for *Under the Sun* (the name she settled on to replace *Starsong*) was drawn from a wider, and perhaps wilder, range of sources. As she worked, she became increasingly interested in popular music, saying, 'Pop music gives me something that by and large other music doesn't do – except for later Stockhausen. It is about something. It speaks for a whole subculture with which I identify myself to a considerable extent. In a way it is my music.'[30]

One reason for Jenny's shifting allegiance was her belief that composers of serious music were failing to reach audiences. 'What goes on in serious art today is utterly irrelevant to the way most people live. Pop is not irrelevant . . . In New Zealand the kids who sing pop music are filling a void left by the lack of serious composers in the country.'[31] To this end she conscripted a local pop band, the Forgiving, to play a leading role in *Under the Sun*. They were front and centre for 'Shadow People', the sparkly pop song that concluded Act Four, and furnished the show with some of the improvised passages called for in the score.[32]

The energy and unscripted qualities of improvisation were further reasons for Jenny's gradual move away from scored art music and towards popular forms. This was quite a shift for her in terms of the ways she expected her own music to be interpreted. In some of her earlier music she had left room for performers to make choices: in *For Seven*, for example, durations were signalled graphically (by the physical distance between noteheads on the score rather than with conventional notation), and players were left to make (admittedly quite modest) decisions about some events: the score called for 'irregular rapid attacks', or instructed musicians to perform a particular bar with too many notes 'as fast as possible'. Even so, Jenny had quite firm ideas about how the music should sound.[33] Bruce Greenfield had first-hand experience of the degree to which Jenny was committed to accurate performances of her work, to scores being played as written. He recalled that while preparing *Piano Piece 1965* for performance, 'I had to learn it with her in the next room and she was absolutely ruthless. She would yell and scream "You're wrong! Too fast! You're slowing down! You missed the accents! Wrong rhythm!" So, I never tried to practise when she was around, but sometimes I was compelled to, which was never enjoyable.'[34]

During the rehearsals for *Under the Sun*, however, Jenny began to embrace improvisation, and to accommodate greater freedoms for performers in the music she composed. She told Elizabeth Kerr, 'There was a rock group in it and one night we got into a jam session. This was something I'd never done before, I'd *never* improvised. We went on till three, four in the morning and when I came out of there I felt completely refreshed, renewed in a way, and this had some sort of message in it for me.'[35] The experience led her towards a new conception of her work as a composer:

> When I think of the whole process of writing down music, the important moments are when you get the idea and when you hear it. In between comes the labour, the realising of an idea on paper. It seems to me it would be better if I could extract that useless middle stuff and throw it away. That's what rock music and Indian music does. Those two moments are together. The idea and the sound are more or less simultaneous so there's no dichotomy between knowledge and experience. In western music – the whole of western culture – the things that should be together have become differentiated and broken up.[36]

Jenny was moving towards the idea that composition might evolve from a top-down autocratic model towards a more distributed activity, where all participants were making choices about how the music sounded. Nonetheless, for a work on the scale of *Under the Sun*, it was still absolutely necessary that most of the music and action be scripted, and she worked closely with the conductors leading the choirs and orchestras, and with Peter Tulloch. Jenny had been so impressed with Tulloch's work on *Earth and Sky* in Masterton and Tauranga, she had asked that he be invited to direct *Under the Sun*. He was eager and said, 'We have a wonderful working relationship because she is so open to suggestion. Jenny can interpret her own creation and this sort of thing from a creative person is incredible. There is a sort of humility about our work together and so things sort themselves out.'[37]

Having things sort themselves out took a good six months of hard work as Jenny commuted to evening rehearsals in Palmerston North. At first she made the trip alone: 'I got to know the old road via Himatangi–Opiki–Shannon so well in the dark I could almost have driven it blindfolded.' Bruce Greenfield recalled that in the final two months leading up to the performance, 'She used to go up three times a week, after work. After teaching at Vic, we'd all pile into her car and drive to Palmerston', returning to Wellington in time for classes in the morning.[38]

The rehearsals took place in the Queen Elizabeth College hall, which had a large space ideal for the floor choirs. Morva Croxson remembered that rehearsals went smoothly, although 'there were always the worries about lateness, parents looking for children to collect, someone not focusing on the task at hand – there were a lot of children to manage,' adding that 'Peter was splendid' in his handling of the youngsters. Jenny had vivid memories of the rehearsal period:

> At the kids' rehearsals Peter was the 'baddie' and I was the 'goodie': one time I remember a whole host of kids literally picking me up and carrying me out over their heads to the middle of the football fields. He had a rhythmic call and response thing he used to shout whenever he wanted quiet and attention from the hundreds of noisy kids: Peter: *Three cheers for Pooh!* Kids: *For who?* Peter: *For Pooh!* Kids: *Why? What did he do?* All together: *He saved a friend from a wetting!* The kids learned this in two ticks, loved it, made it their own – and it *always* worked.

The show, with a final cast of about six hundred, was presented in evening performances (with matinees on Saturdays) between 29 May and 10

June 1971, and played to a collected audience of eleven thousand.[39]

Under the Sun is a work in five acts told – the narrator advises listeners during the first minute – from the point of view of the last men on Earth. Plangent brass casts dark sonorities over the work's opening moments, while thundering percussion and hundreds of voices are raised in cries and screams to offer praise to the sun: creator, preserver, destroyer. Dramatic music with a kind of cyclonic energy accompanies descriptions of the birth of the solar system, the formation of the Earth and the emergence of life. The text – pre-recorded and therefore regulating durations during the performance – describes the physical and chemical evolution of Earth and life on it, and is permeated with the kind of scientism that was so prevalent in the early 1970s: sending men to the moon; nuclear power stations; TV shows like *Doctor Who* and *Star Trek*. Jenny said, 'I have taken the scientific facts and theatre-ised them,' and described the work as 'Darwinian to the core'.[40]

Children's chanting introduces Act Two, which traces the emergence of animals – fish, dinosaurs, birds and mammals, each occasioning a dance sequence – and segues into Act Three which celebrates the arrival of humankind. Once again various 'dance' passages describe human evolution, from hunting rituals and nature worship through war and on to monotheism. A hymn extolling the one true God leads into Act Four, a 'kaleidoscopic sequence of the development of man and his accomplishments on the earth'. Electric bass and organ creep into the mix, and drums lay down a boogaloo rhythm while a kind of pop art collage of headlines and advertising messages brings the action up to date. This all culminates with 'youth speaks . . . the whole world dances'.[41] After an interval, the final act tells of population growth, the pollution of the planet and the exploration of space, the accelerating advances of science and nuclear war. Finally, perhaps mercifully, the sun engulfs the Earth.

Bruce Greenfield recalled issues with the backing track to which the live performance had to be synced and some technical problems on the first night, but the performances largely went according to plan – a remarkable achievement considering the complexity of the show and the number of performers involved. There were certainly some high points to the production. Morva Croxson retained powerful memories of 'The pop group "The Forgiving", with Grant Bridger as the singer' going down well, and 'the appearance of the Sun King, a godlike or Greek statue figure with a gilded body and a sun-ray elaborate headdress – a magnificent sight.'[42] Bruce recalled another particularly memorable episode: 'There was this moment when everybody danced to bring on the rain. We had a corrugated iron roof in the arena, and at the precise moment of the rain dance – it had been dry and hot for days – this huge deluge came out of nowhere and pounded down on the roof. And it immediately stopped once the rain dance music stopped. It was like a sound effect had been turned on and off by God.'[43]

The critical response to *Under the Sun* was mixed. Playwright Bruce Mason described the first two acts, along with *Earth and Sky*, as 'the high points of our artistic achievement'. He concluded his review by suggesting that 'after *Under the Sun*, New Zealand ceases forever to be a provincial society'. Mason was very taken with Peter Tulloch's direction and 'marvelled at the skill which had 440 children performing as a single, wonderfully plastic entity'. But he was less impressed with other aspects of the production, feeling the show was for the most part underlit and lost its narrative force after the second act. He, along with other critics, also felt that the final act was 'a mistake'.[44]

Peter Zwartz, who had been instrumental in commissioning *Earth and Sky*, felt admiration for *Under the Sun* but found it less successful than its predecessor. To his eye and ear the centrality of the taped narration robbed the work of theatrical pace. 'A didactic script, lacking tension, a musical score which illustrates rather than develops the action, a production which only rarely provided those illuminating moments peculiar to the theatre, proved to be obstacles too great to overcome.' Zwartz enjoyed the African dance and the pop song 'Shadow People' but on the whole was unconvinced by the production.[45]

For both Mason and Zwartz, the visual spectacle of *Under the Sun* eclipsed the impact of the music. Jenny's score is frequently melodic – Olivier Messiaen, who called *Under the Sun* Jenny's 'chef d'oeuvre', told her the work contained 'belles mélodies' – but the sheer profusion of sound and event means those melodies get a little lost in the mix.

In places, memorable tunes do come to the fore – the hymn sequence of Act Three; during 'Shadow People', which concludes Act Four – but more often timbre assumes greater importance. That's only to be expected from a composer who was paying attention to Penderecki and Lutosławski, but the textural qualities of the score, combined with the centrality of the pre-recorded narration, tend to make the music subservient to the dramatic action, colouring in the narrators' stories rather than carving out a place for itself independent of the action. This appears to have been Jenny's intention. During the early stages of writing the work she said, 'I prefer music to be associated with extra-musical meaning. Many people think that because I am a composer, I am bound to consider music the most important art: but in fact, I agree with Anthony Burgess when he said that literature is the most important art. So *Starsong* is music associated with words, to give full meaning.'[46]

Reviewers were agreed on the success of the community aspects of the production. 'Jenny McLeod and her collaborator, almost her alter ego, Peter Tulloch, have gone into a community with a project which, for the period of rehearsal and production, becomes that town's collective and ritual life,' Bruce Mason wrote.[47] Morva Croxson was of a similar view: '*Under the Sun* was an epic . . . The impact on the cast and the community was enormous. It was not as succinct as *Earth and Sky*, but it was, as asked for, an event that influenced the lives of so many of Palmerston North's citizens.[48]

Jenny did not think the work had been a success. Although she liked parts of *Under the Sun*, 'I really didn't have the technique to cope with something that big and the players couldn't cope. I'm dissatisfied with a lot of music in it, because it's so primitive, organisationally and rhythmically.'[49] She also had doubts about the tone she had struck for the piece. In her programme note she had written, 'This work celebrates the abundance and tenacity of earthly life,' but as Bruce Mason pointed out, 'she seems less to have celebrated life than recorded its changing forms. "Adapt or die" is her theme for much of the work . . . but finally adaptation proves to be useless.'[50] With hindsight Jenny conceded; 'I don't think my view of things was the right one, although at the time I did. Basically, the piece is rather pessimistic. I don't know why. I can't decide whether I was pessimistic or objective.'[51]

Whatever her outlook as she composed *Under the Sun*, it's clear that writing and staging the show left her exhausted. The following year she said:

> I don't envisage doing anything like that again and I don't think I would want to be involved if it was ever performed again. Once was enough. That whole awful build-up to *Under the Sun*! In retrospect I was afraid it would happen and yet I wanted it to happen. It was hard to separate the two. I was worried it wouldn't come off -- and it bloody nearly didn't . . . I accumulated quite a few grey hairs over that piece.[52]

A triple-album LP recording of the show was released by Philips, a copy of which Jenny sent to Olivier Messiaen. She recalled that he 'had a charitably high opinion of this piece – though he said he would have had a more optimistic ending himself – and had listened to it right through a number of times (which is more, I confess, than I've been able to do).'[53] Messiaen wasn't just saying this to be kind to a former student. Fiona McAlpine, who had studied with Jenny at Victoria between 1968 and 1972, visited Paris a few years later and said, 'I went to Easter Midnight Mass at Trinité church, where Messiaen was organist, and I and my companion, with typical antipodean cheek, bowled up to him afterwards and explained that we had been her students. He said that she had sent him a recording of *Under the Sun* and that it was "remarquable – tout à fait remarquable".'[54]

Whatever Jenny's misgivings, *Under the Sun* – like *Earth and Sky* before it – was to yield fruit in the years to come. Even decades later, she would receive messages from people who had participated in the production and for whom it was a pivotal moment, one that inspired them to pursue a life in the creative arts.

This kind of affirmation is one of the long-term benefits of composing for and working with young and amateur musicians. There were of course occasional costs to doing so. Jenny recalled that during the Masterton season of *Earth and Sky*, 'The first six bars – there were time problems there, the tom-tom players couldn't keep in time with each other.' With *Under the Sun* one of the choirs failed to accurately learn the opening chorus. 'Though it sounded faintly like what I had written, it wasn't the same as what I had written, only I didn't discover this until I was coming for the final rehearsals. They had been rehearsing for months already and by the time I heard it, I realised it was too late to do anything about it.' But she accepted these kinds of stumbles because the mistakes were more than compensated for by the enthusiasm of the musicians and singers: 'I really think that people get together to experience music together for the spirit of the whole thing. If the spirit is good but the notes are a bit missing, you're still getting something good.'

Writing music for non-professionals – work that served communitarian as well as musical ends – had become an activity close to Jenny's heart, and in 1972 she said she preferred working with amateurs and children to working with professionals.[55] As it turned out, most of the music she composed over the next eight to ten years was to be for amateurs, music for which 'the spirit of the whole thing' was more important than the slickness of the production or the accuracy of the performance.

8

The Classroom Loses its Glow

Work on *Under the Sun* was time-consuming, but Jenny had also needed to pay attention to her professorial responsibilities: curricular development; management of the department; service on various university committees. And she had ongoing teaching commitments, for which her enthusiasm had begun to wane:

> For the first couple of years, it was terrific. I really enjoyed analysis but I have this sort of intellect that, if it is allowed to go untrammelled, just goes wild and I got madly ahead of the students. It was getting to the point, in the last few years with the students, that I found it hard to go back and pick them up because I was so much more interested in where I was myself with the material.[1]

Those struggles were not evident to her students, who still responded positively to her teaching. Percussionist Bruce McKinnon, who studied at Victoria between 1972 and 1975, remembered, 'I liked her as a teacher, she had real enthusiasm for the subject . . . Jenny always had a real intellectual vigour. Meeting someone like that when I was 17 really moved my perception of the world.'[2] But for Jenny there was a cost:

I came back from Darmstadt with all this serial language, ideas about music that I had picked up from Messiaen and Boulez and the rest, and that was what I started to teach. After a while those students graduated and a lot of them would go out and end up teaching in schools, so I started getting first year students who were coming in with things that I recognised as stuff that I had taught their teachers. And they were spouting it like this was the Word of God. I wasn't too keen on this attitude because when youth and ignorance take on board all this stuff, they do it without realising that it's just what's happening at the time: it doesn't mean that this is 'the way'; all it means is that this was 'one way'. But that was never the impression I got from them: they were all talking about parameters; in schools they were all talking about parameters. I wondered, 'Where is this going? It can only go next wherever I take it.' When I realised that, I thought I'd better get out quick.[3]

Disappointed with the increasingly doctrinaire attitudes of her students, she also began to lose interest in the work. She said that teaching 'was all so worth doing, but you can't keep repeating yourself for years; well, at least, I couldn't. I just got sick of doing the same thing after a while.'

The new freedoms she had found by embracing rock music and improvisation, and the new avenues of expression she was uncovering in her study of Indian drumming were probably also factors in her growing disenchantment with teaching. They very likely contributed to her nascent suspicion of over-dependence on the intellect when engaging with music. 'It's dangerous to know stuff,' she said, 'and also that whole thing of: you can know too much. Academicism can kill things; knowing too much about the technical side of music. You can know so much that you don't know where to go; the possibilities become so enormous.'

Jenny's scepticism about relying too much on the mind wasn't limited to her understanding of music. She wrote to Fred Page during 1972:

You will be glad to hear that I have 'seen the light' at last (Plato's light outside the cave – in fact the same light that Buddha, Christ, the Hindus and all the ancients were on about too.) This is the most staggering thing – I mean, to actually realise how wrong I've been for so many years to put such faith in the powers of the intellect to arrive at the answers, when now I see that the answers are in fact way beyond reason.[4]

Many accounts of Jenny's work, and most published interviews with her, reveal or make reference to her remarkable mind, her brilliance, the sharpness of her wit and intelligence. She was a lively conversationalist and correspondent – her letters, candid and often funny, are full of acute observations and lively analysis. She was a voracious and omnivorous reader: history, philosophy and religious thought, science, poetry and fiction. Her brother Craig's accounts of her fierce intelligence were endorsed by many others.[5] In light of this, the misgivings she began to express about the value of the intellect in the early 1970s are a little bewildering, but they were voiced at a time when she was also expressing scepticism about what had appeared to be her raison d'être: composition.

On completing *Under the Sun* Jenny had taken time to reflect on her work to date. She concluded that while composing generally involved a great deal of concentrated work, it wasn't particularly difficult for her, and was something she had, in a way, stumbled into: 'I don't think I had any real urge to do it – it was just something that happened. Circumstances made it so I ended up being a composer without ever consciously deciding to be one.'[6]

Jenny's ambivalence about her status as a composer was complicated by a growing dissatisfaction with her motivations. Although she could see that there might be very good reasons for composing music, she confessed that, for her, composing had been 'pretty much an ego trip and all the circumstances went to make it more of one. It made news and people wanted to write about it and talk about it.'[7] For those engaged in creative work that attracts public attention, there is always the possibility – and, perhaps, the danger – that the self-aggrandising agendas of the ego can supplant other drivers. Up to that point in her life, Jenny said, 'This had never entered my head, and indeed I recognised signs in myself, which for a time stopped me in my tracks and brought me down.'

Jenny was on holiday when she experienced a kind of epiphany:

> One day, beside a lake in the bush halfway up the mountain, where
> I was completely alone with the trees and the water, it just hit me. I
> see now it's the same sort of thing that hit the Romantic poets, being
> part of nature, mysticism. Suddenly there were no more problems.
> Everything came together and I realised how much of life I had been
> leaving out.[8]

She came to believe that her professional career as a composer
had been a kind of game. It was a game she no longer wished to play.
During 1972 she cancelled all her composing commitments – including
a commission from the Auckland Festival to compose a rock opera –
and declined all further invitations.[9] While she hadn't ruled out the
possibility that she might compose again, she determined to do so only
if she felt she could do justice to any work requested of her. Her priority
had shifted from composing music to communicating with people, and
only if she thought composing might lead to communication would she
take up her pencil. 'The whole thing is a question of communication. At
the moment it doesn't matter whether I communicate through music or
through something else. Maybe, just by *being* is the best way. I'm wary
now of narrowing my vision too much, to focus just on music, because
everything is so much bigger than music.'[10]

A new awareness

That there was more to life than music might seem obvious to non-
musicians, but for someone as single-minded as Jenny it was a realisation
that came slowly and needed to be helped along. Given the times, it's
hardly surprising that cannabis was to be a midwife to Jenny's expanding
horizons. 'With the dope there came, shall we say, a new awareness, and
it was an awareness that was really great. I became aware of heaps of
things that I hadn't noticed before.'

Jenny had been introduced to hashish in Cologne by friends of some of her classmates. She had enjoyed the experience, although wasn't completely won over by the drug: 'At first the top of my head simply buzzed strangely and I went straight to sleep.' On returning to Wellington, however, her students were eager to show her the way. 'They said, "It's wonderful. Have a go." I did, and they were right.' She became a regular user and a keen evangelist for dope, and cheerfully recounted some of the people she'd introduced to marijuana: friends and colleagues, senior university officials, folk from the Chamber Music Society, even a barrister. 'I don't think I actually turned them on,' she said, 'but I did give them a joint and show them how to smoke it.'

While Jenny enjoyed 'the dreaded weed', as she called it, 'as time passed, I applied this activity more to private meditation and self-examination than simply to pleasure and the munchies. Beginning to see myself more clearly, I truly did not much like quite a lot of what I saw. There was a lot of room for improvement, I thought. This became a spiritual quest which I realised would have to travel well beyond any contemporary association with drugs.'

Percussionist Bruce McKinnon, a student and later close friend of Jenny's, recalled: 'I had the odd conversation about drugs with Jenny. It was the time when some drugs were seen as part of the path to enlightenment and Jenny was definitely in that camp.'[11] This desire for enlightenment saw her broaden her narcotic intake to include hallucinogens. 'I was pretty well educated about soft and hard drugs,' she said, 'so I did actually know what I was doing – and knew very well never to touch any heavily addictive hard drugs such as heroin or cocaine.' Her brother Craig – who briefly shared a house with her in the early 1970s – recalled the range of drugs she experimented with: 'She was doing mescalin, LSD, grass, she even soaked morning glory seeds in a jar on the kitchen window sill because they had hallucinogenic properties.'[12]

The intensity of Jenny's experience with psychedelic drugs varied. With LSD, she said, 'I used to hallucinate; only very mild hallucinations – I'd look at the wallpaper and it would start to move a bit, things like that. It was never very outrageous.' The experience of 'seeing the light' she described to Fred Page was the result of taking mescalin. 'The simple truth is that I took two trips on mescalin (after several rather uneventful ones previously) and had the most extraordinary and miraculous experiences, which I subsequently discovered were those customarily described as "mystical".' While Jenny expressed some doubts about those experiences, she nevertheless concluded, 'They happened, they were shatteringly real, and I'm very glad they did happen.'[13]

As powerful as some of these experiences may have been, Jenny remained securely anchored to Earth. 'Yes, I smoked plenty of dope,' she said, 'but whatever I may have been thinking, I was always wide awake and taking things on board, taking things in.' She may have entertained doubts about the intellect's pre-eminence in life, but she had not abandoned thinking and exploring ideas, and still loved the frisson of intellectual challenge. Nona Harvey, a lecturer in German at Victoria who flatted with Jenny during this period, recalled that joints and hash cookies were shared on a regular basis, but that there was also a rich intellectual current to life; she and Jenny enjoyed a 'profound common interest in myth and ritual and Jungian notions of the collective consciousness'. Nona said, 'I think I can say our common theoretical interests at the time were in structuralism (I was reading Lévi-Strauss in particular) and semiotics, which I have pursued throughout my career.'[14]

With a secure salary from the university, Jenny had been able to raise a mortgage on a property in Ohiro Road, Brooklyn, not far from the university. The big old wooden villa overlooking Central Park was set above and well back from the street, and so was a wonderful retreat from the world. 'Above and well back from the street' might be marvellous qualities in a refuge, but they posed serious logistical problems when she and Bruce Greenfield, with whom she had been sharing a place in Glenmore Street, moved in. 'There was a long zigzag path up to the house from the road. In those days I had about seven thousand books and Bruce nobly carried all of these up the cliff to the house in many, many heavy cardboard boxloads, bless his heart.'

Jenny shared her new home with Bruce and 'a group of intelligent and unique characters' and was described by her sometime flatmate Rob Cameron as 'the benign and tolerant fulcrum of the house'.[15]

Nona Harvey recalled: 'In her role as landlady to four or five tenants, Jenny was indulgent, tolerant and generous to a fault. She was more the genial friend and mentor, an open-minded and interested listener with a wonderful sense of humour. There was a sense of relaxed, chaotic freedom living there, where anything could happen.'[16]

The house was 'like a cultural crucible,' Nona said, 'to which many interesting, if not illustrious people gravitated' for conversation and debate and music.[17] But while 'the company was exhilarating', their shared interests were not entirely highbrow: 'We all watched Monty Python at 6:00pm on a Sunday night.'[18] The property's relative seclusion also meant Jenny and her flatmates felt free to enjoy music, throw parties and indulge their collective interest in drugs. In due course, there were consequences:

> My brother Craig's friend Stephen came back from Thailand bringing a large crate of belongings lined with super-powerful weed – Buddha Grass, as we called it back then – which he unpacked on my bedroom floor and subsequently cut with raspberry tea and weighed out in my kitchen. Stephen also kept a diary, however, and drew attention to himself at the pub. Thus, there came the inevitable day (it was more like midnight) when my house was raided by the drug squad. Windows wide open, lights low, we were having a party, treating the neighbours as usual to the strains of our favourite rock. A loud knock at the door. I thought it was the council, come to complain about the noise. Then I thought these folk had come to join the party, so I opened my arms and my mouth to welcome them in. But no. As they first entered the house to search it, Sergeant Norman Cook said, 'You must be mad! The whole place reeks of it.' My writer friend Jim McNeish, who was staying with us, discreetly offered to take care of anything I wanted hidden. I passed him a few tabs of LSD which he promptly tossed on top of a wardrobe. In the living room, one of the cops actually found our main bag of weed (which somebody had hastily shoved behind a row of books) and was observed quietly putting it back. 'One law for the rich, another for the poor,' Sergeant Cook muttered in my ear as they escorted

Stephen off to jail for the next three years. As they had clearly been instructed, I was not to be charged with anything.

The arresting officers, cognisant of Jenny's position at the university, simply warned her to 'be more careful in future' as they departed.[19] In a letter to Fred Page later that year Jenny wrote, 'It's certainly illuminating to find oneself on the wrong side of the law. Though the laws against pot are inexcusable. How pathetic that Stephen will almost certainly go to jail for giving so many people such a good time.'[20]

In spite of her disenchantment with the law, Jenny was not a vocal advocate for the legalisation of cannabis. But nor was she shy about her fondness for the drug. 'I seem to remember,' she said, 'describing once in an interview how I had "got high and had been high ever since" and they indeed printed this, but there were no particular consequences I'm aware of. Actually, I think such scandalous mischief was more or less expected and tolerated from someone like me, youngest professor in the Commonwealth (when appointed).' Statements of this kind, expected or not, may well have caused alarm among the university's senior administrators, but they didn't particularly trouble her family. Jenny's cousin Carol Markwell recalled that while there may have been 'a bit of disquiet with some of her public statements around marijuana, I think she was just being honest as she always has been, and most of us weren't unduly bothered.'[21]

Perhaps it was the times, but drugs did seem to appear at every turn. When noted Scottish psychiatrist R.D. Laing was in Wellington as a guest of Victoria University, Jenny was responsible for ferrying him around town. His obligations at the university discharged for the day, he went home with Jenny to meet her weed-smoking housemates. One of them was behaving more strangely than usual.

> Ronnie asked me on the quiet if she was always like that. 'Tripping,'
> I explained. Afterwards I took him to a party, where rather shortly
> [after] he passed out. Our Kelburn hosts wanted to call a doctor,
> but Ronnie, still lying on the floor, opened his eyes and whispered
> dramatically, 'No doctor!' By then we were momentarily alone in the

kitchen. 'Why not?' I enquired. 'Cocaine!' said he. Which explained something everybody had really been wondering about – why at his lecture he spoke so exceedingly slowly. He admitted he had been high on cocaine then too.[22]

The soundtrack accompanying drug consumption – and life generally – at 124 Ohiro Road was almost always rock. Jenny had played rock and roll as a teenager – on guitar with her brothers and on piano at dances – and maintained an interest in the genre as a kind of sibling to the art music she had focused on during her years of study. She was fond of the Beatles and the Rolling Stones, but her work on *Under the Sun* had re-energised her interest in pop and rock more generally. One of her Ohiro Road housemates was vocalist and songwriter Tony Backhouse. Tony was then working for the NZBC and performing with local band Mammal. He recalled, 'I'd continually bring home new records. Every night, it seems, we would hit the beanbags with a joint and dissolve into the quadrophonic sound. The current favourite would stay on the turntable for a week.'[23] In this way Jenny was introduced to David Bowie's *Ziggy Stardust*, Stevie Wonder's *Talking Book*, the Rolling Stones' *Sticky Fingers*, Little Feat's *Dixie Chicken* and many others.

Rock music and drugs, as well as being daily features of life in Jenny's home, were also central pillars in the musical *Hair*, which opened in Auckland during February 1972. The show had caused a sensation in the United States on its arrival in 1968 and the simulated sex and drug scenes, profanity and on-stage nudity were considered scandalous. The strongly anti-war theme – at the height of the Vietnam conflict – didn't help the show's reception in conservative quarters, and there were threats and protests and legal action of various kinds against the production. Its arrival in New Zealand was to be similarly contentious. Bruce Mason had claimed that with the arrival of *Under the Sun* in 1971, New Zealand ceased forever to be a provincial society; the moral panic that greeted the staging of *Hair* in Auckland suggests his claims were exaggerated.[24]

Even so, New Zealanders were keen to see it; more than thirty thousand tickets were sold before the production opened. The public's appetite for the spectacle was matched by the enthusiasm of the show's reviewers. Bruce Mason thought '*Hair* is a brave and beautiful piece, at once liberating and integrating.' Iain Macdonald, writing for the *New Zealand Herald*, called it 'Simply terrific . . . Not so much a show as an irresistible experience.'[25] Their admiration was not universally shared: 'The righteous burghers of Auckland railed against what they perceived as the show's depravity and indecency. Its content was an affront to the public standards of the day, they suggested. The filth on show would corrupt and entice vulnerable viewers. It should be stopped.'[26] Attorney-General Sir Roy Jack authorised the show's presenters be prosecuted for the 'distribution or exhibition of indecent matter'.

At the subsequent High Court trial, Jenny, in her capacity as Professor of Music, was called to be an expert witness for the defence. In court she said: '. . . in terms of what I would call emotional highpoints or climaxes in *Hair*, I found more than I have found in any other live experience I have seen. I would be proud if I could do the same thing myself on such a scale.'[27] In a letter she wrote later that year she was a little more equivocal:

> In March I testified at the *Hair* trial in Auckland (about its 'musical merits', which aren't too many actually, but I got around that by telling the jury that I thought it was better than *The King and I*, *Sound of Music*, etc. Which is certainly true, and which they of course took as I intended it, not realising that I thought the latter were complete rubbish). It was quite an eye-opener to see what an utter farce a trial can be. The 'truth' has nothing to do with what goes on in most courts, I suspect.[28]

Although Jenny was pleased with the 'not guilty' verdict, the best thing about the trial as far as she was concerned was meeting Peter Brusey, QC, the Melbourne-based lawyer who led the defence. Brusey was an avid music fan and former president of the Melbourne chapter of the ISCM, and the two struck up a firm friendship. They maintained a 'high-powered correspondence' after he returned to Australia. Later in the year he travelled to Wellington for a case, and spent a great deal of time with Jenny, during which she was pleased to introduce him to the delights of marijuana. The nature of the relationship, and the depth of their mutual identification, led her to write that '[I]n some magical way my life is all coming together. Peter and I are closer than I ever thought possible between two people – I don't mean that we're having an "affair" or that we're "in love". I mean we really love each other. Until now, I'm sure that I didn't really know what that means.'[29]

The search for love

Jenny's search for meaning, for an understanding of life's purpose, became a central preoccupation for her during the early 1970s. A part of that quest was a search for love. Although her parents had been loving and supportive of her and her brothers, they had not been particularly affectionate towards one another. Jenny's brother Craig recalled that Ron and Lorna's relationship had been 'a very strange one; it wasn't a loving relationship. The word love was never mentioned; nobody – not father, not mother, not sister, not brother – ever said "I love you", not once.'[30] Nor were the relationships Ron and Lorna had with their children tactile: 'We didn't hug each other,' Craig said. 'I think that was the Kiwi way, a bit. You didn't want to hug your boys because they might turn out gay.'

As it happened, Jenny preferred to keep her distance in family relationships: 'As a sixteen-year-old in the USA, my American parents had to learn that I didn't like being touched physically.' She conceded, however, 'I couldn't be sure which came first, really – whether this was innate, or more because I was not brought up in the touchy-feely habit.' Jenny also identified cultural reasons why touching and declarations of love were uncommon among members of her family: 'It was much more the case in those days, that the Pākehā world was much stiffer – much more "British" – than it is now.'

Lorna seemed to cope quite well with this undemonstrative environment; she may even have preferred to raise her children in this way. Perhaps her Methodism, with its emphasis on good works and being the best one can be, rather than on kindness and love, was a factor. 'Our mother did indeed love us,' Jenny recalled, 'you could see that in her eyes – I think she just didn't know how to express it (which suggests that Nanna [Perrin], from whom the Methodism stemmed, probably didn't either) and tried to show it by "doing things" for us.'[31] Jenny later heard that Lorna 'bored people terminally raving on about her amazing children,' although, she added, 'not in our presence'.

Lorna appears to have raised her children with the dispassion of an engineer. Even their conception was the result of careful planning rather than the fruit of a warm and loving relationship. Ron and Lorna's separate sleeping arrangements may have been the consequence of a certain coolness between them, or perhaps the result of Lorna's censorious attitude towards sex; it may simply have been because Ron snored loudly and kept Lorna awake. Still, they did manage to have three children. The children, Jenny said, were 'planned by mama to be born *exactly* eighteen months apart for the sake of hand-me-downs, and getting one's grown-up kids out of one's hair as soon as possible, so one can do what one wants'.[32] Jenny thought this – the separate beds; sex as a principally procreative enterprise – must have been a trial for Ron, and years later said simply, 'Poor Dad. Unreal, not natural. But my mother never knew anything else.'[33]

Ron was a quiet and conservative man – he was a National Party voter and kept a firm hold on the household purse strings – and his modest aspirations and retiring personality may have been a disappointment to his confident, outgoing and high-achieving wife. His emotional health, which perhaps had never been particularly robust given his turbulent childhood, suffered in the context of his marriage to Lorna, and Jenny remembered that he experienced at least one 'nervous breakdown'. He underwent treatment at either Ashburn Hall in Dunedin or Sunnyside Hospital in Christchurch, and possibly both. 'Dad quite adored his doctor, intermittently rhapsodising on what a lovely man he was. It was probably the only time anyone had ever listened to my father properly or seriously. I think his doctor was the only one in his life who really loved him.'

Craig and Perrin McLeod had trouble finding love, too. Perrin married designer Sally Hollis-McLeod but eventually came out as gay. Craig, who would marry and divorce three times, thought Perrin 'didn't find a happy relationship until quite late in life. Maybe all of us were

doomed?' Doomed is a strong word, but it's probably fair to say that
finding love, and returning love, was to be a perennial conundrum for
Jenny. Approaching her eightieth birthday, she said, 'It's terrible; it's
taken me seventy years to realise that I don't know how to live with
anybody.'

Whatever the precise nature of Jenny's relationship with Peter Brusey,
it certainly appears to have been important to her. Brusey was married,
with adult children, but she travelled to Melbourne at the beginning of
1973 mainly, it seems, to be close to him. By this time, she said, their
relationship had 'by mutual agreement become almost entirely non-
verbal. It is extraordinary, profound and beautiful.'[34] It was also, to that
point, chaste. This was at least in part because Jenny had become close
to Brusey's wife, Dorothy. And it was this that ultimately scuttled her
relationship with Brusey: 'When Dorothy told me how Peter had lost
his temper and threatened her, claiming he had "another woman", I was
shocked and annoyed – and much too fond of Dorothy to let her be
treated in this way. I informed her immediately that Peter *didn't* have
another woman. And that was the end of that. Peter did little but glare
at me for the rest of my stay, there were no more letters and our paths
never crossed again.'

Later Jenny reflected, 'I was behaving absurdly: too many drugs, too
much silly Californian nonsense about "how to find God" by people
who imagine they have; too much solo reading of "signs", a risky
business at best.' But they were heady times, and that summer the
'signs' had seemed auspicious. She had written to Bruce Greenfield that,
while visiting Brusey, she could 'literally feel vibrations' and had 'started
getting visions once or twice – imperfect as yet and of course they're
hallucinations – but what I do see is quite clear and quite different from
my normal mental/visual imaginings . . .'[35]

What Bruce made of all this is hard to imagine. His own relationship
with Jenny had intensified over the previous two or three years and they
were the closest of friends. Although he was touring a great deal, he was a
perennial help-mate to Jenny, involved with renovations at Ohiro Road,
caring for her dogs when she was away ('rather a love-hate relationship',
Bruce said), cooking meals and taking care of things around the house.[36]

Jenny recalled that she had thought a great deal about Bruce while she'd been away, and in a letter to him wrote, 'When I was in Melbourne I loved your letters, and for a while there I thought that you and I really did get on pretty well, and maybe we should get married.'[37]

In April 1973 Jenny and Bruce did get married. He had proposed during a weekend away at Waitārere Beach, a few kilometres south of Foxton Beach where Jenny had spent her childhood holidays. Her brother Craig could not recall being invited to the wedding, and had the impression the decision to tie the knot may have been drug-fuelled and impulsive. Impulsive or not, the couple were married in a registry office in Wellington's Anvil House, with Bruce's family present.[38] Fred Page was there as a witness, and he and Eve, delighted by news of the wedding, held a champagne breakfast for the couple and some invited friends at their place. 'We passed around a plateful of joints for everyone – Bruce's idea. Fred and Eve had no idea that this was going to happen until it did. And then they laughed.'

The day after the wedding, Jenny left New Zealand for a month-long tour of United States university music departments, thanks to an invitation from the United States Information Agency (USIA), which organised and paid for the visit. It was an exhausting trip, with many stops and meetings, and overall was somewhat dispiriting. A return visit to Decatur, Illinois, to meet the family she had stayed with fifteen years earlier revealed the gulf that had opened up between them. The gap was partly spiritual – her 'sister' Carole Ann had 'become one of the Jesus people – sees Satan all around' – and partly cultural: 'I'd forgotten they were so easily shocked. My conversation was very limited, but they are kind people.'[39]

The university visits, including Princeton, Columbia, Chicago, Indiana, Stanford and Caltech, weren't the fillip she might have hoped for either. While she was interested in the research work being undertaken by Jeanne Bamberger at MIT, and liked what she saw at the School of Music in Indiana, on the whole, she wrote to Bruce, 'if I'm getting any message from this experience, it's that university education is a waste of time'. She was unconvinced by most of what she encountered and confessed, 'I'm surprised to find that our department at Vic is one of the most progressive in the world, which is gratifying maybe, but also depressing.'[40]

But there were high spots too, including some welcome reunions, and Jenny remained grateful to those responsible for planning the trip:

> They saw to it that I caught up at Harvard with my friend Ivan Tcherepnin, whom I had known with his brother Serge in Cologne (and who introduced us to hashish). I duly took off my shoes in California and sat on the floor for an Ali Akbar Khan class, visited a Staten Island social project and the US State Department. They even booked me for lunch in Boston with Leonard Bernstein (who sent a personal apology), took me to a Steve Reich orchestra rehearsal and concert, and a Muddy Waters concert at the Fillmore West (where the guy on my left passed me a joint, and the USIA-er on my right declined it, both without a word), and a way-out concert in a New York attic where we were deafened for 15 minutes solid (followed by the most amazing silence), and I met and talked to John Cage. I said to him, 'Now that I've met you, I don't know what to say to you.' He laughed and said, 'Sweet.' I had a much longer, enthusiastic exchange with the two who had concocted the amazing electronic piece.

The letters Jenny sent to Bruce from the United States are warm and loving, and the security of marriage released within her the desire for children: 'The thought of raising kids by myself always seemed a big drag. Since we got married, or even before, I realised that what really put me off the idea was the fact that they wouldn't have a real home – i.e., a real home means a father as well as a mother. The more I think about it the keener I get.'[41] In their correspondence Jenny began proposing time frames for having a child that would work with her university commitments.

Yet even as she mapped out possible time frames that would accommodate both her present maternal impulses and her teaching work, the scepticism she felt about the academy was deepening. Visiting some of the best music institutions in the States had not provided reassurance.

'I had hoped (or expected?),' she wrote to Bruce, 'to find somewhere here the kind of work going on that would make me believe there was some point in my carrying on teaching. But really as far as teaching is concerned, I've seen nothing to persuade me of that.'[42]

Jenny had long felt that when the student was ready, the teacher would appear. That had been her experience with Fred Page and Douglas Lilburn and Olivier Messiaen, and their instruction had facilitated her rise to a professorship and national acclaim as a composer. Those accomplishments, however, had not led to the kind of fulfilment she may have hoped for, and the dissatisfaction she felt with her professional life became harder and harder to overlook. A new pathway beckoned, one that required a different kind of teacher.

9

Finding Divine Light

Jenny's marriage to Bruce was startling to some of their friends, most of whom knew Bruce was gay. 'I was reasonably amazed,' one of them said. Musicologist Fiona McAlpine, who had flatted with Bruce in 1969 and knew him well, was also surprised, but primarily because 'their music seemed to inhabit rather different fields. Even as a student, Bruce was beginning to make for himself a career as a répétiteur/ rehearsal pianist/pianist for ballet and drama. And that, of course, is where he has ended up. That didn't seem to chime with a commitment to the avant-garde/new composition/New Zealand music' that were Jenny's principal concerns.[1]

The couple's feelings for one another had emerged slowly over several years. Both were musicians of skill and artistry, and their shared passion for music (even if different music) and good food had formed the basis of an enduring friendship. They smoked and drank together, enjoyed talking into the night and shared responsibility for the Ohiro Road house: Jenny had raised the mortgage to purchase it, while Bruce had helped with the maintenance and restoration work the property needed. Little by little, their mutual respect and closeness had deepened and they had become lovers. Craig McLeod, reflecting on the marriage, had also detected what he thought of as a spiritual meeting of minds.

Bruce had grown up in the church and over time developed an interest in the religions of the East. His curiosity about spirituality did not at first appear to be shared by Jenny, whom he had taken to be an atheist. She had attended church with her mother, and even played the organ for services, but churchgoing had been more of a musical than a devotional activity. In her late teens and early twenties, however, her curiosity about spirituality had grown and she read widely on the subject. Even so, she said, 'For a long time in my life [there was] nothing spiritual – not nothing, but it kind of took second place because music was the main thing – and I wasn't aware that I perhaps needed to pay some attention elsewhere in my life than music. And when I did, that was helped by taking dope.'

This renewed receptivity to the spiritual was complemented by her work in the classroom. In 1972 Jenny introduced a course in Indian music at Victoria. She had been taking drum lessons with Balu Balachandran, a Carnatic music specialist, and 'I realised that Hindu philosophy and Hindu music are closely related, so you couldn't really study the basics of Indian music without understanding the basics of Indian philosophy. Well, as I started reading the Hindu philosophy I thought, "Oh, I like this." It was funny – it was a bit like when I first learned to read music – it seemed to come like second nature.' The almost innate understanding Jenny had of the ideas she encountered in the Hindu, and in particular Vedanta, texts had some unexpected outcomes:

> When I read it, and even when I read the old versions of it, I seemed to know all about it already. There was this young Indian guy who'd come to teach in the Religious Studies department – I'd come back from Europe, and after you'd been with Messiaen there was nothing so very strange about any of this, really – so here was this young fellow and here was me telling him all about Hinduism. And he was saying 'You are my guru.' He was getting very excited and I was totally astonished – how did I know all about something I'd never heard of until a few months ago?

Her interest in spirituality also fuelled her conversations with George Hughes, Professor of Philosophy at Victoria, who was an ordained Anglican priest and had supported her application for the professorship.

Already familiar with the works of Søren Kierkegaard, Martin Buber, Jean-Paul Sartre and Albert Camus from her student days, Jenny's reading widened to include Hermann Hesse, Aldous Huxley's *The Doors of Perception* and William James' *The Variety of Religious Experience*. She was interested in Carlos Castaneda and Alan Watts. 'When you started to read the books by all these other people who, like me, were smoking dope and dropping acid and what have you, we were all getting interested in the same new sorts of things, which had to do with anything that wasn't Christian. Christianity had gone off the rails a bit – I think that's what we generally felt – and if we had gone with it, then we had gone off the rails too.' However, Jenny said much later, 'For me, this was all such a private matter I didn't go round talking about it to anyone and everyone . . . something I kept pretty close to my heart.'

It was during this period that Jenny was introduced to the Divine Light Mission. The Mission was established in 1960 by a Sikh guru, Hans Ji Maharaj, and by the 1970s was under the leadership of his youngest son, Prem Rawat, who as leader of the movement was known as Guru Maharaj Ji. His teaching emphasised meditation, service and satsang (telling the truth, or 'coming clean' at group sessions), with some additional instruction, usually in the form of exhortations but without specifying rules or beliefs or a particular ethical orientation.

Jenny's first contact with the Mission came by way of the *Hair* trial, during which she met Lindsay and Kim Field, members of the show's cast and followers of Maharaj Ji. A short time later, missionaries (sometimes called 'initiators') from the Divine Light Mission travelled to Wellington, where a public meeting was held in the Tasman Street Indian Association Hall.[2] The speaker was a retired Indian High Court judge called Rajeshwar. 'He was an incredibly intelligent man,' Bruce Greenfield said, 'and of course Jenny liked intelligent people. So, they got on like a house on fire. This man had been to Oxford and was a Rhodes Scholar and all sorts of things, but he had spent the last twenty years going around doing this missionary work. Anyway, he was the one that talked about Maharaj Ji's philosophy at a meeting.'

Bruce was sympathetic to some of the ideas presented: 'These mahatmas from India – and there's been many of them – they've all got fabulous written sayings . . . books and books of wonderful sayings from the East about how to live.' And he was impressed by the missionary too, saying, 'This man who originally came out and who talked to Jenny was a man of enormous sincerity; not at all interested in wealth or fame or anything.' Even so, he was sceptical: 'I was a religious boy, and I could see through it all.'

Jenny's encounter with Rajeshwar and her introduction to the meditation techniques advocated by Guru Maharaj Ji was profound and life-altering. Bruce could understand the appeal the ideas and practice had for her – 'That's how the spark happened for her, his intellect and all the fabulous Indian philosophy stuff' – but he found the intensity of her response confusing: 'Suddenly, she ceased to be an atheist. Unfortunately, she became a fanatical follower.'[3]

The intensely private nature of Jenny's spiritual journey and concerns meant that when interviewers asked her about these aspects of her life, she tended to quickly pass over the subject, her off-hand responses moving the conversation on to areas she was more interested in discussing. When questioned about her reasons for becoming a follower of Maharaj Ji and joining the Divine Light Mission, she told Elizabeth Kerr, 'I just got zapped.' To Roger Smith she characterised her choices at that time as 'chasing off after an Indian guru'.[4] But her reasons for aligning herself with Maharaj Ji's teaching were serious and sincere: 'Followers follow not so much because they are "externally manipulated" as because their own personal experiences have persuaded them of something. At that point, like many thousands of others, I honestly believed the Lord himself had returned.' With the benefit of hindsight, Jenny also acknowledged the pitfalls that can attend this kind of belief:

How the mind rejoices to be provided with any such potentially enormous creative inspiration (or suggestion) as that 'the Lord has returned' – or (as far as the undiscriminating mind is concerned) quite possibly even the opposite, such as that killing people might be a really good way to salvation. What [the inspiration] is, doesn't really matter at that level. Once triggered by our minds, we are off on 'The Path.' Or I was, anyway. Be we serial murderer or authentic seeker, we start to see magical 'signs' everywhere, because that is what we are looking for, and that is what our minds are now so helpfully 'finding' for us. The mind needs and *loves* to be put to work, but it is a better tool than a master. The mind does not discriminate until it has been taught to. My own mind in respect of anything 'spiritual' had at that stage never been taught to, just as I didn't essentially discriminate between various kinds of music.

Jenny's initial practice as a student of Prem Rawat/Guru Maharaj Ji took the form of attendance at meetings (satsang) and meditating. Maharaj Ji's teaching was predominantly focused on a meditation practice he called 'Knowledge', which consisted of techniques that he and his followers claimed allowed those engaging them to access inner strength and peace. He also offered a few entirely sensible suggestions for living – 'speak to one another with love and humility', for example, or 'appreciating what you have is more important than appreciating what you don't have' – but, other than discouraging recreational drug use among those who wished to practise the techniques he taught, these suggestions were generally not prescriptive.[5]

Already somewhat familiar with Hindu philosophy, Jenny recognised the correspondences between the practices Maharaj Ji encouraged and those advocated by some Sikh and Hindu gurus. They were teachings she found helpful. Years later, she said Maharaj Ji's instruction 'was simply to do "satsang, service and meditation" – speak the truth, lend a hand, and keep your mind (or soul or spirit) clean and clear. That was a "refrain", if ever I heard one. This was, however, and still is perfectly good advice, nothing wrong with it.'[6]

Steve Matthews, a friend of Jenny's who also practised the techniques of Knowledge, confirmed this analysis, saying that Maharaj Ji's fundamental message – 'to experience inner peace, we need to look within' – was sometimes conflated with religious ideas from the East.

'These Indian instructors came out and they were sincere people, but they had their concepts, which they unintentionally mixed in with the real message. What we had then was some Indian concepts translated into a Western culture with mainly young people. Despite this, there was and still is a very beautiful feeling of peace that can be accessed through the regular practice of the techniques of Knowledge and listening to Prem Rawat's message.'[7]

With hindsight, Jenny wondered if her decision to adopt the disciplines advocated by Maharaj Ji was the result of her dissatisfaction with herself as a person. 'I needed to somehow be a bit better than I was, a better person. The sight of myself, once I took up meditation, was not a happy one.' She came to see this awareness as a valuable step on the road to self-improvement.

As she spent more time with other devotees and more time in meditation, she also became dedicated to the Mission's work. Tony Backhouse remembers an Indian instructor staying at 124 Ohiro Road when a Divine Light seminar and meditation course was being delivered in Wellington, and in due course the house became an informal centre for the Mission. Tony recalled coming home from tour 'to find someone in my bed and a bevy of bright-eyed young women in the kitchen baking bread. Ultimately Jenny decided the house should be a centre for the Mission, and asked us tenants to consider joining Divine Light or relocating. I think we all decided to leave the house at that point.'[8]

For the time being Bruce remained, although his relationship with Jenny was tested by her embrace of Maharaj Ji's teaching. At her insistence, theirs had become a 'celibate marriage'. Jenny wrote to Bruce, 'I think you have been, and are, a beautiful husband – it's just that marriage looks different to me now.' She added that the desire for a physical relationship 'has simply left me. I can't explain why because I don't know why, but it seems to me that at a certain point on the path, this becomes inevitable, just as all other "worldly desires" also gradually fall away.'[9] Bruce, hurt by Jenny's withdrawal, had also grown tired of the Divine Light Mission's members – known as 'premies' (or 'lovers of love') – who, at Jenny's invitation, were living in the house. And although he had been curious about Maharaj Ji's teaching, he was ultimately unconvinced by the principles taught, and baffled by Jenny's enthusiastic adoption of them.

Steve Matthews, having experienced the power of the techniques of Knowledge, understood Jenny's wholehearted embrace of the practice Maharaj Ji advocated. He said:

> Based on a strong inner experience, she went, 'Well, this is really life-changing for me, and can be life-changing for a lot of people. I really want to support [Maharaj Ji's] work in terms of getting this message out.' So, Jenny got very involved. These Indian instructors came and they suggested setting up centres or ashrams and I think Jenny was very much at the heart of that. And she was also having a really great experience – I could see that. She was an inspiration as well, in terms of her own focus and her own clarity. Not all of us who learned the techniques of Knowledge were wanting to go and live that ashram lifestyle, but I think Jenny did initially. Out of her enthusiasm and her desire to let others know about this possibility of experiencing inner peace, she chose to make her house available in terms of, 'I want this to be the centre.'[10]

This analysis matches Jenny's contemporary accounts of her experiences of the techniques of Knowledge: 'The all-embracing and permanently transforming effects of this meditation,' she wrote at the time, 'are utterly beyond words. At the same time, it is working gradually and naturally, and patience and perseverance are very necessary. I can say without exaggeration that it is giving me everything I ever wanted.'[11]

In July 1974, Jenny travelled to the United States to attend the annual Guru Puja Festival of the Divine Light Mission. Held that year in Amherst, Massachusetts, the festival attracted twelve thousand of Maharaj Ji's devotees.[12] In a letter to Bruce, written during the journey back to New Zealand, she described the circumstances of her trip and events at the festival. This included a remarkable account of how the festival organisers managed darshan, which for the Divine Light Mission (and in line with Hindu tradition) involved allowing disciples to kiss the feet of Maharaj Ji and to receive 'Holy Breath':

Instead of the conventional darshan line of premies filing past him, he decided to have us stand shoulder to shoulder in a double circle around the racing track of the campus and he drove around it in a seat fixed to the side of a truck with his feet about chest height, so we could just bend down and kiss them as he came by. (Twentieth-century guru, as he put it.) As he approached, a strange intense kind of concentration began to build up inside me, and suddenly it was over. I had kissed his feet, received Holy Breath, given my dedication (flowers) to the truckload of mahatmas towed behind his truck, and received prashad, all in the space of a few seconds. For a moment I was quite dazed, and then the most amazing Something (pure Word, I suppose) went right through me, as powerful as an electric shock, but slower, more rippling and coming in waves from the top of my head to my feet. It made me shake and tremble, and my knees became so weak I thought I might fall to the ground. I've never felt anything like it, it blew me out completely.[13]

Jenny's account of her travel from Wellington to Amherst may have helped Bruce understand her frame of mind. She prefaced her remarks by describing the trip as 'quite an extraordinary series of coincidences and happenings', and went on to find significance in: seeing a rainbow before leaving Wellington and learning the aircraft's pilot was Captain Rainbow; finding all the things she needed to buy at St Luke's Mall in Auckland were on special; discovering that her Los Angeles hotel was only a block from the Hollywood Divine Light Mission headquarters; being the sole passenger on a bus (twice during the trip). The coincidences included repeated appearances of banana cake and fortuitous meetings. 'I found,' she wrote, 'some of my favourite French goat cheese, and made some sandwiches. Shared them later with a girl who turned out to have kept goats, and made goat cheese herself.' She concluded this passage of the letter by saying, 'It just becomes so abundantly clear that everything is meant to happen. What a pattern there is in all these things.' Later in life Jenny was much less impressed by coincidences and not at all inclined to attach importance to them, but during the early 1970s – as her letters attest – she found meaning in them.[14]

Such credulity might be understandable in a very young and earnest neophyte, but was surprising to Bruce, who had fallen in love initially with Jenny's intellectual acuity and creative energy – in short, with her mind. In her letter, it is clear that Jenny was engaged in a kind of pitched battle with her mind, and the world of the intellect seems to have become enemy territory for her: 'After receiving Knowledge, my mind has been getting stronger, sneakier, meaner and more subtle, so that I have come to watch it like a hawk. It tries to deny every beautiful experience of the Knowledge, tries to make you forget, to pretend that it never happened. One just has to hold fast to the real thing, and not to identify with the mind, but to laugh at it, and let it go.'[15]

As distressing as these changes in Jenny might have been, the event that galvanised Bruce to leave the Ohiro Road house was, oddly enough, a powerful premonition of his own. Standing at his bedroom window one day, he had the strong impression he should move out of the house immediately and take his piano with him. 'It was really powerful and so I did. I rang the movers and I moved out the next morning.'[16] Jenny recalled what followed shortly afterwards:

> Those were the days when we were holding (entirely informal) Divine Light Mission meetings at my house, which had a big enough living room to accommodate thirty to fifty people quite comfortably. Neil-whatever-his-name-was from Warkworth had been coming to some of these meetings when he apparently took it into his head that we were possessed by the devil and the house needed to be burned down. A good many of us were sitting in the living room one evening when suddenly the door opened. It was Neil. 'The house is on fire!' he yelled, and took off at top speed. Clearly, he didn't mean us to be burned along with the house. We were remarkably composed, there was no panic at all; we simply moved outside to safety in orderly single file and stood watching the flames roaring up from the basement. Meanwhile some kindly neighbours had already phoned the Brooklyn Fire Brigade, who were with us in less than three minutes, and eventually managed to save the best part of the house. While the firemen hosed the blazing timbers, we sang a selection of

our guru songs (many of which were familiar pop songs, 'My Sweet Lord', 'Stairway to Heaven', 'The Rose', 'Killing Me Softly') to help them along. Later there was a photo in the newspaper of us doing this, with the whole event simultaneously viewed by a surrounding hillside of interested and/or anxious neighbours.

Bruce was grateful to be able to observe these proceedings from a distance: 'I remember, in the *Evening Post*, the front-page photo had a picture of all the attendees at the prayer meeting sitting on the lawn singing, and the headline said "Devotees Sing as House Burns".'[17]

Although the house was saved, many of the documents and records Jenny had stored in the basement, including some of her early music, were lost. Among the scores destroyed was her first piano suite – five short movements she had composed and performed during her first year at Victoria. Also lost were the three e.e. cummings songs for soprano and piano which Maureen Spencer, Jenny's friend from Levin, had performed with her at a student concert, and the incidental music she had written for three plays: the Victoria University Drama Club's productions of *Twelfth Night* and *Troilus and Cressida*; and Downstage Theatre's production of *Hamlet*.

Jenny's determination to rise above attachment – in all its forms – likely mitigated her feelings of loss. She was also busily making new music, music of an altogether different kind.

The Light Brigade

During 1974, the year she had travelled to Amherst for the Guru Puja Festival, Jenny was on sabbatical leave from the university. Ordinarily, academics use such leave to undertake research, often writing books or articles for publication. The university's senior management probably expected Jenny would use the time to compose music – perhaps a symphony or another music theatre piece – but she chose instead to spend the year meditating and exploring rock music in a very hands-on way.

In a report detailing her leave activities, she explained her attraction to the music: 'For years I had lamented the lack of a common international idiom, without realising there was such an idiom staring me in the face.'[18] This realisation – that rock and popular music possessed greater communicative potential than the art music she had formerly composed – had become increasingly clear to Jenny during her work on *Under the Sun*. However, although she was persuaded by the possibilities rock and popular music offered, she was dissatisfied with her first attempts to compose in the idiom, particularly the aborted 'rock opera' commission from which she had withdrawn in 1972. Reflecting on those first attempts she concluded that 'without being a performer of rock music I was simply incapable of composing anything that was really rock'.[19] The long sabbatical leave presented her with an opportunity to immerse herself completely in the rock genre, and so gain the experience necessary to compose such music.

The experience of improvising with the band during rehearsals for *Under the Sun* had been salutary, inspiring her to make her first steps away from the disciplines of art music and towards the looser, improvisational approaches characteristic of rock and pop. She began to train herself as a performer in those styles by reproducing that experience – putting Rolling Stones records on the stereo and playing along with them on the piano while everyone else was out of the house. 'Nicky Hopkins, Billy Preston, Floyd Cramer, Dr John and Allen Toussaint became favourite pianists – and later I admired Harry Connick Jr.' Jenny enjoyed the sounds and the energy of rock, and liked improvising over blues tunes. 'I was attracted,' she said, 'by the common qualities of spontaneity, naturalness, cultural all-pervasiveness and integrity.'[20]

Her next step was to start a band with a few friends, some of whom were also followers of Maharaj Ji. In that context, she began composing songs, and found that the idiom required altogether new approaches from her. 'I wrote lots and lots of pop songs, words and music, and I did it for years,' Jenny told Elizabeth Kerr. 'At first, I couldn't do it very well, it seemed awfully contrived. It was an incredible challenge because it was the first time I'd come across a style that I couldn't imitate. So, then I had to start listening in new ways. There were lots of subtleties there.'[21]

The music also inspired some new ways of thinking:

> I became interested in Lévi-Strauss and structuralism, and particularly in Foucault's theory that any language makes it possible to say certain things but impossible to say others; and that the gaps created by these impossibilities will gradually be filled with a new language, which will ultimately supersede the old (thereby completing a cycle). There came a dawning recognition that (especially) the harmonic language of rock music can be seen as a perfect example of this process, in that it represents a total and literal reversal of past practice. All that was prohibited in classical harmonic tonality has become that which, to my ear, is most characteristic of today's mainstream rock harmony.[22]

The group of musicians with whom Jenny was merrily transacting this reversal of classical music conventions was large: drums, bass, acoustic and electric and twelve-string guitars, sometimes an amplified clarinet, two keyboards and three or four vocalists. The arrangements were loose, close to non-existent, 'more a matter of, "play here, and don't play there"', and the music was rarely notated: 'Sometimes we'd write lead sheets for ourselves but more often it would just be the words and a few chord changes, and then remembering while you're playing what you're supposed to be doing.' Not everyone in the group was associated with the Divine Light Mission, but some of the lyrics were related to the spiritual concerns that preoccupied Jenny and the other followers of Maharaj Ji. There were songs by other artists – 'River Deep, Mountain High', 'Proud Mary', 'Long Train Running' and 'Pinball Wizard' were in the band book – but a lot of the material was original, much of it written by Jenny. She described her music of the time as 'devotional soft-rock songs'.[23]

With the band, known at various points as the Light Brigade, the Divine Light Missionaries, and Roxoffly (or RocksOffly), Jenny played keyboards and sang backing vocals. They performed in the music room at Victoria ('A great gig,' Jenny recalled) and for the annual dance at a school where one of the band members taught, as well as in prisons and old peoples' homes. They didn't perform many concerts, although Jenny recalled that a show at which they supported guitarist Billy TK in

the St James Theatre in Wellington was their largest. They also played
at Auckland's South Pacific Hotel in October 1974, when Maharaj Ji
visited the country and gave an address to followers. Memories are a little
vague, but their performance there was likely to have been to accompany
group singing rather than any sort of concert.[24]

Bruce McKinnon, who was at that time also a member of the
Divine Light Mission, played drums with the group. He said, 'There
was no money involved. It was part of Divine Light activities. I still
did other gigs to make a living. We played a beach sound shell mini
tour from Wellington up to Whanganui.'[25] Those performances, open-
air family concerts, included a play and a wide range of music: rock and
roll, country, the Beatles, Elton John, Cat Stevens, Carole King and a
smattering of originals. Ahead of the tour Jenny had written to town
councils seeking permission to perform at various beaches, among them
Queen Elizabeth Park between Raumati and Paekākāriki. 'We wrote and
they didn't reply so we just went and did it anyway. After we'd done it,
we got a reply saying, "Oh, sorry, no, we can't allow this to happen." It
had already happened.'

The group, which included vocalists Rosie Horsley and Denise Bulte,
second keyboard player Derek Sanders and Martin Jorgensen on bass,
appeared on Michael Dean's TV talk show *Dean on Saturday*, and the
members had sufficient confidence in the band's prospects to consider
becoming a professional unit. Jenny was not interested: she didn't need
the income – her university salary was secure – but more than that did
not want to spend her life as a gigging musician.

That wasn't because she was bored or dissatisfied with the experience
of rehearsing and performing the music. On the contrary, she said, 'The
liberating quality in playing this music is hard to describe. I find its effect
is always therapeutic and always uplifting.' Even so, her engagement
with rock music as a *performer* had been motivated in significant part
by her search for a personal musical style as a *composer*, a style that was
'natural, unselfconscious and spontaneous, a musical language more
articulate than the strange or beautiful effects, gestures and noises of
the avant-garde, a style with room for a good beat and a good tune'.[26]
Having caught a glimpse of 'the possibility of a kind of "classical" music

evolving from the rock language', she had begun to see where her own musical future lay, and it wasn't with Roxoffly. By the end of 1975 the group had drifted apart; Martin Jorgensen went on to play with other groups, Bruce McKinnon moved to Auckland, and Jenny focused on her own songs and her university commitments.

Reflecting on that period, Jenny said, 'It would look to some people as though I had abandoned composing to go and be spiritual for a few years. And I had done, but I hadn't stopped composing, it was just that I was writing pop songs, or religious songs: religious pop songs. Well, they're out of the purview of a whole bunch of my other listeners; they had no idea about a whole other world of music that I was writing.'

The experience of making music with the Light Brigade (and its various subsequent incarnations) was relatively short-lived, but it was important to Jenny: it had acquainted her with the rhythmic subtlety possible in otherwise quite simple music, and introduced her to melodic and harmonic strategies that were to have telling effects on the serious music she was to compose the following decade. Although there are no recordings of the group, there are bedroom demos of some of Jenny's music from this period: light folk-rock songs, Jenny accompanying herself with gentle finger-picked guitar. The lyrics, a kind of home-spun wisdom for the Age of Aquarius, are absolutely of their time and the songs (with just guitar and voice on the demos) would sit comfortably alongside contemporary efforts by Carole King or Cat Stevens. Among them are a couple that Jenny would recycle: the 'Little Owl Song' enjoyed new life as a children's choir piece for an Artsplash festival in the 1990s; and 'There's a Time' became, after some fairly extensive reworking, the final song in Jenny's 1982 cycle *Childhood*.

Leaving Victoria

Given Jenny's youth and relative lack of experience, her appointment as Professor of Music by the university had been a risk. While in some ways it had paid handsome dividends – there had been an expansion of music papers on offer and a deepened commitment to performance training – in other ways her service and the public figure she cut as Professor of Music ran against the grain of the university's culture and overall project. Jenny later characterised the committee that appointed her as 'brave souls' but conceded 'they probably regretted it'.[27]

Fred Page had been a progressive during his time as professor, advocating for new music and seeking to modernise the curriculum; it was he (at Jenny's instigation) who first introduced ethnomusicology to the university and supported Douglas Lilburn to establish the Electronic Music Studio. He was also an administrator who, by being aware of the currents of power in the university, was able to lead the department through the (sometimes murky) waters of institutional politics.

In many ways Jenny had continued in Page's footsteps: modernising the curriculum, delivering excellent teaching, broadening the content of the programme, seeking to serve the best interests of the students. If anything, Jenny may have paid more attention to her pastoral responsibilities than Page. Relatively close to the students in age, sharing their interest in popular music and culture, and being a friendly and approachable presence around the campus, she enjoyed an easy camaraderie with them. As a result, they (and their parents) felt free to call on her for help:

> Called one night by a student's mother (a friend of mine) to their home, I found him very agitated and distant, pacing the front room stark naked. Having no idea what to do, I saw a recording of Mozart, put it on, and sat down. The young man, whom I ignored, was soon putting on his clothes quietly and restored to his right mind – a welcome surprise as I'd simply done the first thing that occurred to me. Another time I woke up to find a music student sitting on the end of my bed in quite a flipped-out state. Alarmed, but knowing more, I put on some Fripp and Eno, which soon brought him back down to earth.[28]

On another occasion, a music student locked himself and Jenny in her office and pocketed the key, 'refusing to open the door until I had "told him about God". Eventually he unlocked us both after I'd said I would "think much more of him" if he did.'

Where Jenny most differed from Page was in the way she minimised the administrative duties she was expected to discharge as a head of department. She said, 'I just had as few meetings as possible. I shouldn't have applied for the job because I didn't want to do administration and I did as little administration as possible.'

While the consequences of these choices may have been felt within the department, it still functioned, students were trained and study options expanded. However, Jenny paid little attention to her obligations as a professor in the broader context of the university: 'I only went to about two professorial board meetings in the whole time I was there. I used to read the agenda and if there was anything relating to the Music Department I'd go, but otherwise I wouldn't.'[29] That might have been a justifiable decision, and would certainly have spared her time in meetings, but may not have endeared her to the professoriate.

Bruce Greenfield expressed confidence in her abilities, but acknowledged that managing a university department was not her métier: 'She was a creator, and administration is not what she was put on this Earth to do. She was very competent at organising curriculum and stuff like that, but once she'd done it for a while, she didn't want to keep doing it and adjusting it and having more meetings about it. She got tired of the job. But she did do a lot for the place.'[30]

Twenty years later, Jenny had the perspective to recognise her tendency to move from one area of intense focus to another. 'I do things until I start seeing holes in them or start getting sick of them, and after five or six or seven years I get sick of a thing.'[31] She had initially intended to stay for as long as fifteen or twenty years as professor, and had made public her intention to strengthen the department's commitment to training performers as well as expanding its offerings in popular, electronic and non-Western music.[32] That said, she had not harboured ambitions to remain at Victoria until retirement:

I never intended spending my whole life being an academic, that's for sure. I took the whole thing less seriously the longer I spent being a professor. At the same time, I was being much more attracted to

popular music because of the energy of it. I was being drawn in a
whole new direction. Whenever something like that happens to me,
I just want to focus on the new thing and be conscious of that alone.
I am aware that I am moving out of something but I am much more
interested in what I am going towards than what I am leaving.[33]

As it happened, senior management were also growing disenchanted
with her service. Negative public perception of Jenny's performance –
which found its most forceful expression in a strongly worded letter
from Robin Maconie published in the student magazine *Salient* –
possibly acted as an accelerant to growing feelings of discontent at the
university. Maconie was then chief music critic for the *Times Educational
Supplement*, on the faculty of the University of Surrey, and a world
authority on the music of Karlheinz Stockhausen, so his blunt criticism
would have been taken seriously. Maconie's perspective was undoubtedly
shaded by the distance from which he observed life at Victoria, and
his priorities as a music educator were quite likely some distance from
Jenny's. Nevertheless, his argument – that 'a teacher of composition
who renounces composing betrays his calling and his art' – and closing
remarks may well have stung Victoria's senior management: 'A University
that will not act to protect its students is unworthy of its scholarly duty'.[34]
Vice-Chancellor Danny Taylor, in a letter to the chancellor, suggested
the department was 'desperately in need of that old-fashioned quality of
leadership which Jenny completely failed to give'.[35]

The university was spared further hand-wringing when in 1976, and
for her own reasons, Jenny resigned. She later confessed 'a yearning to get
out of the academic world', in part because 'I felt I was going over the top
as an intellectual.'[36] It was a decision that surprised some but was greeted
with a sigh of relief by many. The position Jenny vacated was advertised
and David Farquhar was appointed as her successor. The *Dominion*'s
music critic approved: the change would 'bring the department back to a
more academically normal course' after the 'exciting, highly stimulating
interregnum' under McLeod.[37]

Perrin, Craig and Jenny, c. 1946

Jenny picnics with her parents

Perrin, Jenny and Craig, c. 1952

Grandfather John Halford Perrin with his carved figures

Jenny on guitar with brother Perrin on accordion

Jenny at the piano, Levin, 1950s

McLeod family, (from top left: Ronald, Jenny, Lorna, Craig, Perrin)

Igor Stravinsky's New Zealand visit, 1961 (Jenny in the dark jacket)

New Zealand's youngest professor, Victoria University College, 1967

Cover of
booklet
produced to
accompany
Earth and Sky
record, 1970

Publicity shot
from *Under the
Sun* booklet,
1971

Under the Sun rehearsal, Palmerston North's Pascal Street stadium, 1971

Cover of booklet produced to accompany *Under the Sun* record, 1971

Jenny in 1975, still at Victoria but in search of a musical style that was 'natural, unselfconscious and spontaneous'

Jenny unveils her poster-score *Piece for Wall*, designed for the Turnbull Library exhibition *Scores of Sounds: Facets of New Zealand Composition Since 1940*, in the company of fellow composers, 1982

Preparations for
the Sun Festival,
1983

Performer at the
Sun Festival in
Oriental Bay, 1983

Evelyn Page
Jan. 1961

Portraits of Bruce Greenfield and Jenny by Evelyn Page, 1981

Jenny with her Best Film
Soundtrack award for
The Silent One, 1984

Jenny's home studio,
c. 1987

Jenny with parts for *The Emperor of the Nightingale* for the Wellington Regional Orchestra, 1985

Composing Women's Festival, Wellington, 1993 (from left: Elizabeth Kerr, Helen Fisher, Gillian Karawe Whitehead, Tūngia Baker, Keri Kaa and Jenny McLeod)

Jenny at home,
Pukerua Bay, 1980s

Jenny with Peter Schat
at Pukerua Bay railway
station, c. 1990

Hui Aranga, Whanganui, 2002

Hōhepa, produced by NBR New Zealand Opera for the New Zealand International Arts Festival, at the Opera House, Wellington, 2012

Jenny at Pukerua Bay, c. 2001

10

Spiritual Walkabout

On leaving Victoria, Jenny entertained the idea of taking up a teaching role in the newly established Executant Music course of the Wellington Polytechnic, but was unperturbed when the position failed to materialise. 'Thank God,' she later said, 'I was in no way ready to teach popular music.'[1] As it was, her father, living in Auckland, was quite unwell, so Jenny left her house – now mortgage-free – in the care of the local chapter of the Divine Light Mission and moved north to look after him.

Poor health had followed Ron and Lorna McLeod after they moved to Auckland in the mid-1960s. Jenny was in the early years of her professorship when Lorna's health deteriorated – she was at first misdiagnosed with a 'hernia' but was in fact suffering from cervical cancer.

> Failing to make any headway under Dr Herbert Green's 'experimental' regime at National Women's Hospital, my mother turned to Milan Brych for help. Regardless of all the Brych demonising that later went on in the media, she would never hear a word against him. She became tearful, maintaining until her painful death that he had helped her a lot. As with the many other victimised women

concerned, hers was a desperate and horrible situation that none of us understood properly until years later, after the official inquiries were released.[2]

Jenny saw her mother only intermittently during the period of her illness, but said, 'Whatever Milan Brych did or did not do for his patients, I am sincerely grateful to him on her behalf.' She had been close enough to her mother while growing up at home, but their bond was a practical one – Lorna taught and instructed Jenny; they made things together – and not especially affectionate. Years after Lorna's death, Jenny was able to see her mother in an entirely new light when she caught sight of her quite by chance on television:

> I had a peculiar shock many decades later, watching a documentary about the beginnings of TV in New Zealand. Suddenly we cut to a shot of my own Song Spinner mother singing onscreen way back then. She is younger than me watching! Imagine, your long dead mother suddenly jumps up, alive and kicking right in front of you (we were hardly a home-movies family, so I had never seen anything like this before). Almost as if our roles were reversed and I, the elder, was now indeed the mother and she the daughter, such an odd and touching feeling. I think I felt closer to her in that moment, or saw her more as a fellow human being than I ever did while she was alive on Earth.

Lorna's death in 1973 saw Ron move briefly to the North Shore before finally settling in Sandringham, where Jenny joined him. Following prostate surgery (performed by composer Eve de Castro-Robinson's father), Jenny was on hand to nurse Ron through his recovery. It was an arrangement beneficial to them both: Ron had good care; and Jenny enjoyed his financial support: 'I was there for a few years and he paid the bills and I didn't need money for anything.'

Although Jenny was not in any sort of regular paid work, she was still busy, serving full-time as national secretary for the Divine Light Mission. In that context she made time for some music, forming a trio with Rosie

Horsley and Kevin Higgins. 'We all did vocals,' Jenny said. 'Kevin and I played acoustic guitars, sometimes amplified but I think mostly not, so it was all very easy. We performed together a lot in Auckland, usually for Divine Light Mission public and regular meetings.' The group didn't have a name and mainly performed light pop and country music: 'Bette Midler's "The Rose" always went down well, "Here Comes the Sun" and many others.'

In 1977 Jenny was also involved in Mercury Theatre's production of Maxwell Anderson and Kurt Weill's *Lost in the Stars*. Jenny trained the chorus (which included her opera-singing cousin Paul Person) and arranged the score for two pianos, flute and clarinet. For the performances, she played First Piano, with the show's musical director Bobby Alderton playing Second. It was fun to be back in a theatre, and Jenny recalled, 'On the last night at the very end of the show, the back row (men) of the tiered onstage chorus slowly subsided from view as their seating collapsed. Shrieks, squawks, hysterical laughter!'

There was also occasional employment as a music copyist for South Pacific Television. It was familiar work: as a student Jenny had often earned money doing music copying during the university holidays. After a year or so in Auckland, Jenny was deployed by the Mission to Australia, working there for the organisation again (and as always) in a voluntary capacity.

> I didn't get on that well in Australia because I didn't like being told what to do. By anybody. And sometimes I wouldn't do it. I remember this bloke coming into my office – and I was in the middle of the next great operation – and saying, 'Go down town and get me this,' and I said, 'No, you do it. I'm in the middle of this.' I said that to my boss and he didn't know what to say, he just retired in confusion. Shortly after that I was no longer in Australia.

Back in Auckland, she lived for a time in an ashram in Grey Lynn. Towards the end of 1978 she was preparing to travel to the United States to continue her work with the Mission when she received a letter from Bruce Greenfield requesting a divorce. Jenny replied, 'Expected some such would be turning up soon. Actually wrote "divorce pending" on a form for Denver a couple of weeks ago. So yes, no problems.'[3] Bruce and Jenny had not lived together for some years and rarely saw one another after he moved out of the Ohiro Road house. Even if they'd continued to live together, it is not clear their relationship would have survived. Jenny later said, 'You never met such an intensely spiritual person as I was then, I was impossible to live with.'[4]

Jenny's immersion in the practices and work of the Mission was all-encompassing by this time. In her letter to Bruce, she reiterated her commitment to the life and experience she had found through Maharaj Ji, and expressed gratitude for the 'beautiful life he is giving me'. Her gratitude seemed to spring in part from the clear and focused direction she enjoyed day to day. She thought it good 'just to be completely at one with your own experience and not be going in so many different directions at once.'[5]

Life during those years, Jenny said, was 'a spiritual walk-about'. Finding fulfilment in her practice of the disciplines taught by Maharaj Ji, and eager to share her experience with others, she travelled extensively in the United States, spending a year in California and six months in Miami, attending many Hindu festivals and working in various capacities for the Mission. 'I simply went wherever I was assigned to go by Divine Light Mission headquarters in the US,' she said. 'It wasn't at all a matter of me "picking and choosing" various places to go or any particular specific things to do. They dreamed up, organised and paid for everything: travel, food, accommodation. I just got in and out of cars, stayed wherever (houses, ashrams, hotels), ate and drank what I was given (all tasted good), meditated a couple of hours daily and went to whatever meetings, rehearsals, assignments were scheduled for that day.'

In California, she worked with stained-glass artist John Slowski in a small Divine Light Mission enterprise. They operated out of a garage at the house where she and several other devotees lived in a kind of 'artists' ashram':

> We designed, made and sold stained glass as 'Studio West' but we were not paid. Slowski invented the name and had a posh calling-

card printed. The money either went to Divine Light Mission or back into the business (to buy more glass). This was at first in Santa Monica, and then later on I was actually working alone outdoors, at a Malibu house where the weather was great, and we were then living. And then later still in a Trancas Canyon field nearby, in a sort of small shed affair just about big enough for me and the table, with one of those swinging half doors, over which a curious goat would peer in now and then with its strange eyes.

Music wasn't completely set aside. Jenny had kept a guitar with her and wrote religious songs during her time with the Mission in the US, all in the pop idiom. 'I must have written about a hundred of them,' she said. 'I never wrote the music down but I wrote all the words down.' These (and other songs) she would perform on guitar, singing in duos and trios with other premies. 'I enjoyed that, but it wasn't so much a musical enterprise as a spiritual enterprise.'

There were times, however, when her musical gifts were required for more committed ventures. The Santa Monica household in which she lived included a number of musicians and performers brought together by the Mission's headquarters as a kind of 'theatre experiment'. Jenny and Mickey Cottrell, an off-Broadway actor, wrote what she called 'a sort of a musical, called *Ameros*', which they staged at the Loyola Theatre in Westchester, Los Angeles:

Mickey wrote the words for *Ameros* (which I changed a lot) and I did the music. It wasn't so bad, actually, but later I threw it out – too much hidden agenda. The hardest thing was trying to focus on composing something halfway decent at the little upright [piano] in the lounge, with the whole household incessantly coming and going. The Loyola was actually a small local cinema at that time run by the Mission (sometimes we were also ushers and got to see free movies). It had no proper stage but a lower one in front of the (curtained-off) screen, and the small (though maximum) audience was very likely only Divine Light Mission members, who as I recall thought we were pretty useless.

When the 'theatre experiment' was discontinued, Jenny moved to Miami to audition for the main Divine Light Mission band, One Foundation. The group included New Zealand singers Lindsay and Kim Field, members of the cast of *Hair* whom Jenny had met during the show's New Zealand High Court trial. Geoff Bridgford, who had played drums with the Bee Gees, was also a member of the band.

> In Miami Geoff correctly discerned that my sense of rhythm was (still) not steady enough for me to join them as their keyboard player (although it was fine where playing my own songs was concerned and had been well sufficient for all my earlier performing purposes back home and in Illinois). This was a deep and subtly intuitive perception on Geoff's part – one that I now think maybe only a big-time pop-rock drummer could have sensed, someone well aware of the all-revealing exposure of the beat under the magnification of a powerful sound system and the immediate focus of an audience of many thousands. Not that I personally ever got that far (except once on a telethon, and later with the *Sun Festival* at Oriental Bay).

Jenny met many people through her association with the Divine Light Mission: 'Mostly they were really nice dopey people, and some of them were really good people – you just never know who you're going to meet in outfits like that. I'll always be glad I met them.' She would stay in occasional contact with some of them in the years to come. There were other benefits, too:

> I spent about eight years meditating and towards the end I lived in an ashram for some years and so I was getting kind of physical discipline, and the discipline of meditating was quite interesting. This was not so much a matter of having wondrous experiences of light and all this beautiful stuff; it was just of sitting there trying to keep your mind quiet. But of course, your mind won't keep quiet, and keeps reminding you of all the bad things you did, the things of which you ought to be thoroughly ashamed and which you really ought to do something about: apologise, straighten out – this is

yourself talking to yourself, thinking, 'That wasn't very good.' I did learn to control my mind and eventually all that became part of me. But it brought me down – in a good way – sort of recognising that I was far from perfect and there were a lot of things I could do to smarten myself up. That's basically what the experience of meditating was for me.[6]

Jenny contrasted the lessons she learned about herself through meditation with her experiences as a professor at Victoria University: 'There,' she said, 'they put me on a pedestal, and that doesn't help; they thought I was God's gift to whatever. Well, I wasn't.'

The friendships she formed during those years and the self-knowledge she acquired through meditation were certainly a benison. However, despite devoting close to five years of her life to the Mission's work as a volunteer, 'Increasingly, it became clear to me that one of the main Divine Light Mission problems, especially in the USA, was the devotion of followers to the physical personage of the guru, [while] what was really important was an *inner* experience. I advocated this consistently whenever and wherever I spoke, as I did pretty well every day among smaller groups of people in the US.'[7] This growing understanding ensured she kept her distance from the more outlandish behaviours of some of the organisation's members, including the cult-like devotion to Maharaj Ji some followers exhibited. Eventually, the credulity of many of the premies became galling: 'All these earnest young people with their faces shining, eyes bright – all this lovely stuff that you can kind of connect with for a few years – and then after a few years it was "God, help me. Protect me from all these earnest young people".'[8]

Even if it took her some time to develop the capacity to discriminate between the practices (commonly adopted by premies) she found beneficial and those she found unhelpful, Jenny didn't think she ever fully folded herself into the Divine Light Mission community:

Though I always spoke from the heart, I was never much one for 'joining' anything and I kept my deepest responses and feelings well under wraps. Followers themselves were all individuals with their own experiences and responses with which I could sometimes profoundly disagree, whilst meanwhile holding my peace. I actively warned people when I could see that others were essentially trying to 'break their spirit' or get them to 'fall into line'. Eventually my life with the Mission became more what I thought of as 'sabotage from within'.

Highly educated, worldly and frequently older than those with whom she was living and working, Jenny found life among the premies increasingly difficult. She said, 'I thought that battling through all the vicissitudes of this kind of life would be good for me', and she put a brave face on her discomfort. But after six or seven years of close contact with other followers she came to realise it was time to move on.

In fact, as Jenny confessed in a letter to Bruce Greenfield, she had found some of Maharaj Ji's devotees exasperating almost from her first encounters with them. Recalling her early days with the Mission while living in Ohiro Road with Bruce, she wrote, 'Actually, the premies sickened me just as much as they did you – they still do; but I suppose I just put up with them longer.'[9] It wasn't that all of Maharaj Ji's followers were hopeless or foolish or unprincipled; 'some of them were fine,' Jenny admitted, 'but unfortunately not the ones I mostly ended up with . . . it got so that I couldn't speak to them at all, because I knew they wouldn't understand me.' Ultimately, frustration and a sense of isolation in their company galvanised her to leave the Mission. 'I realised that being around the premies was like death for me, on the whole (the company you keep and all that – certainly got to me, anyway) and finally walked out.'[10]

By this stage – sometime during 1981 – Jenny had returned to Wellington and was sharing the Ohiro Road house with other Divine Light Mission members. Deeply unhappy, she recalled, 'I would have done anything that worked to get me out of a situation that I really had had quite enough of. I no longer thought it would be doing me any good at all.' And so, with no clear plan and no work to go to, she left. Fortunately, she had been receiving rent for her house from the Mission. Until then she had simply put the rental income back into the

Mission's bank account; on leaving she took the rent with her, providing her means with which to live.

> I moved into a seedy hotel in Courtenay Place for a few weeks and during those few weeks I was feeling around to relocate myself – wherever that was going to be – inside, especially. The place was really cheap and low – the sort where no visitors are allowed – and also very cold (but no heaters allowed either). I used to leave on my little old toaster, leaving open the side-wings to keep myself warm. I started going to the Public Library (which was warm) and started reading again. I'd read a lot before, but you can read things without the experience of understanding them, which happened when I was a student – I wasn't ready to read half of the stuff I read . . . So, I read. I was feeling lonely – so lonely that if anyone smiled at me in the street, tears of gratitude would come to my eyes – and in the books that I read, New Zealand novels, Patrick White also, and later in Virginia Woolf and Janet Frame, I found my spiritual brothers and sisters. I found in those books things that I recognised for the first time, even though I'd read a lot of these books before. Qualities of character I now valued that I hadn't even noticed before: simple, simple things, like sticking up for something, or recognising what is really important.

Reading New Zealand authors Maurice Gee and Maurice Shadbolt, and branching out to include writers such as Carl Jung and (for a second or third time) poets W.H. Auden and William Blake, proved a balm for Jenny. 'It was an incredible relief. I had been thirsting desperately for this sort of conversation of depth that wasn't constantly concerned with "what is my relationship to God?"'[11] Her response was to begin to write – in the first instance, poetry. The subjects of these early poems were often very personal, concerned with matters of the heart and the spirit. Jenny also thought writing them was therapeutic: 'Poetry became one way I had of . . . moaning; whatever happened to be on my mind, you'd find it in one of those early poems.'

Jenny's poetry from this period covers a lot of ground: expressions

of gratitude, intensely personal confessions of sadness and loss, paeans
to art and its making, complaints about unfaithful lovers, declarations
of spiritual love. The general tenor is often one of sadness, although
rarely regret, and collectively there is a kind of honest self-appraisal and,
with it, growing self-acceptance. This stanza, from 'Of Animals, Fire and
Gods' in her collection *The Eternal Round* (there are six collections of
poems from this period), is illustrative:

> Spring-cleaning my mind
>   is like turning out the spare room.
> I take fresh heart,
>   bask, breathe easy,
>   reflecting happily
>   in this sweet, unexpected
>   newfound peace. [12]

Making sense of the seventies

The title of Francis Wheen's portrait of the 1970s, *Strange Days Indeed*,
could be an apt description of Jenny's life during that decade. A cursory
examination of the facts of the period suggests Jenny was spiralling gently
out of control. Having been appointed as the youngest ever professor at
Victoria University, she was the subject of considerable media scrutiny.
In the interviews and public statements in the years that followed, she
acknowledged drug use, a willing embrace of rock and non-Western
music, and her withdrawal from classical composition. She resigned
from the university after only five years as a professor and joined what
looked to most people like a cult.

These choices are, superficially at least, difficult to reconcile with the
choices she made prior to 1970. However, the pattern of her life and
work during these years becomes more comprehensible when considered
within a larger trajectory.

Reflecting on the period and interrogating why she had been drawn
to meditation and the Divine Light Mission, Jenny said, 'This was all

mixed up – in the beginning, not during the ashram years – [with] me and my students smoking dope.'[13] It would be easy to write off the decade as a series of missteps under the influence of drugs, and some of her associates from this time thought this was possibly the case. However, while marijuana and hallucinogens may have opened a few doors for Jenny, they did not govern her life. The choices she made were conscious ones, and not the product of drug-fuelled impulse or fantasy. 'Amazingly enough, I happen to think that her drug use did not affect her decisions as much as people think,' Bruce Greenfield said. 'I observed her during consumption of all manner of drugs, alcohol, magic mushrooms, LSD, marijuana. The thing that always amazed me – no matter what substance was consumed, her mind stayed remarkably clear and lucid. She may have lost physical balance, but rarely slurred her words. That mind just kept going at warp speed and with great clarity.'[14]

Flatmate Tony Backhouse also remarked on the clarity and speed of Jenny's mind and her attendant powers of concentration. He recalled 'coming into the kitchen of a morning to discover Jenny in the same position we'd left her in the night before, at the kitchen [table] engrossed in a thought process or book or . . . I think she may have once spent twenty-four hours in the same chair, such was her focus.'[15]

Bruce suspected it was this very single-mindedness – her capacity to concentrate on a single idea to such an extent it eclipsed all others – that may have been at the centre of Jenny's wholehearted and apparently uncritical embrace of Maharaj's teachings. 'Jenny is quite fanatical,' Bruce said, 'I would describe her as fanatical.'[16] This is not the word Jenny would have used to describe her single-mindedness, but she did acknowledge a capacity for immoderation: 'Everything I do,' she told Suzanne Court, 'I do to extremes. By the time I have done it to the extreme I've got to the other side of it well and truly, and then I need something very different to balance it out.'[17] She also understood at least one of the reasons why she tended to be so fervent in her interests and convictions: 'A saying from William Blake (or was it T.S. Eliot?),' she said, 'could be the motto of my life: "It's only by going too far that you find out how far is far enough".'[18] However, even if the vigour with which she pursued some of her interests appeared at times intemperate, her decisions to follow particular paths seem always to have been the result of deliberate choices.

Someone once said of Jenny, 'What a mass of contradictions that woman is.' Jenny had her own view of these apparent contradictions. Addressing her search for balance in music and in life, she told me:

> The way in which my life journey proceeded is reminiscent of the way the Fibonacci sequence – with every new number or step – converges gradually upon, or approaches ever more closely, the Golden Mean, or the Golden Section (the ratio of phi, an irrational number that continues to infinity with endless decimal variety). In relation to the central Golden Mean, the Fibonacci series zigzags from higher to lower – the most extreme oscillations occurring at the start and the distances thereafter slowly decreasing. By the fortieth step or number the Fibonacci sequence has pretty well reached the Golden Mean, being accurate to the first fifteen decimal places. The contours of the Fibonacci process could be seen as corresponding to the gradual natural growth within me of (and arrival, eventually, at) my own individual balance – between opposite attractions such as reason and intuition, popular and classical, contemporary and traditional, northern and southern hemispheres (European-American and South Pacific); Māori and Pākehā, with these aspects becoming increasingly incorporated within a single piece of music, and within myself in the form of a growing maturity 'honing in on a mean' – the title of one of my early poems. So I was, to some extent at least, aware of what was happening.

Seen in this light, Jenny's choices during the 1970s begin to make sense. When appointed to a lectureship at Victoria she exhibited the kind of secular values and intellectual interests expected of an academic at the time. Her absorption in structuralist and post-structuralist thought, her enthusiasm for music of the mid-century modernists and the avant-garde, her curiosity about the musical traditions of the East, if not exactly de rigueur for the Music Department at Victoria, certainly chimed with the times. However, those interests and her then-recent compositional work were theoretical, rational, cerebral; listeners might respond to *For Seven* in visceral ways, but the composition of that music was intellectual to the core.

Over the next few years Jenny felt growing uncertainty about her dependence, perhaps over-dependence, on the mind. By 1972 she was experiencing real doubts. In an interview with Jill McCracken in *Landfall* she said, 'In the past I put all my faith in intellect and the power of the mind to reason things out. I had nothing else to hold onto. I told myself that knowledge could take me so far and after that there was nothing.'[19]

That outlook had served her well enough during her time in Europe and her first few years as a junior lecturer, but cracks were beginning to appear. For example, she was experiencing doubts about the value of musical analysis – a cornerstone of both her teaching and her work as a composer. 'There's nothing so difficult as justifying the analysis of music,' she said. 'But sometimes, in little moments, I would see things in the music that made sense – things I saw intuitively and not by adding up a whole lot of analyses. I had experienced this but never attached much importance to it.'[20] Given her confidence in the rational mind, in adding things up, in applying methods and systems, it's understandable that she would dismiss intuitive insights as unimportant. However, their persistence planted seeds of doubt about the sufficiency of the intellect alone to apprehend music clearly, to grasp musical meaning and, perhaps more importantly, to make sense of her life.

Her growing dissatisfaction with a purely intellectual view of music and life led her to investigate ways to go beyond such a rational, analytical outlook. First, and most obviously, she experimented with drugs. Jenny's brother Craig characterised her drug use as part of a spiritual search. That's entirely reasonable, particularly as for Jenny 'spiritual' was mostly to do with self-knowledge rather than anything mystical or religious.[21] Drugs were useful to this end because she found them relaxing; they afforded her the opportunity to slip free of the unremitting and critical commentary her mind insisted on providing. But even that, she came to realise, was not without risk: 'I thought at the time [smoking dope] was having a good effect on my mind because it was helping me to relax, and it did take a few years to dawn on me that what is actually happening – you think you are relaxing and opening up to the whole wide world, but you're opening up to all the shit in the whole wide world, too.'[22]

A crucial new experience occurred in 1971 when, during rehearsals for *Under the Sun*, Jenny improvised with the rock band enlisted for the production. Playing rock music, with its emphasis on spontaneous interactivity and musical creation, allowed her to know at first hand 'the perfect concentration on the moment when one is actually playing', a very different kind of concentration from performing written music or composing music for subsequent performance.[23]

> The chains are cast off and one is directly in touch with that mysterious area which is the source of all inspiration. Music flows through the player; when he is perfectly tuned to the moment, he loses all consciousness of himself as a separate entity making music. It is more as though the music is making him. Afterwards he can only wonder at what happens, what is channelled through him, and where it comes from. He experiences something of the eternal flow which sustains all creation.[24]

Such an insight – whatever others might make of it – was salutary for Jenny. In improvising, she had managed to bypass her mind and touch something altogether 'other'. However, music is ephemeral, and musical experiences of this sort could be only 'a temporary salvation from the infernal clatter of our minds. This interminable commentator rattling on in our heads is the real tyrant. In myriad ways we all seek release from it, only to find ourselves back in its clutches once the music (book, film, game, drink, drug, relationship, etc.) is finished, and/or its effects have faded.'[25]

The uplift and sense of self Jenny had temporarily enjoyed when improvising (which was not unlike the relaxation she felt when she took drugs) fuelled her appetite for more enduring ways to overcome what she experienced as the tyranny of her mind. It was this that fired her interest in the spiritual and philosophical traditions of the East, traditions that appeared to offer the possibility of inner peace and self-knowledge, and that led her to the teachings of Maharaj Ji.

Jenny's enthusiasm for the meditational practices he advocated become understandable when viewed against this background. By practising Maharaj Ji's 'Knowledge of God', Jenny was able to gain some degree of mastery over her mind. She experienced 'the permanently transforming effects of this meditation' as 'utterly beyond words'.[26] Her decision to join (and remain a member of) the Divine Light Mission was, at root, motivated by this experience, which she came to see as key to establishing a greater balance in her life with respect to her intellect and her spirit.

Jenny's experiences with the Divine Light Mission, for all that they were at times costly in personal terms, did offer her a way of living that allowed her to bypass the mind and be open to the intuitive. Adopting the core practices espoused by Maharaj Ji was also a valuable step in her progress toward becoming the better person she aspired to be. These core practices – meditation, speaking the truth, lending a hand, keeping one's mind and heart clean and clear – were ones, she said, 'I practised earnestly and sincerely for some years, and it was good for my soul – if rather less good for my bones. Eventually I found that it all became a part of me, embedded in my unconscious, and that too was good. So, I'm relatively unmoved by remarks about cultish delusions – the best can always be made of any situation.'

Although Jenny ultimately parted company with the Divine Light Mission, over time she came to understand that many of the experiences she'd had as a follower of Maharaj Ji were necessary for her. In 1982 she wrote, 'For the past year or so have been licking my wounds, and thinking what a fool I've been. Except of course that I can think of no other way that would have had such an effect on me, to make me really appreciate the things that really matter in human relationships and give me a solid footing inside.'[27] Years later that understanding had deepened and was leavened with self-deprecating humour: 'I took my spiritual life very seriously, which one must before one can laugh a bit at it. So, I couldn't wait to get out of the university. I was having a wonderful, marvellous, idiotic time. Needless to say, I would never do it again, but what I learned in the next few years, really . . . if I was such a fool that I didn't know all that, I needed to learn it.'

11

Homecoming

Having parted company with the Divine Light Mission, Jenny began to make connections with old friends. Among the first was composer Dorothy Freed, whom she had first met at the Cambridge Summer School in the early 1960s. Dorothy's day job was as a music librarian at Victoria University, and she was able to offer Jenny assistance in a couple of ways. First, she secured Jenny a few weeks of work in the library, providing her with useful occupation and a little income. She also helped Jenny find a place to live.

Dorothy's good friend Jacque Power – with whom 'Dorothy used to play cards and tell jokes and generally have a good time in the evenings' – had a home in Pukerua Bay, thirty kilometres north of Wellington. Jacque's husband Gerard had been posted to Auckland, and just when Jenny needed a place to live their house had become available. Jenny moved in, bought an ancient Mini-Minor (christened Annabelle, and with 'a hole that, if I hadn't covered it with a bit of wood, I would have got wet feet') and roamed the Kāpiti Coast, scouring second-hand shops for furniture and crockery, appliances and floor coverings. 'Praise be, that car never let me down,' Jenny recalled.

A short time later, the house next door became available for purchase.

'I heard about this,' Jenny said, 'and looked over the fence and thought a little place like that would do me just fine. I never even put my nose inside the door; I could tell that this was the place for me.' Jenny, however, had no capital and only meagre income from the rent paid by the Divine Light Mission on her Brooklyn property; it was enough for her to live on but certainly not enough to secure a mortgage. She did approach a lawyer she knew in an attempt to raise a loan, but was unsuccessful. Then one morning Jacque phoned her. 'I said, "Where are you?" She said, "I'm in Wellington. I've come down to get you a mortgage." I said, "What? How did you know about that?" And she said, "I had a dream." In the dream she was told to come down to Wellington and get Jenny a mortgage. Before midday that same day she got me a mortgage from her lawyer . . . Extraordinary.'

Jenny's tumbledown cottage in Te Pari Pari Road on the northern boundary of the Pukerua Bay settlement was to be home to her for the next forty years. Its front windows faced north-west, offering a view across the Rauoterangi Channel to Kāpiti Island. Most of the island, once home to Ngāti Toa chief Te Rauparaha (whose haka 'Ka Mate' Jenny led as captain of her high school hockey team), had for many years been a nature reserve and bird sanctuary. When the winds turned suddenly to the south or clouds poured in from the Tasman Sea, the outlook could change in minutes. The sunsets were often glorious. Jenny said, 'I felt about Pukerua Bay the way I'd never felt about any other physical place. I felt this was my home. It was my tūrangawaewae.'

That sense of homecoming had been a long time in the making. Jenny recalled:

When I was at school in Illinois in America one of my fondest teachers was Justine Bleeks, an artist who taught the art class. She could do a bit of everything, and she taught us a bit of everything. Every six weeks we'd have another block: six weeks of signwriting; six weeks of pottery; six weeks of oil painting. I did this great big oil painting in the middle of Illinois – no sea for many, many miles; most people there had never seen the sea – and here's me painting this coast, with great rocks and close-up sea. This [painting] ended

up on my headmaster's wall – he took it home and put it above his
fireplace. And when my parents eventually decided to go on a world
trip, they visited my headmaster Lee D. Piggott and got their photo
taken beside the painting. I realised at some stage what I had painted
was that coast, below my place at Pukerua Bay. Just along the flat
are two or three big rocks, sort of like landmarks; I recognised that I
had painted that out of my dream vision of missing my homeland.
By then I wasn't surprised that I had actually painted this painting,
and recognised that's what it was.

With a place of her own from which to put down roots, Jenny began
to rediscover her love of the arts. Not long after moving in, she wrote to
Bruce Greenfield: 'I've found myself returning to art as the only thing
I seem able to do that feels worthwhile.'[1] In a poem from that time,
'Honing in on the Mean', Jenny celebrates the artist's work and (in an
echo of W.S. Broughton's 'Epithalamia') aligns this work with service,
acknowledging that to make art requires a kind of surrender of self to
the act of creation:

What more ultimate response to life
Than the supreme, carefree act
    of creation through love
Yet how terrible the sentence
    in this divine indulgence
    of desire set free:
The artist, perforce
    dies to be reborn, lost anew
    in a world, a web
    of his own making.
And yet may well be an excellent reason
For sticking to the truth.

Yet some might say there's a higher art,
    born possibly from a need to serve:

Could it spring out of thanks,
    from a personal joy
    absolutely bound to show itself?
Beyond any joy in the act of creation,
    flow of inspiration,
    feeling of shapes,
    love of colour, tone, texture?
Beyond all pleasure in skills learned,
    tasks accomplished, work well done?

Would it polish to the finest as a matter of course,
    perfection its nature, not its goal?
Would it need to seek the new,
    the original, the meaningful?
Or might it, embedded in the source of these,
    yearn only for a deeper
    expression of itself,
    honing in
    on the golden mean?[2]

From her perch above the sea, Jenny found a peace that had eluded her for some years. 'It was,' she said, 'sort of like things started falling into place in a rather recognisable way. When you're looking for something, something will happen, because you've made a space for it.'

She was delighted to find that Cecilia Wilson, now married to poet Louis Johnson, had also recently moved to Pukerua Bay. Jenny and Cecilia enjoyed an easy companionship, and Louis, whom Jenny had first met in Wellington before leaving for Europe, was great company. Cecilia said, 'She and Louis always got on really well and she really liked my children.'

Jenny and Louis's shared interest in poetry was a significant part of their friendship. Jenny said, 'I used to see his work just after he'd written it; he used to start writing poems when everybody else went to bed. So, he'd be there with it in the morning . . . I started writing poetry and I showed him what I had written, too.' Louis was collegial and supportive, and Jenny fondly recalled, 'He told me he thought I was writing "from the same impulse" that he was.'

Poetry wasn't the only thing they had in common. They also shared what Cecilia described as self-destructive tendencies: both ate too much, drank too much, smoked too much, didn't exercise. She recalled: 'Louis told me the doctor said to him, "You don't want to change; you won't change – you've chosen this. This is what happens." If they'd been sensible, they probably wouldn't have been artistic. They would have been accountants or something. It's part of what they are.'

In her early days in Pukerua Bay Jenny had spent a lot of time with the Johnsons. Cecilia said, 'I remember we used to take her shopping every week – she'd often spend the day with us. She often came to our parties. We saw quite a lot of her.' [3] Cecilia and Louis's dinner parties were memorable. 'Louis was a born host and great cook,' Jenny said, 'and Cecilia produced splendiferous desserts.' Over meals and drinks she enjoyed the company of many of the Johnsons' literary friends: Maurice Gee, Bill Manhire and Marion McLeod, Bill Oliver, Harry Ricketts, Fiona Kidman, Rachel McAlpine, Philip Temple, Kevin Ireland, Lauris Edmond, Peter Bland, Alistair and Meg Campbell, Fleur Adcock, Ray Grover, Marilyn Duckworth. In this company of like-minded people, she joyfully returned to the kinds of conversations and intellectual community she had so missed during the preceding years.

Childhood

Jenny had produced almost no scored music for public performance since *Under the Sun* in 1971, and many believed she had abandoned composition. She had in fact continued to write music, but almost entirely songs for performance in the context of the Divine Light Mission, and with scores that rarely consisted of more than lyrics and perhaps a few chord symbols. Towards the end of her time with the Mission, she resumed composing notated music – music more closely aligned to the art music traditions in which she had been trained.

During 1980, around the time she returned to New Zealand, Jenny had come across Ursula K. Le Guin's *Earthsea* novels. She found them enchanting. It occurred to her that the stories would translate well to the stage, and she began to sketch ideas that might form the basis of a musical drawn from the books:

> I just jotted my ideas down for two pianos, and then I got around to writing to the publishers to see if I could get the rights for it. They wrote back a lovely letter saying how sorry they were, but somebody else had already bought them. I don't know how I would have paid for them, but I am glad I wrote to them because I got such a nice letter back. Well, I didn't think I could do a theatre work about *The Wizard of Earthsea* without having the rights, so I just decided to do a piece for two pianos which I called *Ring Round the Sun* – with obvious reference to David [Farquhar]'s piece. Not that the music is similar, but it's similar in tone, somehow; there's a playful side to it.[4]

Ring Round the Sun, a suite in six movements for two pianos, is a twenty-five-minute work. The music, which is entirely approachable, explores a range of moods. The opening 'Day', for example, is jolly, rarely venturing to minor sonorities, and skips along to brisk dance rhythms. It's followed by 'Thin Air', which is darker, slower, and with chords that hang in the air – Debussy comes to mind. In 'Night Music', the fifth movement, the whimsy of some of the earlier sections is replaced by something more sinister. Even so, the chromaticism of the opening does eventually give way to diatonic melodies harmonised with pop-music straightforwardness. There is music here that recalls Ravel or Debussy, or, given some of the decoration, is acquainted with somewhat earlier music; but it rubs shoulders with chord progressions and melodies that know about Paul McCartney and pop groups like Chicago. It's the kind of thing someone like Rick Wakeman, keyboard player with the group Yes, might have played (in his less garrulous moments).

Jenny likened the third movement, 'Sea Music', to the music of Vaughan Williams – 'it's full of those harmonic changes,' she said – and found in it echoes of her early orchestral piece *Pastorale* (which also owed a debt to the English composer's work, in particular *Fantasia on a Theme by Thomas Tallis*): 'The sense of that piece was that I had never before heard a piece that went on and on and on and was just so glorious – because you don't have to stop; the music really takes you in this wonderful way. I tried to do that with those pieces.'

Jenny thought that it was with this suite that she began to write words to accompany her compositions: a kind of ekphrastic commentary from the composer, welcoming performers and listeners to the work. 'After I'd written those pieces,' she said, 'I felt moved to write a short poem that would go in between each section of the piece. In some of those words, you can get the sniff of *Earthsea*; there's one about houses that would jump upside down. With strange words you are obviously in a strange place.'

Towards the end of 1981, Roy Tankersley visited Jenny in Pukerua Bay. Roy had been a student of Jenny's at Victoria before undertaking postgraduate study at London's Guildhall. On his return to New Zealand in 1974, he had taken over as director of Wellington's Bach Choir, which, with support from the QEII Arts Council, was in the habit of commissioning a new choral work by a New Zealand composer each year. Roy asked Jenny to compose such a piece. 'I wasn't all that keen on doing it,' Jenny said. 'But Roy was fairly insistent and I just gave in.'[5] Roy suggested an a cappella piece, and Jenny set herself to work.

The first task was to find a text for the commission. 'I immediately thought, "What have I just written?" That's what I always do when I have something [new] to do, [ask myself] "What am I doing now? Can it be any help to me?"' Having recently completed the poems to go between the movements of *Ring Round the Sun*, she thought: 'That's it. They're nice poems to set for a little fantasy song cycle about childhood.' The result was the ten songs that make up *Childhood*. In the composer's note that introduces the published score, Jenny described the text as:

> . . . depicting an archetypal childhood – a day in the life of a small
> boy, from the 'inside out' so to speak. The words are the thoughts
> that pass through his mind, unconscious of any audience: his
> spontaneous joys, the things that puzzle and delight him, fragments
> of legend and nursery rhyme, hazy understandings of things his
> parents say – a world where magic, everyday reality and dream are

all bundled together. His parents appear briefly: in No. VII, Father tells a bedtime story and bounces him on his knee; and in the last piece, Mother sings to the sleeping child.[6]

Roy recalled, 'The beautifully handwritten score arrived by mail within three weeks. At the end of the score is the date: 10 January, 1982.' Roy visited Jenny a few weeks later to go over the music, along with the instructions she included with the score. 'The choir began learning it in February. It was a challenge.'[7] Jenny remembered that Roy had sung and recorded each section's part individually (that is, soprano, alto, tenor, bass; or SATB), and given cassette copies to all his choristers so they could learn their parts by ear as well as from the score: 'That, I thought, was a very good idea.'

In the performance notes she wrote to accompany *Childhood* – directions for the choir and their conductor – Jenny remarked that 'any choral virtuosity must be incidental, and not the focus of the performance. The focus is the feel of the song as conveyed by the meaning of the words – the dramatic event. All else is subservient to this.' She also emphasised the 'rather intimate, private-world, family-type feel of the music', and instructed, 'No robes please!'[8] In her final general note about the work, she in effect described the cycle: 'There is nothing of the grand choral style, no great serious or momentous music, nothing "spiritual", nothing "moving", except in a very gentle, simple, unsentimental way.'[9] In saying this, she described the tack her vocal music was to take over the next few years.

Childhood comprises ten short songs for four-part choir with texts by the composer. 'The first performance in Palmerston North was in the pleasantly reverberant acoustic of the Art Gallery,' Roy remembered. It was 'a stunning performance', according to the *Manawatu Evening Standard*, and the cycle was presented again a short while later in Wellington.[10]

The emotional character of the cycle ranges from mysterious and dark in 'Sometimes Things Just Disappear' or 'Hear the Great Ocean'; to jubilant in 'Cocks Crow'; to slightly crazed in 'They Danced All Night'; to the serene, ravishing beauty of the concluding 'There's a Time to Live'. The vocal sounds range equally widely: marvellous glissandi in 'Puss,

Puss, Pussy'; the sibilant mouth-percussion in 'Cocks Crow'; the comic rolled rrr's in 'They Danced All Night'; the laughter in 'Night Again.' All the colours of the rainbow. This considerable variety makes the music fascinating to listen to – there's no chance listeners might nod off – and was a quality Jenny deliberately courted:

> I've written a lot of song cycles, and when you are writing a song cycle you have the opportunity to create a number of little worlds for each song. I like to try and make each one different, so that it suggests a 'this' and a 'that'. And depending on what I've done for the songs preceding, by the time I get to the end I think about what I have *not* really done. I do like writing nice tunes but I haven't always written nice tunes, on purpose, because there is a lot of music that doesn't have nice tunes, and life is not always nice tunes. A cycle is an opportunity to put in, somewhere, a nice tune, just so you've got that side covered.

The cycle has been recorded by the Bach Choir under Roy Tankersley's baton (on *Prisms*, Kiwi Pacific, 1985), and twice by the New Zealand Youth Choir, directed by Karen Grylls: *On Tour in North America* (Manu, 1994) and *Winds that Whisper* (Morrison Trust, 2016). The final movement, 'There's a Time to Live', appears to have become a high-school choir favourite and is frequently performed. It's little wonder: this concluding lullaby is amongst the loveliest of Jenny's songs, with a melody of nursery-rhyme simplicity and concision journeying through a harmonic web that hints at something mysterious – perhaps marvellous, perhaps menacing – in the world outside. 'So hush, my baby', the song advises us, 'no need to wonder why; and I will sing a lullaby.'

Songs for singers

Childhood, which Jenny later confessed to being less than entirely happy with, seemed to mark an opening of the floodgates. New music began to emerge steadily from her little house above Pukerua Bay, much of it triggered by commissions, which came thick and fast for the next five or six years. But in 1982, the year of her full-time return to composing serious music, she completed a song cycle that was motivated not by a specific request but by her affection for the poetry of William Blake:

> I had not long left the Divine Light Mission, feeling finally there was just not enough love. Reading Patrick White, Shadbolt, and other New Zealand writers I felt I had found my true brothers, and I responded similarly to William Blake's poems, which I had of course read before, but there's nothing like personal experience to bring things home. The compassion, the true empathy for others in his poems, also his profound individuality and quirkiness, filled a deep need in my soul and I wrote *Through the World* simply because I was moved to, I had to, just for myself.

Jenny had Wellington-based mezzo-soprano Joan Howard-Jones in mind as she composed the music for solo voice with piano accompaniment. Joan, whom Jenny described as 'a singer of great warmth and humanity', prepared and performed the work privately for Jenny, but retired from public performance before the work could be staged. 'She apologised profusely for this,' Jenny said, 'and then knitted or crocheted me a lovely wool jumper and a holder for spectacles that I still carry.' The work was eventually presented in public ten years later, when Margaret Medlyn sang it in a 1992 Wellington recital, accompanied by Bruce Greenfield.

Through the World is a collection of fifteen songs making use of Blake's poetry, although subject to Jenny's refashioning impulses. 'Lovers of Blake,' she wrote in the notes that accompany the score, 'will observe that I have taken considerable textual liberties, using extracts here & there from longer poems, truncating many of the shorter ones, and in three cases merging two independent poems.'[11] She did not attempt settings of Blake's later, visionary poetry, admitting, 'I don't think I would quite know what to do with it.' Instead, she focused on his earlier verse, drawing on *Songs of Innocence* and *Songs of Experience*:

Blake was very much a poet of ideas – not the ideas of an abstract intellect however, but those of a flesh-and-blood man who observes deeply his own (& others') nature in the light of his own experience of life on this earth. The expression of his understanding was as natural and necessary to him as any other aspect of everyday life . . . His poems are as true and meaningful now as they were when he wrote them. Cruelty, envy, stupidity, greed and kindness, mercy, compassion, love, are still with us. Children still starve under bridges, people are still beaten and chained, babes and fiends are born, angels pass by, lambs frolic (I can see them now from my kitchen window). Tigers lurk, kids get sick of school, philosophers waffle, the church bumbles on, people differ, suffer, love, hate, laugh and weep.[12]

Jenny composed *Through the World* entirely intuitively – which is to say, not by adhering to any compositional system but instead composing 'by ear' – and as a result both her serious music background and her knowledge of popular music and other contemporary idioms are evident in these songs. Some of the harmonic choices in 'Tyger, Tyger' or 'I Wander Thro' & Who Will Exchange' or 'The Vision of Christ', for example, or the melodies of 'Can I See Another's Woe' or 'I Have No Name', could sit perfectly comfortably alongside songs by Randy Newman or Joni Mitchell. The contemporary tenor these choices give to the music emphasise the modern-day relevance Jenny found in Blake's texts. The melodic lines and accompaniment bear a resemblance to the gestures of folk music: diatonic melodies; often spare piano harmonies that frequently include open fifths; the jaunty, dancing accompaniment to songs such as 'Is This a Holy Thing to See' or 'Love Seeketh Not'. Jenny attributed these compositional choices to Blake's verse itself: 'His couplets,' she wrote, 'lend themselves to a folk-like treatment – in fact, they demanded it, I found.' She went on to caution interpreters of the work that 'The "light" treatment is deceptive, however: one must sing from one's heart of one's own human understanding for the performance to succeed. That is, human *and* musicianly qualities are required. If I personally have a musical philosophy, this is it.'[13]

Jenny's decision to set these texts was to some extent inspired by Benjamin Britten's affection for Blake's poetry and his song settings of the same. She had first encountered these as an undergraduate at Victoria, and later came across Britten's cycle *Songs and Proverbs of William Blake* (1965).[14] His 1943 *Serenade for Tenor, Horn and Strings* includes a setting of Blake's 'The Sick Rose' which Jenny described as 'one of the most perfect song-settings I know'. Her affection and respect for Britten's treatment of this poem – 'it could not be improved upon', she said – meant she did not attempt her own setting of it: 'I felt it would be superfluous and uncalled-for.'[15]

The musical implications of his texts seem to have been an important consideration to the poet himself. Jenny noted that Blake was said to have sung his shorter poems to tunes of his own invention, and Scottish poet Allan Cunningham reported that as Blake made the illustrated plates that complemented his poems, 'he mediated the song which was to accompany it; and the music to which the verse was to be sung, was the offspring too of the same moment.'[16] Blake's verse was *made* to be sung. Perhaps, too, the principled earthiness of his musings was especially important to Jenny so soon after her decision to step away from the Divine Light Mission. 'I like the stories about William Blake,' she said. 'He and his wife used to walk around the house stark naked, and once when a friend arrived, Blake pointed to his wife and said "A poor thing, but mine own." I just liked what he was saying and there's nobody like him.'

The music Jenny composed to set these words is mysterious and worldly and various. Musicologist Robert Hoskins identified parallels with Schubert's song setting in the cycle, and thought that in writing the work Jenny demonstrated her capacity to negotiate the psychological terrain of art song. 'In the setting of "The Lamb" for instance,' Hoskins said, 'she creates innocent music that joyously foams over into a rapturous moment of divine presentiment', a reminder of 'what the innocence of childhood feels like'. He contrasted this with her setting of Blake's 'The Tyger', music 'seized with a sudden access of preternatural energy. Each passage seems to gather and discharge an elemental force and it seems we are witnessing a creation being hammered in bronze or welded in a forge where the sparks fly.'[17] The simplicity of some of the texts and the directness of the melodies might lead some to think the cycle naïve. No, these are songs for grown-ups.

Bruce Greenfield, who has played *Through the World* on a number of occasions, expressed fondness for the cycle. 'There are some beauties sitting in there, some really good ones. I like that cycle very much.' He thought one of the reasons the songs are not often performed is because the music is so very challenging: 'There are very few people who can sing it. The piano part is bloody hard too, but it's great.'[18]

Working with text, both her own and that of others, was to be a significant feature of Jenny's compositional work over the next few years. In 1983, event designer (and budding pyrotechnician) Joe Bleakley worked with the support of Wellington City Council to stage the Sun Festival on the city's waterfront. By securing public funding, Bleakley was able to assemble a production crew of eighteen who were paid a weekly wage via the PEP scheme for the months leading up to the festival in December.[19] Together, they planned, prepared and ran rehearsals with schoolchildren, musicians and performers for the event.[20] For the music, Jenny said, 'there was no actual commissioning or contracting – Joe invited me, and I simply joined the festival staff for months as composer.'

Once on staff, Jenny composed what amounted to a cycle of secular hymns that celebrate the sun and its light: the *Sun Festival Carols*. Jenny wrote the music for the songs first. She explained, 'When the length of the piece is not so crucial – you just want it to sound more musical than to do with words or word-based – [you can] write the music first and then fit the words to the music, especially when it's not so wildly crucial what the words are going to be.' This was the approach she had used for many of the songs she composed during the previous decade: 'That's generally the way I've written pop music songs. I've written the music first [so] I've already got a bit of a tune . . . it can just be a few notes, because it's easy to change those things, and it's fun.'

Jenny's song lyrics for the *Sun Festival Carols* responded to the newly composed 'legend' the festival's writers, Jean Betts and Joe Bleakley, had dreamed up for the event, drawing on the physics of visible light and the colours of the spectrum. The seven stars chronicled in the legend were named for the constituents of white light as identified by Isaac Newton, and assume titular roles in Jenny's songs: Vulcan, Ochre, Azure, Henna, Jade, Gentian and Indigo. [21]

As well as the carols, Jenny composed seven processional pieces for the Sun Festival, one for each of seven floats carrying school-aged musicians and leading large groups of children to Wellington's Oriental Bay rotunda. There, supported by the Bach Choir, each group sang a carol to welcome their particular 'star' and acknowledge its qualities.

The songs are all quite straightforward, with largely diatonic melodies and strong, obvious rhythms. The accompaniments are, in places, a little more complex – hints of birdsong in the piano part for 'Henna', for example – but mainly conform to the kinds of harmonic strategies common to hymns and music for civic settings. Even so, there are delicious moments in the writing which, coupled with the generally optimistic texts, make this an attractive suite of choral music with appeal for modern-day non-specialist audiences – absolutely fit for purpose given the occasion for which the music was composed.

After the seven carols of welcome had been performed, a suite of electronic music was played over loudspeakers to accompany a fireworks display. Joe Bleakley had asked electronics whizz Tim Jordan to create the concluding music before bringing Jenny on board. 'When Joe said to me that he was getting Jenny to do the music,' Tim said, 'I must admit to being more than a little put out. However, as I got to know Jenny, I began to like her more and more. She and I would spend many days/evenings in my makeshift studio trying out various ideas for the seven tracks that we needed to make.'[22] Working collaboratively – Tim mainly programmed the synthesisers and ran the studio equipment, although he came up with some of the musical ideas, too – they recorded the electronic pieces that, when played on the night, triggered the fireworks that brought the event to a climax. Joe Bleakley often said that 'the fireworks provided percussion for that section of Jenny's music'.[23]

Roy Tankersley was once again on hand to assist with the performance. 'I rehearsed and directed the Bach Choir,' he recalled, 'which sang the carols accompanied by a wind band plus rock band placed on the rotunda.' As memorable as that (unrehearsed as a whole) first performance was – a cast of thousands, seven torch-lit parades with large, elaborate floats carrying young musicians on a balmy summer night; banners and costumes; musicians floating on pontoons; boaties (who got drunk) in the harbour dragging seven huge fireworks rafts (harbour parallels to the land parades) which at the end burst into flames – such occasions are ephemeral.[24] 'I was conscious of the once-only nature of the Sun Festival performance,' Jenny said, 'and decided I would try to write not just something that would work on the night, but songs that would last and be heard again.' In this she was entirely successful, and the songs have gone on to enjoy a life of their own.[25] Many school and church choirs have performed both the entire cycle and individual songs from it. Roy said, 'I have conducted about ten performances of the carols in various cities since then.'[26]

Over the next three or four years, Jenny was to compose songs which, like the *Sun Festival Carols*, used her own texts: *Dirge for Doomsday*, commissioned for the National Youth Choir (1984); and *Hymn for the Lady*, commissioned by the New Zealand Choral Federation (1984). She also wrote songs using the words of others, notably Edward Lear: *The Courtship of the Yonghy-Bonghy-Bò* (1985) for a-cappella choir, commissioned for and first performed ('wonderfully', Jenny said) by the visiting Cambridge University Chamber Choir under Richard Marlow; and *The Dong with a Luminous Nose* (1986) for soprano, piano and clarinet.

Interviewed in 1984 for the local *Kapi-Mana News*, Jenny described the music she was writing as 'very middle stream' and added that although she had always found it easy to imitate particular styles, 'you know in your gut when something real is happening'. The writer speculated that Jenny, a freelance composer for the previous three years, 'may be the only person in New Zealand making a living this way', and Jenny was happy enough to concede that there was no shortage of work.[27] Even so, making a living from commissions was not easily managed.

The Divine Light Mission had by this time vacated her house in Ohiro Road, but Jenny was able to install new tenants: 'I rented that out because it was a big place, too big for me on my own, and I lived on the rent when I couldn't get a commission. I always got commissions but the rate at which one was paid – and still it's not all that great – I imagine if you were married and trying to raise a family you couldn't really do it on local commissions.' While Cecilia Johnson remembered that Jenny lived in relative penury during her first years in Pukerua Bay, lack of money didn't seem to bother Jenny; she loved living alone and was happy enough to economise, when necessary, to maintain that life: 'I had the rent from my [Brooklyn] house and I just made sure it was enough, basically.'

As it happened, Jenny's return to full-time composition opened doors to a new avenue of work that would fascinate her, and prevent the cupboard from going bare.

12

Music for the Screen

All of her life, Jenny loved the movies. 'I watch a lot of films and I love film,' she said. 'Born again, I'll be a film composer, or something to do with films, whatever it is.' Her fascination with the cinema began in Timaru, 'as a kid, going to the flicks on Saturday afternoons – *Flash Gordon, Buck Rogers*. Then, in Levin, the American musicals: *Oklahoma!, My Fair Lady, Carmen Jones*.' As she grew older her tastes in film were to broaden and, in time, match the breadth of her taste in music. She didn't have a favourite film, but followed certain directors, eager to watch 'pretty much anything by Scorsese, Spielberg, Coppola, Ridley Scott, Ron Howard, Robert Altman, the Coen Brothers'. She had been an early adopter of colour television in the 1970s, and watching TV remained a consuming interest.

Inevitably, Jenny paid attention to the music that accompanied the action on the screen, and her taste in film scores was eclectic. She professed fondness for a broad sweep of film composers, ranging from early work by Erich Korngold and Bernard Herrmann, through composers such as Henry Mancini and Ennio Morricone and more recent practitioners including Alex North and Carter Burwell. She singled out Dave Grusin's work on *The Firm* and John Williams' score for *Schindler's List* as particularly fine work.

Jenny's brother Craig also loved the cinema, and made a career in the film world, training as a sound technician during the 1960s in Britain. On returning to New Zealand, he worked with John O'Shea at Pacific Films, collaborating with filmmakers Barry Barclay, Tony Williams and others. He was the sound technician on Roger Donaldson's 1977 *Sleeping Dogs*, a watershed moment in New Zealand cinema.[1]

Jenny's initial acquaintance with filmmaking was at high school by way of Morrow Productions:

> Bob Morrow was a Scotsman trained in film animation by Hanna Barbera, who had then moved to Levin to make his own educational documentaries. Bob worked and lived in a house pretty much next door to Horowhenua College with two younger Kiwis, filmmaker Mike Walker and composer Chris Small, who was an early Victoria University BMus graduate, thus one of the first students of Freddy and Douglas. But they were interesting local characters and if there were one or two of those, my mother would be sure to work out who they were and get to know them.

Lorna's skills as a painter meant she was able to get work with Morrow, painting in the cartoon backgrounds frame by frame. The cartoons were primarily advertisements to be shown in the cinema and, from 1960 when television broadcasting arrived, on TV.[2] 'Chris, when he wasn't doing stuff at school,' Jenny said of her Horowhenua College music teacher, 'was writing background music for these cartoons.'

Craig's work with John O'Shea at Pacific Films in the early 1970s led to Jenny's first work as a soundtrack composer. 'Craig rang me up and [asked] would I do the music for this *Equation*, which was a film about the aluminium process at Comalco.'[3] Jenny thought it sounded interesting and was happy to have a go. 'There wasn't a great deal to the music actually, a little bit of electronics which I did at the Victoria University Studio which was in its infancy. We had about four tape recorders I think and a few simple sound generators.' Jenny asked her flatmate, guitarist Tony Backhouse, to assist with the music. He called on drummer Mike

Fullarton, also a member of the band Mammal, and Bill Lake of the Wellington group the Windy City Strugglers to join them in the studio. 'We sort of improvised,' Jenny recalled, 'and went back into the control room and said to the others, "How would you like it? A bit more funk, this or that?" It wasn't a lot of work . . . It only involved suitable music for specific shots but it didn't involve any specific timings or anything like that.'[4] Craig wasn't entirely certain the music Jenny recorded was in fact used in the film, which was completed in 1972. Even so, it was a first small step into the world of composing music for the screen.

The Silent One

In 1984 Jenny was contracted by film director Yvonne Mackay and producer Dave Gibson to compose music for a feature film based on a novel by New Zealand author Joy Cowley. *The Silent One* tells the story of Jonasi, a deaf and mute Pacific Island boy who, isolated by his silence and the village priest's antipathy, befriends a rare white turtle.

Jenny had written incidental music for a number of stage and radio productions, and briefly dipped her toes into the world of soundtrack composition with *Equation*, but this was the first time she had to fully confront the complexities of writing for the screen. The challenges of film music composition – over and above simply preparing a score that works in its context – are considerable, and matters of synchronisation, as well as balancing diegetic, non-diegetic and meta-diegetic music and sound, were new concerns for her.

Training for composers wishing to enter the film music world is widely available these days, but in 1984 there was nothing of the kind offered in New Zealand. Jenny wasn't bothered by that, and said, 'I think hands-on is the best way of learning anything.' Besides, even if professional training had been available, there was no time. Jenny had been approached to compose the music very late in the piece, with filming completed and a hard deadline in place for concluding the post-production procedures. This left her only about six weeks to score the music. 'I don't know why they left it so late,' Jenny said. 'It was very daring of them.' All the more so, given that about forty minutes of music was needed for the ninety-five-minute film.

In the absence of training and experience, Jenny was left to look at movies and think about how others had managed the task of composing effective film music. Helpfully, the producers directed her attention to the 1983 film *Merry Christmas, Mr Lawrence*, with a soundtrack by Ryuichi Sakamoto. 'I loved it. It was great,' Jenny said. 'They were giving me a ballpark area in which they thought music could be written that would suit *The Silent One* and I entirely agreed with them.'[5]

Having accepted the soundtrack commission, Jenny confessed her first reaction was one of utter panic. 'I hadn't done any sync work before, and there were so many things to combine. I rang up all my friends and told them not to visit and went underground for six weeks.'[6] She had to work quickly – 'You haven't got time to dwell on things, whether this is the right note or not, you've got to work fast' – and didn't even have time to write the score out properly; the whole thing was done in pencil.[7]

The magnitude of the task was mitigated by the presence of diegetic music – Cook Islands drumming – in the print. The producers planned to include this in the finished film, so those sequences required no input from Jenny. To supplement the Cook Islands drums, she incorporated melodies from local songs into her score, and placed a pre-Christian Cook Islands chant over the opening shots of the deep blue sea, locating the action in the Pacific.

Jenny's considerable experience, and her versatility and familiarity with a wide range of musical idioms, gave her a broad palette from which to draw. Orchestral music was used in many spots, occasionally helped along by the addition of a synthesiser: 'I like the sound of synthesiser mixed in with orchestra,' Jenny said. 'It freshens it up a bit.'[8] She made extensive use of percussion instruments – xylophones, marimba, wooden drums – sounds she liked and that fitted the film's Polynesian setting. She also added a snatch of Chopin (from *Prelude No. 6 in B minor*), although 'It doesn't sound like Chopin at all and nobody has ever noticed it.'[9]

Some electronically generated music was needed for the soundtrack, and for this Jenny called on Tim Jordan, with whom she had collaborated on the Sun Festival. Working with Moog and Korg synths and an Alpha

Syntauri computer synthesiser (possibly the first one in the country, he thought), Tim was responsible for some of the sound effects – spooky electronic versions of natural phenomena (storm sounds and flying insects) for a hurricane scene – and producing the turtle calls. He also programmed the synthesiser Jenny played to 'freshen up' the orchestra.[10]

The final orchestral score was recorded by the Wellington Regional Orchestra directed by William Southgate, whom Jenny had met in Timaru when they were youngsters. Choir direction was again entrusted to Roy Tankersley, and the recording sessions, while presenting some technical challenges, proved an invigorating experience. 'With *Silent One* we got to the end of the booked session and it was about midnight and we still had about three quarters of an hour to finish the recording and the players were magnificent. They all agreed to stay, because they liked the music. It was brilliant.'[11]

In sum, Jenny's music for *The Silent One* made effective use of material that owed a debt to Sakamoto's film score, orchestral music that Jenny described as 'pop-Rachmaninov', and Cook Islands music. She was particularly fond of the score's Pacific elements, drawing attention to the 'strong Polynesian thing in it; I liked building in the Cook Islands singing into the soundtrack and making it integral. That was a real challenge.'[12]

The music is characterful and effective, and the producers were thrilled with the results. The lead actor's lack of speech meant the soundtrack needed to play a central role in conveying his emotions to cinema audiences. Director Yvonne Mackay believed the score achieved this, becoming the most important element in the film after the cinematography.[13]

Jenny's work on *The Silent One* opened doors to a number of other soundtrack opportunities. It was also recognised with the Best Film Soundtrack Award at the 1984 New Zealand Music Awards. Jenny was pleased, although typically self-effacing in her response: 'I like the music and it's kind of nice to feel that other people like it too.' She was most heartened by the reaction of the audience at the event: 'I'd forgotten that there were so many Māori people in the audience and then the Patea Māori Club let out this roar.'[14]

The success of *The Silent One*, and the productive working relationship Jenny established with Dave Gibson and Yvonne Mackay, meant they were soon at work on another collaboration: *Cuckooland*, a television show for children. With scripts by New Zealand children's author Margaret Mahy, the series followed the fantastic adventures of Petunia and her daughters Polly and Patch. Music and singing, in line with the emergence of MTV and the ubiquity of music video in the mid-1980s, were central to the series. The production values of *Cuckooland* corresponded to the more garish music clips of the day, all Day-Glo colours and lysergic visual effects. Jenny recalled: 'Songs were an integral feature and I think I wrote something like thirty. They are quite short songs, each of them in a different popular style. It was me who decided to . . . try and cover as many different kinds of popular styles as I could, just for fun.' Her wide range of skills and diverse experiences – 'you name it, I've done it' – were the perfect foundation for this kind of eclectic practice. Writer and film scholar Deborah Shepard suggested that this, along with Jenny's willingness to indulge her magpie tendencies, made her a 'perfect composer for film.'[15]

Jenny had paid a lot of attention to popular music during the previous decade. She had listened to David Bowie and Queen, the Carpenters and the Neville, Doobie and Allman Brothers, Roxy Music, Elton John. George Martin's arrangements for the Beatles were ear-opening, and the music of Björn Ulvaeus and Benny Andersson had made a strong impression. 'The songs of ABBA, for example, had it all over so many other songs; their arrangements, vocal and instrumental, had so completely "gelled". I knew from the start that ABBA's songs would last, and all these decades later . . . well, no need to crow.' She also recognised that, while her classical orchestration skills were well developed, it 'took a few years for me to develop much in the way of pop arranging skills. By the time I wrote the *Cuckooland* songs, I was much more aware of what was actually going on in pop songs and much better at arranging. Everything in all of these songs was pre-arranged and written out, and by then I was capable of covering a broad range of pop/rock styles.'

The series comprised six episodes, with four or five songs included in each show. Jenny liked Margaret Mahy's text – 'it's a crazy series and the words are mad, so it was really a lot of fun' – but found the song lyrics a little too close to Gilbert and Sullivan, 'so I changed the words to be quite a bit more like pop lyrics'.[16] Once completed, the songs were recorded with the help of session musicians and then captured on film: music videos, essentially. The rest of each episode, connective tissue that tied the songs together, was then filmed, providing a narrative arc for each show. At that point Jenny was called in to record incidental music for these linking passages, matching music to the final footage much as she had for *The Silent One*. 'God, did that happen fast! I did all that on keyboard synthesiser . . . I didn't really know a lot about [synthesisers], so it was kind of hit and miss.'[17] For these passages, Jenny recorded music that resembled the sounds of familiar instruments, while the sound effects for the shows – manic noises, cartoonish diegetic sound effects – were the work of musician and producer Dave Parsons. *Cuckooland* screened on New Zealand television in 1985 and, like *The Silent One*, picked up an award: a Gold Medal at the 1986 New York International Film and Television Festival.

These were busy years for Jenny. There was a further collaboration with Yvonne Mackay and Dave Gibson – an adaptation for television of Margaret Mahy's novel, *The Haunting*, in 1986 – and a string of documentaries: *Plants* and *The Neglected Miracle* with Barry Barclay in 1985; *Beyond the Roaring Forties* with Conon Fraser in 1986; and *The Gift* and *Images of New Zealand* with John King in 1986 and 1987 respectively.

Jenny was a well-trained, experienced and versatile composer, but there were still things she needed to learn in order to achieve good results with her film score work. Synchronisation issues, for example, posed a new technical challenge: 'If you are just doing a piece for a concert, well, you could have things happen any old time. It's the timing that is the real problem in films, and trying to write something that is reasonable music that also meets the timing [requirements].'[18] These concerns had been part of the fun with *The Silent One*, and proved to be so again for *Images of New Zealand*, a tourist film commissioned by the National Film Unit and directed by John King. Ten minutes long, but without commentary, it required careful control of durations so that the music matched the evolving images – Māori cultural performance, stockyard sales, a bio-tech lab, public transport, people playing sports – and sound effects that accompanied them. 'End-to-end music,' Jenny said, 'is not so easy . . .'[19]

Tight time frames – part and parcel of film work – were another challenge: 'The other problem with film composing is the pressure under which you have to work, because the composer is usually only ever called in at the end: you're the last person to make their input. The *Cuckooland* songs, which came first, were an exception.'

Thinking she might do film music for some years, Jenny set up a studio for herself at home. Managing the various kinds of recording and production gear necessary for capturing soundtracks, however, did not come naturally to her:

> I used to have a lot more electronic gear at Pukerua Bay than I ended up with, but I gave it away because it didn't behave for me. When you've got a deadline coming up and suddenly all your wiring is going to pot and you've no idea what is making it sound so dreadful . . . well, I'd just be screaming my head off in the middle of the night and keeping the neighbours awake, because I couldn't fix what was wrong.

But there were moments, too, when everything seemed to come together. Of preparing the score for *Beyond the Roaring Forties*, a documentary about New Zealand's subantarctic islands, Jenny said, 'I found that the music for that one came pretty easily because I related to it so much. Partly because on one of these islands, the only settlers who had actually lived there for some years, and then they had to leave because the life was just so impossible, came from the Shetland Islands. And that's where my mother's family came from.'[20] She added, 'I think your roots often come out . . . and there is quite a kind of quasi-Celtic strain in some of that music.' Jenny liked this soundtrack so much she reworked parts of it to feature in the first movement of the later concert piece *Three Celebrations for Orchestra*.

Another rewarding aspect of soundtrack work was the opportunity to collaborate with energetic and creative people. Over the course of the three screen projects she completed with Yvonne Mackay and Dave Gibson, she came to respect their opinions and instincts, and found it easy to work with them:

> I'd done all that music theatre sort of stuff before, but of course I had done it all [myself], and when it came to productions it was me who had the final say because in that world – I don't know if it's all that healthy, necessarily – but what I said went . . . I was in charge. And when it's a film, well, you're not in charge. You're in charge to the extent that you're the one who creates the sounds, and you have the final say in the recording, but you and the director are a team, and you have to work together.[21]

Working collaboratively in this way could lead to better results, too. During work on *The Silent One*, Dave Gibson wanted to hear mock-ups of the music Jenny was scoring. 'Once or twice, he hated something I did for one particular shot or sequence and on those occasions, well, I'd already learned to trust his instincts so I would just go away and have another think. It only happened two or three times. On every occasion I ended up with something that even I knew was a lot better than what I'd started out with.'[22]

With the benefit of hindsight and experience, Jenny felt she may have been guilty of putting too much material into her film scores: 'I think when I did write film music, mostly I wrote too much music for a situation. I would have, had I been more sparing with my notes, had an effect that might have looked better years later. Nowadays I hear stuff that I did for some film [sound] tracks and I think: "I've used too many notes; I've treated it more as a concert piece than I needed to".' She likened the differences between film music and concert music to the distinctions between poetry and prose; film music, in Jenny's view, presented composers with the opportunity to strip back their writing to the barest gestures: 'The way Picasso's work changed as he got older and became little gestures that would mean a whole world . . . Well, film music can be like that too.'

'I'm not one of those people who looks down their nose at film music,' Jenny said. 'I don't know that I always did it very successfully, but during the time that I did spend in films I liked that challenge, the technical challenge side of it. Of course, once you've done it a few times you think, "Oh well, I can do that now; I'll do something else".'[23] True to form, Jenny did move on to other things, and 1987's *The Gift*, a twenty-seven-minute film celebrating Aotearoa's national parks, was the last film score she composed. She remained fond of some of this screen music, however, singling out *Beyond the Roaring Forties* and especially *The Silent One*. 'I like *The Silent One* music immensely,' she said. 'I really like it. And I've listened to it often, just the music.'

Bruce Greenfield shared her high opinion of this score: 'I think her best work, strangely enough, is her film music for *The Silent One* . . . It's where she allows herself to be bluesy and yet interesting and . . . I think, for me, that's some of her most successful music. She would have made a fabulous film composer; she could have been a New Zealand John Williams, if only she'd got onto that focus.'[24]

13

Popular Music for the Concert Hall

Composing film music was all-consuming work, and when a project arrived it required full-time attention: 'To write a film you have to drop everything for, like, six weeks. People who have already got other jobs can't do that.' Fortunately, Jenny wasn't constrained by a day job, but there was a feast-or-famine quality to these projects, and Jenny had time for other composing work between film score commissions:

> At the same time that I was working on the films, I was also getting quite a lot of commissions for concert music. Most of the concert music that I wrote was rather light, which I just felt like doing; rather light music. And besides, I think serious concerts can just get a bit too much. I was deliberately introducing a rather pop influence or element into serious concert music and actually the audience has always loved it. The critics didn't always like it, but the audiences always loved it.[1]

After the first public performances of *Childhood*, concert music commissions began to flow in, slowly at first but with increasing regularity over the next few years. The first of these came in 1982: *Piece for Wall*, a tongue-in-cheek graphic 'score' – more of a poster, really – for a Turnbull Library exhibition (*Scores of Sounds: Facets of New Zealand Composition Since 1940*); and a short work for choir and orchestra to open Wellington's Summer City Sizzle Festival that year. Rather more substantial was a 1985 commission from the Wellington Regional Orchestra: music for a family concert to be included in the New Zealand International Festival of the Arts the following year.

Jenny decided to make a setting of Hans Christian Andersen's fairy tale 'The Nightingale' and wrote a text based on the 1894 telling of the story from the English-language collection *The Yellow Fairy Book*. After some reflection, she decided to have a narrator tell the story of the nightingale. 'I didn't just use a narrator because it would help kids to understand,' she said, 'but because I thought it was the best way to do it. And that was why I used one in *Earth and Sky* and in *Under the Sun*, as well.'

At close to twenty-five minutes, and scored for orchestra, it was a considerable undertaking and the most substantial single work Jenny had committed to the page since *Under the Sun*. The music illustrates the action effectively, and attractive melodies married to frequently lush harmonies were perfect complements to the narrator's gently droll story. The flute soloist is given plenty to do and, corresponding to the programmatic character of the music, there's an abundance of 'birdsong' throughout *The Emperor and the Nightingale*.

Birdsong deployed in musical contexts has a long history. In art music traditions the practice has been around since at least the fourteenth century, and has found its way into the work of composers including Beethoven, Handel, Delius, Rimsky-Korsakov, Liszt, Milhaud, and of course Olivier Messiaen. In New Zealand the tradition has been continued by composers such as William Southgate, Eve de Castro-Robinson, Gillian Whitehead, Christopher Blake and Jenny. Douglas Lilburn, Ross Harris, Miriama Young and John Rimmer incorporated avian calls into their electro-acoustic works.[2] The incorporation of birdsong into music has a rather longer history in Aotearoa among Māori, and there are several taonga pūoro – the karanga weka and the kōauau, for example – that can be used to imitate birds.

Jenny attributed her use of birdsong to her encounters with Messiaen. 'There are things about him,' she said a few years after his death, 'that have become part of me and I think the bird thing is certainly part of that. Birdsong comes naturally to me . . . but I don't know if it ever would have if I hadn't got fond of Messiaen's music. Before that I think I would have wondered how to utilise a bird.'[3]

Birdsong first appeared in Jenny's music in 1966, with *For Seven*: 'The G sections in *For Seven* are definitely, in my mind, crazy birdsong . . . completely manic birdsong and somehow that was helping me survive Germany.'[4] But incorporating the language of birds into her music wasn't usually a premeditated act:

> When I think about the occasions on which I've been drawn to use birdsong, it's not so much that I've sat down and worked it out, 'Oh, I'm going to use birdsong for this,' it's just that it comes and I find myself doing it and suddenly afterwards: 'Ah! Birdsong.' You just sort of know when you're doing it, you know it's birdsong, but you didn't sit down and plan it. It just comes. I have an affinity for it; or it has an affinity for me.[5]

The inclusion of birdsong in *The Emperor and the Nightingale* was quite deliberate, however, although as was usual for Jenny the bird calls were synthetic, the product of her imagination. 'All my own,' she said. 'For Messiaen it was always real birdsong, but for me I seem to have birdsong in my veins, can concoct a bird call from just about anything.'

Jenny's orchestration for the work, which establishes interlocking rhythms among the various orchestral strata as the nightingale twitters and peeps above, keeps things motoring along. The forward momentum those rhythms give to the work, along with the intermittent exotic effects that decorate the music (perhaps reminiscent of Rimsky-Korsakov, or maybe even Albert Ketèlbey), make it perfect fare for a family concert. The whole piece would sit comfortably alongside similar concert works suited to young audiences – Prokofiev's *Peter and the Wolf*, or Saint-Saëns' *Carnival of the Animals* – and since its premiere under the direction of William Southgate (and with New

Zealand comedian Billy T. James as the narrator) it has gone on to enjoy many performances by regional and youth orchestras around New Zealand.[6]

Three Celebrations

The years 1984 to 1987 were to be some of the most visibly productive of Jenny's life. As well as six or seven projects for the screen, there were numerous vocal music requests and half a dozen major commissions for soloists, chamber groups and orchestra. Following the Wellington Regional Orchestra commission for *The Emperor and the Nightingale* was one from the New Zealand Symphony Orchestra: a concert piece to mark its fortieth anniversary in 1986.

Three Celebrations for Orchestra comprises three movements: 'Journey Through Mountain Parklands', 'At the Bay' and 'A & P Show' – parochial titles for sure, but harnessed to attractive music that sweeps along with plenty of vim. The first movement is energetic, propelled by relentless low strings and punctuated by dramatic gestures from massed brass. Parts of the movement had begun life as film music (in *Beyond the Roaring Forties*, completed earlier that year), which Jenny, with characteristic parsimony, had reworked for the concert hall. The second movement is a little more tranquil; the central section, a kind of bucolic waltz, does get going a bit but on the whole the mood is elegiac. Like the first movement, 'At the Bay' is haunted by echoes of music from the *Roaring Forties* documentary. The final movement, which opens in a jaunty triple metre before settling into a cheerful 4/4, brings Aaron Copland's music to mind.[7]

Some reviewers were nonplussed ('Too American', apparently), but audiences were won over. Perhaps the optimistic directness of this music appealed to New Zealanders in much the same way as Copland's uncomplicated nationalism appealed to audiences in the United States. Jenny received a letter from someone she'd never met, thanking her for *Three Celebrations* and 'relating how the music had made him weep when he heard the NZSO at a concert on his return after years abroad'.

Smiling, she recalled attending a Wellington performance of the work where she overheard, during the applause, a fellow concertgoer say, 'I'd rather have that than Lilburn.'[8] Lilburn had composed music that he hoped would reflect its New Zealand origins; it might have been this quality that concertgoers responded to in *Three Celebrations*. Jenny was not oblivious to the potentially nationalistic overtones of this music, particularly during the first movement: 'In my mind a sort of iconic piece, as Kiwi as Horse, my neighbour's cat.' And she was entirely comfortable writing music that celebrated her homeland: 'I don't mind nationalism – I love my country and I'm proud of it (and us). Civic or triumphalist jingoism is another matter. That's hollow, empty stuff – I think my music is full.'

Music commissions with explicit links to New Zealand were to be a feature of Jenny's work during this period. The previous year she had completed *Goodnight, Christchurch* (for three orchestras, jazz band and four hundred recorders) and *New Wellington March* (music her former landlord Gerard Power suggested she write for the Royal New Zealand Navy Band). The same year as the NZSO commission there was film music for *Images of New Zealand* and *Beyond the Roaring Forties*; and in 1987 the soundtrack for *The Gift*, which chronicled the country's national parks. Coming in the midst of so much music related to domestic themes and locations, *Three Celebrations* – composed to salute the national orchestra – also contained gestures that suggest a kind of musical homage to Aotearoa.

In the liner notes to the Naxos recording of the work, Jenny itemised some of the scenes the music might recall: 'Imagine breath-taking low-flying aerial vistas opening up from peak to peak, or driving through such a landscape, dwarfed by towering alps, with this music blasting away on your car stereo,' she wrote of the first movement; or, for the final movement 'A & P Show', 'a typical Kiwi Agricultural and Pastoral fair, with sideshows, merry-go-round, Ferris wheel and other rides, displays of farm machinery, and competitions for baking and preserving, homegrown vegetables, prize animals.'[9]

As comfortable as Jenny may have been with music intended to evoke an image or spark some kind of association, she was also very clear that

any response listeners had to her music was of their own making, and not
the result of deciphering a musically coded message from the composer's
psyche. What people did (or did not) respond to, she thought, was
mainly 'to do with emotional connections – our own personal or familial
memories or our cultural history'. Conditioning of that sort makes our
responses to music subjective, personal and not hostage to the composer's
(or critic's or commentator's) directions or suggestions.

Such convictions about the very subjective nature of music had made
Jenny wary of notions of an identifiable national music – music of which
an astute listener might be able to say, 'Ah, New Zealand music.' As she
saw it, if music, *any* sort of music, was written by a New Zealander, it was
New Zealand music. Which is to say, New Zealand music was defined
not by any inherent quality it may possess but simply by its provenance.

A more specifically 'New Zealand' music appears to have been
something Douglas Lilburn sought. His essays 'A Search for Tradition',
'A Search for a Language' and 'Search for a Sound' lay out, among other
things, the importance he placed upon the development of a national
music. It was his belief that such music had a role to play in the project of
'the discovery of our own identity'.[10] Jenny respected Lilburn enormously
and was extremely fond of some of his music – works she considered
'decidedly of this place'. She thought the D Major *Sonata* (for violin)
was 'spot on; it hits the nail on the head . . . I like that tremendously',
and said of his early piano preludes: 'Those first four piano preludes
are probably among the best things he ever did.' However, she was less
convinced by some of his more explicitly 'New Zealand' compositions.
Landfall in Unknown Seas, for example, wasn't music Jenny immediately
warmed to, and the perceived nationalism of the work had something
to do with that: 'It's a bit too civic for me, in a way. And he is very self-
consciously a composer.'[11]

It's possible the public's favourable response to *Three Celebrations*
was attributable not to its 'New Zealand' qualities (whatever they might
be), but because it sounded a bit like the kind of orchestral music
general audiences heard most often: film music. A few years later Jenny
remarked that non-specialist audiences – people without advanced
musical training – might think 'a classical composer would be someone

who wrote music rather like what . . . Carl Davis or John Barry might write for a film, or what you might write for a film, and that concert music would be something like that'. Contemporary concert music, she went on to explain, was often difficult and complex. 'It intrigues me,' she concluded, 'that what most people would think of as a classical composer hardly exists. There is hardly anybody who does write the kind of music for concerts, that they would write for a film.'[12]

A curious footnote to *Three Celebrations*, and one that says something of Jenny's attitude to work successfully completed, concerns an invitation she received a few years later. 'One day Johnny Marks (whom I did not and still do not know) phoned me from England offering a commission for a sort of "iconic Kiwi" orchestral piece for a proposed new album,' Jenny recalled. 'I felt I had already written the piece he was looking for with the first movement of my *Three Celebrations for Orchestra*, but he was not interested in that, so I declined.' It would seem that while she was happy enough to reuse musical materials in different pieces, she was reluctant to prepare a new composition that simply duplicated, in its effect, a work already completed.

There were other invitations she was more than willing to accept. Jenny's old friend Bruce McKinnon, along with fellow percussionist Wayne Laird and pianists Michael Houstoun and Diedre Irons, had performed Bartók's *Concerto for Two Pianos, Percussion and Orchestra* with the Auckland Regional Orchestra. Houstoun subsequently persuaded Peter Nisbet, General Manager of the New Zealand Symphony Orchestra, to programme the work. Nisbet was also eager for the quartet of Houstoun et al. to perform Bartók's chamber version of the same piece (a sonata version, which Bartók composed before he drafted the concerto) in some of the nation's smaller centres. Needing a companion piece for the Bartók *Sonata* to complete the programme for those chamber concerts, Bruce (with assistance from the Arts Council) commissioned *Music for Four* from Jenny.

Orchestral percussionists play a lot of instruments – their houses tend to subside under the weight of stored drums and gongs and marimbas and timpani and what-have-you – so determining the precise forces Jenny would write for required some negotiation. 'I think we talked a bit about what instruments she wanted to include and what I actually owned or could borrow,' Bruce said.[13] He recalled that 'Jenny had been writing music influenced by pop music and I think there was some conversation about going that way.' The resulting work was played to very full houses in Nelson, Wellington and Tauranga, and was recorded by Radio New Zealand for broadcast.

Lasting about twelve minutes and consisting of three movements – 'Dolly-Bird', 'Little Song with Cakewalk', and 'Hey-down' – *Music for Four* is cut from similar cloth to *Three Celebrations,* although without the grandness and drama of that piece. A brightly cheerful first movement comprises simple and direct music with folk-like clarity and good humour; breezy and toe-tapping, it sounded a sharp contrast to the darker, sombre work by Bartók it partnered in concert. That had been Jenny's intention: 'to write something completely different from the Bartók, but that would sit well beside it; something completely fresh, like the young wife of an older, more sober husband.' The second movement begins gently, music of tranquil grace and hymn-like dignity, but the stately 'little song' of the title soon enough gives way to a jaunty cakewalk, propelled by stride piano and imbued with the insouciance of a Scott Joplin rag. The final movement – snare drum tattoos, perky tuned percussion and lively interplay between the pianos – closes the work out with suitable élan.

Music for Four is so very different from *Sonata for Two Pianos and Percussion* – even allowing for the brio of Bartók's final movement – one wonders what it was like for audiences hearing the two side by side. Bruce McKinnon thought they worked well together. Having performed Jenny's earlier and more challenging *For Seven*, he contrasted it with the new work, saying, '*Music for Four* came from the other side, being popular in style, but still having enough depth to sit comfortably in a classical concert.' Jenny had described herself, during the 1980s anyway, as 'a composer who for a time refused to "grow up", declaring that writing and performing music should be "enjoyable"'.[14] *Music for Four,* an attractive and ebullient work, is consistent with that characterisation, and as such offered a sunny complement to the darker fare Bartók was offering on the other side of the programme.

A further chamber music commission in 1986 came from the
Zelanian Ensemble. The group – of flute, clarinet, viola and piano –
specialised in performing New Zealand music, and worked with the
New Zealand Music Federation for whom they were touring both in
New Zealand and in the United States. As with *Three Celebrations for
Orchestra*, Jenny decided to use music already composed for the screen
as a jumping-off point. 'I called it *Jazz Themes* not so much because the
themes are suitable for improvisation (I don't think they really are), but
because in the third movement I gathered together a bunch of jazzy little
film stings from the TV series *Cuckooland*, making them into a small pop
sonata-form movement that I thought worked beautifully.'

The music may not lend itself to improvisation particularly, but
there are certainly plenty of jazz-like elements woven into the score: the
melodies often make use of bluesy gestures, and the harmonic games of
some of the movements aren't a million miles from jazz. Rae de Lisle,
pianist with the Zelanian Ensemble, said, 'I'd always loved jazz but
wouldn't have the first inkling about where to begin to play any, and
there it was – all sort of written down – and I rather loved it.'[15]

The mood varies considerably across the work's five (quite short)
movements, the energetic opening 'Zelania' movement flowing into the
gently swinging 'Chaconne' before the third movement's jolly collection
of fragments from the *Cuckooland* scores. The penultimate 'Reverie' is
contemplative, a little oasis of calm before the peppery 'Gypso', which
boasts enough impassioned double-stops from the viola and frantic
clarinet lines to bring the Balkans to mind. 'Chaconne', sweetly melodic
and making use of elements of canon, is unusually contrapuntal for
Jenny, whose writing at this time tended more to concerted gestures. The
movement's weaving lines offer an attractive textural contrast. The
duration of the entire work is just ten minutes, so none of the music
outstays its welcome. Rae de Lisle recalled, 'It was great fun. We took
that all over the place – played it a lot in America and various places –
and we would always end our programmes with it, and people always
liked it. We took it into schools a lot, because they loved it. It was a very
user-friendly piece to have in a concert.'[16]

The Rock Sonatas

A few years earlier, in 1984, Bruce Greenfield had begun teaching pianist Eugene Albulescu, a young Romanian whose parents had moved to New Zealand to escape the Ceaușescu regime. Albulescu was a remarkably talented and hard-working student – Bruce described him as the most exceptional pianist he'd had the privilege to work with – but he had little interest in either classical music of the twentieth century, or New Zealand music. Bruce decided to commission a work for him from Jenny. Albulescu recalled:

> I enjoyed quite a lot of different types of music . . . On one hand I
> was a teenager and interested in Romantic piano music and classical,
> but mostly I took on Chopin and Liszt and didn't have that much
> interest in things like Stravinsky and Bartók. But on the other hand,
> I had a pretty big interest in rock music because I was a student at
> Rongotai College and so of course synthesisers and Van Halen . . . it
> was the 80s. So, Bruce's idea was to work with Jenny to write a piece
> for me that would excite my interest. Their way was: 'Why don't we
> write a rock sonata? We'll give him what he likes but simultaneously
> there will be some interest in new music.'[17]

The rock sonata Jenny composed for Albulescu made the kinds of virtuosic demands customarily expected of a sonata for solo piano, but using the melodic, harmonic and rhythmic language of the popular music that had so interested her over the previous fifteen years.[18] During that time Jenny had formulated what she called an unconscious theory of rock, an informal set of understandings that made theoretical sense of the popular music she liked so much. In essence, she had concluded that rock music, in some ways at least, reversed values central to classical music. For example, the sub-dominant cycles common to rock ('downward' motion from sub-dominant [or IV chord] to tonic [I chord] and pervasive in blues music) were a reversal of the dominant cycles ('upwards' resolution from dominant [V chord] to tonic [I chord]) more common in classical music. Richard Hardie explained: 'When McLeod first formulated these ideas, she tried an experiment with a work by Bach. She took the *Prelude No. 1 in C Major* and inverted all harmonic root movement (while retaining the seventh harmonies) and found that she came out with a very acceptable rock progression. She found that dominant-7 and diminished-7th chords now resolved in quite different ways, familiar to her ears as a standard blues-gospel type progression.'[19]

Jenny first actively listened to rock after her return from Europe, and began to play the music a few years later. 'But to my surprise,' she said, 'I was not very good at it, when I had fairly easily been good at every other kind of music I had met. That presented a new challenge. My sense of rhythm was the weak spot; my own spontaneous rhythms were too old-fashioned.' Playing along with records, and jamming with the musicians in the rock band she had dragooned for *Under the Sun*, had helped develop her feeling for the music. Subsequently, she 'pursued rock for some years with my own band – not commercially, though we did a beach tour – until the idioms had worked themselves into my bones, so that things came naturally and I felt more in tune with the spirit of my time.'

As much as Jenny relished the challenges rock music posed for her as a performer, that was not primarily why she was first drawn to the Beatles and the Rolling Stones; she'd listened to the music because she really liked it: 'My appreciation was full-blooded and enthusiastic. I danced to it too, sometimes all night long.' Her sustained engagement with this music during the 1970s had been fuelled by her growing intuition that pop and rock offered something valuable to her own practice as a composer. 'I had also sensed,' she said, 'the future possibility of a kind of pop-rock crossover classical or art music, which did come to pass, more or less, in my "classical" pop music of the 1980s.' But this was able to occur only once the rock and pop idioms were as natural to her as was the art music she had loved and studied for so long:

> Only after I had learned to improvise rock music was I able to compose and write down, if necessary, music in the same idiom.

And only after these techniques had become second nature was my unconscious mind then in a position to fuse all this with the rest of the musical know-how inside me, i.e., the repository of musical habits acquired from my beloved mentors of the past – Bach, Mozart, Schubert, Chopin and Debussy to name the most important.[20]

Three Celebrations for Orchestra, an obvious example of Jenny's 'classical pop' music, primarily owes a debt to the conventions of film music, and perhaps the light symphonic music of the previous century. However, popular music has clearly left traces on it: the four-square rhythms, triadic harmonies and syncopated diatonic melodies of the first movement are all somehow redolent of the pop music heard on the radio during the 1960s and 1970s. This kind of appropriation, which was by this stage intuitive rather than conscious, seems to have found an even fuller expression in *Rock Sonata No. 1*. With this work, Jenny achieved an effective rapprochement of the materials of popular music and the formal designs and performance strategies of the classical world.

Like a great deal of popular music, *Rock Sonata No. 1* is quite straightforward: the melodies are ones you could whistle walking to the bus, and the harmonies are pretty friendly, rarely confronting listeners with anything more than mild dissonance. At the same time, the music is organised along art-music lines: two of the three movements are in sonata form, with clear subjects, transition themes, classical-type development sections and so forth; and the work makes serious demands on the soloist.

Eugene Albulescu's proclivities, and his virtuosity, were very much in Jenny's mind as she composed the music. 'I was primarily aware of Eugene as a great Liszt performer,' she said. 'He hadn't gone to America yet when I wrote the piece, but his [later] recordings of Liszt won big prizes. That's why – these sorts of things can make you smile – but though it's a pop piece, passages of it are just as difficult as many classical pieces are, and it took him years to play it. It cost him a big effort to learn to play that piece.'[21] The popular-music aspects of the work, which were clearly part of Jenny's practice at the time, were also a good fit for the performer: Albulescu was just seventeen years old when she composed the work for him, and as much as he loved Liszt and Chopin, he also listened to pop music.

Rock Sonata No. 1 is a work in three movements for solo piano. The score suggests a duration of fifteen minutes, although that would require a fairly caffeinated reading; a 2021 recording by Stephen De Pledge clocks in at more than twenty minutes. The first movement ranges from insistently rhythmic to floatingly rhapsodic and covers considerable stylistic ground. The bluesy passages bring Gershwin vaguely to mind, and the more virtuosic episodes owe something to Liszt. Originally there had been no specific title or attribution for the first movement, although a later revision of the work identifies it 'To Absent Friends' and Jenny's programme note lists those friends as 'Beethoven (Mozart, Schubert, Liszt, Debussy, Gershwin . . .)'.[22] There are echoes of all in this movement, but the rhythmic language is definitely closer to Led Zeppelin than to Liszt.

The quieter second movement, marked *andante expressivo*, is softer and gently melodic, and includes the dedication 'In memory of Charlie French (died of aids, 1987)', also added in a later revision of the work. Charlie French, an Australian Aboriginal activist, had been one of Jenny's friends and flatmates in Ohiro Road. Unfolding in familiar ways, the modulations and development sections lend an air of inevitability to the movement, the formal designs of classical music showcasing melodic ideas and rhythms more characteristic of the present day. The final movement reprises the rhythmic urgency of the first, and the ebullient bluesy lines and insistent left-hand chords owe more than a little to jazz, particularly jazz as practised by someone like Dave Brubeck, or the Spanish-tinged music of Chick Corea. Jenny acknowledged this Latin flavour in her programme note, saying the final movement 'is in rondo-sonata form, with a Latino romp as its recurring rondo, a nursery-type second theme, and a development-cum-episode that starts in a quasi-Iberian vein'.[23]

Albulescu received the handwritten score in 1986 and spent time with the work. However, he said, 'I never played it publicly. I learned it, I worked on it but never had the chance to programme it properly and play it.' In 2009, as Director of Orchestral Studies at Lehigh University

in Pennsylvania, Albulescu decided he would like to do something
with the sonata. He was planning a tour with the French Chamber
Orchestra, and thought the middle movement – the elegy dedicated to
Charlie French – would be an ideal piece for him to perform whilst
conducting from the piano. Intending to orchestrate the nine-minute
movement for string orchestra, piano and flute, he contacted Jenny to
seek approval for the idea: 'I explained what I wanted to do and she said,
"That's great." What I have loved about Jenny is she is so eager . . . She's
the most positive musician I have ever worked with; definitely the most
positive composer, where whatever you come up with, she's like "Yeah,
that's good. Let's do this".' Albulescu asked Jenny if she had a computer
score of the work to save him the time of entering the piano part for his
expanded arrangement. She said she'd check and get back to him.

> She got back to me two weeks later, saying, 'Eugene, I had troubles
> converting the file to the latest version so I ended up re-inputting
> it in Sibelius, and while I was doing that I just did it. So here it is,
> I already arranged it for you, you don't have to do it.' About two
> weeks later I got another email from her saying, 'Eugene, I went to
> town and did the rest of the piece too. And the rest of the piece is
> for large orchestra.' So, it's basically a kitchen sink orchestration, for
> the outer movements.[24]

Albulescu was to perform the elegy more than twenty times with the
French Chamber Orchestra, as well as with his university orchestra at
Lehigh. When he learned that his New Zealand colleague Uwe Grodd
was planning to record a CD of Jenny's music for Naxos, he got in
touch and explained the revisions Jenny had made to the sonata, now a
concerto. Grodd agreed to include the entire piece in the recording, and
so Albulescu travelled to New Zealand to capture the work.

With the recording dates confirmed, he contacted Jenny and arranged
to meet with her to go over the score prior to the sessions. 'We met at
Bruce [Greenfield]'s place in Raumati and I went through every note of
the piece and she gave feedback of how it should be. She was also present
for the recording sessions. She was quiet the whole time – she didn't say

anything to anybody. I expected her to come out and say [things] but once we were in the session it was like her work was done – it felt that way.'

Jenny was pleased to orchestrate the work for Albulescu, saying, 'I did sort of revise the whole thing. It's not quite the same piece as the piano piece, but I think it's all right.' However, by 2009 when she prepared the work for orchestra, her compositional practice had travelled quite some distance from the approach she'd deployed when she wrote *Rock Sonata No. 1*. Perhaps it was for this reason that she cautioned listeners in her programme note, 'Though poignant touches can be found, those in search of something deeper and darker must look elsewhere.'[25] Reviewers shared this sentiment. Several commented on the elegance of Jenny's orchestration and the excitement of the piano writing but found the piece a little shapeless, with insufficient contrast between the sections. One reviewer, whose disappointment suggests he either didn't read or failed to take seriously Jenny's programme notes, thought that the sonata's 'treacly tunes, simple harmonies, jaunty rhythms and assorted clichés will please the many who are happy to relegate their music listening to a background distraction'.[26] More generous was the New Zealand reviewer who wrote, 'McLeod's celebration of modern idioms of rhythm and harmonic simplicity results in a work that not only captures the spirit of its time but also stands above it, with continuing relevance today.'[27]

Soon after completing Albulescu's piece in 1986, Jenny accepted a commission for a solo piano work from Auckland pianist Rae de Lisle. The result was *Rock Sonata No. 2*, a three-movement, fifteen-minute work that was premiered at Wellington's New Zealand International Festival of the Arts in 1988. The first movement, marked 'Steady, with contained energy' and beginning in a groovy 12/8 in minor, modulates smoothly to the major before venturing to new pastures. Although some of the juxtapositions are abrupt, the effect is music that traverses varied terrain without obviously losing its way. A reprise of the opening minor 12/8 motif – which once again shifts to the major key – offers a palpable lift to the close of the movement. The second movement, 'Sad Song for the Common Man', is slow and elegiac, and manages to evoke a kind of wistfulness without becoming syrupy. There is greater harmonic variety here than in the opening movement, with a little more dissonant rub in some of the chords and tonal superimpositions, and some surprising turns in the harmonic progression. The chords are voiced in ways that sound superficially like something Billy Joel might play, but they move in a manner closer to Germanic traditions of the nineteenth century. The final movement, a rondo (as in the first piano sonata), skips along brightly enough, although its ebullient melodies mask a kind of ferocity. Jenny's performance note suggests the movement be played 'Fast, chunky' and 'with a certain understated savagery'.

Rock Sonata No. 2 mines similar terrain to its predecessor, although with more minor-key darkness; it is somehow more knowing, more watchful than Albulescu's piece. Where the first sonata was youthful and energetic, a headlong rush in places, the second is a wiser, cagier work. There seems to be greater contrast between the themes, and the potential for dynamic and textural shading is more developed.

Jenny was positive about the work, describing it as 'via Brahms'. She was particularly satisfied with the second movement, 'which I found quite a successful serious classical movement. Its idioms are from rock music, but they're not blatantly from rock music; they don't sound like any other particular composer . . . like neo-classical composers or Debussy. There are things in there that are related [to other compositions] but it's not overtly like anything else.' Having popular idioms filtered through the lens of serious music worked well for Rae de Lisle. She explained, 'My background is all from the classics and the Romantics, and Brahms is always something I've loved to play, so that felt good to me. I really loved the second movement – I thought it was great, it just felt very natural.'[28]

It may have felt natural, but it was still a technically demanding piece. The desire to write music that might extend performers had been a characteristic of Jenny's composing since the 1960s. 'If I was given a professional brief for a commission,' she said, 'that meant I was being invited by people who considered themselves to be musicians. I would like always, even if they were amateurs, to try to stretch them a little bit.' Writing technically demanding music wasn't without risks, however, and Jenny was aware that she had to be mindful of the welfare of performers.

Just as *Rock Sonata No. 1* had been challenging for Eugene Albulescu, so the second sonata tested Rae de Lisle. Jenny recalled: 'It stretched her; I'm glad it didn't ruin her technique.'

Balancing player preferences and welfare with the desire to extend what they are capable of doing requires composers to reconcile competing interests. While Jenny was committed to presenting music to professional performers that would keep them on their toes, she had learned from experience that humility had an important role to play in the relationship between those who write music and those who perform it:

> A young composer writing his or her first piece for orchestra had better watch out, that's all I can say; had better be very humble, and better accept the wisdom of the players. The players can be asked by a young composer to do some wretched things if the young composer really has no idea what the true relationship is of a beginning composer to a professional, long-established orchestra. The thing is, if you're going to be around for years – both of you – you need to be in a good relationship if you're going to work together. Mutual respect is good.

Jenny's desire to challenge performers who commissioned work from her wasn't limited to the technical aspects of the music she composed. She was also interested in creating opportunities for them to play music in new and unfamiliar styles: 'I used to purposely write quite light pop music sometimes to help a classical performer bring themselves out of themselves, basically. Along with that would come all the values that I had learned from the pop side. I thought that would be quite good as part of my [desire] to extend people . . . It meant that they had to expand their little box of values.'

Jenny made a point of not explaining this to the performers for whom she was composing, and was sometimes surprised at the results. On several occasions musicians learned Jenny's pop-influenced classical pieces without input from her. 'They wanted to try and see if they could do it off the page,' Jenny said, 'and they ended up playing a piece at half the correct speed, which really startled me.' Her own familiarity with popular music meant she knew that certain styles gravitated towards particular tempi, and she was baffled when classical performers didn't understand this too. 'Clearly the musicians involved – in taking pieces I've written so slowly – didn't have that background. I suppose I just took that for granted – danger, danger.' But she acknowledged the inevitability of these kinds of misunderstandings, given that 'I had the cheek to try and extend people's backgrounds when I didn't even know what their backgrounds were.'

Richard Hardie suggested that moving out of the 1970s Jenny 'had begun to experiment with ways to combine Rock and Classical ideas. This met with little success until *Rock Sonata No. 1* and *Rock Sonata No. 2*, completed in 1987. These works represent the culmination of her experiments in combining dominant and sub-dominant (rising and falling) forces.'[29] Hardie's emphasis on Jenny's work to accommodate the harmonic strategies of the respective genres is certainly reasonable, but doesn't take into account the ways her contemporary ensemble music also accommodated the rhythms of rock, or managed a marriage of the different ways classical and popular musicians might think about orchestration.

Jenny's orchestration during this period developed along similar lines to the ways popular musicians set words to music. 'All the conventions of [vocal] arrangement that came into pop and rock from the big band . . . all of these things can just get turned into instrumental versions of themselves,' she said. Just as a pop musician might imagine a lead vocalist's line, Jenny would compose a similar line for strings; woodwinds might be assigned parts that resemble what backing vocalists sing, or concerted brass might take over the main melody for a chorus. Scored in this way, the music was developed in layers, often quite different in sound and function from one another. While the value of this approach to orchestration might have been confirmed by Jenny's exposure to popular music, it was also something she had been developing since her student days:

> At university I had studied a first year of sixteenth-century Palestrina-style counterpoint (and at Lilburn's urging had sung in Max Fernie's

legendary choir at St Mary of the Angels). Then came a second year
of Bach-style counterpoint (two and three-part inventions), and a
third year of Bachian fugue. The string trio included in my degree
portfolio has quite a big contemporary fugue as its last movement.
By then I had had enough of traditional counterpoint – for the
time being anyway. But really, I just came to take a different view of
counterpoint. For one thing, why should all the independent voices
be in the same style as each other, I thought. At first, I was interested
in Messiaen's (and early Stravinsky's) horizontal layering of different
'stripes' of sound, so to speak, and this features in *Earth and Sky* and
Under the Sun – it's also a fairly simple way to handle larger forces
texturally. But later I enjoyed more of an African 'interlocking' of
various patterns or sounds that were different and characteristic for
each voice (instrument or section) – a solution much more along
popular lines (for example, Motown, 'Long Train Running' sort of
thing). You'll find this a lot in the *Three Celebrations*, for example,
though I did actually come to it first via African drum music, which
I was 'teaching' (we were playing it in class, thanks to notations and
excellent instructions for building African barrel tom-toms from a
textbook) as part of a non-Western music course I had introduced.

Listening to the first movement of *Three Celebrations* with this in
mind is instructive, and the interlocking rhythms played by the different
sections of the orchestra are quite apparent. It is also apparent that much
of the dynamism of the music, its 'get-up-and-go', can be attributed to
the ways the various strata interact rhythmically.

Richard Hardie's suggestion that the two rock sonatas are more
'successful' as marriages of rock and classical music than *Music for Four*
or *Three Celebrations for Orchestra* is in some ways reasonable.[30] The
technical demands of the solo piano works and their classical formal
organisation, wedded to the rhythms, chord progressions and melodic
vocabulary of popular music, mean the sonatas approach a middle
ground between the genres in ways that some of the slightly earlier
ensemble music does not. However, given Jenny's stylistic catholicism
and perennial curiosity, it may be that she was not trying for an equal

meeting of the genres, but rather something more organic – perhaps the 'kind of "classical" music evolving from the rock language' she had talked about during the 1970s.[31] Jenny claimed that she wrote both sonatas 'completely intuitively (with sonata form as well as rock music by then in my bones)'. Rather than pursuing a very particular synthesis, it seems more likely she was simply curious to play around with music that interested her and for which she felt sympathy, whatever its origins.

'I didn't have a bunch of laws on top of me saying "You can do this. You can't do that." I could just pick what I liked,' Jenny said. 'So, I didn't care if it was pop or classical or whatever; if I liked it, that was the qualification.' With this in mind, perhaps each of these works needs to be appreciated on its own terms. Some of the music from the 1980s, such as *The Emperor and the Nightingale,* is close to models drawn from the classical repertory. Other works appear to owe a greater debt to popular music – the songs from *Cuckooland* are a case in point. And some seem to fall pretty squarely between the classical and pop worlds – the rock sonatas might reasonably be categorised in this way.

Gaining an appreciation of the music Jenny composed between 1980 and 1987 is not so much a question of identifying an ideal balance among ideas drawn from the popular, rock and classical idioms as it is understanding that her music drew from many wells. The final mix she arrived at for a particular piece depended on the commission – for whom she was writing, and for what forces – and her mood and immediate interests as she composed the music. Sometimes she drew close to Brahms, and at other times she was closer to the Beatles.

Coming to a halt

Jenny said, 'My film music was all intuitive, just done by ear, what I felt would work and what sounded right.'[32] She also said that much of the choral music written during the 1980s was similarly composed by ear and intuition.[33] Those intuitive approaches – a 'second nature' feeling for form and orchestration that was the result of her long study of Western art music – were applied to the rhythmic, melodic and harmonic materials of popular and non-Western music that had by then also become second nature to her. The result of this combination was that almost all of her music from this period is appealing, and warmly human. Even when the music accommodates dissonance – during *Through the World*, for example – those moments of discord are resolved so finely that the effect of the music is of return, of resolution. For Jenny, this began to be a problem: 'Cheerful kinds of music – my own – they just make me feel happy, but they don't make me feel exalted or lift me up to heaven or anything like that.'

Jenny began to recognise that the popular and rock idioms she had elected to work with were a limiting factor in the music she was composing. She had been able to achieve good results with those melodic, rhythmic and harmonic materials by corralling them within the formal strategies of classical composition, saying, 'I got to a sort of quasi-deepening . . . somewhat more complex, a little darker, a little bit more moving.' However, it became apparent to her that the kind of depth she aspired to was not something she could access using those materials: 'By the time I got to the end of the second rock sonata I felt I couldn't do any more that was any deeper than what I'd already done.'

As well as recognising the limitations of her chosen materials, Jenny also came to see the cost of composing so much music in such a short period of time:

> I was a full-time composer more or less for a few years there and it nearly drove me nuts . . . During those six or seven years I was pretty much fulltime, but I think that I really wrote too much . . . In those days I used to respond quite well to the pressure of a deadline. But I felt quite burnt out after about six or seven years of that and I felt I was getting to the point where, really, I was writing some real rubbish just to meet the deadline. When it got to that point, I just backed out of that whole way of doing it.[34]

In the middle of 1987 Jenny arrived at an impasse. She had accepted two large commissions and begun to work on them. One was a collaborative project with author Witi Ihimaera, a cycle of poems concerned with Parihaka, a site of Māori non-violent resistance to European occupation in the 1880s, which she was to set as songs. The other was for an event celebrating peace at Wellington's St Andrew's on The Terrace. The commissioning body for these works was the QEII Arts Council, and her letter to them dated April 1988 is worth quoting at length:

> Inevitably, there come times in the life of a creative artist when some sort of regeneration or renewal period is necessary, when one must in a sense 'start again from scratch', and in a way become a 'student' again.
>
> More than fifteen years ago, I embarked on a long-term exploration of the language of popular music, sensing that there was a possibility here for a 'classical' music to come into existence, via what seemed to me still to be a 'common language'. Up until August of last year, I followed this line fairly consistently, until finally I think, in my two rock sonatas for piano (of 1987), I <u>did</u> actually achieve the classical music I had set out in pursuit of so long before – and a long time it took indeed.
>
> I was not prepared, however, for what meanwhile was happening to me. After many years of writing <u>only</u> to commission (and without any break), my inspiration was beginning to flag. I felt more and more like a 'mother' who has been 'milked dry'. Meanwhile I had accepted, and felt committed to, two large long-term commissions . . . both to be finished by 1990. I struggled along desperately with both these pieces for over a year, making very little headway. Meanwhile, moreover, my musical <u>language</u> was running out as well.
>
> The popular language I had worked so hard to achieve turned out finally to be a dead end. Sonata form, though it served me well enough for a time, proved finally <u>deeply</u> unsatisfying, truly a 'dodo', a dead form, and I began to find myself wanting to smash it, and to smash the language, from frustration . . .
>
> There <u>were</u> truly the strains of a 'rock' Beethoven, Brahms, Schubert, Mozart, etc. floating around there, as I had suspected, in

the 'ethers', and I came upon them and mined them many times. But though this was all in terms of <u>present-day</u> popular scales, rhythms and harmonies, I felt the music I came up with was still ultimately so <u>similar</u> to that of its progenitors, that once again I was almost just repeating what they had already done – even though my tunes, and rhythms, and harmonies were new, and sounded as though they belonged in the current age. (*Plus ça change, plus c'est la même chose.*)

The other deep-seated problem that I had to finally confront was the limited <u>expressive</u> potential of my 'chosen language' – it was very, very hard, almost impossible finally, to say anything of real depth or seriousness, in 20th-century terms (i.e., basically post-two world wars, post-Hitler, Stalin and Hiroshima). And I was brought up very much face to face with this particular problem by the <u>subject</u> of my Presbyterian commission – namely, 'peace'.

So, by August of last year, I was really in a complete quandary (and in complete despair) as a composer. I couldn't carry on with my popular language; and I felt I couldn't return to Schoenberg, Webern or Messiaen – I had already come to a dead end there earlier on. Meanwhile the 'minimalists' didn't attract me – not enough character or substance. And in the few serious pieces I had written in the last few years (*Childhood, Dirge for Doomsday*) I had relied on a sort of 'intuitive' contemporary language, to which I felt I could no longer return either: I was by now in need of some much more substantial organisational discipline, but hadn't the faintest idea how or where I was going to find this.[35]

Jenny described these circumstances as 'my own private version of a major crisis'. She decided to withdraw from the commissions and offered to repay the money already advanced to her for the collaborative project with Ihimaera.[36] 'It was a matter of my own development,' she said. 'I needed some time off to work out where I was going to head to next.'

14

The Tone Clock

Time away from composing – which Jenny felt was necessary if she was to identify a new and fruitful direction for herself – came in the form of an invitation to attend a festival in the United States. Friends from the US Embassy in Wellington had asked 'if I'd be interested in being nominated for a list of people to go to this festival in Kentucky with the Louisville Orchestra, well-known for playing contemporary music. They were having their 50th anniversary with a 10-day festival.'[1]

Jenny was initially reluctant but agreed to have her name put forward. In her nominee's statement, 'I told them at length, and sincerely, all the reasons why they didn't want me', and to underscore the point submitted two wildly different scores: *Rock Sonata No. 1* and *For Seven*. 'That'll fox them,' she'd thought.[2] To her astonishment, she was chosen as one of the composers to participate in the Sound Celebration Festival in Louisville during September 1987. She wrote to Barbara Einhorn, 'I should have felt quite proud, but was then in such frightful despair as a composer that it seemed a rather black irony.'[3]

As a guest of the festival, Jenny delivered an address – 'A Composer's Choices', in which she discussed the issues that exercised her as she composed music – and was on hand for a performance of *For Seven*, chosen by the organisers for inclusion in the event. Other composers in attendance included Harrison Birtwistle from the UK; Swede Jan Carlstedt; Argentine Julio Matin Viera; Sofia Gubaidulina from the Soviet Union; Otto Luening, Charles Wuorinen and Ezra Laderman from the US; and Dutch composer Peter Schat.[4]

Jenny had been aware of Schat – he had studied with Pierre Boulez – although she was unfamiliar with his music. 'I knew he was some kind of serial theorist,' Jenny told Elizabeth Kerr, 'and was prepared to dislike his ideas from the outset, and indeed did start by arguing furiously, as serialism was a complete no-no for me. But the more I listened the more I realised that he was not talking about serialism at all but some kind of new tonality system.'[5]

Perennially curious about novel ideas, and acutely aware of the impasse she had reached with her own music, Jenny began to listen more closely to what Schat had to say about his Tone Clock theory of chromatic harmony:

> I was very interested, though, at first, I didn't much like Peter's stuff – he seemed a bit up himself and he couldn't talk about anything except the Tone Clock, and this is always a sign of fanaticism. All the same, he showed me an article and I thought, 'I can really relate to this.' And some of the things that I saw were related to some of the things that I'd already done, especially back in *Earth and Sky* and *Under the Sun*. I thought I'd like to find out more about this.[6]

Jenny hadn't much liked Peter Schat when she first met him: 'We argued, he looked like a typical "po-faced Dutchman", I thought.' But at the conclusion of the festival she decided to travel to Amsterdam to spend more time with him, and stayed just around the corner from his place in the city's red-light district. 'It was really funny because every time I came out and my host held the hotel door, there'd be all these gaping tourists who thought I was a prostitute. So, I would linger in the doorway, smiling . . .' She suspected Schat was a little embarrassed that she had made such an effort to understand his system, and he went to some lengths to supply her with all of his materials, including many articles published in Dutch. Undaunted, Jenny began to teach herself the language so that she could read and ultimately translate his articles.[7]

Jenny spent three weeks with Schat in the Netherlands, working hard to understand his Tone Clock theory. 'The more I did this, the more it became clear to me that, as I had sensed, there was indeed a potential here for me, a "way to go", and I became more and more hopeful, as new vistas and possibilities – a new way of <u>thinking</u> in fact – started opening up.'[8] That realisation wasn't just to do with the power of the ideas; she was also won over by the music Schat had composed using them: 'I heard tapes of Peter Schat's music and was stunned all over again, to find it completely filled the great "void" in my soul: expressed all that I'd been unable to express. The sounds <u>completely</u> turned me on.'[9]

Finding a pathway out of the musical wilderness in which she had found herself was of enormous significance. She was a full-time professional composer, yet uncertain if she was, in fact, a 'real composer'; she had spent the previous year working hard on two substantial commissions but was getting nowhere. She was, when all was said and done, dissatisfied with the music she was writing and the direction she had chosen:

> I had come to a full stop, turned down commissions, given up others in the middle, and spent the official advance payments with nothing to show for it . . . And here was Peter Schat, looking more and more like he could be my 'saviour' and indeed the bearer of very glad tidings from my point of view. As for how he felt about me? For Schat, I was truly God's gift, someone taking him seriously for a change, and not only that but soon galloping away madly with his ideas, and taking them places he'd never dreamed they might go. Somewhere in the middle of all this, fellow feeling, sympathy, excitement and intellectual musical understanding turned into love.

Reporting on events in Amsterdam, she told Barbara Einhorn, 'Of course, I fell passionately in love with Peter Schat, at the same time I fell for his ideas and his music. This took some getting over. But he's basically gay – story of my life. Yet we are two sides of the same coin – have more in common than I'd ever believed possible philosophically and musically.'[10]

In some ways the relationship Jenny enjoyed with Schat resembled the one she had shared with Douglas Lilburn, and was to prove important in similar ways. She described Lilburn and Schat as 'my two "great loves" if I could call them that'. She also conceded that neither of them 'could be said to have possessed a very notable sense of humour, so really we could never have lived together for other than modest intervals'. Nevertheless, both relationships 'were intimately entwined with questions, ultimately spiritual I would have to say, that concerned my whole being and my personal identity. Our respective relationships were not simply a matter of "kindred spirits" (which I think we really were not) or of some "musical affinity" (as essentially I feel we were pretty much worlds apart in our general musical preferences) – but something deeper was involved.'

Returning to New Zealand in time for the summer, Jenny found herself cheerful, energised, and positive about the promise Schat's system held for her. She continued to study his essays and articles, and paid close attention to his music as well. She also began composing again, making her first exploratory steps with the Dutch composer's system.

Put simply, Tone Clock theory involves combinations of three notes.[11] In Darmstadt circles it was widely understood that the chromatic scale contained only twelve different three-note groups or 'chromatic triads'. Schat designated these triads 'hours' (the twelve 'hours' making up the 'tone clock'), each with its own 'flavour' or 'aura'. Putting this idea to compositional work, Schat discovered that all but one of the twelve chromatic triads could be transposed successively onto the notes of a particular four-note group generated from a *different* hour in such a way that all twelves notes of the chromatic scale were generated without repetition. This operation – which he called 'steering' – yielded a sort of twelve-note 'mobile' comprised of four individual groups of three notes each, groups that could be deployed in any order. The notes within each of these groups could also be deployed in any order.

Jenny quickly saw that steering was closely related to 'frequency multiplication', a concept advanced by Pierre Boulez. She had encountered the concept whilst a student in Europe and applied it – in an incompletely understood form – as she composed *Piano Piece 1965*. She recognised, however, that she had not fully grasped the idea or its implications and was frustrated by this gap in her knowledge. 'It eventually got to the point,' Jenny recalled, 'where I said to myself, "I'm going to shut myself up this weekend and I'm not coming out of the house until I've worked out what frequency multiplication bloody well means." And I did that and I focused on nothing but frequency multiplication for hours and days on end and didn't come out of the house until I'd worked it out. And when I worked it out, when the penny suddenly dropped, it was *so* simple.'

Schat, as a student of Pierre Boulez in the early 1960s (he had even lived in Boulez's house) was one of those to whom the French composer had explained his ideas about frequency multiplication shortly after he developed them. Schat, however, had failed to recognise the connection between Boulez's idea and his own theory. Jenny explained: 'I realised, but Pete didn't, that what Pete calls "steering" is what Boulez calls "multiplication". And he was really amazed. He said, "I forgot all about that." He didn't put two and two together at all until I told him, "Look – this is frequency multiplication," and he said, "So it is!" But, of course, he was pleased because he really adored Boulez. Anyone who had been close to Boulez adored him.'

One of the reasons Schat's theory appealed so powerfully to Jenny was because it corresponded closely to the ways she had composed music for her early music theatre works. Tone Clock theory, fundamentally, 'was mine', she said, 'because I'd been doing it for years but I hadn't known what to call it . . . That's the basis of the harmony of my piece *Earth and Sky*. And then it became more detailed in *Under the Sun*. Both of those pieces were written before what Peter Schat did, but Peter's [approach] was way more formulated than mine, because he named the twelve triads, introducing the concept of "hours" and discovered the twelve-note triadic combinatorial properties of all the different hours.'

Musicologist John Croft's analysis of *Earth and Sky* confirmed the presence of Jenny's proto-Tone Clock composing in the 1968 work. He traced some of the techniques used to compose the music back to *Piano Piece 1965*, in which Jenny made idiosyncratic use of Boulez's frequency multiplication and which is closely related to Schat's 'steering'.[12] 'One can also trace in *Earth and Sky*,' Croft wrote, 'a growing awareness of the possibilities of what McLeod would now call "chromatic tonalities", or "hours". As it turns out, the harmonic aspect of the piece is perhaps best discussed in terms of the Tone Clock . . . It should be remembered, however, that at the time of composition of *Earth and Sky* the composer had not yet begun to use the [Tone Clock] terminology.'[13] Jenny said, 'Until Schat came along, I had no effective terminology.'

Jenny found Schat's theories easy to follow, perhaps because they proposed a way of systematising compositional techniques already very familiar to her. But she also quickly discovered that the system, as he'd formulated it, was rigid and limited, more like a prison than a playground, she felt. 'I started thinking about Boulez and his ideas about harmony . . . [Tone Clock theory] wasn't totally the same, but there was enough in common that I saw you could build in all of Boulez's ideas into a bigger version than Peter had conceived of. So, there were all these freer ways you could use it – it was up to you how systematic you wanted to make things'.[14]

Schat tended, in Jenny's estimation, to be quite inflexible in his application of Tone Clock ideas. For example, he routinely used three-note groups steered by four-note groups which, if there are no note repetitions, yields a twelve-note chromatic field. 'As soon as I saw that,' Jenny said, 'I thought, "Ah, well three by four is also four by three",' and the many regroupings to which the system could be subjected revealed a world of possibilities to her. 'And that's how come I got into it so readily. That startled Peter – he really was surprised and saying things like "How do you be so free?"' To which she replied, 'How do you not "be so free" with it?'

Perhaps the greatest attraction of Tone Clock ideas was their capacity to analytically account for *any* music that used the chromatic scale. 'I saw where it could go,' Jenny said. 'I saw how the whole thing could become the basis of an understanding for the whole of the chromatic system.'[15] She had long been familiar with numerous systems for harmonic organisation, and the all-encompassing potential of the Tone Clock approach was compelling. 'It already included everything we know – it doesn't exclude anything. Another thing that Boulez said: anything that you use (in terms of tempered pitch and harmony) – any kind of wider system or theory you make up – it needs to subsume the past.'

It was this potential to accommodate past systems, while at the same time accounting for phenomena that those earlier systems failed to explain, which completely won Jenny over. She found that certain of Messiaen's music, which he, a profoundly knowledgeable theorist, had been unable to define except by listing the intervals or actual pitches of the note complex, could be readily described using Tone Clock nomenclature. She also recognised that Tone Clock approaches offered a more robust analytical framework for thinking about Debussy's music, for example, revealing it to be rather more systematic than might at first appear to be the case. 'Debussy's 24 *Préludes* are themselves remarkable precursors as regards the use of the twelve chromatic triads/hours and of steering (or multiplication),' Jenny wrote. 'They are not 12-note, of course, yet are fully chromatic – and in respect of the 12 hours (triads) so is Stravinsky's *Le Sacre du printemps*.'[16]

Small music

Jenny read and translated Schat's articles, maintaining an extensive correspondence with him as she did so. She and Schat also had long conversations about his theory, first in Amsterdam and later when he stayed with her at Pukerua Bay and they'd gone over her translation of *The Tone Clock*. Together, these experiences rewarded her with a deep understanding of his system. That understanding also revealed to her the limitations of the guidelines Schat had formulated for applying the system. 'Due to the inherent textural monotony of so many triads,' Jenny recalled, 'I soon began to think of Schat's invitation to other composers as something more like "Welcome to my cage!" Peter had made his own quite strict Tone Clock rules and he was determined to live with them, but I didn't see why I had to.'

Adapting Tone Clock principles to her own purposes, and in this way expanding the possibilities Schat's ideas offered, Jenny began using the system to compose music. This work – a combination of careful theorising with charts and tables, and composition at the piano – progressed steadily over the early months of 1988. By April of that year, she wrote that she was composing 'small music, piano music, nothing large or ambitious, and I feel this is how I will have to carry on'.[17] It was the first time in many years she had written music that was not commissioned, that was not the result of a request or a performance deadline but instead emerged from her own musical curiosity and appetite. Composing those pieces, Jenny said, was 'something that I did want to do; that had been quietly there in the background and building up. When I wrote the first lot of Tone Clock pieces, those were pieces that I really had wanted to write.'[18]

The composing block Jenny had experienced over the previous year or so was broken, and music flooded out. Between March 1988 and February 1989, she completed seven pieces for solo piano, all of them resulting from her exploration of Tone Clock theory. In the essay that accompanied the 2016 recording of all her Tone Clock pieces for solo piano, Jenny documented her compositional process.

First, she established foundational principles to guide her work. These ranged from general and quite liberal – for example, 'I can stay as long as I like, anywhere I like' – to rather more specific and rigorous: 'Every group or sub-group (whether regrouped or not) within a specific harmonic network needs to appear at least once in the piece of music for which it was created. Its constituent notes need to be (musically, texturally, registrally, dynamically, etc.) disposed in such a way that the group itself is recognisable as a group – in order to maintain the integrity of the deep structure.' This 'deep structure' was the 'specific, quite limited pitch network' she chose (or generated) for each piece.[19]

With these underlying principles in place, and with pitch networks determined in advance for each composition, Jenny improvised with the materials she had assigned herself. 'Thus, the music itself is born of my creative intuition operating via a predetermined rationale, the spontaneous or improvisatory element being thoroughly reined in and controlled (but also impelled) by the logic of the predetermined deep structure.'

Jenny considered the Tone Clock piano pieces to be among the most precisely organised she had written for some years. Part of her motivation for working along such exacting lines was her desire that, 'as part of my life's work, so to speak, there had to be some really technically solid thing there, so that I could compare it with the intuitive side' of her composing. 'I wanted to reach that point in order, maybe, to never have to go there again.'

In many ways the rigour of the Tone Clock music corresponds to *Piano Piece 1965* and *For Seven*, works also composed by means of strictly applied theory. Even so, with the detail of the Tone Clock pieces emerging from improvisation, the theory that predicated this music was leavened with Jenny's musical proclivities and habits, her taste and the preferences of her ear. In this respect the music seems analogous with her character, which balanced the competing demands of a brilliant, sharply focused mind and a passionate, generous and earthy nature. Jenny reflected:

> Essentially, what I consider to be (in principle) valuable for one's work I also consider to be of value in one's life. One of my chief aims in this respect has been the long search for some semblance of balance, both my life and work having at various points consisted of such extremes. In both respects I have understood the need to 'pull myself together'. The predetermined nature of a musical deep structure can be seen as corresponding to the life values learned and embedded as we grow up and mature, which have become our invisible and inherent support and guide, our 'second nature'.

This analysis is consistent with Jenny's response to Elizabeth Kerr, who asked if, for the first time, an 'inner necessity' had driven her to compose the Tone Clock pieces. 'Absolutely the first time,' Jenny replied. 'In my little piano music, I feel at last that my own true and original voice is starting to be heard.'[20]

The 'little piano music' is categorically different from the music Jenny produced prior to leaving for Kentucky in 1987. *Three Celebrations*, *Music for Four* and *Rock Sonatas No1* and *No2* tend to emphasise melodic clarity, possess a freshness that can feel youthful, are consistently and often energetically rhythmic, and are painted in something akin to primary colours. The Tone Clock pieces are concerned with a more nuanced colour palette: Monet's aqueous canvases replacing the bolder colours of Matisse cut-outs. And they inhabit deeper, more contemplative emotional waters. That's not to say the Tone Clock pieces are all quietly meditative – they can be urgently rhythmic too – but there is depth, even darkness, in the music that is largely absent from the pieces Jenny composed earlier in the decade. The music is also more open, more ambiguous, less conventionally resolved. That may be a function of the chromatic mobility of the pieces; or perhaps because, relative to her slightly earlier music, there are fewer predictably voiced chords, fewer (traditional) major and minor triads.[21]

The results, at various junctures along the way, can sound something like Messiaen, like Debussy, like Lilburn, can even be reminiscent of Chopin. Taken together, the music is rather more than the sum of its influences. It is also of its place. Pianist Emma Sayers, when preparing *Tone Clock: Piece IV* for performance, discussed the work with Jenny. 'She did tell me that it had a sub-title in her mind of "The sea and me", which is always how I thought about it anyway – that you'd just be on the beach, because one of those themes is very wave-like.'[22] In the essay that accompanied the complete recordings of this music, Jenny wrote:

> In the *Tone Clock* pieces, the listener will hear all sorts of sounds that (as I usually recognised later) probably originated in my own natural environment. There is lots of birdsong, though I made it all up (there are no 'real' birds in the Messiaen sense; that is, I have never sat at home knowingly transcribing any actual local birdsong). But somehow it all comes out in my music, and also other elements reminiscent of natural sounds – water, waves, wind in the trees or the flax, crashing, cliffs and rocks – also more mysterious 'inner' sounds that I have always loved, bells and chimes small and large, 'crystals' or 'jewels', gongs, liquid and wood-type sounds, gestures that Debussy or Messiaen might have identified as 'arabesques', or Boulez as 'ornament', quasi-fanfares, other cadenza-type flourishes that might be closer to Bartók, and sounds suggesting incipient movement of all kinds.[23]

The first of the Tone Clock pieces, composed for David Farquhar's sixtieth birthday, was performed by Margaret Nielsen in April 1988 at a Radio New Zealand studio concert broadcast to mark the occasion. A further six were completed over the following year and received a New Zealand premiere from Margaret in 1989, although not before Jeffrey Grice performed them at the New Zealand Embassy in Paris.

When offered an opportunity to deliver a recital in the salons of the embassy's residence, Grice decided a programme of French and New Zealand music would be ideal. Having selected music by Ravel and Fauré, Grice contacted Jenny. 'I had heard,' Grice wrote, 'that Jenny McLeod, having discovered the "tone clock", was then writing her first Tone Clock Pieces. It seemed exactly what I needed for this programme, something totally fresh.' It was also a perfect match for a Paris concert: Jenny had studied there with Messiaen; Grice with Messiaen's wife, Yvonne Loriod. But preparing to perform music still being composed, and with the concert fast approaching, was challenging. Grice recalled, 'Working from the manuscript, I started on what I had so far, one page at a time. Some days, Jenny would fax me a new page that I would quickly learn before the next. All this remained a secret between Jenny and I until the first publication of the *7 Tone Clock Pieces* when she acknowledged that I had given the first performance on March 17, 1989.'[24]

As her composing and theorising advanced, Jenny felt a growing sense of freedom within the chromatic universe. Tone Clock thinking, she said, 'pulled the shutters away so that what previously seemed unknown became gradually known. If I had been a sailor, I wouldn't set off without a map. It was like a map and that was why I called the Tone Clock theories – my actual charts – "chromatic maps", because they permitted me to discover in what area of the chromatic system I was.'

Jenny had continued working with Schat's materials, eventually translating all of his Dutch articles and essays. That work resulted in the publication in 1993 of *The Tone Clock* by Peter Schat, translated and with an introduction by Jenny. In a letter to Barbara Einhorn during this period, she said:

> I was writing increasingly long letters to Peter Schat – about much
> but particularly about my own experiences with the Tone Clock.
> After a few months of this he wrote back one day and said 'do you
> realise you're writing a book about the Tone Clock?' He was right
> of course, that was exactly what I was doing, I'd half suspected as
> much. So, then I got down to it seriously . . .[25]

She titled her expansion of Schat's Tone Clock ideas *A New Guide to the Chromatic System* and shared it with fellow composers and university music schools. Jenny was delighted that they understood it. 'People here, like Ross Harris and Gillian [Whitehead], were the first ones who saw it, and they both thought it was great, and Lyell [Cresswell] has been using it in Edinburgh.'[26] Nonetheless, Jenny was dissatisfied. *A New Guide to the Chromatic System* – a sort of user's manual – might have been concise, but it was incomplete. She sat with the ideas for a year or so before coming to the conclusion she had a lot more to say about Tone Clock theory. 'I decided to do this academic version, which I wrote off the top of my head without consulting my notes but using my many charts.' This more complete book she titled *Tone Clock Theory Expanded: Chromatic Maps 1 & 2*. 'In some respects,' she said, 'it's just a different version of the set theory classification, but I think it is a much more helpful one.'[27] There was some negotiation with publishers to have the book produced for market, but eventually Jenny decided to publish the work online, making it freely available for anyone interested.[28]

Completing those texts consumed much of Jenny's time during the late 1980s and early 1990s: 'I got a lot of pleasure out of that too. I didn't write anything for a few years, I spent so much time tabulating and making charts.' In fact, her interest in the theoretical work she was doing supplanted her desire to compose music. She told Neville Glasgow, 'I haven't got great ambitions as a composer at all. I think my real work is this theoretical work, actually.'[29] In due course she did start composing again, but it was 1995 before she resumed writing Tone Clock pieces for piano.

Douglas Lilburn had retired from Victoria University in 1980 but his legacy, particularly in the form of the Electronic Music Studio, was a constant reminder of his contribution to the Music Department. In 1995 the faculty decided to throw an eightieth birthday concert for Lilburn, and the school's piano tutor, Judith Clark, requested a piece from Jenny for the event. 'Having written the first one I found there were several more waiting in the wings, so I wrote those as well (while Judith became increasingly alarmed). I just kept saying to Judith, "Well, there's another one coming", until finally she said "Stop! No more. I've got no more students".'[30]

Over the following fifteen years Jenny went on to compose a further thirteen Tone Clock pieces, all of which were commissioned. *Tone Clock: Piece XII*, written for a piano competition to be held in Paekākāriki – just up the road from Jenny's place – emerged as a musical response to the Kāpiti Coast. Complete with birdsong and what might be the susurration of waves, echoes of Messiaen and Debussy cast glorious light over the score.

Tone Clock: Piece XVIII, Landscape Prelude was commissioned by pianist Stephen De Pledge and also found its inspiration in Jenny's environment – in this instance a renewed appreciation of the beautiful place she called home. During 2006 and 2007 Jenny and many other locals had battled with Transit New Zealand, opposing a plan to put a motorway along the coast north of Pukerua Bay that would cut through numerous private properties, including Jenny's own. Jenny composed a poem to accompany *Landscape Prelude* that responded to (or in some way 'expressed') the music – a reversal of her more common practice of composing music that responded to text. 'The poem's subject as the "image" of the music,' Jenny said, 'came out of the very landscape itself; namely the fragility of the awesome natural splendour in which we are so lucky to live, and in which I had earlier so gloried (in No. 12).'[31]

Tone Clock: Pieces XIII–XVII were composed on commission for Jack Richards to mark composer Jack Body's sixtieth birthday, hence the title: *From Jack for Jack*. Jenny titled the second piece *Lullaby for the World*, although after Body's death from cancer in 2015 she came to think of it as *Lullaby for Jack*.[32] All five pieces were composed using pitch fields generated from a six-note chromatic group favoured by Pierre Boulez. In the 1970s Boulez had composed birthday music for his patron Paul

Sacher, basing the work on the musical spelling of SACHER: e♭, a, c, b, e, d.[33] For Jack Body's birthday commission, Jenny decided to use this chromatic group, 'feeling it had a sort of "mantle" over it'.[34]

The final six Tone Clock pieces were commissioned by pianist Michael Houstoun. 'I commissioned the six in order to complete the set,' he said. 'I knew that Jenny had 24 in mind.'[35] These final pieces also owed something to Boulez. Jenny explained in her programme note, 'The deep structure of this last group is based quite strictly on a "tone clock-via-Boulez" treatment of the old 12-note series of my *Piano Piece 1965*.'

These last six pieces all possess evocative titles. Sometimes Jenny composed music with a title in mind, but only when it was part of the brief. That was the case with *Landscape Prelude*, in which she found ways to allow her feelings for the subject to creep into the music. More generally, Jenny said, 'I never think I'm going to write a piece about . . . the forest, for example. If I wrote a piece about the forest, it would be that I wrote the piece and when I finished it, or perhaps halfway through, I discovered it was about the forest.' The final six Tone Clock pieces have titles such as *Moon, Night Birds, Dark Pools* or *Te Kapowai (The Dragonfly)*. 'As for where the colourful, sometimes enigmatic titles came from,' Jenny confessed, 'I cannot tell – simply out of my deep subconscious, I suppose.'[36]

The Tone Clock pieces have been performed singly and in combination by probably hundreds, possibly thousands, of pianists. As such, they likely represent the subset of Jenny's music most extensively abroad in the world. They also held a special place in her own affections:

> The 24 *Tone Clock* pieces constitute my most personal, independent and intimate music. In between times the music I wrote was more free, but still always conceived in tone clock terms (though not so specifically 12-note). Coming back each time to continue this piano collection, I always took pleasure in the renewal of a discipline without which, in fact, there can be no real freedom.[37]

15

Finding Whānau, Finding Faith

On her return from the Netherlands in 1987, Jenny decided to accept no further commissions, and withdrew from the two outstanding composition requests she'd had on the go. Without commitments, she was able to completely immerse herself in the new ideas she had encountered in the United States and Amsterdam. 'During those years,' she said, 'I was living hermit-like, only working with and thinking about the Tone Clock, gradually expanding it and putting together (largely for my own benefit) a new guide to the chromatic system, my *Chromatic Maps*. This was a time of dwelling on all these fresh ideas, and once again letting them work their way into my bones, or into my second nature.'

The rhythm of her life outside of work was also changing. She had established some enduring friendships in the years after her move to Pukerua Bay, and was particularly close to Louis and Cecilia Johnson. Louis's sudden death in 1988 was a terrible shock to his family and a loss to Jenny, too. He had been a good friend and kindred spirit. She also found there were fewer opportunities to socialise with Cecilia, who had returned to work and had little time for much beyond her professional and family commitments. Miranda and Lucien, Louis and Cecilia's children, had been very attached to Jenny and spent a lot of time with

255

her as youngsters. As they grew older, that began to change. Cecilia thought that, 'By the time they were teenagers, she probably didn't see too much of them.'[1]

Jenny didn't really see too much of anybody for a few years during the late 1980s and early 1990s. It wasn't that she avoided people, but Pukerua Bay was just far enough from Wellington to mean she rarely had casual visitors. Besides, the modest footprint of her home combined with the intensity of her work habits tended to put people off: 'I've got my whole set-up [here] and when I want to work, it sort of totally discourages visitors. The kitchen and the bathroom are about the only rooms in the house that are not overflowing with paper and books and piles of this and that that have some bearing on my many activities.'[2]

Completing her translations of Peter Schat's essays and articles and getting those away to Harwood for publication did seem to draw that chapter of Jenny's life towards some sort of close, opening up space for her to consider other pursuits. In May 1993 she was delighted, and intrigued, to receive a telephone call from Greg Tata (Ngāi Te Rangi, Ngāti Tūwharetoa), the musician – and later music educator – who had played the part of Māui in the Tauranga production of *Earth and Sky*. An executive member of the New Zealand Choral Federation, Tata had a proposal that offered Jenny an opportunity to return her attention to composition.

He Iwi Kotahi Tātou

During the 1990s the Choral Federation held the Sing Aotearoa festival over a long weekend in October every third year. Tata had called to ask Jenny if she would consider writing a piece for the 1993 event. The first festival, held in Ohakune in 1990, had been hosted by Maungārongo Marae, and the iwi had agreed to host the second festival as well. Although Jenny had not composed serious music since 1989 and at that point felt no particular desire to do so, the involvement of local tangata whenua immediately sparked her interest.[3] 'When I heard that [the] iwi up there had been very involved in the first one,' Jenny said, 'and they had cooked all the meals, they had people sleeping at the marae . . . I liked the sound of that and I thought "Oh, good, I'd like to be involved in that. And I'd like to involve the tangata whenua in this piece I am going to write".'

Jenny had long felt that her connection to te ao Māori was ancestral. Her great-grandmother Matilda Montgomery (who married John Edmund Perrin) and Matilda's mother (by adoption) had been the first Pākehā women to travel with Māori by canoe up the Manawatū River to Hokowhitu, where they settled in the area of Papaioea that later became Palmerston North. There, Matilda and her adoptive parents attended Sunday morning church services at the local Ngāti Rangitane marae, and would likely have been invited to join the traditional communal meal that followed. Matilda, in turn, baked bread most days, and family lore has it that 'a few Māori used to smell the bread as it was baking and turn up for a little visit, sitting outside and smoking their pipes until it came out of the oven'. The family used to smile about these well-timed visits, but the fresh bread they shared – an open-handed return acknowledging the generosity of the local people – reflected their mutual friendliness. Matilda's adoptive father, George Snelson, was 'clearly loved and respected by the Māori . . . a number attended his funeral in November 1901, one named Tapeta from Awahuri wailing and waving a willow branch in mourning, and they placed on his coffin a Māori mat which was buried with him.'⁴

The depth of Jenny's feeling of connection to tangata whenua is perhaps most powerfully illustrated by an experience she had visiting her old friend, author James McNeish:

> Jim lived at Te Maika which is on the headland opposite the Kāwhia Harbour. In order to get to Te Maika you had to catch a boat, and the only boat was a little fishing boat. The Māori couple who had the boat lived at Te Maika and they had to take their catch over to Kāwhia. So, if you wanted to get to Jim's place, which I did on this occasion, you had to get a ride in the boat. This one time . . . Pat, the Māori fisherman, decided to take us right along the Kāwhia foreshore, just Jim and me and Pat . . . Jim must have been there

a lot of times because it was the land of his iwi; the marae is there, just further along, and there was a rock sticking out and he said, 'The *Tainui* canoe is buried there.' And I thought 'God! The *Tainui* canoe? Whoa!' I'd already, long before this, written *Earth and Sky*, and my connection with Māori wasn't as developed as it is now, but it was very powerful. Suddenly to be told that there, right there, is buried one of the great waka of the great migration – that has been, to me, an inspiration. The great migration is a wonderful thing. At almost the same time, we were standing, not sitting, just alongside the side rail of the boat and something amazing came in the top of my head, went straight through me, down through my feet, down to the deck of the boat. I don't know what it was, but at one stage I described this feeling to my friend Tūngia Baker and she said it's called a tohu – which means a sign; well, I suppose it was a sign – and I just started to weep and I couldn't stop weeping. It went on for days. I couldn't think about it without completely silent tears just suddenly . . . it was for that whole thing that you wept, for the whole amazing story. And that the bloody thing was still buried right there. I could have gone – although you never would – and wiped away a bit of soil and touched it. I couldn't explain it; I can't explain it now, but a wonderful thing. It would be easy for me to start crying again, just [thinking] of the whole amazing enterprise and courage that brought those people here with such slender means.[5]

Another pivotal experience was reading New Zealand historian Michael King's biography of Te Puea Hērangi shortly after it was published in 1977. 'I was profoundly shocked and horrified by it,' Jenny recalled. 'At first I too felt completely betrayed by our own past successive supposedly "Christian" governments. Before and immediately after *Earth and Sky* I was still completely unaware of our own pathetic litany of governmental treachery, but after *Te Puea* I resolved firmly in my heart that I would be ever after a Pākehā whom Māori could trust.'

Shortly before being asked to compose a piece for the Choral Federation, Jenny had attended a conference at which Keri Kaa had extended, in te reo Māori, a welcome to both her and *Earth and Sky*.

Jenny was touched by the welcome, and grateful for the acceptance it implied of both her and her work among tangata whenua. Jenny had been invited by the conference organiser Jonathan Mane-Wheoki to contribute to proceedings, and her participation took the form of a discussion paper, 'The Arts and Humanities: Some Bearings, Observations and Suggestions'. Amongst other things, Jenny wrote in some detail about the role Māori had to play in shaping creative endeavour in Aotearoa. Explaining that Māori understood art and love to be inseparable, she concluded:

> Channels of communication are opening up, and need to keep on being opened up, so that Māori and Pākehā can have more ways of meeting and getting to know one another as friends and human beings. (On both sides I feel we are often shy or afraid of breaching protocol, and though we might like to get closer we have no idea how best to go about it.) Marae are the most natural communal focal points in New Zealand society, and the whanau feeling – that abundant generosity of spirit & glad acceptance of our common humanity – had better be at the heart of the 'new society' or it will fail like all the others.[6]

It was in this context – shaped by many years of disappointment (and at times, anger) at Pākehā treatment of Māori, and at the same time being personally welcomed by Māori she met – that Jenny determined that her piece for Sing Aotearoa would both honour Māori, and contribute to improving relationships between tangata whenua and Pākehā:

> When I was invited by the New Zealand Choral Federation to write *He Iwi* for their festival, my first impulse and desire was to centre the new piece on the tangata whenua at Ohakune – and my second impulse was then, that in this case, I must first get to know them, that we would need to get to know each other face-to-face, before they could ever trust me enough to allow such a joining-in to happen.

Her intention was to transcribe a suitable Ngāti Rangi song, and use its pitch materials (that is, the notes of the melody) as the basis for her composition. 'I had this idea,' Jenny said, 'that I'd ask them to sing one of their songs – just in the way they normally sang it, without anything different about it – in the middle of my piece.'[7] She recalled: 'So, I went up there and met them, and when I met them, I fell in love with them. They agreed and sang me a few songs. I taped it all and I went home and I decided, "I'll use this piece".' That choice – a waiata tangi that in Jenny's cycle was entitled 'Waengapū Manu' (or 'Bird Interlude'), though the original song has no separate title – was made on the basis of the words of the song and her subjective response to it ('the one that I liked best and that felt right') rather than because of its musical materials, which at that point she had yet to consider.[8]

Shortly before that first trip to Ohakune, Jenny had been thinking about Boulez's music, considering permutations of the SACHER series: e♭, a, c, b, e, d. When she wrote down the Ngāti Rangi song she had selected, she was astonished to find that the pitch relationships of the melody were identical to that series. More remarkable, the kuia who had led the singing the day Jenny recorded the song had a cold and so sang it a little lower than was usual; as a consequence, it was in the same transposition as the SACHER series. 'Clearly this chromatic group had been handed to me on a plate,' she wrote at the time, 'and I was in no doubt that these were the notes I was to use for this piece.'[9]

Jenny composed her text in te reo Māori. She had tried to learn the language before, with limited success, but was determined to make greater progress this time around so that she could 'write some very simple words from my heart' for the Ngāti Rangi hosts. Kaumātua Joan Akapita, whom Jenny had met on her first visit to the marae, asked if she could see the words in advance:

> So, I showed them to her (the score was already collated) and we
> sat there together while she read through them all, along with my
> translations. She corrected 'Kua tae te wā' to 'Kua tae ki te wā.'
> When she got to my big long haka addressed to Ruapehu, she asked
> me to show her how it went – so I performed the whole thing

straight through for her, sotto voce. Afterwards, Joan told me that she 'couldn't do that' – and she was herself a lifelong composer of songs, the chief living composer and song-leader of Ngāti Rangi.

Describing the completed text, Jenny wrote: 'I have tried to provide a vehicle for the members of the New Zealand Choral Federation and other Pākeha to be able to express something of their (and my own) real affection for the Māori people, and also of their own feeling for this land.'[10] She titled the piece *He Iwi Kotahi Tātou (We Are One People)*, after words spoken by Governor Hobson at the signing of the Treaty of Waitangi. It took Jenny fourteen weeks to complete the twenty-five-minute work, finishing with just enough time to get herself – and the score – to Ohakune for Sing Aotearoa.

Robert Sund, the festival's guest conductor from Sweden, directed the work at the event's final concert, but Jenny assisted at some rehearsals. That assistance partly involved teaching (male) choristers the haka she had written. Among the observers were some of the older men from Ngāti Rangi. 'They were listening like mad,' Jenny said, 'and one of them came over to me and said, "It's too fast." I nearly went, "What? You're telling me how fast my piece should be?" He was, because there are things attached to haka, like tempo, that matter. When it didn't happen the first time after he'd told me, he came and told me again. Then I *had* to slow it down.'

He Iwi Kotahi Tātou was the first specifically Māori piece Jenny had composed since *Earth and Sky*. What is striking about the work is how different it is from the music she composed in the intervening twenty-five years, and yet how closely it corresponds to that earlier music theatre piece. '*He Iwi* follows on directly (if some 25 years later) from my *Earth and Sky*,' Jenny wrote. 'Only at this point (after a thorough investigation of, and self-training in, the chromatic system during recent years) was I really equipped to realise the implications of, and to develop much more fully, the chromatic techniques that appeared there in embryo and only half-consciously.'[11]

The work is for Māori choir, a chamber choir and large choir (of about 250 for the Ohakune performance), with two pianos for accompaniment. Comprising seven movements, *He Iwi* reflects the order of events on a marae, beginning with a mihi (greeting) and concluding with a poroporoaki (farewell). The music ranges from monophonic chanting through concerted unison melodies and on to passages of complex rhythmic counterpoint woven amongst the various choirs and their sections. While the songs are often clearly chromatic, dissonances are artfully balanced with passages of more harmonically restful music. This is perhaps most elegantly – and most beautifully – achieved in the central movement, 'Waengapū Manu'.

That movement begins with a long introduction from the pianos, spare and gentle birdsong that cools the temperature after the preceding haka and turns the mood from declarative to one of contemplation. The Ngāti Rangi choir sings the first verses of the ancient waiata tangi as the pianos' birdsong continues, but from the beginning of the third verse, the manuhiri (guest) choirs add a hummed background. Initially long, sustained notes in unison across altos and tenors, these background lines subtly pull towards other tonalities, and expand to trace consonant, hymn-like chords as the piece progresses. At those hymn-like moments – during which the Ngāti Rangi song, the accompanying massed voices of the (mainly Pākehā) manuhiri choirs and the chromatic birdsong of the pianos combine – Jenny's vision for the work seems reified: 'I wanted to write something that might celebrate this coming-together of Māori and Pākehā,' she said.[12]

Mindful of the fraught history of Māori–Pākehā relations, Jenny recognised that a coming together or reconciliation of the respective peoples needed work, and so she embedded in the piece an acknowledgement of past wrongs committed against Māori: 'In one of the bigger songs of that cycle, I put an apology, in Māori, that the Pākehā had to sing to the Māori. The words said, "Can we start again? Get off to a new beginning?" Acknowledging wrong; not specific wrongs but wrongs on the side of the Pākehā. So, it was important to me from that point of view.'

The text was not simply an acknowledgement of Pākehā culpability. Having lamented the misdeeds of European ancestors, the song went on to express hope that Māori and Pākehā might paddle their canoes together, towards a better future:

Ko tēnei tō mātou tūmanako
He tīmatanga hōu
E hoa mā, kia haere tahi tātou . . .
Ki roto ki te moana o te wairua . . .
Ki roto ki te moana o te rangi . . .
Ko reira te ike rawa . . .
Ko tō tātou kāinga

This is our hope
A new beginning
O friends, let us travel together . . .
Into the ocean of the spirit . . .
Into the ocean of the sky . . .
Behold there the highest place . . .
Behold our home[13]

That song, 'Hoea Ngā Waka' ('Paddle the Canoes'), is the most challenging of the work, harmonically abstruse with angular melodies and plenty of rhythmic mischief. Composer Gillian Whitehead described it vividly as 'the most complex movement, with layers of singing, chanting, slapping, and stamping superimposed in the exciting paddling song, which is followed by the sweep up into the oceans of the sky'.[14]

It's not as though the rest of the music was a cakewalk, however, and Jenny's analysis of the score reveals extensive use of complex chromatic networks (and particularly Messiaen's 'Mode 3'), subject to various manipulations that grew out of her interest in the music of Messiaen, Boulez, Iannis Xenakis and Schat.[15] Gillian Whitehead observed, 'The technical skill of the piece is highly impressive, but not obtrusive – the surface hides the complexities. There is much use of symmetry, in the structure of the whole piece as well as vertically and laterally.' Whitehead also identified correspondences between the musical ideas and the text – evidence of the careful and comprehensive thinking that Jenny invested in the work.[16]

The overarching structure of *He Iwi Kotahi Tātou* was of considerable importance. Jenny's decision to organise the cycle to reflect the order of events on the marae had the effect of transforming the concert stage into a marae. She did this because Māori understood that on the marae the meaning of the song or haka and the history behind it were what really mattered.

The difficulty of the music and the challenges posed by the Māori text meant the (mainly Pākehā) performers probably weren't aware of the meaning of the words and the apology they contained; they were simply trying to get their mouths around the syllables and make it through to the end. But Jenny wasn't particularly concerned with how Pākehā might respond to the work, 'because I was not really talking to them in the piece, I was speaking to the Māori'. Those Māori in attendance, including Joan Akapita, understood the meaning of the words – and the sincerity with which Jenny had expressed them – perfectly well, 'and they appreciated it', Jenny said.

'Ever after the whānau referred to my piece as "The Opera". Cousin Luke innocently thought Robert Sund was somehow making up all the music as he conducted it, and remarked in wonder what a clever man he must be.' Jenny's close friend Tūngia Baker appreciated *He Iwi Kotahi Tātou* too, if for slightly different reasons: 'I told Tūngia, who was Ngāti Toa – we went to America together as AFS students so we knew each other well – she was on her deathbed when I told her what I did with this piece. She laughed and laughed. Just the fact that I'd made all these Pākehā sing this big apology, and they never knew what they were doing. Oh dear . . .'[17]

As Jenny was composing the music, she had not known that the choirs would have only six hours to rehearse the cycle. It was nothing like enough time to do the work justice. Robert Sund agreed: 'I thought it was far too difficult, and I have experienced that many times before. You commission a work for a specific group or occasion, and it turns out to be impossible to do. Anyway, I worked on it, because I thought it was a very interesting concept.'[18] Jenny recalled:

> It was a hideously difficult piece . . . Robert Sund didn't want to
> do the whole thing, and he was right, but I was desperate. I just

wanted the whole thing to be got through. We got reasonably good performances in the rehearsals but it was a big piece and they didn't know it well enough and by the time we came to the actual performance they went astray in several serious respects.[19]

Sund may have hoped for a stronger reading of the work, but given the circumstances he was positive about the performance: 'There was too little time to do it justice, but I was pleased that we got through it with some pride still left.'[20]

There were positive responses from the choristers, too. 'The Jenny McLeod work is wonderful,' one of them said. Another participant felt that the festival and *He Iwi Kotahi Tātou* achieved exactly the purposes Jenny had in mind:

> There's a depth and a richness and a mystery about what's been going on. The striving on the one hand to get to grips with Jenny's piece, to try and get it right, almost an impossible task in the number of hours we had – that on the one hand. And on the other hand, the coming together of the people and doing the haka together, and the meeting of minds and spirits. That's where I think the depth is. I think if New Zealand choral singing could capture some of that depth of emotion and mystery on the one hand, and the excellence of the detail in the piece on the other hand, it would be earth-shattering, spell-binding.[21]

Audience members were taken with the piece too, and not just by the sentiment of the words. After the performance, Jenny recalled, a Māori man 'came up to me because [*He Iwi*] was full of my pitch strategies, and he said to me, "I'd really like to talk to you one day about, how do you come up with sounds that are so different from what music normally sounds like".'

Jenny was not troubled by the shortcomings of the public performance. Fellow composer David Hamilton recalled, 'In Jenny's workshop on her piece, she said that for her the work had achieved what she set out to do. Even if the performance didn't go well, it had brought the peoples together.'[22] Gillian Whitehead confirmed this view: 'Not every movement peaked at the public performance on Sunday night (some peaked earlier) but with such a piece, perfection in performance is secondary to the journey of exploration, with Māori and Pākehā combining and sharing their ideas, their voices, their breath.'[23]

He Iwi Kotahi Tātou cost Jenny three and a half months of hard work, not only to realise the score – twenty-five minutes of complex, substantial music – but also to gain enough competence with te reo Māori to write the libretto in 'simple words from my heart'. *He Iwi* was also a pro bono effort. 'The Choral Federation didn't have any money at that stage to commission it, but they asked me to write a piece and so I wrote a piece for which I wasn't paid.' She doubted she would have accepted payment even had it been offered: 'The important thing, and the honour, was my even being invited – and by a Māori, Greg Tata – to write such a piece.'

The work was performed only once. As something of a site-specific work – it incorporates a song that belongs to Ngāti Rangi; the 'Mihi' movement includes specific references to the people of Maungārongo Marae – it is not a cycle that can easily be performed, as written, elsewhere. Further locking the work to that time and place, there is no acceptable recording of the cycle that might be circulated.[24] As a result, *He Iwi* is hardly known at all beyond those who participated in the 1993 festival.[25] That Jenny confessed satisfaction with the project when so much of her expertise and effort had resulted in a single, indifferent performance to a packed-out, but still relatively small, audience in the high school auditorium of a small central North Island town is revealing.

Robert Sund reflected, earnestly, that 'It was a beautiful idea to involve the Māori of Ohakune in the piece. It was a gesture of great humility.' Jenny might have attributed any humility on show to the tangata whenua of Maungārongo, for graciously welcoming the manuhiri choristers and sharing their ancient waiata tangi with them. Even so, Sund's analysis is correct: Jenny did approach the task and the occasion with humility and grace. This is evident in remarks she made to Richard Hardie that year; he reported that she was 'very satisfied with this work, and believes she has now found a way to balance her own needs with the needs of those for whom a work is intended'.[26]

When asked if she was disappointed that the work had lived only in that moment in 1993, she said, 'I don't mind. Of course, you're always happier when something gets heard . . . When this gets a good performance, it will be well received, but it doesn't matter that I'm not there because I know the piece.' The work was of significance to her 'particularly because of the words,' she said, 'but also because of the music. Because of both . . . If [recognition] were the reason why you were trying to write something you'd better give up, I think. How could it be that you could seek fame and fortune as a reason to do something? It's not a reason; it doesn't fill you up. Love fills you. And trying to help a situation fills me.'

The performance of *He Iwi Kotahi Tātou* may not have marked a watershed moment in relations between Māori and Pākehā in Aotearoa, but it marked such a moment for Jenny and the people of Maungārongo Marae: 'Even though Matiu [Māreikura] said to me at one point, "But we're *not* one people!", "We are in our hearts," I replied. Ngāti Rangi took me at my word in this piece, they took me in, and ever since our hearts have been pretty much as one, which is what I had meant by the title.' The work was also of considerable significance to the choristers and audiences for whom it was intended. In that moment, as the piece was prepared and performed, there was a meeting of hearts and minds.

A foot in both worlds

Jenny's introduction to the people of Maungārongo Marae and participation in the Sing Aotearoa festival laid the groundwork for a number of deep, powerfully meaningful relationships. In particular, Jenny formed a close friendship with Joan Akapita (known on the marae as Aunty Joan), who invited her to join the Tira Hoe Waka from Ngāpuwaiwaha Marae at Taumarunui to Pūtiki Marae in Whanganui the following summer. Jenny recognised the invitation as 'a response to me personally – both in her own right and on behalf of Ngāti Rangi – to my hopeful request for a "new start"'. The journey was normally open only to members of the river tribes, and Jenny felt privileged to be invited.[27]

It's really for the whānau, for the young to get to know their heritage. They stop at old defunct maraes; they stop at existing maraes . . . That river – especially in the upper river that you can't get to by road – is so beautiful, incredible. The oldies, the aunties, they karanga to the forest out there on the river. You'd be in the waka and suddenly this call – in Māori – would go out to the forest, mixed with the bird song and no other sound . . . You suddenly feel that this is the voice of the land in a way that you don't quite get – it doesn't have the same effect – when you hear it in a city or somewhere [else]. Magic, magic.[28]

She was well aware of the dangers of travelling such a long way by canoe. She was also well aware of the long history of aggression and dispossession her companions had suffered at the hands of European settlers and their governments. It was during this journey that she heard a recitation of the ancient Māori words – ancient but *living* words, as it turned out – that she had used in *Earth and Sky*. Her desire for the establishment of good relations between Māori and Pākehā – a new beginning in the wake of historic colonial injustice – was thus complicated by the knowledge that she too had taken something precious from Māori without first asking.[29] While it was to be a year or two before she was able to seek forgiveness for her use of Whanganui creation poetry in *Earth and Sky*, by the end of the trip she did feel she had been welcomed as a member of the tribal family. 'Doing that long trip down the river, I started out feeling very Pākehā and then, as the whole trip went by, I just gradually forgot that I was Pākehā.'

Over the next few years Jenny spent more and more time in Ohakune. The fleeting high school interactions she'd had with Ōtaki Māori were 'not the same as being on the marae,' Jenny said, 'with the ātea outside where the kids would be playing touch [rugby], and you'd be in the kitchen, sitting there with your cup of tea doing as little as possible. Well, you don't dare do as little as possible until you've been there a few years and you've earned that right by doing as much as possible. When you feel you can come and go in that situation, that's when you belong. And you *can* come and go – they don't have to do a big welcome for you when you come because it's your marae.'

She went on: 'I knew that there were Māori people but I didn't know how big the Māori world is and how the Pākehā just don't even know it's there. And you only find out what something is by actually stepping into it and living with them and finding out what their values really are.'[30] Jenny's interactions with the people of Maungārongo Marae were overwhelmingly positive. Within a few years of meeting them, she said:

> I know a particular group of Māori who are actually a particularly wonderful group of people. The way they're never in a hurry to pass judgement, they're very patient and they hear you. They'll sit there and they're really such great listeners and they just take things on board and you make boo-boos left and right culturally speaking. It doesn't worry them. The first thing they're interested in is who you are and once they're satisfied, once they feel they know who you are and they like you, then everything flows from that.[31]

During the mid-1990s Jenny's deepening relationship with her friends in Ohakune helped her establish a healthier work–life balance: time mostly alone at her home in Pukerua Bay where she could work on music and writing; and time with her Māori whānau in Ohakune. She told Di Fairley, 'I've got a foot in both worlds and it's nice because I'm able . . . you can get too far into one world and you can become too extremely individual and then you stop caring about people. Or you can get so involved in a communal society that there's no real space for you. So, I sort of balance both.'[32]

The ease Jenny had found in her relationships with Ohakune Māori represented a kind of fulfilment of the feelings she had expressed in an interview in the late 1980s. Discussing the depth of her affection for the creation poetry and its role in the genesis of *Earth and Sky*, she told Elizabeth Kerr, 'I loved that Māori poetry, I'd always wanted to do something with it, and then *Earth and Sky* came up, as an opportunity. I've never felt separate from the Māori people. The mere fact that I responded like that to the creation poetry and that I feel the way I feel about Pukerua Bay. To me I am a Māori.'[33] It's a startling claim from someone well aware of their European ancestry, and reveals that, for Jenny, a sense of kinship with Māori involved something other than blood relationships.

When Jenny spoke about this it was clear that, for her, the wholehearted affection and respect she felt for te ao Māori and her love of the land were evidence of a very deep connection. Her responses to the creation poetry served only to confirm this conviction: 'The words speak to me (I *feel* them!) as coming from a source deeper than the Book of Genesis. I love this creation poetry because intrinsically it moves me – as somehow a great river of I Am.' It wasn't that Jenny wanted to be Māori; rather, that 'Beneath my skin I feel I simply am, and I always have been.'

Michael King claimed to feel 'nothing but sadness for Pākehā who want to be Māori, or who believe they have become Māori – usually empty vessels waiting to be filled by the nearest exotic cultural fountain – who romanticise Māori life and want to bask forever in an aura of aroha and āwhina.'[34] It's impossible to know whether King would have characterised Jenny in this way. What can be said is that her feelings for – and identification with – Māori were deep and sincere.

Those feelings of kinship were mutual; Māori at Ohakune welcomed Jenny, describing her as 'a whangai to us of Maungārongo Marae and the Māramatanga of our tupuna Hōri Ēnoka Māreikura.'[35] 'Welcome home!' rangatira Matiu Māreikura said to her the second time she arrived on the marae. The local iwi, it seems, claimed her as their own. Had this welcome into the whānau simply been politeness or good manners, Matiu would not have asked her to document the story of his kinsman Hōhepa Te Umuroa. Jenny said, 'I don't recall feeling I really had much choice in the matter.' This was evidence of a family dynamic – something confirmed by Vera Māreikura, Matiu's older sister: 'We adopted her as a cousin to my family, the Māreikura family. And the cousins from the [Hawke's] Bay, when they see her, they call her cousin. "Hi cousin Jen," they say.'[36] Jenny said:

> Those Māori I do know well – who mostly call me whānau, Ngāti Rangi, kui or aunty – have always loved me best just for being myself. Karakia, snoring, breakfast, whare paku, feasting, kōrero, laughing (till crying), singing, rejoicing, washing-up, lamenting,

cleaning, listening, welcoming, learning, practising, packing up, parting, looking for your shoes or a blanket . . . this is what it's all about, it's just you and your mates or your rellies.

For Jenny, Governor Hobson's 'He iwi kōtahi tātou' was both her experience (with her Māori friends and among her Maungārongo whānau) and a promise. And that promise – that the respective peoples be reconciled with one another – became an article of faith which informed her personal and professional choices over the following decades.

As well as composing music for Māori (*He Iwi Kotahi Tātou*, and later hymns and her opera *Hōhepa*), she also made room for Māori concerns in her music: thematically and in her use of te reo Māori. Eventually, her work as a composer reflected both the way she lived, with 'a foot in both worlds', and the partnership principles of the Treaty of Waitangi – Māori and Pākehā together. Which is to say, hers was the musical practice of a single composer drawing respectfully on the wells of tradition offered by the two cultures.

It was on the basis of her deepening relationships with Māori that Jenny was compelled – 'I'm part of the whānau now, and I felt that I had to tell them', she said – and able to approach Matiu Māreikura and other Ngāti Rangi elders to explain her use of ancient Whanganui texts in *Earth and Sky*, seeking forgiveness and asking permission for the work to be performed again.[37] 'Had I not done that,' Jenny felt, 'me and them would still be two worlds. So, the Māori in my life have been a big deal. And if there's any purity in my heart, I owe it to them, I think. Not just to them, but to the way they treat sacred things.'

Jenny was grateful for the forgiveness and acceptance she received: 'This was really led by Matiu,' Jenny said, 'from whom the others took their cue.' But she had also come to understand the significance of what she had done: 'I would never dare touch a subject like that now, but that is only because I know a lot more about where it comes from and that it is not mine to touch; not mine to even look at.'

The more time she spent among Ngāti Rangi, the more involved she became in their music. 'Finally, they asked if I would be their permanent choir judge for the Easter Hui. How lovely. I couldn't think of anything nicer than having a permanent reason to keep coming back and seeing them. So, I said yes. I didn't realise that they wanted me to write choir test pieces in Māori every year and be the choir judge every year – but that was all right and I kept on doing that.'[38]

Jenny enjoyed writing music for Māori choirs a great deal. For one thing, songwriting was comfortable and familiar work; it had been one of the very few constants of her musical life. Her earliest songs had been composed during her first year at university; later, as a lecturer, she wrote songs for plays and for her music theatre pieces. During her time away from the profession, with the Divine Light Mission, her principal musical activity was composing and performing songs, and on her return to serious music the song cycles *Childhood* and *Through the World* were among the first works she completed. This was work that came naturally to her.

The request for Māori choir test pieces was also welcome because it kept her in the compositional saddle. 'Messiaen used to say "Don't stop" and I've taken that fairly seriously. Even if it's the simplest kind of pieces that I wrote for the Māori choirs and what have you, there were still things, merely by my writing stuff down and having people sing it back to me, that I was learning about choral music.'

The music Jenny first wrote for the choirs made noticeable use of chromaticism:

> Because quite a lot of what I heard in the old waiata would be rather unexpectedly chromatic, that led me to a view – a mistaken view – that if I wrote some quite chromatic things, they would find them easy. No, no, no. They found them terribly hard, even though they were more like their own stuff . . . The more diatonic my music for them became, the easier they found it. As I became more and more familiar with the things that they liked and normally did themselves, then they kept asking me to do stuff for them. I was also still getting the pleasure of working with amateurs who really, really wanted to do what I was asking them to do. Then, you become part of their family, and they start laughing when they hear your music – 'Ah, that's Jenny.' They can recognise things that I would do just because they sounded good (or familiar) when they did them. Most of the

time for those pieces I would have a high, loud ending, because they
loved to sing things like that, and their audience loved to hear it.

Vera Māreikura, a soprano in the choir, sang for me, from memory,
one of Jenny's hymns. 'Jenny doesn't make them easy,' she said. 'Especially
the "amens". We have good fun with the choir.'[39]
The choral test pieces Jenny composed for the annual Hui Aranga
(or Easter Hui) of the Māori Catholic church sometimes used existing
text – for example, 'He Honore, He Kororia' is a setting of a traditional
(post-European) prayer – but at other times featured words Jenny wrote
herself. Her work was not limited to composing the pieces and judging
the performances, either. Because almost none of the choristers – or
their conductors, for that matter – could read music, she also assisted
by making cassette tapes (and later CDs) of each of the four parts for
standard SATB choir configurations. 'This is a very private CD,' Jenny
said, 'because they are forbidden to let Pākehā hear this.' The reason?
Because Jenny sang all the parts herself. 'So, we have rather high bass
parts and rather low soprano parts so I can sing them. And it still sounds
terrible.' She went on:

I've been so embarrassed sometimes. One time I turned up at
Christmas, up at Ohakune, cos I go up there at Christmas. And
bugger me, in the marae kitchen, which was right next door, I heard
my voice on this damn CD, looped, going on and on while the
basses in the kitchen were learning their parts. When I first started
doing this, they thought I was getting other people to help and they
heard me singing the bass part and they said, 'Is that Jenny?' 'No',
[someone would reply], 'it's that priest . . .'[40]

Jenny wasn't thrilled with the sound of her own voice on the tapes,
although it delighted small children who, she understood, rolled about
with laughter when they first heard the recordings. But she was thrilled
to hear her music sung by the choirs, particularly on the Easter Sunday
morning when, directly after Mass, all of the choirs would get together
and sing the test piece for the rest of the large congregation – a high

point of the five-day hui. 'By the time they get together for the massed version they're all listening. The ones who know that they didn't get it right in the competition, are listening to the ones [with] strong voices who have got it right. And somehow, by magic, it always comes out that everything is right, and everything is there, and everybody adores this.'

During those years in which she drew close to her Maungārongo family, Jenny was delivered a sobering reminder that she was still her mother's daughter. In the mid-1990s she, like Lorna before her, was diagnosed with cancer. Jenny had not been particularly health conscious – Cecilia Johnson reckoned that Jenny's appetite for booze and smokes and food had done her no favours.[41] 'It was pretty serious at the time,' Jenny said. 'It certainly put a new gloss on my life. My house and surroundings bloomed with a kind of radiance as it dawned on me that I wasn't quite ready to leave this beautiful Earth just yet, and my priorities underwent some fairly serious review.'

The support she received from her brothers was especially meaningful, the dark humour that had always been a feature of their relationship a particular benison. 'Both my brothers were pretty good at black humour. After dad died [in 1985], my brothers referred to him as "our father who art in heaven". When I got cancer, that sort of lifted me above all the people that got so upset that I got cancer; I'd have to deal with them rather than the other way around, and my brothers coming back with all the black humour made it possible to laugh at everything.'

Jenny's cancer proved operable, and after surgery and with support from friends and family, she enjoyed a full recovery. 'In fact,' she said in 2021, 'me and my medicos have forgotten all that – there's been a lot of water under the bridge since then.' Positively, Jenny gave up smoking entirely, and managed to forgo drinking alcohol – for a while and to such degree, at least. Cecilia Johnson recalled that Jenny even began exercising, taking the neighbour's dogs for walks down to the beach and around the coast at Pukerua Bay. 'This continued every day for the next sixteen years,' Jenny said. 'I loved the dogs, and just being out there. Nature is a great healer.'

Music and spirit

Whether because of her illness, or the closeness she felt to her many Māori friends who were practising Christians – 'Karakia at seven each morning and evening is the unvarying custom at our marae and I had always liked being there, though mostly I didn't understand a word' – or possibly the result of watching early-morning television evangelists, it was around this time that Jenny returned to the church.[42] Although as an adult she had become preoccupied with matters of the spirit, as a child she had not given much thought to spirituality; the 'lovely little Croft's pipe organ – two manuals, pedals – that I got to play' in the Methodist church in Levin, and singing in the church choir, meant her attendance had more to do with music than faith.

Her ambivalence about Christian belief – she once suggested that even her participation in church youth groups was mainly driven by her interest in boys – may itself have been edged towards scepticism by an awareness of something unspoken in her brother Perrin's church experiences: 'My brother, who wouldn't call himself any kind of Christian, was an Anglican choirboy. My mother put both my brothers into the Anglican Boys' Choir at the cathedral in Timaru, though she was a Methodist. I think [Perrin] may have been abused in this situation – something went on there that I never found out about and that he never talked about. He departed the church quite swiftly.'

Jenny's willing embrace of Guru Maharaj Ji's teaching doesn't particularly complicate the impression of a longstanding scepticism regarding the existence of God: Prem Rawat's teachings didn't involve any sort of specific theism. However, many of the Eastern trappings that had become attached to Rawat's message and to the Divine Light Mission may well have seen her move towards some kind of belief in a deity. Whatever her convictions about God prior to the mid-1990s, at some point during her recovery from cancer Jenny began to attend services in St Luke's Methodist Church, joining the small congregation for their meetings at Pukerua Bay. 'I think I felt I wanted somebody's company – with a mind similar to my own . . . There was no pressure, I just did it because I felt like it.'[43] Jenny's return to the fold was to open a new musical chapter for her, one closely related to the test pieces she had been composing for the Māori choirs competing at the Hui Aranga.

Jenny knew the Wellington-based Presbyterian minister John Murray – John had officiated at Craig's wedding (to his first wife, Leslie) while serving as Victoria University's chaplain. John's wife Shirley Murray was a well-known hymn lyricist, collaborating with composers who crafted musical settings for her texts. Jenny came across Shirley Murray's hymns when – because she had not prepared herself to say 'No' – she ended up playing organ at St Luke's. She liked Shirley's hymns in particular, because the small congregation sang them with such gusto, even managing to stay in tune:

> Some of those words that she wrote, I liked them, and as has happened from time to time with me, I just started writing music to some of them, ones that often [New Zealand composer] Colin Gibson had already written music for, and that were already known with his music. So, I wasn't particularly thinking that anyone was going to sing them. The tunes came very readily, so I wrote a bunch, quite a few. She liked them – I gave them all to her – and one or two of them ended up in collections by her, published in America.

Jenny's settings of Shirley's texts first appeared in print in the 2003 collection *Faith Makes the Song*, and would find their way into some anthologies as well. Initially motivated by her own positive response to Shirley's words, rather than by dissatisfaction with the existing settings (although she admitted that did happen once or twice), 'It was as though the floodgates opened and all the hymns that I had ever wanted to write came out.' Between the late 1990s and around 2010 she completed more than one hundred and thirty hymns, in a variety of styles and for all kinds of occasion. About half a dozen of those written using Shirley's words made it into print. From time to time, she even had the opportunity to accompany her own hymns 'on a fairly dim electronic organ' during services, 'but the tiny congregation, half elderly and half Cook Islanders, was not very good at – and little interested in – picking up new songs, so I ended up simply playing them as organ music before, during and after services'.

While Jenny enjoyed being in the company of the St Luke's congregation, being rostered to play the organ regularly became increasingly burdensome: 'These small churches, they don't have many people but they insist on having all this damned organisation. So, you've got councils and committees and you end up with no room in your life for anything else but running this tiny little church. After a few years of that I needed to move.'[44]

Moving on from the Methodists developed entirely naturally. Jenny's Ngāti Rangi friends were all Catholics, and she liked how she felt when she was with them. She wondered if in fact they were the first truly Christian people she had met. 'They were very devout and I just liked being with them . . . They never tried to ram anything down your throat and they had a very realistic attitude to life, it seemed to me. It didn't begin and end with the church – you had your work [as well].'[45] Within a few years, Jenny said, 'I felt I belonged with these people. Every time I saw them, I said, "My family, my family, I love you." Things I never really said to my own family.'

Prior to the Easter Hui in Whangārei in 2003, Jenny asked the Māori bishop, Max Mariu, if he would receive her into the Māori Catholic church. 'He never questioned the fact that I wasn't a Māori to be accepted into the church – I was already baptised. So, I was received into the Māori Catholic Church.' She was touched, too, by the bishop's acknowledgement of her place among them. 'In the middle of one of his sermons, I was sitting up there – we were part of the band at one of the Easter services which he used to take before he died – and he was going on and suddenly I realised he was standing behind me, massaging my neck, and telling the whole congregation "This is a national taonga – look after her." Well, I've loved Bishop Max Mariu ever since.'

In joining the Catholics and finding acceptance among them, Jenny discovered a kind of relaxed freedom she'd always hoped for but rarely found in her spiritual life:

I like the Catholic Church a lot, but I only go to church if I'm
with the Māori. Aside from that I don't think about church at all
– I don't think anything theological at all – and I'm very glad not
to. I don't feel it's necessary (for me) to go through all this church
performance. I think that's there for people who like it or who want
it – it's a very safe place for people to stay if they don't want to move.
If I'd stayed there and tried to write serious music it would have
been like Messiaen – they would have heard the devil in the pipes.
It wouldn't be so overtly mediaeval as that, but it would be that I
would upset people, and there's no need for me to upset people.[46]

The freedom and ease Jenny experienced as a member of the Māori
Catholic community also led her to a new understanding of the
relationship between her spiritual leanings and her work as a musician.
It was an understanding that enabled her to recognise and accept, finally,
her vocation as a composer.

In interviews up until the late 1990s Jenny consistently expressed
uncertainty about her status as a composer. In 1988 Elizabeth Kerr asked
her, 'As a student did you think of yourself as a composer?' Jenny replied,
'No. Not ever! In fact, I still don't think of myself as a composer.'[47] In the
mid-1990s she was asked, 'When and how did you feel that you were a
composer?' Jenny said, 'I've never felt that. I still don't know.'[48] And later,
'I didn't exactly know what a "real composer" was because I had never
felt like one. But I did instinctively feel that there *was* such a thing as
being a real composer.'

It wasn't doubt in her abilities that made Jenny unsure about her
professional standing: 'I knew I could do that; I had proved that to my
own satisfaction,' she said. So, exactly why Jenny remained uncertain
of her status as a composer for so long is hard to determine precisely. It
may have been because she had never felt a sense of vocation or calling.
From quite early in her career, she had said that composing hadn't
been something she felt compelled to do, it was simply something that
happened. 'Circumstances made it so I ended up being a composer
without ever consciously deciding to be one . . . I didn't really know
what I was doing, why I was writing music,' she told *Landfall* in 1972.[49]

Neither was she driven by a need for self-expression through music: 'I don't really write pieces to express myself, I don't understand that whole thing because I just don't experience it like that. But I know, well, most other people that regard themselves as composers, they do seem to feel that.'[50]

Perhaps the absence of these drivers, so common (or at least commonly professed) among the composers she met, led her to doubt she was a 'real' composer? It may also have been that received wisdom suggested the work of 'real' composers exhibited mastery, complexity, gravity and power – principally masculine constructions that, while sometimes evident in her music, were no more important than other qualities, including simplicity, delicacy, humour and humility. Or perhaps it was her unwillingness to dedicate the whole of her life to music that fuelled her uncertainty? When young composers approached Pierre Boulez seeking to study with him, as Peter Schat had done, Boulez would ask them, 'Are you willing to devote your entire life to music?' If they agreed they would indeed be willing, Boulez would take them on, teaching them at no charge. 'This was why I never went to him,' Jenny said, 'because I didn't think I could say that, really. Not at that time.' She was deeply committed to pursuing other things besides music: personal relationships, the written word, spiritual sustenance. That being the case, she couldn't claim to be just or only a composer, and therefore perhaps was not a 'real' composer at all.

This last priority, a recognition of the need for spiritual sustenance, seems to have been particularly significant. For a long time, Jenny had experienced the musical and spiritual dimensions of her life as independent. The acceptance she found in the Māori and wider Catholic community allowed her to see these apparently separate strands in a new light.

> If you're a fulfilled Catholic then you know it and you won't be bothered by going to church or not going to church. Enjoy whatever, do whatever, but you're a free soul, basically. That helped me out because they had, to me, a very helpful and I think true relationship to the arts. If you're going to be a practising creative artist and you're

also hooked up with some religious outfit or other, they need to recognise what you're doing is your way of growing, is your way of finding a much more personal religion than you will find for yourself in a church.

The Christian community in which she found herself was not exclusive or absolutist in its beliefs, but comfortable with plurality. That context, Jenny said, was 'demonstrably effective in *showing* me things: it gradually brought me closer to an understanding of the way the most important things had all along been operating in my life.' This understanding was one she expressed by invoking the metaphor of the braided river: at times and places the river flows as one, and at others it breaks apart into separate strands – yet it is always the same river. Jenny grew to realise that – like the braids of the river – music and spirit might at times appear independent, but for her they were always part of the same overarching whole: 'I was splitting things up where there was no actual split.' She linked this realisation to William Broughton's poem 'Epithalamia', which she had set as song in 1963:

> The whole kaupapa of the text actually became the story of my life, as I sought alternately (and more than once) to 'rectify' my own spirit and to be 'wedded to my craft'. Today it is largely by practising my craft that I rectify my spirit. My religion is ultimately my craft. In all this I find I am supported by my Māori Catholic family and priest and sister friends. I recognise that it isn't *good* for me not to be composing something, be it words or music – without this I die, I become intolerable. The result has been that both [my spirit and my craft] have grown and prospered.

With this awareness, Jenny was able to confidently state: 'My spirituality is my music, and it's very broad. This realisation, this understanding, dawned on me from within, and ever since then I have simply known that I am a composer. It also has nothing to do (sorry, Pierre) with "dedicating one's entire life to music" – I can be doing anything I like, but I am still a composer.'

It wasn't just Jenny who had come to recognise her status as a composer. In 1997 she received a letter from Governor-General Sir Michael Hardie Boys, advising her that she had been nominated for the New Zealand Order of Merit (ONZM) for services to music in the Queen's Birthday Honours. Among those also honoured was Ian Harvey, with whom Jenny had taken piano lessons in Levin and who had been musical director of the Auckland production of *Earth and Sky*. Publisher and painter Janet Paul, whom Jenny knew well – they had enjoyed a mutual friendship with Fred and Eve Page – was also honoured that year, as was Sister Dorothea Meade of the Sisters of Compassion. Jenny had got to know Sister Dorothea through Joan and Ritchie Akapita, and they had become close friends.

Having met the Queen and Prince Charles during the Auckland season of *Earth and Sky*, and as a supporter of the monarchy in general, Jenny was pleased to receive the award and happy to have the Queen's signature on her wall. 'Though of course,' she added, 'so much effort from others had as usual played a big part, and one had no opportunity to say as much.'

16

Jenny McLeod | Composer

The breadth and volume of Jenny's compositional output (hymns and songs, chamber and orchestral music, film scores and theatre pieces, ranging in style from the abstraction of *Piano Piece 1965* to the sing-along pop of *Cuckooland*), as well as her extensive theoretical work and creative writing (poetry, essays), make it hard to get an exact bead on what it is she has done. And what she did from day to day, and from year to year, is a moving target as well. Even after coming to terms with her vocation as a composer – accepting that she was, in fact, a composer – Jenny's practice continued to develop and expand. It seems fair to say, however, that by the late 1990s she had settled on a more or less consistent set of approaches to making music, and had firmly established her values as a musician.

Jenny told me, 'It is difficult to be a real composer. It's difficult to find yourself, if that's what you are looking to do.' Music histories are full of 'great men' narratives, full of stories about composers who write music out of some inner compulsion – music that somehow discloses their own true character. Jenny said:

There's a lot about the kind of 'search to be yourself' that I don't necessarily agree with. There grew up in the nineteenth century a whole tradition of what it meant to be a composer, half of which you can agree with very well because it produced some brilliant, real composers. The rest, it just got [composers] into a way of thinking that was dangerous, that was full of hubris; they took themselves far too seriously and set themselves up for the pedestal. I think probably Beethoven was responsible (after his death) for the growth of a whole tradition like that.

Beethoven was a real composer in Jenny's estimation, but not because he was able to 'translate feeling into sound' or was in some way Goethe's musical cognate, composing works that captured the emerging spirit of humanism characteristic of Romantic thinking. Beethoven made the grade, Jenny believed, because 'anyone whose work has lasted – has met the test of time and that we still listen to – is a real composer.' Real composers, she said, are those whom other composers look to and learn from:

Even someone like Rimsky-Korsakov, who wrote a few wonderful pieces – we can all learn from the artistry of those particular works. Even if they have written just one piece that we can learn from, like Khachaturian. If we are still plumbing these works and learning something from them – rather than just resting in them – then I call that a real composer, somebody who didn't just compose on Sundays. A real composer has something that is not just about music – there's something deeper. Music can already be very deep, and what can make it [more] so is what the composer is aspiring towards: being something that is going to last, that is going to help people to be human beings in the world.

She believed the work of a real composer involved 'plumbing the depths'. Real composers thought about where music came from and where it might be going to. That kind of project inevitably requires that composers go beyond what they already know; are unconstrained by what others might think or say. In this she had two immaculate examples:

Olivier Messiaen and Pierre Boulez. Asked if these men were happy to
go beyond what was known, happy to advance their music whatever the
cost, she said, 'Not just happy to, it was necessary for them. They could
never have been satisfied with just doing more of the same.'

Curiously, although she listened to and analysed their music, Jenny
did not study composition with either of them: with Messiaen she
studied analysis; and with Boulez she did not study formally at all, simply
observed his teaching and read his work extensively.[1] Even so, together
they formed a kind of twinned pole star about which she oriented her
musical thinking and values.

Jenny was to say that her arrival at a kind of peace with herself as a
composer was partly attributable to her coming to terms with these two
very different role models. And to do that, it was necessary to understand
the things they'd done. 'Messiaen was much easier to understand, and
besides, Messiaen never behaved as though anyone ought to do anything
the way he had done it. But Boulez sort of did. I think he would have
regretted that people might have felt like that, but otherwise, why did he
write as much as he wrote along the lines that he wrote, which were so
often about how to do something?'

The musical materials Jenny drew most obviously from Messiaen
were related to his modes of limited transposition, and to his use of
birdsong. However, she left these – and in particular his modes – largely
to one side of her compositional practice for many years. 'I got hold of
[his *Technique de mon langage*] before I went to study with Messiaen,
and that's where I got his ideas. The extent to which he used his modes
was so personal that – well, that's partly why I felt I needed to leave
them to him . . . I didn't get into them myself purposely until after he
had died.' Echoes of Messiaen's modes sound in much of Jenny's Tone
Clock music – they are, after all, simply particular chromatic groups,
nestled among all the other chromatic groups that might be described
or generated using Tone Clock theory – but it wasn't until *He Iwi Kotahi
Tātou*, composed a year after his death, that she made deliberate and
extensive use of them. There's quite a lot of birdsong in *He Iwi*, too.

In Boulez's music, Jenny observed and subsequently adopted various
techniques and methods, such as frequency multiplication, the basis

of Schat's 'steering' when composing using the Tone Clock hours. She spent considerable time working out for herself how Boulez developed his harmonic systems, and also paid attention to ideas he explored in his books. For example, she endorsed Boulez's view that all the harmonic cells derived from a (frequency multiplication) network as the basis for a piece had to appear at least once, after which the work could be considered complete. She also took seriously his suggestion that if a composer was going to fully organise one of the musical parameters, it was not necessary to fully organise all the others: 'I believe that's a good idea. I do that, mostly. In *For Seven* it was the rhythms and the durations and what have you that were fully organised. But after that, well, nearly always it was the pitches that I organised and let the rhythms take care of themselves.'

Both Boulez and Messiaen devised strategies for composition, systems to facilitate the choices they made as composers, but both adopted attitudes towards those systems that Jenny found invigorating. 'One must never be a slave to anything,' Messiaen suggested to Jenny, which she reported was 'advice he certainly followed himself. For although he invented and used numerous systems (sometimes in startlingly simple ways), these could be combined with completely extraneous elements . . . The fact that he liked the sounds concerned was, for him, quite sufficient reason for them to be there.'[2]

Boulez, who could be doctrinaire about compositional processes, was also capable of comparable flexibility. Jenny recalled:

> In quite early days . . . he said he had suddenly, in the middle of a piece, whatever system he had created to generate the music so far, he suddenly threw it all away. In the middle of the same piece, even in the same movement, [he] wrote completely instinctively with no intellectual basis for what he was doing at all. And he said later on he couldn't tell the difference. That, for him, was a big kind of release – if you can't tell the difference, then there's not too much to worry about.

While Messiaen's *Quatuor pour la fin du temps* had galvanised Jenny to leave New Zealand in search of a new world of musical colour, and Boulez's *Le Marteau sans maître* opened doors to a startling array of new musical possibilities, the importance of their example extended beyond just the musical:

> I needed and loved them both, almost as two opposite ends of a spectrum: Boulez for his dedication, his heart and mind, and his incomparable writings perhaps more than his music – though its purity is matchless and I love it for this. His standards in the end became largely those against which I must measure my intellectual thought. But Messiaen, in his greatest moments, for the sound, and truth, and power, and beauty of his soul, and for being who and what he was – for me a kind of guardian angel, as well as my teacher and friend.[3]

It would seem that while the way these composers worked was important to Jenny, who they were was of equal consequence. And both of them were completely comfortable with who they were. She said, 'Boulez, he had a very strong sense of who he was, of what his position was. He knew very well how good he was, but he didn't say it – although you could read it in his face.' And of Messiaen she wrote: 'He never told others how they should do things. In a way he was a sort of reverse iconoclast, not by design, but by nature. He didn't set out deliberately to provoke, or to upset our preconceptions of what music is, or "should be." That he sometimes did (and was not unaware that he surely would) was simply a by-product of his remaining constantly and triumphantly himself.'[4]

Perhaps the almost Janus-like opposition Jenny found in the characters of Messiaen and Boulez sounded an echo with her own apparently contradictory nature. A devout Catholic, Messiaen was comfortable with mystery and embraced the spiritual. His capacity to see the best in people, his humility and his deep love of the natural world were qualities Jenny loved and revered and, in truth, shared. Boulez, who moved beyond the Catholic church to a life apparently without faith, was an iconoclast. 'Boulez – I never heard him do this,' Jenny said, 'but he did it when he was younger, could improvise like Beethoven and laugh at it.' He was worldly and urbane and fiercely intelligent. Although Jenny rarely (if ever) demonstrated the kind of arrogance of which Boulez was capable, she – like Boulez – was an intellectual and needed to make sense of the world, needed to arrive at a rational understanding of the things she encountered (or at least those things that were responsive to rational analysis).

By coming to terms with the two very different examples Boulez and Messiaen had set, Jenny was able to arrive at her mature voice as a composer. Similarly, by coming to understand that music – which was what she did – and her orientation to the spiritual – which was who she was – could live together, she was able to accept her vocation as a composer. 'The music spiritual thing sorted itself out,' she said. 'It just went away. I stopped worrying. What was I worrying about?'

Composing women

Jenny's university years coincided with the beginnings of second-wave feminism, a time when ideas about sexist power structures, the changing roles of women in the workforce and ending discrimination were receiving widespread attention. In spite of her proximity to these social movements she described herself in 1993 as being 'up to now a confirmed non-feminist'.[5] It wasn't that Jenny didn't believe in or value equality between the sexes. Rather, she was confident that, for the most part, she did enjoy equality with men.

She was asked from time to time about the ways in which her biological sex might have been disadvantageous to her professionally. These were questions to which she responded with varying degrees of impatience. Did she think starting out as a composer was harder because she was a woman? 'Oh, it wasn't any different. No, no, no . . . If anyone had ever suggested to me that because I was a woman, that it was going to be impossible, I would have just ripped them to pieces . . . a bloody absurd idea. So, everything I did, I never thought for a moment about being a woman.'[6] Had she been inhibited by the lack of a female role model? 'Why would I want a female role model? It never entered my head.'[7]

As far as Jenny knew or could remember, being a woman had not made any difference to how she had fared professionally. 'My whole life long, I never ever got the slightest flak from anyone at all about the fact that I happened to be a female; possibly they sensed I'd have withered them with scorn if they tried this. Consequently, it never entered my head that this could possibly be an issue.'[8] As a result, she was reluctant to include biological sex as part of her definition of a composer. 'I never would have given tuppence, myself, to say there was a difference between men and women composers. I never wanted to be a "woman composer". In fact, I privately took it as a kind of insult for the first few years.'

Nonetheless, looking beyond her own professional circumstances, she was not blind to the effects of sexual discrimination and prejudice against women. She said, 'There have been many, many woman composers about whom we know nothing. Why? Because they didn't consider to put them in the history book. That's discrimination.'[9] And her awareness of why that might have been the case was to develop significantly during the 1990s.

In 1993, the centenary of women's suffrage in New Zealand, Jenny was invited by Elizabeth Kerr to take part in the inaugural Composing Women's Festival in Wellington. The following year, and in her capacity as Music Manager for the QEII Arts Council, Elizabeth invited Jenny – along with Keri Kaa, Tūngia Baker, Mere Boynton, Gillian Whitehead and Helen Fisher – to join a party of New Zealand musicians participating in an equivalent festival in Melbourne, Australia.[10] And in 1996 Elizabeth was involved in organising a further New Zealand event which Jenny also attended. Jenny enjoyed the music and the community of the women, saying, 'I was pleasantly surprised. I discovered there *was* a difference between men and women composers.' She also confessed that she could not have imagined herself making such a claim before. 'It's just that women – well, these women – did get on together much better than I thought would ever be the case. And I found myself part of this and quite enjoying it, really.'

Jenny was pleased to discover, among other things, that women composers were comfortable making music that did not rely on prevailing orthodoxies, and were open to all kinds of influences and people. She found that relationships with younger composers were calmer: 'You realise, in women's company, that they are a lot less competitive, less threatening, they like to please people and not make divisions between high art and low art.'[11] Women, Jenny thought, were inclined to regard music as communication rather than competition, so 'they don't necessarily write a piece to shine in the eyes of the audience, but to speak; and are quite happy to do this in quite a small and modest way if that's how the piece comes out. But, of course', she felt the need to add, 'there are also male composers who are quite capable of doing that, too.'[12]

Jenny found that the experience of being among so many women – talking with them and listening to their work – got her thinking more about the distinctions between men and women:

> I think a lot of feminist-type cultural analysis is totally valid. It's just that I didn't start thinking about it until quite late and when I did – and a lot of this whole thing about 'what is a composer?' and 'what does it mean to compose?' – then I began to sort of realise that, well yes, it has been pretty much defined by males. And maybe that is why I was just never able to fit into it, couldn't see where I fitted in because I didn't feel any of those things.[13]

Jenny's view, one she believed was shared by her contemporaries, was that so-called masculine and feminine qualities were not the exclusive province of the respective sexes. 'There are some quasi-stereotype masculine and feminine-type qualities,' she explained. 'Now, they exist within men and women in different proportions and in proportions that can change from day to day. I mean, I think you need a fair share of both of them to be any kind of decent composer. Any composer that I've ever really liked is able to deal with what I would call both sides of that.'[14]

However, she had come to see that many common conceptions about what a composer was tended to be dominated by masculine constructions. She described these common conceptions as 'the generations of the "masterpiece syndrome" and all the assumptions, the older assumptions, about what music is and what a composer is and what [composers] are aiming for'.[15] Those presuppositions appear at odds with her notion that creative artists possess both feminine and masculine qualities, yet as a younger composer she too had been captured by them. Of her time in Europe, and in the years after her return to New Zealand, she said:

> I was trying to do more in those days and I was still caught up in the 'masterpiece syndrome', in what I would call now a male definition of a composer: you have to write a great masterpiece of music – there is no room for writing popular music. But I didn't consciously think of any of those things till years afterwards. I stopped thinking about the masterpiece syndrome after *Under the Sun*.[16]

The pervasiveness of these ideas was attributable, Jenny thought, to the almost complete invisibility of women amongst the ranks of composers, historically and even until quite recently. It wasn't that women weren't composing music. They were, but their work was almost entirely missing from the standard narratives. As a result, some of the different stories that might have been told about what a composer could be and do were marginalised. Jenny's intentionally cultivated indifference to critical opinion, and her determination to blaze her own trail, had to a large extent insulated her from these issues. Besides, she'd had plenty of commissions and her reviews had generally been good. Nevertheless, her growing awareness of the consequences of composers being defined and valued in masculine terms enabled her to understand the reasons for the gap between what was fêted and what was equally valuable but often overlooked.

Jenny was optimistic that the work of women composers was being recognised, and felt that in New Zealand, 'women composers were judged on the quality of their music rather than on their gender'.[17] She also sensed that received wisdom was beginning to evolve to accommodate a wider variety of ideas about what composers had to offer. She observed, 'They're starting to dig up a few women composers from the past and you find that their whole approach has been quite different. They haven't been mad keen to write the world's greatest masterpiece, they've often been happy to spend their lives writing music maybe for children or for teaching purposes or for the kinds of things that women see as important, or just as important.'[18]

New Zealand music

The notion that women composers might be somehow categorically different from male composers has a geographical cognate in the idea that New Zealand music is in some way categorically different from music composed elsewhere. That there might be a New Zealand music, or a New Zealand voice in music, was an idea that had circulated in the communities within which Jenny moved, but it was not one that concerned her particularly. Her agnosticism about a so-called 'New Zealand voice' was fuelled in part by her belief that it was an idea linked to masculine notions of composition. 'I'm rather inclined to think,' she said, 'that this is all a male thing, this New Zealand voice business and self-expression and all this stuff.' The potentially exclusive nature of those ideas was also problematic to Jenny. 'To have one and only one voice, which is your New Zealand voice or Australian voice or wherever you come from, to have only one voice for all the different kinds of people does seem, to a mother or a school teacher or someone like that, a bit daft.'[19]

Douglas Lilburn had been exercised by the idea that New Zealand needed a music of its own, music that might 'satisfy those parts of our being that cannot be satisfied by the music of other nations'.[20] It was an idea consistent with the thinking of an informal group of artists, writers, musicians and publishers he had known in Christchurch during the 1930s. Described by historian Peter Simpson as 'Bloomsbury South' (after London's Bloomsbury Group of the first decades of the twentieth century), the group harboured the desire to synthesise European modernism with a nationalistic agenda in the hope of arriving at a unique, local art.[21] These were ideas that Lilburn addressed formally on a number of occasions.[22]

But Jenny said, 'I never thought about them. I wasn't worried about

stuff like that. I was just worried about getting through the next piece.'
She was aware that some older people in the arts community were
conscious of these concerns. 'But just quietly,' she said, 'I really felt: these
people don't feel at home here . . . They'd probably contradict me and
say, "Of course I felt at home here" – but that's not what I observed.' She
was disconcerted by older composers 'who kept talking about home, in
Britain', and who gravitated to Britain to study, just as she was dismayed
by radio and television announcers who affected a British accent, and by
the commonly held idea that New Zealanders were in essence Britons
transplanted from one side of the globe to the other.

While Jenny did travel abroad, she missed New Zealand terribly: the
sea and sky, the bush and the birds. She was always clear that her home
was there, and always intended to return. In Europe her longing for
Aotearoa was partly assuaged by her immersion in the Māori creation
poetry, but really only by returning was she able to once again feel
completely at home.

'Feel' is the right word to describe Jenny's response to New Zealand's
environment. She wasn't oblivious to how the country actually looked
when she returned from abroad: 'The light itself is so bright; when you
get back it hurts your eyes. It's harsh, this bright light. The hills look
black, they don't look blue. All the rest of the colours – it's as though
something had covered them up.' But her relationship to the country
was 'not so much visual as . . . it is within me; I feel this place more than
I hear or see it.' That said, the sounds she heard in New Zealand were
also a part of her appreciation of the country. 'I hear things like the birds
and the wind and when it rains, those sorts of sounds. I love them – but
I love those sorts of sounds anywhere. Well, the birds are different. Our
birds are just over the top. Our birds really know where they are.'

Given her strong identification with New Zealand it followed that
whatever she wrote would in some way be of the place. Composers who
lived and worked in New Zealand were, by Jenny's reckoning, making
New Zealand music: 'I never consciously looked for a New Zealand
music. I think it's daft. I think you should just be trying to write music
that is truly yours and it *will* be New Zealand music because you're a
New Zealander.'[23] How that relationship to the country might materially

affect the music local composers wrote, however, was not something she felt a need to comment on.

Jenny did have thoughts about how New Zealand musicians might nurture the music they developed as a result of their relationship with the country. In particular, and like Lilburn before her, she cautioned composers (and other artists too) not to get swallowed up by newly minted international styles; not to lose themselves in worldwide trends.[24] Peter Schat had approved of the development of international or global styles of music, but Jenny feared that the spreading-out that attended such styles – the dissolution of the particular in a more general gestalt – might rob local scenes of the things that were unique and close and, as such, precious. 'I was never so keen on that,' she said. '*For Seven* was the only piece I ever wrote that was in that vein and deliberately in that vein.'

But even in a work as deliberately international as *For Seven*, Jenny's links to New Zealand managed to assert themselves. Elizabeth Kerr said, 'When you listen to *For Seven* now, you can hear the New Zealand influence so strongly – the birdsong and the way she's structured [it].' Elizabeth recognised that even while clearly understanding and making use of 'that middle European way of doing things,' Jenny (like other New Zealand composers working in that idiom) had somehow 'found a clarity in those textures'.[25] Jenny elaborated:

> At the time I was thinking of [*For Seven*] mostly in fairly abstract terms. Only years later did it dawn on me that the piece is actually full of 'insect life' and the sounds of the bush. The manic woodwind 'bird-song' was certainly conscious, but not what I now hear as sudden little chatterings and flurries of insects, wings, or leaves, or the microscopic detail that for me now evokes the intense activity of the forest floor, as studied at close hand, say, from some meditative seat on a fallen punga log. Clearly Gondwana was asserting itself despite the black depths of Cologne (which I hated).[26]

This echo of Aotearoa arrived from somewhere beyond the level of conscious thought. Jenny wrote that with *For Seven*, 'what I had thought of as an abstract modernist idiom was actually much closer to my own real experience than I dreamed'.[27] Perhaps for a composer like Jenny, deep experiences can potentially find expression in any music they write, irrespective of the style or the instruments chosen, or even their conscious intentions? She had come to the conclusion that if there ever was to be a local musical tradition that somehow reflected or expressed its provenance, it would emerge in this way – organically, unconsciously – rather than by being planned, engineered or mapped out in advance. 'I don't believe you can just say, "Oh well, now we're going to create a local tradition." I don't think it happens [that way]. It's going to be funny as hell if you came to it with that attitude.'

Even the idea of a 'national identity' was one Jenny found dubious, however much had been said about it over the years. But while she remained sceptical about monolithic statements of what it meant to be a New Zealander, she did feel positive about what New Zealanders might offer to the world:

> What I like is the sense that out of all the misapprehensions and misgivings and injustices and awful things that came out of colonialism – all over the world, and for similar sorts of reasons – that we could maybe start to get over that and be ourselves. But not just Māori and Pākehā (and there's all the others as well), not for our prime senses of difference between us and the Māori, but for our sense of what is common between us – as Māori and Pākehā – and other places in the world. Because of the way at least some of us are working and have been working on our own inter-relationships and growing friendship, it releases us to be creative in a fresher, more positive way.

What the creative outputs resulting from these burgeoning partnerships might actually look or sound like was of little concern to Jenny. They would certainly be particular to New Zealand (given their twinned provenance in Māori and Pākehā cultures), but for her the relationships required to make such work were of greater importance than anything they produced. It is these values – of dialogue, sharing and collaboration – that informed Jenny's approach to the composition and performance of *He Iwi Kotahi Tātou*. They are also values a very long way from what she has described as the 'masterpiece syndrome'.

In nuts-and-bolts terms, such partnerships often involve stylistic crossovers, and Jenny was very comfortable with approaches of this sort:

> I love it when Māori start taking in other things, or their own styles start to adapt themselves, because my view is you don't lose anything through all this kind of interaction (or appropriation, if the attitude is wrong – the attitude is really important). Meaning that all the old things are still there unchanged; anything new is simply added to them. When all of us are sort of reaching out and doing what releases us, then that's going to be good for the world and it's going to be something that they can't do yet – because they haven't been through what we've been through, and are going through still.

It is likely that Jenny's optimism about this kind of syncretism was at least partly a result of the success she had enjoyed with her own trans-cultural projects. Those works – *Earth and Sky*, her hymns for Māori, *He Iwi Kotahi Tātou*, and later compositions such as *Hōhepa*, *He Whakaahua o Maru* and *Te Pūroto Kōpua* – created the opportunity for her to work with Māori, as well as Māori materials and te reo Māori, to explore themes and compose music that in some way reflected values absolutely to do with living in Aotearoa. Importantly, they were projects that moved beyond reductive notions that equated New Zealand music only with the local landscape. Jenny had laid the groundwork for this kind of practice with her first major commission, and it was this undertaking that gave her confidence to believe she could be a composer with something to say in New Zealand:

> For me to write a piece like *Earth and Sky*, that did involve Māori people and not just the land, that was like my Warrant of Fitness. I don't think I could ever have been a composer without having written that piece. I had already written *For Seven* and the first big piano piece – that meant I was a European composer, because those

are European pieces, the whole approach is European, and that's
where *For Seven* was first performed. I thought they were pieces that
would stand up in Europe. They would stand up here, but it was of
less consequence to me if they stood up here than that they stood
up over there. But *Earth and Sky* was something that wouldn't have
cropped up anywhere in Europe; it is so <u>not</u> Europe, and it is much
closer to my heart.

Whether *Earth and Sky* represents 'the sort of truth in New Zealand
music we have been looking for, for a long time', as Owen Jensen had
it, would depend on who you asked.[28] Less contentious, however, is the
suggestion that with that work – and for all the problems we might
identify viewing it through a lens fashioned in the twenty-first century –
Jenny McLeod made her first steps towards music that genuinely sought
to communicate something that was truly hers, and so by extension
something of what it was to be a New Zealander.

17

Words and Music, Poetry and Song

The routines of the new century were to be the most stable of Jenny's life. Living quietly in Pukerua Bay, with occasional visits to Wellington, she also made regular trips to Ohakune to spend time with her adopted whānau at Maungārongo Marae. Her working days were divided between writing words and composing music. While some of the music she composed was instrumental – a handful of chamber works and a further ten Tone Clock pieces for piano – much of it was for voices, including quite a few settings of texts by New Zealand poets.

Her compositional approach had also to some extent stabilised. Jenny's earlier work as a composer, which ranged widely in style and tone, had been informed by the music she had heard and studied, and by the theory she had read. Her mature music emerged from the sum of her intuitions – themselves the product of years of experience across many styles and approaches – shaped by the insights offered by Tone Clock thinking. It wasn't as though she had calcified into fixed ways of doing things – growth and change were as essential to her, and as deep-rooted, as they had ever been – but the changes were becoming less dramatic and the shifts in her work from piece to piece evidenced a more subtle evolution. However, where ideas came from, and what triggered particular decisions in particular pieces, remained mysterious to her:

> Who knows why you write something, because the whole thing, it hasn't stopped since I was a five-year-old – the process of taking in and having music running around in your head. When I wrote the *Little Symphony*, my experience of listening to classical or contemporary music was way smaller: then, I didn't know much music, I was still learning, being introduced to music that I didn't know, that I would come to love. Then I went to Europe and I heard more new music. You were just taking in new stuff all the time. By the [early 2000s] I'd completely forgotten about other composers. I'm not trying to be like anybody; I'm trying to be like me.

Having developed her own ways of navigating the chromatic firmament – by means of her chromatic maps, which transformed that firmament from a forest of sharps and flats into familiar and comfortable terrain – Jenny was able to compose music that reflected her growth as a musician and musical thinker: music that is not quite like anybody else's. That music was the product of an ongoing and intensifying awareness of her personal and musical values, which in turn were coloured by her deepening relationships with Māori, her acceptance of the twinned nature of her musical and spiritual lives, and to some extent her relationship with the written word.

The written word had always been close to Jenny. An omnivorous and voracious reader, she was also an inveterate writer. At one point she'd thought that, had she not been a composer, she may instead have pursued a career as an author – writing words, she said, came to her more easily than writing musical notes. Her deposits in the Alexander Turnbull Library include essays and extended accounts and reflections on various aspects of her life and thought. Her letters are marvellous, acutely observed and richly written. Poetry was also an important part of the way she reflected on life, and during the early 1980s she wrote a great deal of verse, some of which found its way into her songs: *Childhood, Sun Festival Carols, Dirge for Doomsday, Hymn for the Lady*.

During the later 1980s and 1990s her writing had been focused on musical matters and the Tone Clock in particular. She did compose text, entirely in te reo Māori, for *He Iwi Kotahi Tātou* and for many of the hymns she wrote as test pieces for the choirs participating in the Hui Aranga, but poetry per se ceased to be a regular feature of her writing practice. She had continued to read poetry, however, sometimes finding words she subsequently set as song. Composing art songs in this way had been a consistent facet of her compositional work since 1961 when she had made songs with poems by e.e. cummings as a first-year student at Victoria. During the 1980s and '90s William Blake, Edward Lear and hymnist Shirley Murray had enjoyed her attentions.

In the early 2000s, after her move from the Methodists of Pukerua Bay to the Roman Catholic congregation at St Theresa's in Plimmerton, Jenny had been shown the poetry of Anne Powell, a Cenacle Sister with the Catholic church in Wellington. Powell's first published collection of poetry, *Firesong*, interrogated people's relationships with the land, and celebrated nature and womanhood. 'I just liked the poems a lot and felt like setting quite a few of them to music. They were very Kiwi poems. A little bit like a sort of *Sings Harry* for women, maybe?'[1]

Written for mezzo-soprano and piano, *Under Southern Skies* consists of twenty-one settings of Powell's poems, and was Jenny's most substantial song cycle – a good forty-five minutes on paper, although she expected it would be longer in performance. 'The musical style is free, personal, not systematic in any respect, though always aware of Tone Clock aspects. Spare but expressive and illustrative piano accompaniment. I think it's some of my best music, but I wrote it for myself – it wasn't commissioned.' By 2021 it had still not been performed, but Jenny was sanguine about this: 'There are some good songs in there, but it's all right, somebody else will hear them one day. I'm quite optimistic about things like that.' She was proud of the cycle and confident that, when performed, it would be considered a major work.

The next art song Jenny composed was commissioned, so did enjoy public performance. This time she worked with texts by Walt Whitman and Virginia Woolf to produce *A Clear Midnight*. The genesis of the song's text, a 'found poem' that mixed a brief snatch of verse from Whitman's *Leaves of Grass* with lines cherry-picked from Woolf, offers an insight into the ways serendipity played a role in Jenny's compositional practice:

> What I need suddenly, if I need to do a vocal piece, is words. If it happened that I was working already on some words, well, I might use them. I did that for my friend Anna Wirz-Justice. We were students together – she was at Otago when I was at Vic – and we went to Europe on the same ship when we were just graduates. We got to know each other so well that we've been friends ever since. She spent her life in Switzerland; she became a famous scientist whose work was in light therapy – the good effects that things like sunlight have upon us, to get us out of our depressions and what have you, and she spent the rest of her life in Basel married to a Swiss architect, Hans Wirz, a lovely guy. She retired after a lifetime's work in Basel and there was going to be this evening of recollections and celebration for Anna's retirement. Her husband played the piano a little bit and he wrote to me quietly, behind Anna's back: he wanted to commission a piece of music for somebody to sing at her retirement thing. I had been reading Virginia Woolf's *The Waves* again after many years and just loving some of the passages in it, which are just so full of what seemed to be – if you're away overseas – recollections of New Zealand; about the sun through leaves and water and images like that. When Hans's request came, I thought, 'I can use some of those, they'll be appropriate words.' Then he suggested Walt Whitman as a possibility for some words: there was a poem in *Leaves of Grass* that had references to ivy which relates to the academic [world] and Anna's work. So, I put the two together in a sort of joint poem, both of them luckily out of copyright so I could do whatever I liked with them. That way I got words that were perfect for the occasion, but if I hadn't already been reading *The Waves* it would never have come out that way.

It wasn't the first time Jenny had subjected poetry to this kind of structural revision. When she composed *Through the World*, using William Blake's poetry, she had mixed and matched passages from different poems to arrive at her final text. She was surprised when people expressed confusion over her willingness to do this, saying, 'I was just working with the material.' *A Clear Midnight* differs from the Blake settings in that it mixes texts by two quite different writers, but for Jenny the process was much the same. For her, words out of copyright were fair game. 'I would take stuff and just do it like that, because that's part of the whole activity. If you can, work something else out. I've used different words, found items – objets trouvés – plucked stuff out of somebody else's work and put it together in different ways.'

A Clear Midnight was performed in Basel by Hans Wirz at the piano with expatriate New Zealand singers, tenor Keith Lewis and bass Martin Snell. Although it has not enjoyed further performances, it did lead to Jenny's most fertile engagement with a single writer's work: that of Janet Frame.

The Janet Frame song cycles

In 2006 Keith Lewis, having recently performed *A Clear Midnight*, commissioned Jenny to compose a song cycle using Frame's poems. He had come across *The Goose Bath*, a posthumous collection of her verse, and had thought some of the poems would make excellent songs. Jenny had read many of Janet Frame's novels but was less familiar with her poetry. She recalled, 'I got *The Goose Bath* and then I got the earlier collection, *The Pocket Mirror* from 1967, which I didn't have. I thought they were fabulous poems. I picked a mixture, perhaps a dozen or so, and Keith had already suggested one or two, so we just sorted them out from there.'[2]

As she selected texts for Lewis' commission, Jenny discovered rather more poems that would work well as songs than she needed. A short time later, however, she was invited to write a twenty-minute piece for chamber choir and string quartet, and some of the Frame poems she liked but that were surplus to requirements for Lewis' cycle were a good fit for the new project. 'Well, I just got on a roll,' she said. Eventually she completed three song cycles using Frame's verse: *Peaks of Cloud* for Keith

Lewis; *The Poet* for Voices New Zealand and the New Zealand String
Quartet; and *From Garden to Grave*, commissioned by Jack Richards.

Although *Peaks of Cloud* was requested first, it was the last to be
performed: in 2010 by Lewis with pianist Michael Houstoun. The poems,
including the quirky 'I Met a Man' and the bleak, wintry 'Promise',
are rich and strange, and oddly personal. 'I think Janet Frame makes
some people a bit nervous,' Jenny said. 'There is something formidable
and weird in her work.' But not too strange for Jenny, who loved the
humour and the darkness lurking in the poems: 'To me she's got just
about everything. I'm startled at the extent to which I relate to them
personally.'[3]

Jenny's settings are quite varied, matching the broad emotional
sweep of the poems she and Lewis had selected. The songs range from
the malignant blast of 'Promise' to the oddly tender 'Before I Get into
Sleep with You'. But even at its most melodious, this music reflects the
century of Frame's birth: a little crazed, with few obvious tonal centres
– meat and potatoes for composing with the Tone Clock hours, but
not a good fit for *Sing Along with Mitch*. Jenny described the music as
'fiendish', saying, 'With two brilliant international performers I would
be stupid to do something lighter for them, that other people could do.'[4]
She elaborated:

> It was a hard piece, the idea being that if it was too hard, they should
> tell me. I ended up having to change quite a bit of it and that was
> only after the first performance in the [Wellington] Town Hall. But
> [Keith] managed to scrape his way through it. I said, 'Why didn't
> you tell me?' and he said, 'Oh, but I just thought I was supposed
> to do it, so I did it.' I love working with this kind of attitude – the
> harder the better, almost.

The slightly unsettling nature of this cycle is not just attributable to
its frequently jagged music. It is also a function of the enigmatic quality
of the texts, a quality amplified by the intimate 'piano and solo voice'
presentation. A rather less personal sensibility was needed for *The Poet*,
written for chamber choir and string quartet, and for which Jenny

selected quite different poems. 'The kinds of poems that are needed for a group, like a choir – I have in my head that it's civic music, rather than lyrical [music] which is individual,' she said. 'I think it goes back to the ancient Greeks: there was lyric poetry which was individual, personal poetry, and there was civic poetry.'

The massed voices of the choir invest *The Poet* with considerable warmth, and the words, being less confessional, do suggest this is a kind of communal music. Frame's idiosyncratic humour creeps into the music as well: 'Prejudice' – with dirty bathwater its central metaphor; the choristers sounding somehow unhinged and accompanied by horror-movie strings – must have been great fun to sing. The choir is front and centre throughout the cycle, with the New Zealand String Quartet largely assigned accompanying duties. Jenny suspected some listeners may have been less than happy that the quartet did not receive a greater share of the limelight:

> If it had been up to me, I would probably have . . . I don't know, I might have just used a piano or something. But they wanted a piece for the Tower Voices Choir and the string quartet together, so my way of handling it was to make the string quartet not so important in the scheme of things. Had it been an orchestra, for instance, I would have probably had to write some more . . . but I was already up to twenty minutes without making a big feature of the string quartet as well . . . If I had made [the string quartet] more important the whole piece would have gone over.

The Poet was premiered in March 2008 at the New Zealand International Arts Festival. In November that same year, Jenny's third Janet Frame cycle – *From Garden to Grave* – was performed at a private concert to mark Bruce Greenfield's sixtieth birthday. The music is manic in places – a good fit for the words. Jenny described 'Freesias', for example, in this way: 'The singer is singing to a little pot of freesias on her desk, and the way that suddenly rises up to become another huge world . . . She's a startling piece of work, is our Janet.'[5] There are also moments of tenderness, 'My Mother Remembers Her Fellow Pupils at

School' a poignant nod to the passing of the years, with spare piano gestures that speak in the language of the Tone Clock but that know about Debussy and Messiaen, too.

For the concert Rosemary Barnes performed the piano part, but Bruce Greenfield was on hand to accompany soprano Margaret Medlyn when the cycle was recorded. Bruce had mixed feelings about the Tone Clock music and found the work challenging to play. He was laughing as he said, 'It is *so* difficult. It is just so hard.' But he had this to say about Jenny as well: 'Her ability to set words is outstanding – about on a par with Benjamin Britten. He set text and words better than anybody, and she'd done a brilliant job of that.'[6]

The year turned out to be a busy one, with premieres of two of her Janet Frame cycles and a new choral commission, but it was also visited by grief. 'I had a little Māori friend, he was just a child, but he loved to hang out with the oldies, and he loved what he called "hopera", meaning "opera", of all things.' Jenny said Jago 'would often sleep next to me on the marae (wherever we were), and chat away happily. One day, on the beach at Napier, a freak wave suddenly washed him out of his mother's arms and he was drowned.' Jenny put together a 'found poem' by selecting various lines from Louis Johnson's *Collected Poems* and *True Confessions of the Last Cannibal*, and gave them to Jago's grandmother (her friend Kere Robinson), hoping it would offer her some comfort.

On being commissioned to write an a cappella work for Wellington vocal consort Baroque Voices, Jenny used this text to compose *Obscure as the Theology of Mountains*. 'I did not think at all about the style of the music – except that it had to be singable by SATB with two voices per part (that was the brief of the commission). I just thought about the feeling, the meaning of the words. Louis had invited me more than once to set something of his to music, but alas, I only managed it after he had died.' The resulting work is mysterious, burnished with awe and hauntingly beautiful. Hints of the Polish composers Penderecki and Lutosławski, who so intrigued Jenny in the 1960s, sound in this music, which might be mistaken for a sacred chant from some lost continent.

It was around this time that Jenny returned to writing poetry. In the preface to a volume of her verse published in 2011, she wrote: 'As well as writing music, I have written poetry on and off for years, till now mostly unpublished, unless as song or music texts. My earlier poems tended to be more inward-looking, more for myself than for others. I was later brought back to poetry with a jolt by events in my own life which demanded a poetic expression as the only effective means to say what I felt needed to be said.'[7] The events that triggered her renewed interest in poetry had nothing to do with her love of the arts, however.

'My house at Pukerua Bay,' Jenny recalled, 'came under threat from the proposed four-lane coastal highway – also all the houses in our whole street, as the street would have disappeared altogether. I spent about a year full-time fighting this proposal, read lots of law and local history in the process, and put together several submissions, one very lengthy.' A change of government finally saw a different proposal accepted, an inland route replacing the coastal highway that had been on the table. Until that change was confirmed, Jenny felt 'incredibly helpless, outraged and angry, fighting the government's Land Transport Agency and all its career lawyers. I felt as if I had no voice – or had lost my voice . . . I finally realised that poetry was the most effective and condensed way for me to strike my blows. So, I turned one of my submissions into a series of poems instead.'

The blows Jenny sought to strike with her poetic submission are of the bare-knuckle variety. Never one to pull her punches, in 'Voices in the Western Corridor' her anger is unconcealed.

> imperative is, the motorist shall have a better road
>
> to this end we will lie, cheat, misinform
> conceal information, violate
> trust and promises,
>   go through a whole charade
> of public consultation
>   but refuse point blank
> to clarify who is under threat, putting
> scores of angry residents under extreme stress

and we shall confuse them, disorient them
   and indeed make every little last thing
as difficult as we possibly can
(whether by design or incompetence)
   all under the pretext
of helping people to have their say [8]

Cat Dreams

Poetry might have been a hammer in Jenny's hands as she clashed with the New Zealand Transport Agency, but it could also be balm, an aid in the expression of grief. When her brother Perrin died painfully from cancer during 2007, writing poetry was one of her ways of coming to terms with his passing. She had been extremely fond of Perrin, who, like her, could be a bundle of contradictions. Jenny described him this way:

> Torn between intense shyness and a desire to be outrageous, he was once judged (by whom I forget now) to be the 'best-dressed man in Auckland' – and so advertised in the newspaper. At this stage he lived with his partner on one floor of an empty downtown warehouse overlooking the railway station, and his main apparel consisted of a long hairy goatskin jerkin designed and made by himself. Yet he was also so shy that he would wear sunglasses indoors, including at his own parties.

Perrin shared his father's passion for cars. 'In Auckland,' Jenny remembered, 'he drove around in a huge Lincoln convertible for fun, while sporting a silver headband with little wings over the ears and waving regally to the occasional passer-by. This was in the weekends. The Lincoln was so enormous it wouldn't fit into a regular city parking space, so he kept it parked in a Mount Eden driveway and had to buy a motor scooter for everyday city transport.'

Perrin's health had begun to deteriorate in the early 1990s, when he designed and made costumes for Jane Campion's celebrated film *The*

Piano. 'It was nearly the end of him: the pressure of deadlines got to him, he had a heart attack, developed a kidney affliction, and more or less retired as a semi-invalid, taking to a spinning-wheel, spinning natural wools of different hues into thread, and knitting beautiful beanies and headbands' – which he sold bearing his own 'Perrin' logo.

In his final years Perrin and his partner Martin were adopted by two stray cats, and it was their antics Jenny recorded in her sequence 'Cat Dreams', an elegy to her dead brother. 'The poems are about his two black cats, the only way I could handle the subject: that is, at a distance. The cats are nuts, and comical – the cancer too is nuts, but grotesque.' When composer Michael Norris commissioned a chamber work for the Wellington new music ensemble Stroma in 2008, it was to these poems that Jenny looked for inspiration. *Cat Dreams* is a nineteen-minute work comprising nine movements, one for each stanza of her poem. Jenny's programme note for the work was a paraphrase of the epigram she later used to introduce the poem in her 2011 collection *Mutterings from a Spiry Crag*:

> In memory of my brother Perrin – he and his partner had two black cats. Doris, the elder (& undisputed boss) was half the size of Stanley. The cats arrived one day quite unheralded, realised they were onto a good thing and promptly settled down as rulers of the house. In old age, Doris went slightly spastic and wonky. We all thought she would go first, but she outlived my brother. [9]

It wasn't the first time Jenny had used her own texts as a leaping-off point for a composition. The poems she had written to sit between the movements of her collection *Ring Round the Sun* were the spark that gave life (and lyrics) to her song cycle *Childhood*. 'When you're stuck, words can be quite a help. Even if you didn't actually use them overtly in the piece, they could be behind the piece, they could affect the way you think about it.' That was the case with *Cat Dreams*: the words appeared in the score, but were not sounded during its performance.[10]

The music, for nine players – woodwinds, various percussion, harp and piano – recalls Boulez's *Le Marteau sans maître*, partly for the sounds (flute and tuned percussion foregrounded; the textures afforded by Boulez's guitar finding some analogue in Jenny's piano and harp) but also for its unpredictability, its 'guess-the-next-note' melodic and harmonic shapes. *Cat Dreams* also has a distinctly New Zealand flavour: a kōauau joins the woodwinds, perhaps Jenny's timbral substitute for the alto who sings René Char's surreal text in *Le Marteau*. Those words, utterly European and sung in a style reminiscent of the Second Viennese School, are replaced by the beautifully elemental sounds of the Māori flute. This music absolutely knows about European traditions, but it also evokes the country of Perrin's birth.[11]

The quirky, skittering qualities of the piece, along with verses that document the adventures of the cats and accompany the score, might have led some who heard it to assume Jenny had comic intentions with this music. 'People thought, even Jack [Body] thought, and I think Michael Norris who commissioned it, they thought it was another fun piece, but it isn't. It's a piece about my brother's death. And that emotional area is so immediate, so close to us, but so difficult to find.' The spiky, comedic qualities of the music reflect the complicated and elusive emotions concealed within Jenny's text: there is humour here, but it is dark and forlorn humour. Jenny likened the effect to what she heard in some of Edward Lear's poetry. There is, she said, 'a lot of the emotion in *The Courtship of the Yonghy-Bonghy-Bò*. It's terribly sad. I can hear his own unrequited love . . . I'm sure that's what it is. He wrote about these things in order to unburden himself, but everyone takes it for a joke. And that's what happened a bit with the *Cat Dreams* piece: they thought "Jen's written one of her funny pieces again".' *Cat Dreams* was premiered in 2009 by Stroma under Hamish McKeitch, with composer Ross Harris performing on kōauau.

In 2009 Jenny composed a second chamber work commemorating a relative lost to cancer, albeit one at some remove. *Airs for the Winged Isle*, for string quartet, was dedicated to 'John MacLeod of MacLeod, Dunvegan (1935–2007), 29th Chief of the Clan MacLeod – with affection and respect for a prince of a man'. Jenny had met John on her Christmas visit to Dunvegan Castle in 1964 and he had made a lasting impression on her. A collection of brief airs, laments and reels, some of the tunes in the work were drawn from hymns Jenny had written the previous decade. 'Amongst this great outpouring of hymns,' she said, 'was a whole lot of Scottish [hymns]. They'd come through me, but they were Scottish and I just recognised them as such. Some of them ended up, minus their original words, in *Airs for the Winged Isle*.' For Jenny, those melodies felt utterly authentic, and evoked memories of Dunvegan, 'especially of the snow-bound car journey outward ("Road to Portree")'. After learning of John's death, the suite came together naturally. 'I think, I hope,' Jenny said, 'he would have loved it.'

The music had to wait more than ten years to be performed (at the Martinborough Music Festival, in 2021). Elizabeth Kerr was on hand to report:

> The droll programme notes for the ten miniatures tell of a heavy-hearted MacLeod putting the flat-topped Black Cuillin mountains (also known as 'MacLeod's Tables') on the market to raise funds to repair the roof of Dunvegan Castle. There was no sale and for the 10th movement the composer offers a picture of MacLeod 'muttering ancient prayers and imprecations to ward off the rain' and frantically rushing around his castle setting plastic buckets under leaks. [12]

The music is playful and melodic, and the livelier tunes would sound perfectly at home at a cèilidh: these pieces might be two hundred years old, or could just as easily have been written last week.

One of the melodies also had life beyond its inclusion in *Airs for the Winged Isle*. The fourth movement, 'Dunvegan Fastness', had already appeared as the hymn 'Whatever this Life Has Been' with words by Shirley Murray.[13] But, Jenny said:

> I liked the tune so much that I wrote more, different words . . . a hymn for a funeral. I also wrote Māori words to it and dedicated the hymn to an old Māori friend, Auntie Pī Grey, when she died, but I couldn't manage to sing it, so [her husband, Uncle Mark Grey, at Kuratahi] got the words but he still doesn't know what the tune

sounds like. Then I did another set of Māori words, but they're not so much religious words – they're words about the nature of love and they have their roots in Māoridom . . . there are three or four verses of that, to that tune. And then I did a sort of street song to the same music. Street songs are generally very short – they don't have verses much; they can be only four bars and it would be considered a song – but this is more like three verses or something, it's more substantial than that. You see, I'm not getting sick of this thing I've written: four different songs to the same tune.

Jenny's willingness to reuse her materials in this way is a curious facet of her oeuvre. She attributed her parsimony to 'Scottishness' and it has been a quiet feature of her output. She said, 'I don't want to waste anything if you can get a bit more mileage out of it. And besides, nobody ever noticed.'

Revisiting older material also happened in more explicit ways during this period. In 2009 she revised *Rock Sonata No. 1* to produce the *Rock Concerto*. Recorded for Naxos with Uwe Grodd at the podium, the concerto sits comfortably alongside *Three Celebrations for Orchestra* with which it appeared on the 2011 recording. The release also included an updated arrangement of *The Emperor and the Nightingale*. In revisiting that piece, Jenny did admit some of the lessons the Tone Clock had offered her in the intervening years. The music to accompany the arrival of the emperor's watchmaker made use, fittingly enough, of Tone Clock sounds, and goes around some surprising corners – the pizzicato strings, piano and woodwinds hopping about chromatically during that passage add a delicious sharper edge to the otherwise conventionally tonal music.

18

Hōhepa

Although Jenny's output across the first years of the new century was somewhat modest she had not been idle, spending a great deal of time working on a project she had begun the previous decade. In 1996 Matiu Māreikura, a Ngāti Rangi kaumātua and Jenny's close friend, asked her to record the story of Hōhepa Te Umuroa, a Ngāti Hau warrior (from Hiruhārama [Patiarero] on the Whanganui River) arrested in 1846 during the New Zealand wars, found guilty on dubious charges and transported to a penal colony in Tasmania. Contracting tuberculosis, he died there the following year. In 1988 Māreikura, his sister and his wife were members of a mission of Whanganui elders who, after a protracted legal process, travelled to Maria Island off the Tasmanian coast to collect and repatriate Hōhepa's bones.

Jenny accepted responsibility for the project: 'It's the sort of subject that I would never have dreamed of touching had it not been requested of me. Matiu asked me quite early on if I would do this, and I was very honoured to be asked. I also looked forward to having something that would tie me to these Māori people because I am, and was, really fond of them.'[1]

Māreikura supplied Jenny with the materials he had collected as he pieced together Hōhepa's story, 'a stack about a foot high, of notes and letters and copies of newspaper cuttings and photographs and maps of the island, cos they went there. So, he had all this material from his side.'[2] To supplement those materials Jenny began searching in the Alexander Turnbull Library. Among the library's holdings she found records of some of the first Pākehā settlers in the upper reaches of the Hutt Valley, two of whom, Thomas and Jane Mason, had made their home close to Ngāti Rangitahi, with whom Hōhepa lived for a time. Along with Thomas Mason's letters, Jenny found a large, illustrated family history published by the present-day Mason family. She also uncovered (online, in a New York bookshop) a nineteenth-century British Quaker pamphlet that recounted tales Thomas Mason and his daughter had told of their encounters with Māori. With these and other resources she was able to piece the story together.

At first Jenny had thought she would write a book to recount Hōhepa Te Umuroa's life. She had completed a draft when American anthropologist Karen Sinclair, who had been working with the iwi for thirty years, published *Prophetic Histories*, telling the story of Hōri Ēnoka Māreikura and the Māramatanga.[3] Because that book included a chapter on Te Umuroa and contained a lot of the same material Matiu Māreikura had given to her, Jenny set the project aside for the time being.

A few years later New Zealand Opera got in touch with Jenny, asking if she would be interested in writing an opera for performance at the 2012 New Zealand Festival of the Arts in Wellington. Hōhepa's story came to mind. 'Now, up to that point,' she said, 'I hadn't thought of it in terms of an opera at all, but when they asked me that, I started to think, "This could be, at a pinch, an opera."' It would be challenging to write, but Jenny figured she could find a way.

Already intimately familiar with the material, Jenny began to shape the story for the stage. She said, 'I took as my guideline all the bits that I liked best. When I read a story there are particular points that strike me, that I think are to do with human things or morals or ethics – the things that are the bones of a real story to me.'[4] She also emphasised some of the spiritual elements of Te Umuroa's life. To invite the magical dimensions of his biography into her account, she included Hōhepa's tokotoko – his ceremonial walking stick – as both a narrator and a character in the story:

The thing about *Hōhepa* – I had so much to tell in such a short time. Anyway, it is not entirely an opera because it has the narrator and then the narrator is there on stage too – the Tokotoko. That became an extended part of the whole thing. Using recitative and narrative you can cover a lot of ground quickly with a lot of material in it. This is what upset [music critic] William Dart about *Hōhepa* – that there were so many words. But he doesn't know how many words I left out.

The libretto, about a third of which is in te reo Māori, took several years to write:

The reo is so beautiful – it is so wonderful to work with. By trying hard to do good things with the reo, that teaches you. It doesn't just teach you about the reo and the subject, but about all your life. Learning any kind of language does that for your relationship to the culture, but it is particularly strong with Māori, and I always celebrated privately that I had another occasion to do it, to try and do it.

Although Jenny completed the libretto before she made a start on the score, the choices she made as she assembled her text were informed by the knowledge that the words would be set to music:

Words have their own rhythm and their own ways of cutting through the air – with consonants and so on. Some consonants are softer and some are harder, so they give you a different edge to your line. I would nearly always end up writing trial or draft lyrics – whether it be a solo song, little groups in dialogue, a duet, whatever it is for that particular passage – so you're getting your words increasingly into shape. This is before you've even got any notes, but . . . you are shaping it in preparation for notes. Your contours, your ups and downs and what have you, are coming along – you're just kind of welcoming them, or hunting them out while you're shaping the sound of the words into something that will work as music. And in

that process, you are coming more and more towards what will be
the tune that will go with those words. More often than not I will
then try and put a formal rhythm to the words. And more often
than not I will do that twice or three times maybe, and it comes out
differently each time. Finally, I find it will settle somewhere, so that
when I come back to it later it still stays the same.

With the text complete, and with it a sense of the libretto's rhythmic
and melodic shapes, composing the music came a little more easily: 'I set
all the words to their own melodies first, in the same sort of way that I
had put together the whole libretto – as an imaginary solo performance
for a single character onstage. Only after that did I start splitting it up
into different roles.'

The music that emerged from this process, Jenny thought, revealed
Stravinsky's influence. 'If you listen to *Hōhepa*,' she said, 'there are quite
a few little passages in there that could easily have been written by a
Stravinsky, by a pre-serial Stravinsky.' Douglas Lilburn, whom Jenny
did not really consider a musical influence, managed to surreptitiously
work his way into the piece, too. As she was orchestrating the work, she
wrote a piccolo line that reminded her strongly of a melody from one
of Lilburn's early *Four Preludes* for piano (1942–44). 'What I heard was
not strictly what Douglas had written, but it was so similar. My mind
had done that, had come out of somewhere with something that he had
done, but that I had done my own version of. It was nobody but Lilburn
basically, and I knew that, and I was really pleased, too.'[5] The Tone Clock
hours were ever-present in her mind as she composed, and though they
certainly informed the music, they did not reduce it to a single style.
'Quite the opposite,' Jenny said. 'The twelve hours operate more to
expand one's awareness of different styles and bring them together in a
consistent and logical framework.'

As well as drawing from her European art music palette, Jenny also
made use of musical colours from the Māori world. The opera includes
waiata and haka, including a haka performed in English. With these
pieces she was inclined to be faithful to the idiomatic conventions of
the forms. 'I'm aware of general characteristics of a particular kind of

waiata, for instance,' she said. 'The words for my waiata, sometimes they're deliberately of a style that will be taken as an old song.'[6] She had learned quite a lot about waiata by studying ethnomusicologist Mervyn McLean's collections of Māori song, but most of her knowledge was from first-hand experience.

Jenny had grown so familiar with her Ngāti Rangi friends and their music that she came to see the *Hōhepa* score as continuous with their practices. In Jenny's view, while it had started out as 'their music', it had become, to her, 'a sound that is us: this is us; this is our music; this is how we do it.' However, she understood that kind of musical assimilation could only be the product of a sincere and abiding relationship: 'It's just been a growing depth and closeness. The more you become like that, the less you're afraid to do something involving aspects of their own work, which you need to if you're going to do something like *Hōhepa*.'

As well as accommodating her love of both Māori and European music, Jenny found that writing the opera called on sensibilities she had developed as a composer of music for the screen. Her work on numerous documentaries as well as *The Silent One* and *Cuckooland* had taught her that scenes could be long or short, and that you could have as many scenes, or as many items in a scene, as you liked. She often watched film and television analytically, thinking about how scenes changed, how one shot might cut away to another, how long particular scenes or transitions might be. She thought about the nature of the sounds and music used to accompany scenes and changes between scenes, and the various effects that sound or music could have. 'All these things, which are part of film, I always thought they ought to be and could be part of opera. If opera was going to grow and mean something, those techniques would just automatically be embraced.'

Applying these approaches to the detailed and complex story she was seeking to tell, Jenny ended up with fifty-two scenes for an opera lasting less than two hours. The director of the 2012 Wellington production, Sara Brodie, said, 'Jenny's musical writing doesn't allow for transitions – we just cut from one thing to the other . . . There are fifty-two separate pieces that make up this opera. It goes by like an absolute rocket.'[7]

The epic scope of the story and the number of scenes required to tell it, combined with Jenny's eclectic musical practice, resulted in an opera of remarkable musical diversity. Marc Taddei, who conducted the first season of *Hōhepa*, said, 'Quite often the Māori choruses are done in a modal style and then she'll go to quite frankly syrupy tunes from time to time, and then she'll go to very challenging atonal turns of phrases. And from time to time she'll break into a haka . . . it's an amazing amalgamation of different styles.'[8]

Hōhepa is a chamber opera of just over a hundred minutes for a cast and chorus of about thirty-five, including half a dozen kapa haka performers for its first season in 2012. The twelve-piece orchestra is deployed ingeniously to produce a remarkable range of colours and styles. To compose the music Jenny trusted her instincts, saying 'I just decided to let it come how it's going to come.' She admitted the mixture of styles evident in the music had surprised her, but in the final analysis, also thought it sounded more like her than anything else she had done.[9]

The challenges of the opera were not limited to its composition and performance. Jenny was well aware of the potential for misunderstanding among Māori with regard to her telling Hōhepa Te Umuroa's story. Matiu Māreikura, who died a year or two after he had asked her to record the story, had not told anyone else of his request. Jenny recalled:

> I was in a bit of a difficult situation because he had asked me to do this using his authority as the leader of the mission to [Maria] Island, which was not the same as the mana of the family that are actually descendants of the person in question. But seeing that he had asked me this I figured it was not my place now to go to the family and say, 'Is this all right with you?' He had the power to ask me to do it and I had said 'Yes', so that was it, I was going to do it. And the whole relationship with the family came much later – long after I'd finished it.[10]

As a condition of her agreement to undertake the project, Jenny had asked the opera company to pay for buses to transport Māori of the Whanganui tribes to the dress rehearsal. She also made sure there was a supper for them after the show – 'You can't invite Māori and not have something to eat,' she said. She had been in touch with Hōhepa Te Umuroa's direct descendants, and at first they had declined to be involved, perhaps unsure of her bona fides or anxious that their ancestor's memory was being exploited in some way. It was a cause of concern for Jenny, who had spent years searching for the best way to tell Hōhepa's story. 'They were real people that lived that I was writing about; not only real, but they had living descendants, and that's really important . . . you'd better not do anything that offends living descendants. But more important is to try and say well, and with point, the things that need to be said.' It came pretty close to the wire: 'Hōhepa's direct descendants did not agree to be part of it until the week before the dress rehearsal. The buses were all booked and everything and suddenly I got a phone call, the only phone call I ever got from them, saying "Jenny, we do want to be involved." I said, "Thank you. I'm so pleased." It had come so close to them not even turning up.'

The season, a dress rehearsal and three public performances, received mixed reviews. 'A welter of words,' said the *New Zealand Herald* reviewer. Among other concerns were a lack of balance between singers and orchestra ('Rubbish!' Jenny said), a longing for more expansive writing, and 'not enough tension built between the main protagonists or within the events which happen'. According to one review, it was 'a great but flawed opera'.[11] Other commentators were taken with the 'prismatic, rich beauty' of the production, describing *Hōhepa* as 'a must-see for anyone interested in what we can now muster in New Zealand with regard to this most demanding form of theatre and what we can do in the future'.[12] Yet another reviewer identified elements of ritual in the production, and noted that in Māoridom, whānau, hapū, iwi and the associated whakapapa are more important than individuals. *Hōhepa's* tragedy, the review concluded, 'was essentially a communal one', and the opera was, perhaps, 'about a darker aspect of this country's history than about what actually happened to him'.[13] Indeed, it is right to view *Hōhepa* as oral history – the very reason Jenny became involved in the project in the first place. Consequently, she was vitally interested in what the Māori audience at the dress rehearsal thought of the work, needing to know that the opera had said well, and with point, the things that needed to be said:

> I did find that out, because when they came down, my old closest mates – [they're] like my older sisters: Biddy and Mona, the wives of Matiu's two dead older brothers – sat one either side of me in the front row, holding my respective hands and crying their eyes out. So, I knew then. And also I knew by what happened at the end that what I said was good, was right, was the thing to have done. Māori, if they like something, they'll do a haka. When I heard the haka breaking out in different parts of the hall, I thought 'Thank God.' That was the reception that concerned me – more than the Pākehā reception, much more – because it was their story.

Sara Brodie, who directed the season, believed *Hōhepa* was a story relevant to all who live in Aotearoa: 'I see it as a New Zealand story, fundamentally. It's a story about our past and our present and reconciling what that is and what that means . . . Jenny has a very great sense of there being something that needs to be reconciled and I think that shows within the piece and her writing.'[14] The desire for reconciliation, and the promise of unity that will flow from it, was something that performers actually experienced in the staging of the opera. Lead soprano Jenny Wollerman said:

> It was amazing to be part of a group that was that cohesive. I think part of that was having all the soloists sing in the ensemble as well. What that meant was everybody was on the same footing all the way, and we were much closer as a group. Opera is incredibly hierarchical [but] it was a completely different thing in *Hōhepa* – we were all part of the same group, and we got very close. Through this closeness I learned some stuff – and I think a lot of the other Pākehā singers learned stuff – about what life is like for Māori in New Zealand today that we had no idea about.[15]

The opera's closing song, a dénouement featuring the full cast singing together, reflects Wollerman's experiences and confirms Brodie's analysis:

Troubled hearts need to be shared
Song and story and laughter in the air
Give our wounds a chance to heal
Acknowledge the pain
And the wounds we bear are deep and real
Imagination and love
See through other eyes
And help us grow wise

Although *Hōhepa* has yet to be restaged, it was captured on film. The idea to do so came from Jenny's brother Craig, who was in New Zealand for an extended stay around the time the opera was going into production. He later told Jenny that the whole reason for his return was so that he could film *Hōhepa*.

When approached, New Zealand Opera said that because the performers' contracts had not included film rights, and with their budget already fully committed, it would not be possible to make a film of the performance. Craig was unfazed and suggested they instead produce a film of the making of *Hōhepa*: footage of rehearsals, interviews with performers and the creative team, that sort of thing. The company agreed.

Craig had begun capturing some rehearsals when he chanced to meet Jack Richards, an old friend from his days at Victoria (and Jenny's predecessor on the Box Hill, Khandallah postal round). Craig recalled:

Jack took us out to dinner one night and we were talking about the opera. Jack has always been a great admirer and supporter of Jenny throughout the years and he was so excited. He said, 'Oh Craig, you're doing the film of the opera?' I said, 'I am, but unfortunately we can't shoot the actual performance because we don't have the rights.' He said, 'Well, what do you need?' I said, 'We need a bit of money to do it', and he said, 'I'll pay.'[16]

Discussions with the opera company revealed that if the film were to be made available at no charge rather than sold, filming rights could be accommodated within the performers' existing contracts. The documentary idea was abandoned and instead Craig, with a small team and four cameras, captured all of the performances.

Craig had planned to set up a few microphones for sound – not ideal for a music production, but a necessary compromise given his resources. As so often happened in Jenny's affairs, fortune smiled at that point. Craig said, 'I was very lucky that Radio New Zealand were doing a recording of the opera for radio broadcast – they set up 36 microphones all over the place – and they gave me the soundtrack which I was able to synchronise with the footage. And it's a very good soundtrack, a beautiful recording. Hats off to Radio New Zealand.'[17]

Working alone after the season had concluded, Craig selected the best of what he'd captured across the four shows and edited the footage to make a complete performance. 'Jenny wasn't all that involved,' Craig said, 'and luckily she loved it. She was very happy with it, particularly because the sound was so good.' The full opera was posted online two years after the Wellington performances.

He Whakaahua o Maru

Soprano Jenny Wollerman, who played Jane Mason in *Hōhepa*, was very taken with the opera. 'The experience of *Hōhepa* was incredible. After that some part of my brain clicked and went, "I have to ask Jenny McLeod to write a song cycle in te reo." It was one of those things that you just have to do.'[18] Wollerman approached Jenny, requesting a full-length cycle – about twenty-five minutes of music, with an optional flute part. 'She wanted something that she could pin a programme to, in Māori,' Jenny recalled. 'She also wanted some songs within the framework of the cycle that she could take out and sing in other programmes and . . . she also wanted some songs that she could use for teaching. So, I think she got a bit of everything.'

After completing *Hōhepa*, Jenny had read New Zealand journalist

Mike Nicolaidi's autobiography, *A Greekish Trinity: Tales from the Book of Michael*. It struck her that Nicolaidi's life story could easily have been that of anyone who had grown up on a New Zealand farm, Māori or Pākehā. It also seemed to her that many passages in the book would translate elegantly into te reo Māori, and would call for richer language than she had used as she wrote *Hōhepa*. On accepting Wollerman's commission, she approached Nicolaidi for permission to use excerpts from his book as text for the cycle. He agreed.

Jenny began by identifying key sentences and passages from the book that she thought would offer suitable material for songs: an accidental bush fire on a local hill; Nicolaidi's relationship with his mother; the death of his father. Drawing on a range of dictionaries as well as her now quite extensive writing experience, she translated these passages into te reo Māori.

During the production of *Hōhepa*, musician and educator Teina Moetara had been brought in to offer advice on the reo in the opera. Jenny had liked him – she described him as 'a rare flower, basically' – and had found his insights valuable. Having completed her texts for Wollerman's cycle, but before writing a note of music, she asked him to look over the words she had written:

> And after he sat on the words for weeks and weeks, I asked him – I probably sent him an email – what did he think of the words, and he said, 'It all depends on the context,' which is absolutely true. 'In the right context they could all be all right.' And I thought, 'My God, this is what I need.' That just set me loose . . . When Teina said that, I went away and I had a think and I thought it was time for me to take all my own risks, so to speak, and just go with what I felt would work, would be okay. And I've done that ever since. So that's what I said to Teina: 'I'm going to take this as my sign to go with what I feel will be good and won't pay attention to anybody else.'

One further translation task remained. Jenny wanted to include both the Māori text and an English translation in the programme notes for the piece, so that audience members not fluent in te reo Māori would understand what the songs were about. To achieve this, she re-translated her Māori words – the found poems, objets trouvés from Nicolaidi's book – back into English. 'This was such a fantastic experience of getting to understand better what the differences are between the Māori language and English,' Jenny said. 'I love working with words as well as working with notes: just change a wee word here, change a little word order, change a little bit of this or that, leave out a punctuation [mark], put one in . . . the subtleties are so glorious, and what a process that was.'

He Whakaahua o Maru (A Portrait of Maru) is a cycle of fifteen quite short songs that offer vignettes primarily of the protagonist's relationship with their father, although the implications of that relationship for the mother and the narrator's love for her also feature. 'It made me think,' Jenny said, 'of how for some children their parents occupy such a huge place in their lives; that a parent (or parents, or some figure in their family) can be like a god. Like a Māori god in this case. I looked around the spectrum of gods and thought Maru would be a good one, because he's god of war – a big figure.' Jenny described the cycle as:

> The depiction of an initially godlike figure bursting with exuberance, power, fury, who over the years gradually declines in all his dimensions becoming the incompetent farmer whose burn-off destroyed half a mountainside; the unfaithful husband unaware that his hard-worn wife (herself once lovely) knows; and eventually the small shrunken pathetic disappointed figure who lies staring at the wall from his soon-to-be death-bed – all as seen and finally accepted through the eyes of the child, son, adult, who manages nevertheless to arrive at his own sense of homecoming.

The spare libretto – thirteen poems of her own and two traditional Māori texts – includes moments of gentleness and beauty, as when a loving mother is recalled or the splendour of the land described. Overall, however, there is a fearful, bewildered quality to the cycle that culminates in a kind of sad acceptance. The concision of Jenny's texts – it's hard to imagine the story could be told with fewer words – and the clarity of the accompaniments give the work an austerity reminiscent of some of the Tone Clock piano pieces. As is the case with those works, Debussy and Messiaen can be heard whispering from the rafters throughout the cycle. Scored for soprano, piano, and flute or piccolo, the work is more contrapuntal than much of Jenny's music.

Given the New Zealand provenance of the story and its strong links to the land, it's little wonder Jenny introduced Māori cosmology and gestures into her setting. The cycle begins with a description of Hine-ahu-papa, one of the 'props of heaven', who, embedded in the Earth, holds up the sky. Against this backdrop, Maru – one who subdues anger and can turn harm away – is invoked. This context had implications for the music that followed. Jenny said, 'Of course I made my accompanist use a poi here and there – it was [pianist] Emma Sayers, and she was all into doing that. She did a great job.' The cycle included two haka, which called on the soprano to provide rhythmic foot-stamping to accompany the music. 'Jenny Wollerman went out and bought a pair of shoes that would be good for doing haka-stamps,' Jenny said. 'This whole thing being in Māori was her idea, after she had sung in *Hōhepa*, and her Māori pronunciation is spot-on, bloody good.'

It's an arresting cycle, with music of considerable range and covering richly varied emotional terrain. Jenny believed the music and te reo text-setting were helped by the work she had done for her opera. 'Everything I did after *Hōhepa* benefited from the amount of focus, in that work, that there was on music that was appropriate to set the Māori language to.' Completing *He Whakaahua o Maru* and hearing the cycle performed at the Adam Chamber Music Festival in Nelson in 2013 was deeply satisfying: 'That is my best Māori work,' she told me.

'Ko ngā riu', the song that concludes the cycle, is concerned with mortality: the hills and valleys, the landscapes in which we live, 'nakedly portray giant human forms, of all desires and persuasions, resting in peace'. As the song draws to a close, the melodies and accompaniment spiral slowly downward; the formerly cohesive ensemble delaminates, the music somehow unwinding as it comes to rest. Jenny likened the effect – the music seems to relax and loosen and gently descend to Earth – to that achieved in the last song in her 2007 cycle *The Poet*: 'There is in both *Maru* and *The Poet*, a strong and intentionally sought feeling in the music of "coming home" and of finding ourselves at home, here in this land of ours. Some of the closing bars still please and satisfy me most in the context of a life's work – to me a recognisable feeling of warmth, thankfulness, relief, is shared by both pieces.'

19

The Shape of a Life

In 2016 Jenny celebrated her seventy-fifth birthday. Although she had been a diligent student of her own past music, always seeking to learn from what she had just done, always thinking about its implications for her future composing, she tended to look forwards rather than backwards. In interviews she had often recounted important episodes from her life, and had written essays on particular aspects of her experiences – her childhood years; her encounters with Olivier Messiaen – but autobiography had not been a significant driver for her. An invitation from the Lilburn Trust in 2016 to deliver the annual Lilburn Lecture gave her reason to look back across her career and to reflect on the shape of her life.

The Lilburn Lecture series, inaugurated in 2013 with an address by composer and Lilburn biographer Philip Norman, offers a forum for respected New Zealand musicians and commentators to share ideas about music in Aotearoa. Jenny, as a friend and colleague of Douglas Lilburn and a composer whose music had left a mark on the country's cultural matrix, was an obvious person to invite to deliver an address. Asked to consider offering a survey of her work, Jenny decided to give a comprehensive account of her own musical journey, illustrating it with brief examples. The rich diversity of her experiences and the size of her oeuvre meant that compressing a meaningful survey into a single lecture was going to be a challenge:

> Having only fifty-five minutes to speak, there was no way I could do it in a 'lecture', I had far too much to say. Poetry was the only solution – giving me a more intense focus, a completely free range, both of expression and content, able to jump from anywhere to anywhere, didn't have to be grammatical (correct grammar uses up far too many words that are unnecessary, when what you mean could come across in only a couple of keywords). Freedom! Poetry gave me back my voice – or perhaps I should say, my speaking voice.

Writing in this style, Jenny reflected, 'you could leave out half the words and still be understood. Just do one powerful image of something – if you want to make a punch you've got to leave out everything inessential and hit them with four or five words and let them get over that while you patter on. It's much more like just writing music.' Preparing in this way was an effective gambit, and the kind of chiselled concision that gave *He Whakaahua o Maru* so much of its power is a prominent characteristic of her lecture.

Jenny illustrated her talk with thirty-six short musical extracts, judiciously edited to work as thirty-second miniatures. Preparing an excerpt from *Piano Piece 1965*, originally composed by means of meticulous and systematic manipulation of a tone row, Jenny said, 'I changed the bars around. I just chopped [and] edited it and extended a bar here and there, so that [it] was a little bit more satisfying as an example on its own.'

Her lecture touched on the events and values most important to her, from her musical baptism in Levin in the 1950s to her immersion in te ao Māori with Ngāti Rangi, which had carried over into the new century. The musical examples ranged chronologically from 1962's *Cambridge Suite* through 2013's *He Whakaahua o Maru*, and stylistically from the light pop of *Under the Sun*'s 'Shadow People' to the rigour of *Piano Piece 1965*; from the whispered haka of 'Matiti nei' to the declamatory voices of 'Prejudice'; from the astringency of *For Seven* to the lush symphonic sweep of *Three Celebrations for Orchestra*. Concentrated into less than an hour, it's a remarkable précis of her life and work up to that moment.

One of the most arresting aspects of her summary is that it made evident the remarkable range of music she had composed. It is that breadth, and the stop-start nature of her career, that has led to some misconceptions about what Jenny has actually done. While many people are aware of *Earth and Sky*, they may not have come across her European works *Piano Piece 1965* and *For Seven*. Jenny said that most of those she met among Ngāti Rangi were not aware even of *Earth and Sky* – it had been too long ago and, besides, they rarely went into the cities or followed national publications. For them, Jenny was a composer of choir pieces that they sang at the Easter Hui. Concertgoers might know her orchestral and chamber works but have no idea about the hymns she had composed, or the film score work she had done.

The limited degree to which recordings of her work have been available exacerbated the public's incomplete knowledge of her music, and the very low public profile she had maintained since the mid 1970s was a factor, too. During her first years as Professor of Music her life had been highly publicised. Fêted for her music theatre pieces and a source of interesting copy on music and drugs and spirituality, she was often in the papers. After her resignation from the professorship at Victoria University, however, she had avoided the attention of the media. 'I'd had enough of glory,' she said. 'I just wanted to be an ordinary person that people didn't recognise in the street.' Given her very private nature, that retreat from public scrutiny was hardly a surprise to those who knew her.

The Lilburn Lecture was the most public and most complete picture Jenny was to offer of herself and her music. By telling the story of her life she was able to cast light upon the values that had animated her work, and reveal their sources. The origins of her eclecticism, for example, became apparent as she detailed the diversity of her musical interests and activities as a young musician in Levin. And the gamut of that musical endeavour – 'Bartók, standards, show music, old-time dance music, hymns, anthems, opera, *et cetera*. Folksongs . . .,' the list goes on – was summed up:

To me it was all
one <u>huge</u> tradition, a riotous profusion!
And all of it mine! [1]

Being grounded in such an abundance of musical styles, and happily owning all of them, makes sense of the diversity of Jenny's music. In fact, the seeds of almost all of her subsequent musical undertakings can be traced back to the music that exercised her as a young person. Those seeds were, in many cases, to flourish for a season before being supplanted by a different set of ideas or approaches.

Cecilia Johnson, a friend since university days, described Jenny as someone always searching for something. She went on to say, however, that when Jenny did find things that held her attention, she would often become quickly disillusioned with them. Cecilia was talking about Jenny's search for personal meaning, but a survey of her career suggests that this analysis also applies to the music Jenny made: fairly conventional concert music reflecting the work of composers she respected as a student at Victoria; rigorous high modernism in her European pieces; eclectic music that mixed modernist tendencies with vernacular (and in particular Māori and popular) music for her music theatre works; concert music composed intuitively, drawing on pop music materials and classical forms; a return to chromatic and abstract music but managed with the chromatic maps of her expanded Tone Clock theory; sacred music for Māori choirs and congregational singing. You'd think, from the kind of serial monogamy Jenny practised with these various styles, that she was simply trying on a different set of ideas for a few years before discarding them in favour of something new, blown about by the winds of musical taste. But while Jenny did (to some extent) rely on circumstances to lead her – what was commissioned; what she was reading; ideas that had recently commanded her attention – she was hardly passive in her response to those circumstances. She had always dug deeply into her current interest, mining it for what was useful to her before moving on to new and richer seams. 'I keep what's valuable,' she said, 'and just let the rest go. For me it's all a matter of growth.'[2] Her migration from composing using popular music materials to composing using the Tone Clock was indicative of this tendency. She described that evolution in the Lilburn Lecture:

> After the second Rock Sonata, I had to concede:
> my musical language
> of the past fifteen years or more
> had finally proved
> too familiar, too limited,
> too like some dear old well-darned
> patched-up poncho –
> essentially incapable
> of the kind of deepening
> I now understood
> was for me a necessary citadel.
> Long dead in the water
> was my back-breaking modernist youth.
> No respite there.
> I had no idea where I might strike out next,
> was in a state of despair, ready to turn up my toes,
> when I met the Dutch composer, Peter Schat,
> in Louisville, Kentucky.

Jenny's biography reveals that when she had exhausted the seam she was working, she would step away from composing. Breaking off from work created space, an opening from which something new always emerged. And yet each 'something new' was never entirely new – there was always a precedent for what came to light:

> What have looked like these enormous zigs and zags, to me have always been a carry-on of something that was [already there]. The whole world is like this: it looks like a big change is happening somewhere but if you go back fifty years, you can see where that change started, in these little places here and there, and just grew and grew and it was growing all along. Meanwhile the opposite,

over here, wasn't growing – it was decaying, until there comes a time when one puts its head above the other and suddenly, we're into a new trend. But wake up, it was there all along. It's like that all the time in your life, I think. It's not these big zigs and zags that people look at and think, 'Oh, did she give up something because something else looked more attractive?' That was partly it, especially when I sort of swung over to pop music, but I was playing rock and roll when it first came in, as a kid.

Two of the core values that Jenny outlined in her lecture seem central to understanding her priorities as a mature composer. The first was to do with the communitarian values that underscored a great deal of her work:

When it comes to those leading lives
of 'quiet desperation'
I have a tender sympathy –
I'm not worried about their souls.
I'll write them a piece that goes
with a cold beer, and a welcome-home,
and a put-your-feet-up.
I don't call this 'commercial' (far from it!)
I call it fellow feeling.
These folk work
hard enough already.
They don't need me making
more demands.

Jenny wrote music, first of all, to please herself. But even as a young composer she did not lose sight of the fact that musicians would perform the pieces and audiences would listen to them. It was their needs she remained mindful of as she worked. Each commission almost invariably served different audiences, a new set of performers and a distinct context, but her desire that the music communicate with those who performed and heard it remained important to her. That had been true when she composed *Earth and Sky* – which Jenny never intended or imagined would be anything more than it was: a work for schoolchildren and amateur musicians – and just as true when she composed *Childhood* and *Three Celebrations for Orchestra* and *Hōhepa*. That was why the positive responses of performers and audiences of those works so pleased her. In the Lilburn Lecture Jenny contrasted the critical appraisal of *Three Celebrations* ('Too American!') with feedback from musicians ('The deputy leader is reminded of Brahms') and audience reactions:

> Somebody mutters during the applause,
> 'I'd rather have that than Lilburn'.
> Time for a quiet grin.

Jenny's desire to create a communicative experience through the music she wrote was one of the reasons she remained fond of working with, and for, amateur musicians. Such groups often spent a lot of time working on a piece, particularly longer compositions or those that might be receiving their first (and quite often only) performance: groups who, in Jenny's experience, 'did the best they could and were happy with what they'd done'. In those situations, the music-making experience is also a community-building experience. 'You spend a lot of time together,' she said. 'You end up . . . it becomes like a family, the people who work together on a particular piece.' In the context of this family, and the intense and focused activity of creating music together, people frequently find something of great importance to themselves. Jenny recalled a message she'd received when her song cycle *The Poet* was performed again in 2021:

> Christine Archer-Lockwood, who was conducting the choir, emailed and told me how as a third former or something she had been in one of the choirs for *Under the Sun*, and how it had completely changed her life. She tells me that now, and *Under the Sun* was fifty years ago . . . It's happened a few other times as well; people much older tell me they were in a choir [for one of my pieces] and it changed their life. After that they focused their life on theatre or music or both, or on the arts. So, even if nothing else ever happened from

what you've done, you'd feel a contentment, a pleasure, a feeling that
you are part of something bigger in your own country.

A second core value Jenny drew attention to in her lecture was her
closeness to Māori, and the importance of those relationships to her.
Outlining her early experiences with Ngāti Raukawa and her encounter
with the *Tainui* waka, she went on to recount the events around *He Iwi
Kotahi Tātou*:

> I put into the mouths of a massed Pākehā choir
> a humble apology in Māori.
> Alas, the singers had such trouble
> pronouncing the words
> that the meaning largely escaped them.
> My old friend Tūngia of Ngāti Toa,
> twenty years later, laughed till she cried
> when I told her what I had done.
> But the listening Ngāti Rangi back then
> honoured my own pained request
> for a tīmatanga hōu.[3]
> I promised myself,
> for the rest of my days
> I would be a Pākehā they could trust.

Jenny's close friendships with Joan Akapita and Matiu Māreikura,
with Raana (Biddy) Māreikura and Teina Moetara, with Tūngia Baker
and Amy Taylor, with Gillian Whitehead and James McNeish, and the
many relationships she formed among Ngāti Rangi in Ohakune, were
of supreme importance to her. They had become her family, and she a
part of theirs. Those relationships also added an important dimension
to her compositional practice, both with the hymns and choral test
pieces she wrote, and in her music for the stage: *He Iwi Kotahi Tātou,
He Whakaahua o Maru* and, particularly, *Hōhepa*. And it was Jenny's
closeness to them that revealed to her that love among friends trumped
all, and certainly trumped all musical values:

I am listening with my whānau.
The words of the country song
I would have described
as mawkishly sentimental.
But these are the people I love best.
They are broken-hearted, weeping bitterly
for the young one they have lost.
I will honour their reality, not mine . . .
and so much for aesthetics.

Jenny's Lilburn address concluded with an explanation of her understanding of what it meant to be a composer, of what was necessary for her before she could freely compose:

Something that's there before the music, telling us
nothing about the music
beyond a kind of global call,
something hidden, that must first be lived with.
We must have it in our bones
before we can work with it.
The way in which we work with it (and it with us)
is our own algorithm.
The spontaneous living language
– what we hear with our living ears –
is the music itself.

And this she linked to her home in Aotearoa:

We have it in our senses,
in our bones and blood:
the sweet smell of home,
the presence of the land,
Aotearoa-Gondwana.
The difference others feel

but cannot put their finger on
lies here: they sense by instinct
a living algorithm
other than their own.

dark bright night

Jenny spent the remainder of the decade enjoying the views from
her home above the Tasman Sea. She continued writing poetry and
composing music – an orchestral suite of music from *Hōhepa*; a
musical titled *The Amazing Head* and peopled with characters from
Margaret Mahy's books; the piano trio *Seascapes* – but only a few of
these pieces were publicly performed. Deteriorating health and the
need for care at home saw her move north to Horowhenua in 2021 – a
move that coincided with the surprise arrival of two almost identical
commissions:

> I got commissioned within two or three weeks to do two pieces
> for piano trio, seven minutes long. That was terrible because I
> was ready to write the first one and I launched into it and got
> it written pretty fast. I enjoyed it; it went well. And I thought,
> 'Thank goodness, I really felt like writing that.' And then there
> was an email from the New Zealand Trio: can you write a piece for
> us, seven minutes long? I just could not believe it. I thought 'Oh,
> Jesus, I've just written that piece.'

Commissioned and performed by the New Zealand Chamber
Soloists, *dark bright night* begins slowly but soon develops a head of
steam, then roars through to the end. Jenny said, 'You never know –
until you find out for yourself – that there are going to be some really
hard moments in being a composer. And there are going to be some
other beautiful moments where suddenly a fantastic piece pops out.
[*dark bright night*] was sort of almost like a new idiom for me. It just
really surprised me, that piece. Surprised and pleased me.'

Part of her delight may have been because *dark bright night*, while cut from similar cloth to other chamber pieces she had composed in the preceding decades, charted new territory. She expressed pleasure with the obvious quality of the work:

> You're always hoping you'll write a good piece. It doesn't happen that often. If it did, we'd learn to just take it for granted and that would not be helpful at all; we'd be writing bad ones and thinking they were good ones . . . This *dark bright night* commission came up very suddenly. I wrote it much sooner than they thought I was going to. I read the email and started to write the piece. I wasn't expecting to write a piece of . . . I wouldn't say it was a piece of consequence, but it has got a bit of oomph – and it just pleased me to be going out on that sort of note, rather than some groaning or moaning away like a stuffy old fart.

The second commission, for the New Zealand Trio, was entitled *Clouds* and proved a difficult birth. 'It's like I paid for all the easiness of the first one,' Jenny said, 'with all the difficulty of the second one, to find something to write about.' In five short movements *Clouds* balances passages of rhythmic eventfulness with episodes of calm; dark textures with airier melodic lines; and moments of drama with repose. The dissonances are so finely handled they're not unsettling – they're simply another colour among the many that parade through the piece. The work is episodic but, like the arc of Jenny's career, its disparate moments somehow hang together to disclose a rich and beguiling coherence. The poem that accompanied the piece – and that Jenny offered as a programme note – reinforces this impression:

> cumulus?

> not so much
> white fluffy puffy
> as here there
> high bright low
> wild, raggedy

dense, dark, hymnic
calmo, agitato
with a bit of cirro-
cumulo-nimbo-stratus
thrown in
     more like
McLeody sort of clouds . . .

Epilogue: A Braided River

All those clouds – different shapes, sizes, colours and densities; at different altitudes and temperatures. But all of them water vapour and all suspended in the same sky. Jenny's music is a little like that. Her life choices, too. Her suggestion that the (sometimes extreme) zigs and zags she made in her career and in her personal and spiritual life ultimately tended to hone in on some sort of mean, makes sense to me. I also find reasonable her claim that what look like radical changes in direction have always been a further step on a pathway that was already present, already in mind.

As my work on this biography was drawing to a close, I was in regular contact with Jenny, asking questions, seeking clarification, confirming details, checking dates. One of the late questions I posed was around her identification with Māori. While her long answer spoke to my question, it also revealed that the ways she thought about relationships between Māori and Pākehā were of a piece with both her thinking about the range of music that engaged her, and the variety of her spiritual experiences:

> Think of a braided river: at certain times and places it flows as one, and at others it breaks apart into separate strands, all depending on the contours and the weather. So, I love the haka and the Highland pipes, Bach and Palestrina, Beethoven, the Beatles, Messiah, the great old British hymns, our tribal waiata – and so much more. The river

itself just keeps on flowing – essentially, it's all one. Sometimes there are currents, snags, rapids, points that are dangerous, elsewhere it is broad, deep, placid – or again shallow, tinkly, sparkling. Religions are deltas (that can also be mudflats), and beyond it all is the mighty sea.

Her remarks brought to mind a paper she'd presented in an Honours seminar at Victoria in the early 1970s. Jenny's friend, anthropology professor Jan Pouwer, had invited her to participate in one of his graduate courses. It was at a time when semiotics and structuralist symmetries were of considerable interest to her, 'the height of my intellectual days,' she said. 'I remember applying the dictum "either/or – both/and" widely and enthusiastically. First, as exemplifying the difference between two individual opposites (e.g. "either high or low"); and second, as a spectrum, which incorporates the two (e.g. "both high and low") – the thought being that the spectrum itself is as essential as the two opposite ends.' That the spectrum itself – the full gamut of possibilities – is as necessary as any single possibility within the spectrum corresponds precisely to the braided river: essentially, it's all one.

Jenny once asked Fred Page what 'categorical imperative' meant – she'd had a crack at Immanuel Kant but found him unreadable:

He told me a categorical imperative was 'that which must be'. Well, I immediately understood that. The creation poetry spoke to me irrevocably of 'that which is'; the categorical imperative for me then was: I must follow this. But back to the braided river, *not* 'I can *only* follow this' . . . I've always followed those feelings that were deepest within me, which were also always the ones I felt most certain about. They were also not passing – they have remained. They have come before and stood above (and beyond, and within, or at the heart of) all the actual human connections. I have not followed outer things, am not interested in success, fame, glory and the rest. When I did seem to have them for a time, I found I hated them. I've always followed inner things – it may have looked as though I was influenced by someone or something 'out there', but

I was always actually following my own inner response to whatever it was. The recognition comes: 'Here is what moves me.' One's own categorical imperative naturally follows: 'I will go with this, I will follow it, this was meant for me.' Right from the time when I first saw the big black music notes on the Primer One wall, it has always been like this.

By following the inner things, the things that moved her, Jenny was to experience two homecomings: at Pukerua Bay and at Maungārongo Marae. She came to think of Pukerua Bay as her tūrangawaewae, 'only that was to do with the landscape (earth, sea, sky), whereas at Maungārongo it concerned the people'.

During her early childhood Jenny had believed there were 'people in the sky' who were watching her at night. 'Privately I called these people The Watchers. As a young child, the presence of the Watchers could sometimes disconcert me to the point of tears, whereupon my mother would close the curtains and tell me there were "no people in the sky". (I knew she was wrong.)' When she was welcomed by the people of Maungārongo, Jenny learned that Ngāti Rangi meant 'Sky People' and she was, at first, a little afraid of them, too. In October 2022, she wrote to me, saying:

> The sense I now have of the stars or the 'people in the sky' – as being not any remote, cold, forbidding 'Watchers' but my own beloved oldies – has somehow 'rounded off' my feeling of a life having come full circle. I arrive more or less back where I started but now with an understanding that essentially all is and was always well – and that all was also always grace. Suddenly I'm reminded of Messiaen – in my mind I hear that vast solo horn call echoing through deep (inner) space – the solo from *Des Canyons aux Étoiles*. Of course, Messiaen too is one of my 'beloved olds' along with Aunty Jane, and Joan, and Biddy, Matiu, Dean . . . and Bach, Mozart, Boulez, Beethoven, Chopin, Debussy . . . and Fred, Eve, Douglas, Peter Schat . . . and Mum and Dad and Grandpa . . . ah, the cosmic braided river.

The following month, a few weeks after her eighty-first birthday, Jenny suffered a severe stroke and was admitted to Palmerston North Hospital. On 28 November 2022, her friend Sheryl Boxall was sitting with her, joined by Aroha Māreikura over the phone. As Aroha sang one of the hymns composed for the Hui Aranga, Jenny slipped quietly away to join her beloved oldies.

Notes

Preface

1   McLeod, 'Aspects of Myth', p2.

Introduction

1   McLeod, 1996, p3 [corrected JMcL, 2022].

2   Ibid.

Chapter 1: Beginnings

1   McLeod, 'Liberated Learning', p3.
2   McLeod, 'Family Background', p9.
3   McLeod, 'Some Early Memories', p1.
4   McLeod, 'Family Background', p10.
5   Ibid., p12.
6   McLeod, 'Some Early Memories', p2.
7   Ibid., p2. 'So much,' Jenny said, 'for [my later] notions that my parents had nothing to teach me.'
8   Ibid., p3.
9   Ron McLeod and Lorna Perrin were married in November 1940.
10   Jenny believed Ron had struggled with his non-combatant status during World War II. 'In wartime New Zealand, any fit young man still in the country might be handed a white feather, signifying pretty much "Why aren't you over there fighting, you coward?" Living in daily fear of the feather was no match for the terrors faced by Kiwi soldiers, but Dad suffered sorely from this during the war years. He even considered wearing a sign on his back: "Flat Feet".'
11   McLeod, 'Liberated Learning', p5. Paul Person was a foundation member of the first New Zealand Opera Company and later, with Cyril Kelleway, founded the Perkel Opera Company in Auckland; Ronald McLeod (junior) along with his wife Catherine Styles-McLeod composed the musical *Mr King Hongi*, based on the life of Hongi Hika.
12   Gillett, 1999[a], Alexander Turnbull Library; McLeod, 'Some early memories'.
13   Ibid., 1999 [corrected JMcL, 2022].
14   Smith, 2009 [corrected JMcL, 2022].
15   McLeod, 'Liberated Learning', p1.
16   Ibid., p5
17   Ibid., p6.
18   Smith, 2009.
19   McLeod, 'Some Early Memories', p2.

Chapter 2: Levin | Horowhenua College

1   Smith, 2009.
2   Ibid.
3   Jensen, 1968.
4   McLeod, 2016.
5   Smith, 2009.
6   Craig McLeod interview, October 2021.
7   Small, 1998, p9.
8   McLeod, 'Liberated Learning', p6.
9   Small later changed his mind and took
     a serious interest in contemporary
     classical music.
10   McLeod, 'Liberated Learning', p6.
11   Smith, 2009.
12   McLeod, 'Liberated Learning', p6.
13   Ibid.
14   Another of Bleeks' students while Jenny
     was at Decatur High was sculptor.

Preston Jackson, who said, 'Decatur was
heaven. Everything I did there brought
a smile to my face. I . . . played football
for a while, I stopped because my art
teacher told me I shouldn't be playing
football – I should be studying art. Her
name was Justine Bleeks . . . She was a
savior.' (*PEORIA*, July 2021, pp68–76,
www. peoriamagazines.com
15   Galbreath, 2008; Anon., 'Post War
     Development', March 1981.
16   Smith, 2009.
17   McLeod, 'Liberated Learning', p7.
18   Kerr, 1988, p8.
19   McCracken, 1971.
20   Fairley, 1997, p58.

Chapter 3: Victoria University College

1   Auckland and Canterbury were also
     'university colleges'; Otago University
     alone enjoyed the title of 'university',
     having negotiated to keep it when
     joining the national university in 1874.
     For student numbers, see Barrowman,
     1999, p106.
2   Page, 1986, p90.
3   McLeod, 2016.
4   Jensen, 1968.
5   Jenny told Elizabeth Kerr, in 1988, that
     it might have been *Festival Overture* she
     first heard by Lilburn on LP (p8). This
     is likely, given that work was released
     commercially by HMV in 1959.
6   Gillett, 1999[b], p8.
7   The concert, including electronic music
     by Stockhausen, was a special evening-
     long event to celebrate the opening of the
     University Little Theatre. (Robin Maconie,
     email correspondence, October 2022).
8   ATL Eph-A-MUSIC-

VUMS-1950/1981.
9   Page, 1986, p94.
10   Fairley, 1996, p58.
11   McLeod, in Page, 1986, p161.
12   Ibid., p162.
13   Ibid., p164.
14   McLeod, 'Liberated Learning', p7.
15   McLeod, in Page, 1986, p166.
16   Later in life Jenny's view of her parents
     softened. She said, 'I used to come back to
     Levin from my exploits as a student and
     thinking, "Now I understand about the
     world", which [at that age] you obviously
     don't. God, I so badly put my parents
     down in my younger days. But Mum and
     Dad *were* interested in things . . .'
17   McLeod, in Page, 1986, p163. It was
     a film by Fellini, Craig told me. (Craig
     McLeod; email correspondence, August
     2022).
18   McLeod, 'Liberated Learning', p7.
19   Lilburn had studied with Vaughan

Williams at the Royal College of Music in London during the late 1930s, so his advocacy of the English composer's music is understandable. See Norman, 1983, pp50–52.

20 Pruden, in Dodd, 2003. For Pruden at Cambridge, see also Robert Hoskins' introductions to *The Larry Pruden Collection*, Vols 2–4 (Promethean Editions).

21 Rimmer, in Dodd, 2003.

22 Kit Powell, email correspondence, November 2022.

23 Maconie, in Dodd, 2003.

24 McLeod, in Dodd, 2003.

25 Rimmer, in Dodd, 2003.

26 McLeod, in Dodd, 2003.

27 Craig McLeod interview, October 2021.

28 Three movements of the *Cambridge Suite* were later recorded by a youth orchestra conducted by Juan Matteucci, and released on the album *Music and Youth*, Kiwi-SLC-72, 1969.

29 'Waitangi Day Concert, 1964', ATL MST7-0612.

30 I couldn't find any other accounts of this rehearsal, but Robin Maconie recalled Stravinsky's attendance 'at the University Little Theatre of rehearsals of *The Soldier's Tale*, parts of which conductor Peter Zwartz found hard to negotiate. A nimble Robert Craft stepped up to assist.' (Robin Maconie, email correspondence, October 2022).

31 Anon. 'Unashamedly Tonal', 1964, p276. The *Cambridge Suite* and the *Little Symphony* weren't the only pieces Jenny composed that were fêted at this time. In 1963, her *Toccata for Brass* (and William Southgate's *Toccata for Brass Choir*, jointly) won the Philip Neill Memorial Prize (administered by Otago University) for excellence in composition. She also won the 1962

and 1963 Wellington City Council Music Prize for submitting the 'best musical composition for performance at this university'. Norman, 1983, Vol. 2, p726; Victoria University of Wellington Calendar 1967, pp239–40.

32 *String Trio* had been performed the previous year at an ISCM concert in Wellington. See Norman, 1983, Vol. 2, p716.

33 McLeod, in Dodd, 2003.

34 From *Minor Poems*, 1930.

35 *Auckland Star*, 11 January 1964.

36 Body, in Dodd, 2003.

37 McLeod, in Dodd, 2003.

38 Craig McLeod interview, October 2021.

39 McLeod, 1992, p3. John Kennedy taught at Cambridge in January 1962. Given that commercial recordings of Messiaen's music had been available in the US since 1949 (and in Europe from 1952), it is possible some of them had reached New Zealand prior to Kennedy's visit. They certainly arrived soon after. Robin Maconie told me, 'In 1962 or 1963 I remember entering the music room in Kirk House and finding Fred Page, a baffled conductor Georg Tintner and Roger Savage listening to a freshly delivered LP box set of Messiaen's *Turangalîla* symphony, upholstered in shocking pink' (Robin Maconie, email correspondence, November 2021). This would have been the Vega recording, released in April 1962. The tape of *Quatuor pour la fin du temps* Kennedy played was most likely the recording he'd made with an Australian quartet in 1961, released on the W&G label.

40 Robin Maconie, email correspondence, October 2021.

41 McLeod, 1992, p3. Jenny performed

the work again at Cambridge the following summer. (John Rimmer, email correspondence, October, 2022.)

42 Smith, 2009.

43 McLeod, 1992, p3.

44 APRA: Australasian Performing Rights Association.

45 An Honours degree was ordinarily a four-year undertaking, but Jenny's extramural study allowed her to propose a programme of study (duly approved by Fred Page) that meant she could satisfy the requirements of the qualification in three years.

46 McKay, 1990, p192.

47 McLeod, 2016.

48 In 1969 Baxter, by then sober and a committed Catholic, established a spiritually oriented commune in the small Whanganui river settlement of Jerusalem.

49 McCracken, 1971.

50 Robin Maconie, email correspondence, October 2021.

51 There is a copy of the score of *Diversions for Orchestra* in the Alexander Turnbull Library. ATL MSY-2340.

52 Jones, 2003; Hardie, 1994, p15.

53 Kerr, 1988, pp8–9.

54 McCracken, 1971.

Chapter 4: Europe | Paris

1   Cecilia Johnson, email correspondence, September 2021.

2   Kerr, 1988, p9; McLeod, 1992, p3.

3   Cecilia Johnson interview, September 2021.

4   Boulez, 1959/1986, p404.

5   McLeod, 1992, p4.

6   The previous year the topic of study had been religious music, and the works examined included: Mozart's *Magic Flute*, Bach's *Mass in B Minor*, an introduction to Gagaku ceremony and instrumentation, Stravinsky's *Symphony of Psalms*, Debussy's *Le Martyre de Saint-Sébastien*, and some of Messiaen's own music. (Robin Maconie, email correspondence, November, 2021.)

7   McLeod, 1992, p6.

8   Ibid., p4.

9   Ibid., 1992, pp4, 5.

10 Robin Maconie, email correspondence, November 2021.

11 McLeod, 1992, p7.

12 Ibid., p6.

13 Ibid., p8. Jenny said his performance on that occasion was 'indescribable' and that he layed like a 'complete madman' who was 'totally *gone*!'

14 Ibid., p7.

15 Smith, 2009.

16 Page, 1986, pp112–13.

17 McLeod, 1992, p12.

18 A twelve-tone matrix is a tool for generating the inversions (or mirror image, in intervallic terms) and transpositions – and their retrograde versions – of a series of pitches.

19 Letter to Fred Page, 29 January 1965, ATL MS-Papers-5558-2.

20 Jenny commented, 'The ancient Greek metrical rhythm known as the "Sapphic Major" is fundamental here. Derek Sanders (while living in Australia years later) spent months learning this very hard piece so he could perform it for his Greek friends.'

21 Hardie, 1994, pp23–30.

22 Richard Hardie, email correspondence, January 2022.

23 Brownlee, 1971.

24 Cecilia Johnson interview, September 2021.

25 Letter to Douglas Lilburn, April 1965, ATL, MS-Papers-7623-191.

26 McLeod, 1992, p8.

27 Ibid., p11.

Chapter 5: Europe | Basel, Darmstadt, Cologne

1   McLeod, 1965, p13.

2   McCracken, 1971.

3   Letter to Fred Page, 8 July 1965, ATL MS-Papers-5558-2.

4   Anon. Darmstädter Ferienkurse, 1965/2013.

5   Page, 1986, p106. He continued by saying, 'A hearing in West Berlin a few weeks later of Beethoven's Seventh quickly cured me of that notion.'

6   Lilburn, 1963, pp2–3.

7   With the guitar as his point of reference – an instrument harmonically limited compared with the piano (which most composers favour) – Berlioz would likely have developed circumscribed ideas about harmony. 'The reasons for that,' Jenny understood, 'are completely musical; they're not to do with anything extramusical at all. It's just that there are certain demands in writing for guitar and other demands in writing for piano.'

8   Smith, 2009.

9   Court, 1996, p2.

10 McLeod, 1992, p12.

11 Robin Maconie, email correspondence, November 2021.

12 Court, 1996, p2

13 Smith, 2009. That was how he seemed to Jenny at first, but she added that, 'When he wrote to me (just once) he was completely open, genuine, humble and friendly.'

14 Ibid.

15 The original title *Fourches* means 'Forks'. This, Jenny said, 'related to the fact that the initial structure was an open form in which the sections could come in different orders based on the predetermined fork-like mathematical ratios of their relative lengths – a very satisfying overall structure . . . However, I later decided not only that I preferred one particular order, but also that I liked certain sections less. So, I ditched those, closed the open form, and changed the title.'

16 Stockhausen did eventually compose such a piece: *Für Dr. K* (1969) consists entirely of accelerandi and ritardandi, and was composed as a birthday present for Dr Albert Kalmus, the director of the London branch of music publishers Universal Edition. (Robin Maconie, email correspondence, October 2022.)

17 In this regard her approach resembled Stockhausen's work on *Studie 1* (1953), where numerical values were used to determine aspects of the work. In both Stockhausen's work and in *For Seven*, it seems to me, the use of numerical ratios was not the fundamental premise of the piece, but rather a tool used to achieve a musical/conceptual objective.

18 Robin Maconie, email correspondence, October 2022.

19 Letter to Fred Page, 29 November 1965, ATL MS-Papers 5558-2.

20 Kerr, 1988, p9.

21 Ibid.

22 Letter to Fred Page, 29 November 1965, ATL MS-Papers-5558-2.

23 Lilburn, 1985, p13.

24 Smith, 2009.

25   Craig McLeod interview, October 2021.

26   Letter to Douglas Lilburn, April 1965, ATL MS-Papers-7623-191.

27   This is amongst Jenny's papers in the Alexander Turnbull Library: MS-Papers 7349-225.

Chapter 6: Junior Lecturer | Journeyman Composer

1   Lyell Cresswell, email correspondence, October 2021.

2   Ibid.

3   Ibid. The ideas of Lutosławski and Penderecki fitted perfectly well with Jenny's point of view at the time; she had, after all, used them in the 'background music' of *For Seven*. The reason their music wasn't included in the syllabus was more prosaic: 'It was more that there wasn't a lot in that music to analyse. The way it was made was perfectly obvious from a quick look at the score.'

4   Roy Tankersley, email correspondence, September 2021.

5   Elizabeth Kerr, email correspondence, October 2021.

6   Lyell Cresswell, email correspondence, October 2021.

7   Jenny enjoyed playing *Rhapsody in Blue*, saying, 'His piano arrangements [of his other music] were really quite difficult, my hands too small.'

8   Jack Richards, correspondence, March 2022.

9   Anon. 'Wairarapa Schools' History', n.d. Norman, 2006, suggests 1965 (p251).

10 Court, 1996, pp4–5.

11 Ibid., p5.

12 Jensen, 1968.

13 Ibid.

14 Smith, 2009.

15 Jensen, 1968.

16 Kerr, 1988, p10.

17 Jensen, 1968.

18 Foreshadowing her compositional practice of the late 1980s and beyond, these were the same chromatic triads Jenny pressed into service when composing music using Tone Clock theory. See pp 244-247.

19 Kerr, 1988, p10. Jenny added, 'In *For Seven*, by contrast, it is largely the beats themselves that are absent (silent). They are indicated by the conductor but quite rarely are they articulated in sound. This only happens at the beginning and end of an accelerando or ritardando.'

20 Jenny added, 'Peter Zwartz marvelled that I had "dared" to mark the arrival of the Nothing with a sudden total blackout in the theatre – from which we then heard (pre-recorded) the cosmic sound of a tiny baby whimpering. It had never entered my head that this might be somewhat risky, given the inevitable family audience – but (as far as I know) it has always worked like magic.'

21 Smalley, 1970.

22 McLeod, 1993[a], p19.

23 Tulloch, in Anon. 'Jenny McLeod's Earth and Sky', 1993, p25.

24 Anon. 'Prime Minister was impressed', 1968.

25 Hill, 1968.

26 Saunders, 1970; Page, 1969.

27 Mason, 1969.

28 Morrissey, in 'Jenny McLeod's Earth and Sky', 1993, p27.

29 Tulloch in Anon. 'Jenny McLeod's Earth and Sky', 1993, p25.

30 Kerr, 1988, p10.

31 McLeod, 1993[a], p19.

32 Ibid.

33 Jenny recalled a further production by 'a Catholic girls' school in Auckland' (ibid.) but I've not been able to find records of that event.

34 Shieff, 2002, p67.

35 Ibid, p72.

36 See also Court, 1996, p3.

37 Court, 1996, p3.

38 Ibid., p4.

39 Shepard, 1996, p15.

40 Ibid. With the benefit of a further twenty-five years to think about it, Jenny said, 'I think now however that the end should remain as it was, even if it does end in the spirit world. I may have been a little bit too hasty to accommodate traditional views, tacking on a sort of corny "happy ending" that will more likely bring the audience down. Death is where we will all end up in any case, though this earth and our descendants carry on. The point of the story's end is that Māui *failed* to conquer death, just as the rest of us will. The old ending is much more powerful, and leaves us face to face with the very fact of our own mortality.'

Chapter 7: Professor of Music

1 It appears that this is close to what Page had in mind in 1964 when he asked Lilburn to redraft the degree. In a letter to Robin Maconie dated 21 March 1964, Page wrote, 'You may have heard that I'm putting up a scheme to the University authorities to admit students in 3 streams: to BA in Music, with five units in Music; in B Mus, with <u>nine</u> units; in B Mus for performers, with nine units . . . performers will do three stages on an instrument, with various subjects. We want to give a degree and not a diploma, which is important.' (Courtesy Robin Maconie, October 2022.) The introduction of performance for academic credit towards a degree was thus pioneered by Page; the addition of a major in composition appears to have been Jenny's idea.

2 Smith, 2009.

3 Norman, 2006, p249; Norman, 1983, p139.

4 Lilburn interpreted Jenny's work on the curriculum as 'her first real bid for power'. He was not pleased when Jenny was later appointed Professor of Music, attributing her success to game playing – 'Jenny played her cards well, all too well . . .' – and Page's favouritism: 'David, Margaret [Nielsen] and I built that Dept for him, saw him through all his hapless administration crises, then watched him opt for Junior lecturer [i.e. Jenny] and latest bandwagon.' Norman, 2006, pp249–51.

5 Ibid, pp248–49.

6 Ibid, p255.

7 Her other referees were Professor Peter Platt (head of the Otago University Music Department), George Hughes (Professor of Philosophy at Victoria, who had attended some of Jenny's Honours seminars) and Owen Jensen (*Evening Post* music critic and former director of the Cambridge Summer School of Music).

8 Barrowman, 1999, p307.

9 Smith, 2009. The vexed circumstances experienced in the department at

this time are elegantly summarised in Norman, 2006, pp248–55.

10   McCracken, 1971.

11   Ibid., 1971. Fifty years later Jenny's views had softened considerably, and she hoped 'not too many orchestral hearts were dismayed on reading this, for all its truth at the time'. Times change, and Jenny was gratified that in the new century youth and regional orchestras were well established and thriving, the universities had orchestras of their own, and that in 2022 Gemma New, Principal Conductor of the NZSO and 'in demand by orchestras around the world', was a music graduate of Canterbury University. But in 1971, 'I still had the modernist bit between my teeth; but as Boulez said, 'J'ai la droite d'avoir tort' – I have the right to be wrong.'

12   Anon. 'Kitchen sink', 1970.

13   J .McLeod, 1970.

14   Anon. 'Kitchen sink', 1970.

15   R. McLeod, 1970.

16   Ibid; 'Kitchen sink', 1970.

17   McLeod, letter to Kevin Ireland, 4 May 1991, ATL 94-180-1/19. Regarding 'A Whiter Shade of Pale', Jenny said, 'Actually I must confess I quite like it nonetheless – I also have the right to enjoy a bit of crap' She added that her earlier 'scathing attitude was still fairly subject to the avant-garde or Boulez-ian perspective'.

18   'Kitchen sink', 1970.

19   Barrowman, 1999, p306.

20   White, 2020.

21   Morva Croxson, email correspondence, November 2021.

22   Ibid.

23   Chamberlain, n.d.

24   Ibid.

25   Ibid.

26   Morva Croxson, email correspondence, November 2021. Children's artwork illustrating the action was projected at both ends of the arena during the production, adding a further visual dimension to the performance.

27   McCracken, 1971.

28   Bruce Greenfield interview, October 2021. While a great deal of work was accomplished during this four-week period, Jenny spent a further two weeks at Morva Croxson's place in Palmerston North completing the score.

29   Ibid.

30   McCracken, 1971.

31   Ibid.

32   The Forgiving were a Palmerston North band playing original music on the pub circuit and included brothers Gary and Paul Hunt, and Garry Powell. For *Under the Sun* Grant Bridger was added on vocals. www.ricko.co.nz

33   She said of *For Seven*, 'Players can in fact follow this visual notation surprisingly accurately and, given the slight individual vicissitudes of tempo inevitably present in any live performance, I don't believe any more perceptible accuracy would have been achieved by overlaying conventional notation.' (McLeod, 1992, p30).

34   Bruce Greenfield interview, October 2021.

35   Kerr, 1988, p11.

36   McCracken, 1972, p342.

37   McCracken, 1971.

38   Bruce Greenfield interview, October 2021.

39   White, 2020; www.manawatuheritage. pncc.govt.nz

40   McLeod in '*Starsong* now *Under the Sun*', 1971; McLeod, 'Author's Note', *Under the Sun* LP liner notes.

41   McLeod, 'Synopsis', *Under the Sun* LP

liner notes.

42 Morva Croxson, email correspondence, November 2021.

43 Bruce Greenfield interview, October 2021.

44 Mason, 1971.

45 Zwartz, 1971.

46 Chamberlain, n.d. Fifty years later Jenny said, 'I don't agree with Anthony Burgess now – even though I've also been writing poems and such for years. What I think now is that any of the arts may take precedence over any other, depending on what is needed or will

work best at the time, or whatever art one happens to be focussing upon.'

47 Mason, 1971.

48 Croxson, in 'Jenny McLeod's Earth and Sky', 1993, p28.

49 Kerr, 1988.

50 McLeod, 1971; Mason, 1971.

51 McCracken, 1972, p339.

52 Ibid., pp339–40.

53 McLeod, 1992, pp9–10.

54 Fiona McAlpine, email correspondence, February 2022.

55 McCracken, 1972, p343.

Chapter 8: The Classroom Loses its Glow

1 Court, 1996, p6.

2 Bruce McKinnon, email correspondence, November 2021.

3 Smith, 2009.

4 Letter to Fred Page, 1972, ATL MS-Papers-5558-2.

5 Craig McLeod, interview, October 2021. For example, see McCracken, 1972; Hardie, 1994; Glasgow, 1995; and Shieff, 2002, which was drawn in significant part from interviews conducted by Elizabeth Kerr. Kerr, who knew Jenny well, said 'She's got a very big brain'. (Elizabeth Kerr interview, December 2021).

6 McCracken, 1972, p336.

7 Ibid. More recently, Jenny said, 'As I peeled off the layers, I did get back much more to the real thing. I wasn't wrong, there was plenty of ego and self-deception; I needed (and will always need) to keep up the conscious work that only comes from taking a good hard look at oneself – but by no means was it *all* ego. Underneath was still the bedrock.'

8 McCracken, 1972, p337. It was, Jenny recalled, beside Lake Rotopounamu, above Lake Taupō.

9 Anon. 'Jobs for the Boys – Says Jenny', 1972. Jenny withdrew from the commission in part because she had concluded that a rock opera would be better composed by the group that was to perform it (perhaps *Tommy* by the Who was the model she had in mind) than by a composer independent of the performers.

10 McCracken, 1972, p338. Jenny qualified this in later years, saying, 'This is true up to a point, but in point of fact when we are actually focused on music, there is nothing else until we have to come to the end [of life].'

11 Bruce McKinnon, correspondence, November 2021.

12 Craig McLeod interview, November 2021. 'The morning glory was a flop,' Jenny told me. 'I ground up the seeds into a kind of soup and swallowed them, but they tasted disgusting.'

13 Letter to Fred Page, 1972, ATL MS-Papers-5558-2.

14 Nona Harvey, email correspondence, February 2022.

15 Rob Cameron, correspondence, March 2022.

16 Nona Harvey, email correspondence, February 2022.

17 Ibid.

18 Tony Backhouse, email correspondence, October 2021.

19 Rob Cameron, correspondence, March 2022.

20 Letter to Fred Page, 1972, ATL MS-Papers-5558-2.

21 Carol Markwell, email correspondence, November 2021.

22 Laing, a psychiatrist, championed the use of mind-altering drugs, particularly LSD, in the treatment of some of his patients. He was also an enthusiastic experimenter with drugs. His biographer (son Adrian Laing) reported, 'He tried heroin, opium and amphetamines, but they were not to his liking. Cocaine was fine if you could afford it.' (Laing, 1996, p71.)

23 Tony Backhouse, email correspondence, October 2021.

24 Mason, 1971.

25 Shiels, 2019.

26 Ibid.

27 Ibid.

28 Letter to Fred Page, 1972, ATL MS-Papers-5558-2. In 2022 Jenny told me, 'I wouldn't be nearly so scathing today. "Something Wonderful" is well felt and beautifully shaped, and "Edelweiss", for example, has lasted pretty well. There really isn't anything in *Hair* that is better or as memorable, though "The Age of Aquarius" isn't bad.'

29 Ibid.

30 Craig McLeod interview, October 2021.

31 In her fifties, Jenny became close to Ngāti Rangi of Ohakune and said: 'What a relief it was finally to connect with the Māori for whom fondness and affection are expressed naturally and daily in multitudes of hugs, embraces, kisses, and physical comforting and reassurance.'

32 Craig said, 'I was a mistake; I was a faulty condom, my mother told me', although his arrival did fit in with what appears to be a well-managed timetable. Jenny remembered Lorna telling her that 'Craig had arrived "a few days early" (born 8 May, with Perrin 12 August and me 12 November). The leaky condom explains why.'

33 Smith, 2009. Later in life Jenny wondered if her mother had been a lesbian. 'It would explain a good deal. For quite some time she was very close to a theosophical lady friend who lived in the next street. Mum spent a surprising amount of time there; I would come home from work and she was never there, she was always over in the next street.'

34 Letter to Bruce Greenfield, January 1973.

35 Ibid. Jenny later said, 'I had taken to reading people's hands – something at which I found I was now eerily gifted. Things just "came to me" as I spoke them, faces would grow pale, people would start to sit up, as apparently what I had said was true or in some way significant to them.' Oliver O'Brien, a friend of the Bruseys, gently pointed out to her that she was 'saying some big things'. Jenny went on, 'That was enough. I recognised at once that he was right, and that this was a benign warning. Reading a "sign" more lucidly for a change, I was instantly restored to a good path.'

36 Bruce Greenfield, email correspondence, October 2021.
37 Letter to Bruce Greenfield, April 1973.
38 Bruce Greenfield, email correspondence, June 2022.
39 Letter to Bruce Greenfield, 7 May 1973.
40 Ibid.
41 Ibid.
42 Ibid.

Chapter 9: Finding Divine Light

1   Fiona McAlpine, email correspondence, March 2023.
2   Shieff, 2002, p69.
3   Bruce Greenfield interview, October 2021.
4   Kerr, 1988, p12; Smith, 2009.
5   A fuller context for the first quote: 'You should love one another and behave lovingly because when love comes, everything comes. You should speak to one another with love and humility. Love is the essence.' Prem Rawat, Ram Lila Grounds, Delhi, India, 29 October 1966 (translated from Hindi). In *Divine Light* (UK), 1 April 1973, Vol. 2, Issue 7.
6   'Satsang' in the context of Maharaj Ji's teaching involved regularly meeting with other followers so that they might speak from the heart about their own experience of inner truth. The purpose of the meetings was to provide ongoing support and inspiration for each participant's own practice.
7   Steve Matthews interview, July 2022. Steve stressed the point that the Divine Light Mission (and later Elan Vital) were organisations that, while associated with Prem Rawat, were distinct from him and his teaching. Their function was primarily facilitative – booking halls for meetings, organising festivals, arranging travel for Maharaj Ji and his instructors – but they were often seen 'as this Eastern, guru-based religion'. Rawat's teaching, Steve said, 'isn't [that], but that's how it was originally perceived in the West'.
8   Tony Backhouse, email correspondence, November 2021.
9   Letter to Bruce Greenfield, July 1974.
10 Steve Matthews interview, July 2022.
11 McLeod, 1975, p4.
12 www.prem-rawat-bio.org
13 Letter to Bruce Greenfield, July 1974.
14 Ibid. In 2021 Jenny wrote, 'The amount of synchronicity in my own life has been, and still is, so considerable as to be almost staggering – until I simply began to get used to it, and more importantly to cease looking for any particular significance (especially any personal meaning) in all the ongoing coincidences – sometimes as many as three or four in a single day. That way lies very possible insanity.'
15 Letter to Bruce Greenfield, July 1974.
16 Bruce Greenfield interview, October 2021.
17 Ibid.
18 McLeod, 1975, p1.
19 Ibid.
20 Ibid.
21 Kerr, 1988, p12.
22 McLeod, 1975, p2.
23 Shieff, 2002, p69.
24 Bruce McKinnon, email correspondence, July 2022.
25 Ibid.

26 McLeod, 1975, pp3–4.

27 Kerr, 1988, p7.

28 Guitarist Robert Fripp and producer Brian Eno recorded electronic music subsequently characterised as 'ambient' and which was valued by many listeners for its contemplative qualities.

29 Court, 1996, p6.

30 Bruce Greenfield interview, October 2021.

31 Court, 1996, p6.

32 Barrowman, 1999, p307.

33 Court, 1996, p6.

34 Maconie, 1975. For a broader context, see Maconie's 'Tender Roots or Mature Dwarfs', in *Salient*, 4 March 1969. Jenny did not in fact teach composition – that work fell primarily to David Farquhar. She told me, 'I didn't really think composition could actually be taught. Both Messiaen and Boulez had felt the best way of teaching it was through detailed analysis of existing works, which was my own view also. I taught harmony and music history myself.'

35 Barrowman, 1999, p308

36 Kerr, 1988, p12.

37 Barrowman, 1999, pp308–9

Chapter 10: Spiritual Walkabout

1   Kerr, 1988, p12.

2   Brych was a Czech-born refugee who arrived in New Zealand claiming to have medical training. He practised as a cancer therapist in Auckland until an investigation of his qualifications led to his removal from the medical register in 1974.

3   Letter to Bruce Greenfield, September 1978.

4   Kerr, 1988, p12.

5   Letter to Bruce Greenfield, September 1978.

6   Smith, 2009.

7   Steve Matthews reiterated this point, saying that some of the those who encountered Maharaj Ji during this period were inclined to assign him some kind of messianic role, yet '[Prem Rawat] said, "I have no interest in setting up a religion, I have no interest in setting up some sort of a spiritual thing" . . . He has always said, "I'm a human being. I'm not God. If you want God, go inside and find that experience within".' (Steve Matthews interview, July 2022)

8   Smith, 2009.

9   In 1976, while still living in her Ohiro Road house, Jenny had become so exasperated she moved out, staying in Steve Matthews' house in nearby Devon Street during her final year teaching at Victoria.

10 Letter to Bruce Greenfield, August 1982.

11 Kerr, 1988, p13.

12 From a collection of Jenny's poems, 1981–82, ATL MS-Papers-7349-124.

13 Smith, 2009. Jenny (more or less) stopped using drugs when she became an adherent of Maharaj Ji's teaching.

14 Bruce Greenfield, email correspondence, November 2021.

15 Tony Backhouse, email correspondence, October 2021.

16 Bruce Greenfield interview, October 2021.

17 Court, 1996, p1.

18 Ibid., p6. The quote is from Blake's *The*

Marriage of Heaven and Hell, mixed with a little T.S. Eliot: 'Preface' to Harry Crosby's *The Transit of Venus: Poems.*

19   McCracken, 1972, p337.

20   Ibid.

21   While Jenny did have some drug experiences that might fairly be described as numinous – 'seeing the light' on mescalin, for example – with hindsight she was dismissive of them. She said, 'Nowadays I wouldn't give you tuppence for such experiences, they come and they go, essentially they mean nothing.

They don't mean you are some wondrous being blessed from on high. You can interpret them any way you like, and doing so on your own can even become quite risky, depending on the craziness of some momentary inspiration or other.'

22   Smith, 2009.

23   McLeod, 1975, p3.

24   Ibid.

25   Ibid.

26   Ibid., p4.

27   Letter to Bruce Greenfield, August 1982.

Chapter 11: Homecoming

1   Letter to Bruce Greenfield, August 1982.

2   From the collection 'Another Life', from Jenny's poems, 1981–82, ATL MS-Papers-7349-124.

3   Cecilia Johnson interview, September 2021.

4   David Farquhar's *Ring Round the Moon*, originally incidental music for a 1953 play of the same name, later developed into *Dance Suite from 'Ring Round the Moon'.*

5   Kerr, 1988, p13.

6   McLeod, 2003.

7   Roy Tankersley, email correspondence, October 2021.

8   McLeod, 2003.

9   Ibid.

10   Roy Tankersley, email correspondence, November 2021; Bach Choir programme, 21 September 1982.

11   McLeod, 1995, piii.

12   Ibid.

13   Ibid.

14   Jenny's teacher, Douglas Lilburn, studied with Ralph Vaughan Williams, who also set William Blake's poetry,

notably in *Ten Blake Songs* (1958).

15   McLeod, 1995, piii.

16   Cunningham, 1832/2017, p482.

17   Robert Hoskins, correspondence, February 2022.

18   Bruce Greenfield interview, October 2021.

19   The Project Employment Programme was a subsidised work scheme introduced in New Zealand by Robert Muldoon's (1975–1984) National government. It was discontinued in 1985.

20   Joe Bleakley interview, September 2022.

21   Bleakley, n.d.

22   Tim Jordan, email correspondence, October 2022.

23   Joe Bleakley correspondence, September 2022. The electronic music included a 'pulse track' that activated the fireworks. As far as Tim knew, the Sun Festival marked the first time this was done in New Zealand.

24   There is an excellent description of the event with many vivid photographs at www.joebleakley.com

25   'Indigo II' is included under the title 'Light of lights beholden' in *Carol our*

Christmas, a book of New Zealand carols. Jenny said the song 'has even become something of a favourite at weddings and funerals . . . and the words were quoted by a spiritual columnist

in the *Evening Post* years later for their relevance to our time.'

26   Roy Tankersley, email correspondence, November 2021.

27   Campbell, 1984.

Chapter 12: Music for the Screen

1   Craig McLeod interview, November 2021

2   'Morrow Productions', www.ngatoanga. org.nz. Among the company's most memorable advertisements were those for Four Square and Chesdale cheese, whose cartoon characters Ches and Dale featured on New Zealand TV screens for several decades.

3   Pacific Films made many sponsored short films. *Equation*, commissioned by Mobil Oil NZ Ltd, NZED for Comalco, and NZ Aluminium Smelters Ltd, was one of many such projects in the 1970s. See Reid, 2018, pp239–40.

4   Shepard, 1996, p1.

5   Ferreira, 2010, p87.

6   Lang, 1984, p13

7   Ferreira, 2010, p82.

8   Ibid., p82.

9   Ibid., p85.

10   Tim Jordan, email correspondence, October 2022.

11   Ferreira, 2010, p86. Ferreira identifies composer and orchestrator Craig Utting as the arranger of the music for *The Silent One*. Utting did make

an arrangement of the title theme for a children's massed choir event in an Artsplash festival in Wellington some years later, but the music in the soundtrack was composed and arranged by Jenny. She said, 'I would never permit any of my written-out music to make its first appearance arranged by anyone but me, since as far as I'm concerned, the arrangement is half the work. Later cover versions are another matter altogether.'

12   Shepard, 1996, p11.

13   Ferreira, 2010, p81.

14   Lang, 1984, p13

15   Shepard, 1996, p12.

16   Ibid.

17   Ibid., p13.

18   Ibid., p6.

19   Ibid., p10.

20   Ibid., p4.

21   Ibid., p7.

22   Ibid.

23   Ibid., pp6, 7.

24   Bruce Greenfield interview, October 2021.

Chapter 13: Popular Music for the Concert Hall

1   Shepard, 1996, p17.

2   See Sanders, 2004.

3   Ibid., p100.

4   Ibid., p99.

5   Ibid., p98.

6   In 2012 *The Emperor and the Nightingale* was performed by the NZSO under Hamish McKeich at the New Zealand International Arts Festival, where it was paired with *Peter*

and the Wolf.

7   Jenny had first heard Copland's music
     as a high school student in the United
     States: 'I remember hearing Copland's
     Fanfare for the Common Man, which I
     liked a lot, it's remarkable as a sort of
     "anthem"; and *Appalachian Spring, Billy
     the Kid, Lincoln Portrait* – also Ferde
     Grofé's *Grand Canyon Suite* – these were
     some of my youthful predilections, and
     so was *West Side Story* when it first came
     out.'

8   McLeod, 2016.

9   Liner notes, *Emperor and the
     Nightingale,* Naxos 8.572671, 2011.

10   Lilburn, 1946, pp9, 10.

11   Jenny thought this self-consciousness
     was attributable to Lilburn's European
     roots predominating over his New
     Zealand roots. 'First, Douglas was a bit
     of a snob – he couldn't really help it.
     This was the strait-laced "buttoned-up"
     Lilburn, to whom Aaron Copland was
     "vulgar" because he gave the fingered-
     circle sign to an American orchestra
     after a good performance. This was
     "Lilburn: The Composer" as he walked
     around the place fairly self-consciously,
     in short, having a reputation to live up
     to as the quasi-composer laureate – as
     Curnow was more or less acting as
     a quasi-national poet laureate when
     he wrote *Landfall in Unknown Seas.'*
     Jenny suspected this attitude came
     partly from Lilburn's 'quasi-upper-
     middle-class education as a boarder
     at Waitaki Boys' High – like Christ's
     College and Whanganui Collegiate,
     the New Zealand equivalent of an
     English public school, to which well-off
     Rangitikei farmers could afford to pay
     to send their isolated sons.' It was also
     attributable, she thought, to 'that later
     Christchurch/post-European literary

(etc.) "lost-soul-ness" about the "need
to find a national language".'

12   Shepard, 1996, p17.

13   Bruce McKinnon, email
     correspondence, November 2021.

14   Liner notes, *Emperor and the
     Nightingale,* Naxos 8.572671, 2011.

15   Rae de Lisle interview, February 2022.

16   Ibid.

17   Eugene Albulescu interview, February
     2022.

18   By the mid-1970s Jenny's interest in
     popular music as a point of reference for
     solo piano pieces saw her compose a set
     of simple 'pop piano exercises' for herself.
     These were collected as *Once Upon a
     Twinkle* and submitted to Price Milburn
     to be considered for publication. These
     pieces were eventually withdrawn but
     possibly marked Jenny's first small steps
     towards the later rock sonatas for piano.

19   Hardie, 1994, pp40–41. Jenny inverted
     the roots, so that in the key of C: C
     stayed the same; D(m) became Bb;G7
     became F7, etc. 'My thought was that
     the pop composers rather typically
     (as a reversal or kind of unconscious
     "rebellion") used not the classical/
     traditional 12-note cycle of fifths, but
     its inversion or reverse, the 12-note
     cycle of fourths. Bach's entire harmonic
     vocabulary, for example, and pretty
     much that of the entire late baroque
     period is based on the cycle of fifths
     (viz. the theory of Rameau as it is still
     traditionally taught). The so-called
     "perfect cadence" extends to the
     secondary dominants and so forth. The
     pop guys favoured the "opposite" plagal
     cadence, which extended typically to
     Bb–F–C – not a recognisable classical
     progression, in fact a recognisably *non-*
     classical progression that came as new
     and fresh.'

20 McLeod, 1975, p4.

21 Albulescu's recording *Piano Music of Franz Liszt* won the Grand Prix du Disque Liszt in 1994.

22 Liner notes, *Emperor and the Nightingale*, Naxos 8.572671, 2011.

23 Ibid.

24 Eugene Albulescu interview, February 2022. Sibelius is music notation software.

25 Liner notes, *Emperor and the Nightingale*, Naxos 8.572671, 2011.

26 SGS, 2011; Byzantion, 2012.

27 Goss, 2011.

28 Rae de Lisle interview, February 2022.

29 Hardie, 1994, p41.

30 Ibid., pp40–41.

31 McLeod, 1975, p4.

32 Shepard, 1996, p14.

33 As well as relying on intuition, she did make conscious use of the cycle of fourths in preference to the cycle of fifths.

34 Fairley, 1996, p59.

35 McLeod, 1988, pp88–169.

36 Jenny said the project with Ihimaera, *The Clio Legacy*, was 'a commission that Dorothy Buchanan later took up, and to which she did full justice, bless her'. To their credit, the Arts Council forfeited the advance paid to Jenny for her preparatory work on the project, treating it as 'a contribution to the time that you are devoting at the moment to exploring new directions in your work'. Letter from Brendan Smyth, of QE II Arts Council, November 1988. ATL MS-Papers-4788-02.

Chapter 14: The Tone Clock

1   Smith, 2009.

2   Body, 2011.

3   Letter to Barbara Einhorn, December 1988, ATL MS-Papers-4788-02.

4   Shieff, 2002, p70.

5   Kerr, 1988, p40.

6   Smith, 2009.

7   This resulted, eventually, in *The Tone Clock* by Peter Schat. Translated and with an introduction by Jenny, it was published by Harwood Academic Publishers in 1993.

8   McLeod, 1988, pp88–169.

9   Letter to Barbara Einhorn, December 1988, ATL MS-Papers-4788-02.

10 Ibid.

11 Interested readers are referred to Jenny's helpful essay '24 Tone Clock Pieces: A Commentary and Memoir' included with the Rattle CD *24 Tone Clocks*. For the full, weapons-grade exposition of Tone Clock theory, see Jenny's *Tone Clock Theory Expanded: Chromatic Maps 1 & 2*, www.archive.org

12 Musicologist Fiona McAlpine reiterated this point, saying, 'I have been very struck by her 1965 *Piano Piece* . . . [with its] embedded 3-3 sets (to use Fortean terminology), as if she was using the Tone Clock before it had even been thought of.' (Fiona McAlpine, email correspondence, February 2022.)

13 Croft, 1993, p20.

14 Smith, 2009.

15 Jenny was referring to the equally tempered twelve-note chromatic system. New Zealand-born composer Jeroen Speak subsequently applied Tone Clock principles to a quarter-tone scale and identified forty-nine possible chromatic triads in the twenty-four-tone octave.

Arabesques (2000) and *Comme le son évolue* (2002) were composed using this approach.

16 McLeod, 2016, p43.

17 McLeod, 1988, p2.

18 Fairley, 1996, p67.

19 McLeod, 2016, pp25, 27–28.

20 Kerr, 1988, p40.

21 Jenny's expansion of Schat's Tone Clock ideas identifies major and minor triads in seven other hours as well as the traditional natural triad(s) of the Eleventh Hour.

22 Emma Sayers interview, March 2022.

23 McLeod, 2016, p27. Jenny confessed that a 'fondness for Debussy can be detected' at one point in these notes, a correspondence also noted by musicologist Fiona McAlpine (McAlpine, 2011).

24 Grice, n.d. A typo in the liner notes to *24 Tone Clock Pieces* [fn. 52] suggests the Paris concert took place in 1990; 1989 is the correct date.

25 Letter to Barbara Einhorn, December 1988, ATL MS-Papers-4788-02.

26 Court, 1996, p1.

27 Ibid.

28 It's available through the SOUNZ website, or at www.archive.org

29 Glasgow, 1995, p102.

30 The four pieces Jenny wrote for Lilburn were composed using matrices (or 'magic squares', an approach used most notably by English composer Peter Maxwell Davies, and subsequently by his pupil, and Jenny's good friend, Gillian Whitehead) to generate steering networks created by using the horizontal, vertical and diagonal rows of the magic square (the numbers equated, via set theory, to pitches) to steer one another. See McLeod, 2016, pp34–35.

31 Ibid., p38. *Piece XII*, the only other singly composed piece in the Tone Clock collection, was also accompanied by a poem written after the music, rather than before it. New Zealand composer William Green later set that poem to music of his own.

32 Jenny added, 'I think you will also hear some echo of Gillian [Whitehead]'s Lullaby for Matthew for piano, which I much admired (and hence that title).'

33 *Messagesquisse*, 1976.

34 McLeod, 2016, p37.

35 Michael Houstoun, email correspondence, January 2022.

36 McLeod, 2016, p45.

37 Ibid., p47.

Chapter 15: Finding Whāuna, Finding Faith

1 Cecilia Johnson interview, September 2021.

2 Fairley, 1996, p62.

3 McLeod, 1993[b].

4 McLeod, 'Family Background', pp5–6.

5 In 2022 Jenny said, 'This was one tohu that was far from any "risky business". I still have no idea what it was, but am still powerfully affected – it has never faded away, as most of the other great so-called "spiritual experiences" did.'

6 McLeod, 1993[e], p5.

7 Smith, 2009.

8 McLeod, 1993[c], 1; 'Ohakune – 2 Ngāti Rangi songs', 1993, ATL MSC-11829.

9 McLeod, 1993[c].

10 McLeod, 1993[b].

11 McLeod, 1993[c], p2.

12 McLeod, 1993[b]. ·

13 'Paddle the Canoes', McLeod, 1993 [b]. As Jenny's first mature attempt at translating her texts into te reo Māori, *He Iwi Kotahi Tātou* is solid work. It does not, however, match the high standards she was to achieve in her later works, *Hōhepa* or *He Whakaahua o Maru*, for example.

14 Whitehead, 1994, p54.

15 McLeod, 1993[c], pp1–3. Xenakis was a Greek composer who, on Messiaen's advice, did not formally study music but instead composed works shaped by his training as an architect and his knowledge of mathematics.

16 Whitehead, 1994, p54.

17 Tūngia Baker's iwi affiliations also included Ngāti Raukawa, Te Āti Awa and Te Arawa. (www.komako.org.nz)

18 Hamilton, 1994, p13.

19 Smith, 2009.

20 Hamilton, 1994, p13.

21 'Sing Aotearoa '93', Radio New Zealand Concert, producer Kerry Stevens, ATL MSC-11820.

22 Hamilton, 1994, p54.

23 Whitehead, 1994, p54.

24 An amateur recording of the work is lodged in the Alexander Turnbull Library. Given the poor fidelity of the tape and the problems of the performance itself, it's not a recording that will see release. 'He Iwi Kotahi Tātou: for choir', 1993, ATL MSC-11820. Radio New Zealand also recorded the performance.

25 The last movement, 'Poroporoaki', was performed under Michael Vinten at a later New Zealand Composing Women's Festival in Wellington, and also, Jenny said, 'by a courageously unfazed Australian choir (with improvised calls contributed by Tūngia Baker and Keri Kaa) at an equivalent festival in Melbourne'.

26 Hardie, 1994, p56.

27 Shieff, 2002, p72.

28 Smith, 2009.

29 In the 1960s, when she made use of the words, Jenny had thought they were forgotten, dead to the tangata whenua. She was astonished and ashamed when she discovered they were in fact living words.

30 Fairley, 1996, p63.

31 Ibid.

32 Ibid.

33 Kerr, 1988, p10.

34 King, 1985, p238. See Keam, 2006, pp25–26 for further discussion.

35 Korty Wilson, email correspondence, April 2023.

36 Vera Māreikura and Kaye Oliver interview, November 2022.

37 Shepard, 1996, p16.

38 Smith, 2009.

39 Vera Māreikura and Kaye Oliver interview, May, 2022.

40 Smith, 2009.

41 Cecilia Johnson interview, September 2021.

42 Jenny was an inveterate TV watcher, often leaving the set on while she slept. She began watching TV evangelists in the mid-1990s simply because they were on, although seeing them repeatedly she came to 'like them as people'. At first she thought them 'nice idiots', but was eventually persuaded by their sincerity and began to read the Bible again. McLeod, 2000, pp7–9.

43 Smith, 2009.

44 Ibid.

45 Ibid.

46 Ibid.

47 Kerr, 1988, p8.

48 Fairley, 1996, p58.

49 McCracken, 1972, p336.

50 Fairley, 1996, p58. While Jenny may have been uncertain about composing music as a self-expressive activity, she later added, 'I do however very definitely write poetry to express myself.'

Chapter 16: Jenny McLeod | Composer

1   She also met and talked with Boulez on a number of occasions, and corresponded with him.
2   McLeod, 1992, p7.
3   Ibid,, p12.
4   Ibid., 1992, p7.
5   McLeod, 1993[e].
6   Fairley, 1996, p64.
7   Ibid., p68.
8   McLeod, 'Liberated Learning', p1.
9   Fairley, 1996, p67.
10 Elizabeth Kerr interview, December 2021. Elizabeth made her invitations on the basis that these artists 'were the ones collaborating with Māori. They were the ones who were drawing on Māori culture in their music.'
11 Court, 1996, p7.
12 Fairley, 1996, p65.
13 Ibid., p66.
14 Ibid., p65
15 Ibid.
16 Court, 1996, pp5–6.
17 Fairley, 1996, p69.
18 Ibid., p62.
19 Ibid.
20 Lilburn, 1946/1984, pp9,10.
21 Simpson, 2016.
22 In particular, *A Search for Tradition* (1946) and *A Search for a Language* (1969).
23 Sanders, 2004, p104.
24 Lilburn, 1946/1984, pp15–16.
25 Elizabeth Kerr interview, December 2021.
26 McLeod, 1992, p31.
27 Ibid.
28 Anon. 'Jenny McLeod's Earth and Sky', 1993, p18.

Chapter 17: Words and Music, Poetry and Song

1   *Sings Harry* (1951) is a cycle of fourteen poems by New Zealander Denis Glover. Douglas Lilburn set six of those poems for baritone and piano in 1954. See Norman, 1983, pp409–10.
2   'Jenny McLeod', Radio New Zealand Concert, 4 March 2010.
3   Ibid.
4   Ibid.
5   In the performance notes, Jenny wrote: 'The poet addresses the freesias on her desk in terms both witty and grave, speaking in her own voice and from the imagined point of view of the flowers, whence an unexpected elevation and enlargement, as the "giant" now "smells blood". See McLeod, 2011[b].
6   Bruce Greenfield interview, October 2021.
7   McLeod, 2011[a], p7.
8   McLeod, 2011[a], 45. 'Voices in the western corridor'.
9   McLeod, 'Cat Dreams', 2011[a], p38.
10 Jenny subsequently revised the score, saying, 'In future, the words should be read aloud at the start and between each movement, as they are in the Concert FM recording (Craig and I added the

poems afterwards; he read them aloud and recorded himself – and then wept.)'

11   Jenny said, 'My main reason for the (optional) kōauau or piccolo was that dear Biddy, my oldest Māori mate in Ohakune, had immediately opened her freezer and given me a large bag of whitebait to take to Perrin as soon as she learned he was in such pain he couldn't keep his food down, and was fixated on the idea of some whitebait fritters he hoped might do the trick.'

12   Kerr, 2021.

13   Murray, 2003, p44.

Chapter 18: *Hōhepa*

1   Nurse, 2012.

2   Ibid.

3   The Māramatanga is a movement based on the prophetic sayings of, among others, Hōri Ēnoka Māreikura. The movement continues to the present day, and is centred in the Ruapehu district. See Sinclair, 2002.

4   Nurse, 2012.

5   When we discussed it, Jenny was at first not convinced Lilburn's music had directly influenced her own. On reflection, she confessed to being 'completely unaware of the extent to which his first little piano prelude, No. 1 "Allegro grazioso" (from *Four Preludes* [1942–44]) had entered my subconscious. Playing it through very early on, I remember thinking, "Oh yes, pretty little piece," and that was about it. Now I see there are bits of this in *Three Celebrations* No. 2 – chains of thirds, anticipatory pairs of thirds, octave leaps. Anticipatory pairs of octaves, up and down (or one octave down, then down another) became my own signature in *Piano Piece 1965* and other piano pieces thereafter, especially as grace notes – which I'm happy to say Lilburn didn't do. And my *Silent One* signature (short, short, long, long) is already partly Douglas as well – already in that first "Allegro grazioso".'

6   Nurse, 2012.

7   Ibid.

8   Ibid.

9   Ibid.

10   Ibid.

11   Dart, 2012; Daly-Peoples, 2012.

12   Gilchrist, 2012.

13   Mechen, 2012.

14   Nurse, 2012.

15   Jenny Wollerman interview, April 2022.

16   Craig McLeod interview, October 2021.

17   Ibid. The video of the opera is available for viewing on the SOUNZ website.

18   Jenny Wollerman interview, April 2022.

Chapter 19: The Shape of a Life

1   McLeod, 2016. All subsequent quotes from the lecture, op cit.

2   Court, 1996, p6.

3   tīmatanga hōu: a new beginning.

List of Works

Details for most of these works can be found under the entry for Jenny on the website of the Centre for New Zealand Music, SOUNZ: www.sounz.org.nz. The order in which compositions were completed within each year is not specified.

*Indicates the score has been withdrawn, discarded, or lost.

1961
Suite *   piano
Three cummings songs *   piano, soprano. Text: e.e. cummings
Pastorale *   orchestra

1962
Cambridge Suite   orchestra
Six Little Pieces *   piano
Three Serial Pieces *   strings

1963
Dialogue on a Northern Shore *   music for a radio play
Epithalamia   piano, baritone. Text: W.S. Broughton
Four Profiles for Solo Cello   cello
Little Symphony   orchestra
Song of the Nativitie   choir . Text: unknown
String Trio   string trio
Toccata for Brass   brass quintet
Troilus and Cressida *   incidental music
what a proud dream horse   choir, chamber group. Text: e.e. cummings

1964
Diversions for Orchestra *   orchestra
Metamorphosis *   violin, piano

1965
Piano Piece 1965   piano

1966
For Seven   chamber group

1967
Hamlet *   incidental music
Twelfth Night *   incidental music

1968
Earth and Sky   music theatre for children, amateurs.
                                         Text: McLeod

Mister Brandywine Chooses   music for a radio play
  a Gravestone

1971
Under the Sun   music theatre for children, amateurs.
                                         Text: McLeod

1972
Equation   music for documentary film

1980
Ameros *   musical comedy. Text: M Cottrell, McLeod
Just Music *   two pianos
Nicholas and the Easy Chair *   songs. Text: McLeod
Ring Round the Sun   two pianos

1982
Childhood   choir. Text: McLeod
Piece for Wall   graphic score
Summer City Sizzle   chorus, orchestra
Through the World   piano, soprano. Text: W. Blake

1983
Sun Festival Carols   choir. Text: McLeod
The Cherry Orchard   music for a radio play

1984
Cuckooland   music for TV series. Text: Mahy

Dirge for Doomsday	choir. Text: McLeod
Hymn for the Lady	choir. Text: McLeod
The Neglected Miracle	music for documentary film
The Silent One	film score

1985

Africana	wind quintet
Goodnight, Christchurch	three orchestras, jazz band, 400 recorders
New Wellington March	military band
Rock Sonata No. I	piano
The Courtship of the Yonghy-Bonghy-Bò	choir. Text: E. Lear
The Emperor and the Nightingale	orchestra, narrator. Text: McLeod

1986

Beyond the Roaring Forties	music for documentary film
Images of New Zealand	music for documentary film
Music for Four	two pianos, two percussionists
Suite: Jazz Themes	flute, clarinet/soprano sax, viola, piano
The Dong with a Luminous Nose	clarinet, piano, soprano. Text: E. Lear
The Haunting of Barney Palmer	music for TV film
Three Celebrations for Orchestra	orchestra

1987

Rock Sonata No. II	piano
The Gift	music for documentary film

1988

Tone Clock: Pieces I–VII	piano

1993

He Iwi Kotahi Tātou (We Are One People)	choir, chamber choir, marae choir, two pianos. Text: McLeod/iwi

1995

Tone Clock: Pieces VIII–XI	piano

1997
Little Owl Song (The Ruru)   three choirs, ensemble. Text: McLeod

2003
Tone Clock: Piece XII   piano
Under Southern Skies   piano, soprano. Text: A. Powell

2004
Tone Clock: Pieces XIII–XVII   piano

2006
A Clear Midnight   piano, tenor, bass.
                                    Text: V. Woolf, W. Whitman

2007
The Poet: A Song Cycle   choir, string quartet. Text: J. Frame
Tone Clock: Piece XVIII   piano

2008
Cat Dreams   chamber group, kōauau
From Garden to Grave   piano, soprano. Text: J. Frame
Obscure as the Theology   choir. Text L. Johnson.
  of Mountains

2009
Airs for the Winged Isle   string quartet
Rock Concerto   piano, orchestra

2010
Peaks of Cloud   piano, tenor. Text: J. Frame

2011
Tone Clock: Pieces XIX–XXIV   piano

2012
Hōhepa   opera. Text: McLeod

2013

He Whakaahua o Maru (*A Portrait of Maru*)	piano, flute/piccolo, soprano. Text: McLeod

2015

Seascapes	violin, cello, piano

2016

The Amazing Head	music theatre for children, amateurs. Text: McLeod

2021

dark bright night	violin, cello, piano
Clouds	violin, cello, piano
Nā Kui ki a Tama: Te Pūroto Kōpua (Big Sis to Little Bro: The Deep Dark Pool)	piano, soprano. Text: McLeod

2022

Study – Mirror Echoes	piano

Music for beginners and intermediate players

Once Upon a Twinkle (1974–6) *	piano
18 Easy Pieces (1996)	piano
Mysterious whirly square dance (2009)	piano
Loss (2009)	piano

Hymns, Godsongs and choir test pieces

Fifteen collections of *Godsongs* and numerous Hui Aranga test pieces are lodged with SOUNZ. The collection *Twelve Maori Songs* is in the Alexander Turnbull Library. Together, these total (allowing for duplications) more than one hundred and forty songs. There are a further six of Jenny's hymns included in Shirley Murray's *Faith Makes the Song*. Also:

Light of Lights Beholden (1983)	Text: McLeod
Two Hopkins Hymns (2009)	Text: G. Manly-Hopkins
A New Zealand Blessing (2012)	Text: unknown

Recordings

Earth and Sky
Philips – 6503001
1970

Under the Sun
Philips – 6641009
1971

The Silent One (original soundtrack recording)
Jayrem, JAY321
1984

Composer Portrait: Jenny McLeod
Wai-te-ata Music Press, WTA 005
2003

Jenny McLeod: Vocal & Choral Works
Wai-te-ata Music Press, WTA 012
2011

The Emperor and the Nightingale/Three Celebrations/Rock Concerto
Naxos 8.572671
2011

24 Tone Clocks
Rattle, RAT-DO-66
2016

Portrait with Piano
Atoll, ACD223
2022

Anthologies

Piano Music by New Zealand Composers
Kiwi Pacific KP SLD-19, 1968
Tessa Binney – piano
Includes *Piano Piece 1965*

Youth and Music: Ashley Heenan, Jenny McLeod, David Farquhar, Edwin Carr
Kiwi Pacific SLC 72, 1969
National Youth Orchestra
Includes *Cambridge Suite*

Prisms
Kiwi Pacific KP TC SLD-74, 1985
The Bach Choir
Includes *Childhood*

Music by New Zealand Composers
Flora Series Vol. 4
Kiwi Pacific TC SLD-94, 1985
The Bach Choir
Includes *Childhood*

New Zealand Youth Sings to the World
Tartar TRL-063, 1987
National Youth Choir of New Zealand
Includes *Dirge for Doomsday*

On Tour in North America
Manu CD 1471, 1994
New Zealand National Youth Choir
Includes *Childhood* (three songs)

New Zealand Composers
Continuum CCD 1073-2, 1995
New Zealand Symphony Orchestra
Includes *Little Symphony*

Winds that Whisper
Trust Records MMT2016, 1998
Tower New Zealand Youth Choir
Includes *Childhood*

Burning Bright: Music by New Zealand Women Composers
Kiwi Pacific SLD 110, 1999
Margaret Medlyn – voice
Bruce Greenfield – piano
Includes *Through the World*

Landscape Preludes
Rattle Records RAT-DO46, 2014
Henry Wong Doe – piano
Includes *Tone Clock Piece XVIII: Landscape Prelude*

Sarajevo: A Collection of New Zealand Piano Works
Atoll ACD 217, 2017
Jian Liu – piano
Includes *Tone Clock: Piece XX, XXIII*

Exiles
Rattle, RAT-D116, 2021
Michael Houstoun – piano
Includes 'Twenty-Three Fifty-Nine', a remix of *Tone Clock Piece XXIII*

There are further recordings of many of Jenny's pieces available through
the Radio New Zealand website, generally of live performances captured
for broadcast. There are also audio (and video) recordings of performances
of some of Jenny's music on the SOUNZ website. A number of live
concert recordings, no longer in circulation, are archived in the Alexander
Turnbull Library.

Sources

All unattributed quotes are drawn from my interviews and correspondence with Jenny between 2019 and 2022. Where things Jenny told me also turned up – in some cases almost verbatim – in other published (and unpublished) interviews and articles, I have sometimes added a note to that effect, particularly where alternative sources shed greater (or different) light on the matter at hand, or where they contribute useful context.

Some of my sources were newspaper items or magazine articles cut out and stuck into scrapbooks, often without attributions or an indication of date or provenance. Such finds can be gold for a researcher but a nightmare for bibliographers. Some of the citations listed are incomplete for this reason. The abbreviation ATL refers to the Alexander Turnbull Library.

Anon. (2013, 2 July). *Darmstädter Ferienkurse 1946–1966*, www.issuu.com

Anon. (1993). 'Jenny McLeod's Earth and Sky', *Music in New Zealand*, No. 22

Anon. (1972, 6 September). 'Jobs for the Boys – Says Jenny', *New Zealand Herald, Weekend Magazine*

Anon. (1970). 'Kitchen Sink Training for Music Prof', *Star*

Anon. 'Morrow Productions', Ngā Taonga Sound and Vision, www.ngataonga.org.nz

Anon. 'National Film Unit Collection', www.archives.govt.nz

Anon. (1981, March). 'Post War Development', *The Chronicle*, 75th Borough Jubilee issue, www.horowhenua.kete.net.nz

Anon. 'Prime Minister was Impressed', in 'Scrapbook Concerning McLeod's Productions'. ATL MSY-4023

Anon. 'Staging Hōhepa'. *Te Ara – The Encyclopedia of New Zealand*, www. teara.govt.nz

Anon. (1970, 8 August), '"Starsong" now "Under The Sun"', *Evening Standard*

Anon. 'The Silent One', *New Zealand Films*, www.nzvideos.org/silentCD.html

Anon. 'Timeline of the Early Career of Prem Rawat aka Maharaji aka Guru Maharaj Ji', www.prem-rawat-bio.org

Anon. (1964, 14 May). 'Unashamedly Tonal', *New Zealand Listener*

Anon. 'Wairarapa Schools' History', www.wairarapaschoolhistory.co.nz

Barrowman, R. (1999). *Victoria University of Wellington 1899–1999: A History*. Victoria University Press

Bleakley, J. *Sun Festival*, www.joebleakley.com

Body, J. (2011). 'Jenny McLeod', *Composer of the Week*. Radio New Zealand Concert

Boulez, P (1986). *Orientations: Collected Writings*. (ed. Nattiez). Harvard University Press

Brownlee, C. (1970). 'There is no such thing as silence', ATL MSY-4023

Byzantion. 'Jenny McLeod'. www.MusicwebInternational

Campbell, B. (1984, August). 'Composer Jenny McLeod at Home in Pukerua Bay', *Kapi-Mana News*

Chamberlain, L. 'Production plans made by composer of "Starsong",' *Evening Standard*, n.d.

Court, S. (1996). 'Interview with Jenny McLeod', ATL MS-Papers-7349-127

Croft, J. (1993). '*Earth and Sky*: The Music', *Music in New Zealand*, No. 22

Cunningham, A. (2017). *Lives of the Most Eminent British Painters, Sculptors and Architects*. Forgotten Books

Daly-Peoples, J. (2012, 19 March). 'Hōhepa – a great but flawed opera', *National Business Review*, www.nbr.co.nz

Dart, W. (2012, 19 March) 'Concert Review: Hōhepa', *New Zealand Herald*, www.nzherald.co.nz

Dodd, T. (2003, 25 May). 'Cambridge Music School', *Composer of the Week*. Radio New Zealand Concert,

Fairley, D. (1996). 'Interview with Jenny McLeod', ATL MS-Papers-7349-127

Ferreira, R. (2010) 'Music for *The Silent One*: An Interview with Jenny McLeod', *Screen Sound Journal*, 1

Galbreath, R. 'Agricultural and horticultural research – Department of Agriculture research', *Te Ara - the Encyclopedia of New Zealand*, 2008, www.TeAra.govt.nz

Gilchrist, M. (2012, 16 March). 'A must-see for anyone interested in what we can now muster in New Zealand', *Theatre Review*, www.theatreview.org.nz

Gillett, S. (1999[a]). 'Interview with Jenny McLeod', ATL MS-Papers-7349-127

Gillett, S. (1999[b]). *Exceptional Women: Exceptional Schools?* [Paper presentation] New Zealand and Australian Associations for Research in Education Conference, 28 Nov–3 Dec 1999, Melbourne, Australia, www.aare.edu

Glasgow, N. (1995). *Directions: New Zealanders Explore the Meaning of Life*. Shoal Bay Press

Goss, T. (2011, September). 'Critics Chair'. Radio New Zealand, www.naxos.com

Grice, J. 'The New Zealand Connection', n.d., www.jeffreygrice.com

Hamilton, D. (1993/1994). 'Robert Sund & David Hamilton: A Conversation', *Music in New Zealand*, No. 23

Hardie, R. (1994). *Jenny McLeod: The Emergence of a New Zealand Voice*. Master of Music thesis, Rice University

Hill, C. (1968, 4 October). 'Earth and Sky', *New Zealand Listener*

Jensen, O. (1964). 'Waitangi Day Concert', Radio New Zealand, ATL MST7-0612. Originally broadcast 1964

Jensen, O. (1968). 'New Zealand Composer Profiles: Jenny McLeod', Radio New Zealand, Ngā Taonga | Sound and Vision, Ref. 250266. Originally broadcast 1968

Jones, M. (2003). 'Composer Portrait: Jenny McLeod', liner notes for *Composer Portrait: Jenny McLeod*. Wai-te-ata Music Press

Keam, G. (2006). *Exploring Notions of National Style: New Zealand Orchestral Music in the Late Twentieth Century*. PhD thesis, University of Auckland

Kerr, E. (1998). 'Jenny McLeod talks to *Music in New Zealand*', *Music in New Zealand*, No. 2

Kerr, E. (2021, 9 November). 'Jenny McLeod at 80: to me I'm always me', *Five Lines*, www.fivelines.nz

Kerr, E. (2021, 6–12 November). 'McLeody Clouds', *New Zealand Listener*, 45

King, M. (1985). *Being Pākehā*. Hodder & Stoughton

Laing, A. (1996) *R.D. Laing: A Biography*. Thunder's Mouth Press

Lang, R. (1984). 'The Silent One', *Onfilm*, Vol. 2, No. 1, 13

Lilburn, D. (1946/1984). *A Search for Tradition*. Wellington: Alexander Turnbull Library Endowment Trust 1946/1984

Lilburn, D. (1963). 'Notes from Darmstadt', *Composer*, 12

Lilburn, D. *A Search for a Language*. Wellington: Alexander Turnbull Library Endowment Trust 1969/1985

Maconie, R. (1969, 4 March). 'Tender Roots or Mature Dwarfs', *Salient*, Vol. 32, No. 1, 4, www.nzetc.victoria.ac.nz

Maconie, R. (1975, 29 May). 'Jenny McLeod in the Clouds', *Salient*, Vol 38, No 19, 29, www.nzetc.victoria.ac.nz

Mason, B. (1969, 29 August). 'Mainly Music', *New Zealand Listener*

Mason, B. (1971, 21 June). 'After Under the Sun,' *New Zealand Listener*

McAlpine, F. (2011). 'The Blue, Blue Sky and the White, White Mountains',
    Landscape Preludes. (ed. Samuel Holloway). Score Publishers

McCracken, J. (1971, 31 May). 'Painting Pictures with Music', *New Zealand Listener*

McCracken, J. (1972, December). 'Composer in Transit', *Landfall* No. 104

McKay, F. (1990). *The Life of James K. Baxter*. Oxford University Press,

McLeod, J. (1965, October). 'Boulez at Basle', *Conductor*, No. 17

McLeod, J. (1971). 'Author's Note', *Under the Sun* LP liner notes. Philips 6641009

McLeod, J. (1975). 'Report on Leave – Professor J.H. McLeod', ATL MS-
    Papers-7349-128

McLeod, J. (1987). 'A Composer's Choices'. Address at the Louisville New Music
    Festival, ATL MS-Papers-7349-237

McLeod, J. (1988). 'Letter to Composition Panel, QE II Arts Council', ATL 88-169

McLeod, J. (1992). 'Messiaen Through the Eyes of a Small Pupil', *Canzona*

McLeod, J. (1992, Spring). 'The Composer Speaks: Jenny McLeod on *For Seven*',
    Music in New Zealand, No. 18

McLeod, J. (1993[a], Spring). 'The Composer Looks Back', *Music in New
    Zealand*, No. 22

McLeod, J. (1993[b]). 'Notes', in *He Iwi Kotahi Tātou* [musical score]. ATL MS-
    Papers-7349-209

McLeod, J. (1993[c]). *He Iwi Kotahi Tātou: A Pitch Analysis*. ATL MS-
    Papers-7349-109

McLeod, J. (1993[d]). 'Introduction' in P Schat, *The Tone Clock*. Routledge

McLeod, J. (1993[e]). 'The Arts and Humanities: Some Bearings, Observations
    and Suggestions'. ATL MS-Papers-7349-237

McLeod, J. (1994). *Tone Clock Theory Expanded: Chromatic Maps 1 & 2*.
    Informally published, www.archive.org

McLeod, J. (1995). 'Notes', *Through the World*. Wai-te-ata Music Press

McLeod, J. (1996). 'People, Pathways and Power: Reflections on a bicultural
    journey', *Music in the Air*, No. 2, Winter

McLeod, J. (2000). 'A wee bookie for my brother'. ATL MS-Papers-12630-04

McLeod, J. (2003).'Composed for A Cappella Choir', *Childhood*. Wai-te-ata
    Music Press

McLeod, J. (2011[a]). *Mutterings from a Spiry Crag*. Steele Roberts Aotearoa

McLeod, J. (2011[b]). *From Garden to Grave*. Wai-te-ata Press

McLeod, J. (2016). *Prosaic Notes from an Unwritten Journal: The Lilburn Lecture*, www.rnz.co.nz

McLeod, J. 'Aspects of Myth'. Unpublished manuscript. n.d.

McLeod, J. 'Correspondence – Jenny McLeod'. ATL 94-180-1/19

McLeod, J. 'Correspondence'. ATL MS-Papers-4788-02

McLeod, J. 'Family Background', 1980–2001. ATL MS-Papers-7349-225

McLeod, J. 'Inward Correspondence – Jenny McLeod'. ATL MS-Papers-7623-191

McLeod, J. 'Letters to Frederick Page'. ATL MS-Papers-5558-2

McLeod, J. 'Liberated Learning: Women as Facilitators of Learning'. ATL MS-Papers-7349-224

McLeod, J. 'Some Early Memories', 1980–2001. ATL MS-Papers-7349-225

McLeod, R. (1970). 'Jenny's Music Will Jump', *Sunday Star Times*. ATL MSY-4023

Mechen, P. (2012, 15 March). 'Great Enthusiasm at Jenny McLeod's "Hōhepa" Premiere', *Middle C*, www.middle-c.org

Messiaen, O. (2000). *Technique of My Musical Language*. Paris: Alphonse Leduc

Murray, S. (2003). *Faith Makes the Day*. Carol Stream, IL: Hope Publishing Company

Norman, P. (1983). *The Beginnings and Development of a New Zealand Music: The Life, and Work (1940–1965), of Douglas Lilburn*. PhD thesis, Canterbury University

Norman, P. (2006). *Douglas Lilburn: His Life and Music*. Canterbury University Press

Nurse, A. '(2012, 8 March). The Making of Hōhepa.' *Appointment*. Radio New Zealand

Page, F. (1969, January). 'New Zealand', *Musical Times*, Vol 110, No 1511

Page, F. (1986). *Frederick Page: A Musician's Journal* (eds J.M. Thomson and J. Paul). John McIndoe Ltd

Reid, J. (2018). *Whatever It Takes: Pacific Films and John O'Shea 1948–2000*. Victoria University Press

Sanders, D. (2004). *Song of the Kokako: Birdsong in New Zealand composition*. MA thesis, Victoria University of Wellington

Saunders, L.C.M. (1970, February). '*Earth and Sky* Outstanding', *New Zealand Herald*

SGS. '(2011, December). McLeod: The Emperor and the Nightingale', *Classical CD Reviews*, www.classicalcdreview.com

Shepard, D. 'Interview with Jenny McLeod. 1st May, 1996'. ATL MS-Papers-7349-127

Shieff, S. (2002). *Talking Music: Conversations with New Zealand musicians*. Auckland: Auckland University Press

Shiels, R. (2019, 12 March). 'Hair on Trial', *Audioculture*, www.audioculture.co.nz

Simpson, P. (2016). *Bloomsbury South: The Arts in Christchurch 1933–1953*. Auckland University Press

Sinclair, K. (2002). *Prophetic Histories: The People of the Māramatanga*. Bridget Williams Books

Smalley, D. (1970, 8 July). 'Earth and Sky (1968)', *Salient*, Vol. 33, No. 10, 8, www.victoria.ac.nz

Smith, R. (2009). 'Interview with Jenny McLeod'. ATL OHDL-001799

White, T. (2020, 26 September). 'Glory Days of City's Centennial Brought to Life for Sesqui Celebration', *Manawatu Standard*, www.stuff.co.nz

Whitehead, G. (1993/1994, Summer). 'Jenny McLeod's *He Iwi Kotahi Tatou*: An Appreciation', *Music in New Zealand*, No. 23

Zwartz, P. (1971, 21 June) 'After Under the Sun', *New Zealand Listener*

Further Reading

Boulez, P. (1990). *Orientations* (Ed. Nattiez). Harvard University Press

Glasgow, N. (1995). *Directions: New Zealanders Explore the Meaning of Life*. Shoal Bay Press

Lilburn, D. (2014). *Memories of Early Years and Other Writings* (ed. Robert Hoskins). Steele Roberts

McLeod, J. (2011). *Mutterings from a Spiry Crag*. Steele Roberts Aotearoa

McLeod, J. (1994). *Tone Clock Theory Expanded: Chromatic Maps 1 & 2*, www. archive.org/details/toneclock-BO1095DS

Norman, P. (2006). *Douglas Lilburn: His Life and Music*. Canterbury University Press

Samuel. C. (1986/1994). *Olivier Messiaen: Music and Colour*. Amadeus Press

Schat, P. (1993). *The Tone Clock*. London: Routledge

Small, C. (1998). *Musicking: The Meanings of Performing and Listening*. Wesleyan University Press

Stockhausen, K, and R. Maconie. (1989). *Stockhausen on Music: Lectures and Interviews*, (comp ed. Robin Maconie). Marion Boyers Publishers

Thomson, J.M. and J. Paul (eds). (1986). *Frederick Page: A Musician's Journal*. John McIndoe Ltd

List of Illustrations

All photos courtesy of the McLeod family and archive, except where noted.

1a. Perrin, Craig and Jenny, c. 1946

1b. Jenny picnics with her parents

1c. Perrin, Jenny and Craig, c. 1952

2a. Grandfather John Halford Perrin with his carved figures

2b. Jenny on guitar with brother Perrin on accordion

2c. Jenny at the piano, Levin, 1950s

3a. McLeod family

3b. Igor Stravinsky's New Zealand visit, 1961

3c. New Zealand's youngest professor, Victoria University College, 1967
Tapuaka—Heritage & Archives Collection, Victoria University of Wellington, ref. vimas09

4a. Jenny conducts a rehearsal of *Earth and Sky*, 1968 *Wairarapa Times-Age, 17-101-005-032-199 frame 05*

4b. *Earth and Sky* rehearsal, Masterton Town Hall, 1968 *Wairarapa Times-Age, 17-101-005-032-274 (frame 01)*

5a. Celebrating the premiere of *Earth and Sky* at the Masterton Town Hall, 1968 *Wairarapa Times-Age, 17-101-005-032-275 (frame 02)*

5b. Jenny chats with Pat Hanly at the Victoria University Arts Conference, 1970 *Photographer Ans Westra, courtesy of Suite Gallery*

6a. Cover of booklet produced to accompany *Earth and Sky* record, 1970 *Photographer Michael Tubberty*

6b. Publicity shot from *Under the Sun* booklet, 1971 *Photographer Barry Woods*

7a. *Under the Sun* rehearsal, Palmerston North's Pascal Street stadium, 1971 *Manawatu Standard, Stuff Limited*

7.b Cover of booklet produced to accompany *Under the Sun* record, 1971 *Photographer Barry Woods*

8a. Jenny in 1975 *Stuff Limited*

8b. Jenny unveils her poster-score *Piece for Wall*, 1982 *Alexander Turnbull Library, PAColl-7480-4-04*

Acknowledgements

The greatest debt of gratitude is owed to Jenny McLeod: for her willingness to contribute to this project, her generosity and grace, her stories and the laughter that accompanied them, and her music. Arohanui, Jenny. Moe mai rā e te wahine toa, moe mai rā.

For their generosity, insights, recollections, suggestions, advice and permissions, thank you: Anna Wirz-Justice, Barbara Einhorn, Bill Manhire, Bruce McKinnon, Carol Markwell, Carole Brungar, Cecilia Johnson, Charles Royal, Denis Smalley, Elizabeth Kerr, Emma Sayers, Eugene Albulescu, Fiona McAlpine, Graham Parsons, Jack Richards, Jenny Wollerman, Jeroen Speak, Joe Bleakley, John Rimmer, John Thornley, Kaye Oliver, Kit Powell, Korty Wilson, Lyell Cresswell, Michael Houstoun, Michael Norris, Morva Croxson, Nona Harvey, Peter Galvin, Philip Norman, Rae de Lisle, Richard Hardie, Roger Smith, Ross Harris, Roy Tankersley, Sara Brodie, Sarah Shieff, Steve Garden, Suzanne Court, Tim Jordan, Tony Backhouse, Vera Māreikura.

In particular: Robert Hoskins originally suggested this project – although not quite in the form it has finally taken. He was its first reader and a quiet voice offering encouragement and reminding me of the duty of care we have to one another, and to music.

Glenda Keam and Jim Gardener provided valuable encouragement and support and a wealth of material on Jenny and New Zealand music generally.

Bruce Greenfield, one of Jenny's oldest friends and her husband during the 1970s, was generous beyond my expectations and offered me many valuable insights into Jenny's music and life.

Robin Maconie offered acute comment, provided detailed historical background on New Zealand music and Karlheinz Stockhausen, and drew my attention to several excellent sources I might well have over-looked.

Tim Dodd was able to guide me to a number of Radio New Zealand recordings that were of enormous value to me as I prepared the manuscript.

Rob Cameron's long, long letter provided a beautiful window for looking in on life at 124 Ohiro Road in the early 1970s.

Steve Matthews was a patient and thoughtful correspondent and his insights helpfully made sense of several matters I'd found confusing.

Roger Steele's generous advice and suggestions on the manuscript were of enormous value.

Craig McLeod, Jenny's brother, answered questions, offered helpful suggestions and shared some wonderful photographs with me.

Sheryl Boxall, Jenny's housemate in recent years, made visits to Jenny even more agreeable and was a great help in some important ways. Without Sheryl, this book would not exist in its present form, and possibly not at all.

At the Alexander Turnbull Library I received generous assistance above and beyond the call of duty from music librarian Mark Hector. Special thanks to the library's music curator Dr Michael Brown. And for their friendly and patient help, thanks also to Keith McEwing, Katrina Hatherley, Paul Diamond, and Audrey Waugh.

Grateful thanks to editor Jane Parkin whose generous and expert attention to the manuscript made a world of difference. At Te Herenga Waka University Press, I'm sincerely grateful to Anna Knox, whose patient and careful editing added a further lustre to the writing I could never have managed alone. Rachel Barrowman was a brilliant proof-reader. Thanks to Todd Atticus and Ruby Leonard. And thanks to Fergus Barrowman for his sharp eye, his good humour and deft touch, but mostly for his friendship.

Thanks, of a global variety: Irene Meehan, Hannah Griffin, Blair Latham, Lance Philip, Andrew Laking, Paul Dyne, Julien Dyne, Hayden Chisholm, Colin Hemmingsen, Steve Cournane, Nick van Dijk, Thomas Voyce, Roger Manins, Jeff Henderson, Daniel Ryland, Michael Stewart, Steve Hemmens, Keith Hill, David Long, Steve and Viky Garden, John Cousins and Colleen Anstey, Neil Aldridge and Charlotte Crichton, Adam Levy and Brigid Feehan, Andy Whittaker and Rhian Salmon, Sue Prescott, Tim and Cathy Denne, Alan and Hazel Kerr, Chris Bourke, Elizabeth Hudson, Yorroh Batchilly.

Special thanks to two of my closest friends: George Mason, who reminds me to listen for the low hum; and Calum MacLean who, survived by Cathy and Ben and Martha, is sorely missed, and who reminded me to listen to Don Cherry.

The ones who make it worthwhile, and who make it possible, too: Suzi Kerr, Hazel Meehan, Roma Kerr.

Index

Bulte, Denise, 172
Burgess, Anthony, 141, 349 (n46)
Burt, Gordon, 109
Burwell, Carter, 208

Cage, John, 158
California, 52, 158, 180
Caltech University, 157
Cambridge Suite (McLeod), 59–62, 66, 72,
  97, 110, 326, 343 (n28), 343 (n31)
Cambridge Summer School of Music, 40–41,
  45, 47, 57–66, 68, 192, 343 (n39), 347 (n7)
Cambridge University Chamber Choir, 206
Cameron, Rob, 149–150
Campbell, Alistair, 196
Campbell, Meg, 196
camping, 85
Campion, Jane, 306–307
Campion, Richard, 111
Camus, Albert, 162
Can (rock group), 96
'Can I See Another's Woe' (McLeod), 202
cancer diagnosis
  Jenny McLeod, 274
  Lorna McLeod, 177–178
  Perrin McLeod, 306–308
cannabis, 147–152, 154, 161–162, 187,
  189–190
Cantéyodjayâ, 65–66
Cargo, Allan, 50
Carlstedt, Jan, 242
Carmen Jones (musical film), 208
Carnival of the Animals (Saint-Saëns), 220
Carpenters, The, 213
Carr, Edwin, 47
cartoons. *see* animation
Caruso, Enrico, 54
Caskel, Christoph, 95, 100
Caskie, Helen, 134
Castaneda, Carlos, 162
Castel Felice (ship), 74
Cat Dreams (McLeod), 307–308, 359–360
  (n10)
Catalogue d'oiseaux (Messiaen), 80
'categorical imperative', meaning, 338
Catholic faith, 80, 277–280, 286, 299
Ceaușescu regime, 227
Cello Quintet (Schubert), 64

cervical cancer, 177–178
'Chaconne', 226
chamber music, 47, 97–102, 224–226,
  231, 297, 301–303, 307–309, 316, 327,
  334–335
Chamber Music Society, 148
Char, René, 308
Charles, John, 45
Cheltenham, 91
Chicago (pop group), 197
Chicago University, 157
childhood, 20–27, 339
Childhood (McLeod), 173, 198–200, 218,
  240, 272, 298, 307, 331
children, desire for, 158
choir judge, 271–274
Chopin, Frédéric, 22, 30, 46, 48, 79–80, 211,
  227, 229–230, 250, 339
choral music, 198–200, 204–206, 237, 256,
  259–267, 271–274, 327, 332
Christ, 145
Christchurch, 121–122, 155, 291
Christianity, 162. *See also* Catholic faith
chromatic system, 251–252, 255, 261, 263,
  272, 284, 298, 328, 346 (n18), 356 (n15)
cinema. *see* films
Cinque variazioni (Berio), 83
Clan MacLeod, 23, 86, 308
Clark, Judith, 132–133, 253
Clouds (McLeod), 335–336
cocaine, 148, 152
'Cocks Crow' (McLeod), 199–200
Coen Brothers, 208
coincidences, 167, 351 (n14)
collaboration benefits, 216
Collected Poems (Johnston), 304
Cologne, 89–90, 93, 95, 101–104, 148, 158,
  293
Cologne Course for New Music, 94–95, 98,
  101, 104
colonialism, 294
Colquhoun, Neil, 17
Columbia University, 157
Comalco, 209, 354 (n3)
commissions, earning living from, 207,
  238–239, 243
commissions, withdrawal from, 240–241,
  243, 349 (n9)